The Economics
of Industries
and Firms

The Economics of Industries and Firms

THEORIES, EVIDENCE AND POLICY

Malcolm C. Sawyer

SECOND EDITION

First published 1981
by Routledge

Second Edition 1985

Reprinted 1991
by Routledge
2 Park Square, Milton Park, Abingdon, Oxon, OX14 4RN
270 Madison Ave, New York NY 10016

Transferred to Digital Printing 2006

British Library Cataloguing in Publication Data
Sawyer, Malcolm C.
    The Economics of Industries and Firms: Theories,
    Evidence and Policy — 2nd ed.
    1. Industrial organization (Economic theory)
    I. Title
    338   HD2326

ISBN 0-415-06604-2

CONTENTS

ABBREVIATIONS

A	Advertising expenditure
AC	Average costs
a_i	The degree of interdependence indicated by the expected response of other firms' output to firm i's output change
C	Costs (total)
CRn	n-firm concentration ratio
EC	Executive compensation
e	Price elasticity of demand
e_A	Advertising elasticity of demand
e_g	'Goodwill' elasticity of demand
g	Rate of growth
HI	Herfindahl index (sometimes called Herfindahl-Hirschmann index)
i	Rate of discount/interest
K	Capital stock
M	Profit margin on sales
$m.e.s.$	Minimum efficient scale
$N.O.$	Net output
q	output
r	Retention ratio
S	Sales
s_i	Market share of firm i
v	Valuation ratio
V	Market value of firm
W	Wages and salaries
σ	Standard deviation
ϱ	Rate of profit (on capital)
π	Total profits

PREFACE TO THE SECOND EDITION

The second edition retains the structure and purpose of the first edition. The changes in the second edition are mainly those of updating the material and extending the coverage. There has been updating of the empirical work surveyed and of the policy discussions in Chapter 16. The extended coverage brings in discussion on multinational enterprises, price behaviour, vertical integration and diversification, organisational structure of firms and the theory of contestable markets.

I am grateful to reviewers of the first edition, teachers of courses using the book and third-year undergraduate students at University of York taking courses in industrial economics in the early 1980s for comments which have led to changes in the second edition.

PREFACE TO FIRST EDITION

A complete study of industrial economics requires a knowledge of microeconomics (especially theories of the firm) and of elementary econometrics. I have endeavoured to write this book so that someone with only a one-year course in economics behind them could follow the line of argument. But without a further study of micro-economics they would miss the significance of some parts of the argument, and without a knowledge of econometrics would have to take many of the empirical results on trust. In writing this book, limitation on space and a natural inclination have led to an emphasis on providing the framework(s) of industrial economics. Thus I have not attempted to write a book which attempts to survey everything written on industrial economics. Further reading, indicated by the references in the text, is required for a fuller appreciation of the subject — rarely can a few lines in a text be an adequate substitute for the original paper or book.

This book is loosely based on lectures on industrial economics given to third-year economics students at University College London, over the years 1975 to 1977. Comments by those students on those lectures and comments on an earlier draft of a number of chapters by Sam Aaronovitch are gratefully acknowledged.

PART ONE:

ECONOMICS OF INDUSTRY

1 AN INTRODUCTION

The central aim of this book is to provide an overview of the ways in which economists have studied the operation of privately-owned industry under the general heading of industrial economics. Industrial economics has many facets which are reflected in this book. One has been the development of theories of firm behaviour. Some of these theories group firms together in industries and explore the consequences of the operation of independent firms within an industry. Other theories treat firms as individual entities. But the theories share the common feature of postulating objectives for the firms (whether profit maximisation, growth of sales maximisation, satisficing, etc.) and investigate the consequences of the pursuit of these objectives. Another facet, which is given particular attention here, is the examination of the empirical validity of the various theories. This examination requires that predictions be derived from the theories in a form amenable to empirical investigation and that the relevant variables can be measured. Undertaking these tasks can prove rather difficult as our discussion below will show.

The performance of privately-owned industry is of central importance for the overall productive efficiency of a private enterprise economy, and consequently it is not surprising that economists have not been slow in drawing out the implications of their theories and evidence for public policy. The discussion of government industrial policy provides a third major facet of industrial economics.

It would be misleading to pretend that there is one widely accepted approach to industrial economics. The aim of this book is to present the major approaches to industrial economics (and to specific parts of it) and to examine the evidence relevant to these various approaches. The decision on which approach, if any, is acceptable is left to the reader. Four particular approaches to industrial policy are outlined in Chapter 15, and that chapter provides a summary of the essential points of the major approaches to industrial economics.

The unbiased presentation of conflicting approaches is difficult, if not impossible. There is the need to make a selection of which approaches and which parts of particular approaches to discuss. Thus references are provided for the reader to follow up any particular approach. But anyone writing a text-book must become immersed in its subject matter, and form views on the validity or otherwise of the various approaches. The views

3

of the current author are essentially contained in Aaronovitch and Sawyer (1975a).

This book does not intend to cover everything ever written on industrial economics, but rather to provide a framework within which the student can pursue further study. It seeks to indicate the major issues of industrial economics, to relate the important theories and evidence pertaining to those issues, and to give guidance for further reading. A satisfactory study of industrial economics would require that many of these references for further reading be pursued. The references given are of three types. There are references which serve to indicate the source of a particular piece of information, theory or evidence. There are references for further reading on the topics discussed, and both of these types of references are generally given in the text. Finally, there are references given in notes for reading in areas of economics which have been taken as part of the reader's knowledge and for those parts on economics on the boundaries of industrial economics. References are given in terms of the author and year of publication (with the suffixes a, b, etc., used where more than one publication in a year by the author is referred to) and the full references are given in the Bibliography at the end of the book.

A common format has also been used with symbols. Throughout the book, each symbol retains its own meaning, which is explained on its first usage in each chapter. Thus, for example, A is used throughout for advertising expenditure. A list of the symbols used and their meaning is given on page vii. In presenting regression results, we have adopted the common format of presenting standard errors in parenthesis under the estimated coefficient even when t-ratios were used in the original source.

One of the major aims of this book is to present and discuss the alternative approaches in a manner which leads to the derivation of hypotheses which can be confronted with the evidence. In doing this, we accept the line of argument that an important aspect of the acceptance (or rather non-rejection) of a theory is the ability of that theory to generate testable predictions which are in line with observations. But in applying this approach we must be careful of falling into the trap which says that only theories which provide predictions are worthwhile (Friedman, 1953). Thus there are many other desirable characteristics of a theory besides ability to predict adequately. These desirable characteristics could include explanation, insight and simplicity. Further, a theory may predict well, but only make predictions about features which are regarded as of little importance. The important features of the real world which we hope a theory will explain and for which we hope it will make testable predictions have to be decided.

When the hypotheses and predictions of the theories are subject to empirical investigation, the form of that investigation will generally be in the form of the use of econometric regression analysis. An outline of econometric techniques widely used in industrial economics and the problems which often arise are given in Chapter 2.

Two other techniques by which theories can be appraised are also widely used. The first is the use of case studies to investigate a particular industry to see whether that industry conforms to a particular theory. More usually case studies are used to illustrate theories rather than test their validity. As the price of computer time to estimate regressions has fallen and the price of research time to conduct case studies has risen, industrial economics has made relatively less use of case studies. The work reported in this book reflects this, although there are some areas (notably Chapter 4 in the use of the engineering approach in the estimation of cost conditions) where case studies have been used.

The other technique of appraisal is essentially direct calculation of the phenomenon under review across a larger number of firms. For example, part of the appraisal of the view that there has been a 'managerial revolution' which has changed the objectives of the firm involved is through a direct investigation of the extent of managerial or owner control in large corporations.

There has been intermittent discussion of the relative merits of these different techniques, particularly between regression analysis and the case study approach. Regression analysis has the advantage of being able to make allowance for the impact of many variables on the variable of interest. Whilst with the advent of computers the estimation of regression equations has become an easy undertaking, nevertheless regression analysis is limited to variables for which statistics are readily available (often from government sources). Case studies in contrast tend to be labour intensive but may be able often to investigate the impact of factors which are difficult to measure. The results reported from the use of either technique are likely to be influenced by the judgement of the investigator. With case studies it is clear that the judgement of the investigator is involved when trying to assess the impact of factors which are difficult to measure. But also the investigator using regression analysis has often to choose between alternative measures for the variables and between the large number of regressions which the computer produces.

In many respects much of industrial economics rests on a deductive approach which proceeds from a set of assumptions and seeks to produce predictions from those assumptions, and this is followed by seeking to test those predictions against reality. The deductive approach has largely taken over from the inductive approach which often used an intensive and largely descriptive study of a particular industry to generate general ideas concerning the operation of industry. The two approaches are not as separate as might appear, for many of the assumptions which are used as the basis of the theories have been generated by intensive case studies.

There are two basic approaches to industrial economics. One of these approaches focuses on the interaction of firms within a particular industry, where the characteristics of the industry in terms of number and relative size of firms, ease of entry, elasticity of demand for products, etc., are important determinants of the performance and behaviour of that industry. Within this broad approach, the structure-conduct-performance paradigm has been widely used. In Part One, our attention falls mainly on this approach. We systematically explore the key characteristics of industrial structure in terms of the number and relative size of firms (Chapter 3), the cost conditions (Chapter 4), and the behaviour of firms including collusion and attitudes to new firms (Chapter 5). Then we investigate the impact of structure on profitability (Chapter 6), advertising (Chapter 7), technical progress (Chapter 8) and price changes (Chapter 9). In each of these chapters we consider the topic in a broader context than merely the impact of industrial structure on that element of performance. The final chapter in this part provides a critical assessment of the structure-conduct-performance approach (as well as the broader approach of focusing on industries rather than firms).

The alternative approach, which underlies Part Two, is to treat the firm as central in the analysis, and implicitly pay little regard to the influence on a firm's behaviour and performance of the industries in which it operates. Thus firms are taken as central, industrial structure as peripheral. There will be some effect on, say, a firm's profits arising from the general profit experience of the industries in which it operates but this is taken as dominated by the nature and efficiency of the firm itself. In Chapter 11, we survey the empirical literature relevant to the managerial theories of the firm including the questions of whether there has been a shift of control from shareholders to managers (the so-called managerial revolution) and whether growth and profitability are influenced by differences in control as between owner-control and manager-control, and the determinants of managerial income, and possible incentive effects arising from those determinants. This chapter also addresses the question of whether the internal organisation of the firm influences its performance. The relationship between growth, profitability and size of firm is the first topic investigated in Chapter 12, which is followed by a discussion on the forces influencing horizontal and vertical integration and diversification. In Chapter 13 theories of acquisition and mergers are outlined, and then the empirical evidence relating to those theories and on the consequences of acquisitions is examined. This list of topics indicates that it is features of the firms, rather than features of industries in which they operate, which are the central features of the analysis.

In the third part of the book there is a discussion of public policy towards industry and firms. The discussion is undertaken in three stages. In Chapter 14, the question of whether the welfare losses imposed on consumers and the economy by monopoly are substantial is examined. These welfare losses are intended to be a measure of the extent of resource misallocation, and arise from higher prices (relative to costs) under monopoly as compared with perfect competition. In Chapter 15, four basic approaches to public policy are examined, and these policies range from minimal government intervention through to government control of prices and investment and public ownership. These approaches are discussed in terms of the theoretical positions which provide their foundations, and the type of empirical evidence (widely interpreted) which would be consistent with each of these approaches. Finally, Chapter 16 discusses the types of policies pursued in the post-war period, particularly in the United Kingdom, with a brief look at policies in the United States and the EEC. This policy discussion covers monopoly and mergers policy, policy on restrictive trade practices, policies for restructuring industry and other forms of intervention such as price control.

2 STRUCTURE, CONDUCT AND PERFORMANCE: AN OVERVIEW

The dominant approach to industrial economics is the one which is usually described as the structure-conduct-performance approach. In this approach the key to understanding and predicting the performance of an industry in terms of profitability, growth, advertising, technical progressiveness, etc., is to be found in the structure of the industry. The structure of an industry covers factors like the relative and absolute size of the firms involved, the ease of entry into the industry, and the elasticity of demand for the output of that industry. The conduct of firms covers the objectives of the firms, price-setting behaviour, and attitudes to rivals (actual and potential). The conduct of firms, which is expected to be heavily conditioned by the structure of their industry, generates the performance outcome for the industry. The notion that the structure of an industry largely conditions the activities of the firms involved and thereby the performance of the industry means that emphasis is placed on the nature of the industry rather than on the nature of the firms in the industry.

The various dimensions of structure and performance, and the influences of structure on performance, are discussed below. The conduct and behaviour of firms is highlighted in Chapter 5. A critique of the general approach is undertaken in Chapter 10.

One possible starting point in deriving the structure-conduct-performance approach is the theories of perfect competition and monopoly. The structural features of perfect competition are a large number of firms of roughly equal size with free entry into the industry. In perfect competition, in long-run equilibrium price equals marginal cost, and also equals average cost, and profits are at a 'normal' level. Under monopoly, the industrial structure is one firm with high barriers to entry; and the outcome is that marginal cost is equated with marginal revenue, price is above marginal cost and there are super-normal profits. These two models provide description of the extremes (an infinite number of firms versus one firm, free entry versus blockaded entry), and all industries in practice can be seen as falling somewhere between them. The position of any particular industry can be located along this spectrum by looking at the structure of that industry in terms of the number of firms, ease of entry, etc., and from that the performance of that industry predicted, particularly in respect of profitability. Thus as we move through the spectrum from industries with a large number of firms to industries with only a few firms, it is postulated that profitability will rise from the normal level towards the super-normal level of monopoly.

This general idea can be formulated by taking the Cournot model of oligopoly, under which it is assumed each firm makes its output decision in the belief that its rivals will keep their output constant (see, for example, Sawyer (1979a), ch. 4). Take the simple case of a linear demand function, so that price $p = a + bQ$, where Q is the output of the industry, which is a homogeneous product. There are n firms of equal size in the industry. For firm i with output q_i, profit $\pi_i = p \cdot q_i - d \cdot q_i$, where d is the constant unit cost of production. The maximisation of profits yields as a first-order conditions $d\pi/dq_i = b \cdot (dQ/dq_i) \cdot q_i + a + bQ - d = 0$ and the Cournot assumption that each firm believes that other firms hold their output constant gives $dQ/dq_i = 1$. Summing over all n firms gives $Q = n(d - a)/(n + 1)b$, and then $p = (a + nd)/(n + 1)$. Under conditions of perfect competition price equals marginal cost, so $p = d$, and then $Q = d - a$. Under monopoly, in the above $n = 1$, and then $p = (a + d)/2$ and $Q = (d - a)/2b$. This analysis indicates that as the structure of an industry moves from perfect competition through to monopoly, that is from n at infinity through to $n = 1$, so price and output change from perfectly competitive level to the monopoly level.

Now this analysis has been based on a rather naïve assumption of the Cournot model. The use of a more general model does not alter this basic conclusion but draws out the importance of other factors. This general model retains the assumption of firms producing a homogeneous good, but the assumption of heterogenous goods would not change the basic results but complicate the analysis. Firm i seeks to maximise profits $\pi_i = p(q_i + Q_i)q_i - C(q_i)$, where q_i is the output of firm i, Q_i the output of its rivals, p the price in the industry which depends upon total output $Q = q_i + Q_i$, and C are the costs of production. The first-order profits maximising conditions yield for each firm i:

$$\frac{d\pi_i}{dq_i} = q_i \left(\frac{\partial p}{\partial q_i} + \frac{\partial p}{\partial Q_i} \cdot \frac{\partial Q_i}{\partial q_i} \right) + p - \frac{dC}{dq_i} = 0$$

where the term $\partial Q_i/\partial q_i$ arises since the rivals are likely to adjust their output in response to firm i's output change, and this term reflects firm i's belief about this reaction.

Manipulation yields $-\dfrac{q_i}{Q}\left(\dfrac{Q}{p}\cdot\dfrac{\partial p}{\partial q_i}+\dfrac{Q}{p}\cdot\dfrac{\partial p}{\partial Q_i}\cdot\dfrac{\partial Q_i}{\partial q_i}\right)=\dfrac{p-c_i}{p}$

where $c_i = dC/dq_i$ is marginal cost. Now the elasticity of demand $e = (p/Q)\cdot(\partial Q/\partial p) = (p/q_i)\cdot(\partial q_i/\partial p)$, the perceived response of rivals $a_i = (\partial Q_i)/(\partial q_i)$ and the share of firm i, $s_i = q_i/Q$. So we can write the above equation as

$$\frac{s_i}{e}\,(1 + a_i) = \frac{p - c_i}{p}$$

To arrive at the average mark-up of price over marginal cost in an industry we take the above equation for each firm i weighted by the firm's share s_i, and hence can derive $\Sigma s_i^2(1 + a_i)/e = (p - c)/p$ when $c = \Sigma s_i c_i$. (Recall that by definition $\Sigma s_i = 1$.) Thus the mark-up of price over marginal cost depends upon the elasticity of demand (e), an indicator of the degree of industrial concentration (Σs_i^2, which is labelled the Herfindahl index discussed further in the next chapter), and a measure of the degree of collusion between the firms (a_i). The first two of these factors are elements of the structure of the industry. The third factor relates to the behaviour of the firms, although it may be heavily conditioned or even determined by the structure of the industry. It can be seen that as Σs_i^2 varies from zero (its value under perfect competition) to unity (its value under monopoly), the mark-up of price over marginal cost rises. When $a_i = 0$ (for all firms), then the Cournot solution arises, and the mark-up of price over marginal cost depends on industrial concentration and the elasticity of demand. When $a_i = Q_i/q_i$, then $\Sigma s_i^2(1 + a_i) = \Sigma s_i^2\cdot(1 + Q_i/q_i) = \Sigma(s_i^2(1/s_i)) = 1$ since $q_i + Q_i = Q$ and $\Sigma s_i = 1$. Then $(p - c)/p = 1/e$, and the outcome is one of joint profit maximisation, and is analogous to the outcome under monopoly.

This type of approach forms a basis for the view that structure (in this case industrial concentration and the elasticity of demand) working through behaviour (profit maximisation and the output response of rivals) determines performance (the mark-up of price over marginal cost). In later chapters we will discuss alternative ways in which structure may influence profits, and how structure affects other dimensions of performance such as advertising, technological advance and price behaviour.

Elements of Structure and Performance

What are the main features of the structure of an industry? Much of the discussion on the 'structure-conduct-performance' approach begins from contrasting perfect competition and monopoly. Those two polar extremes differ in two major dimensions of structure, the number and relative size of firms and the extent of barriers to entry into the industry.

The number and relative size of firms is usually placed under the general heading of either the size-distribution of firms or industrial concentration. Most industries do not fit neatly into the category of a large number of small firms or of one firm. In most industries, since the size and importance of the constituent firms varies from the small and insignificant to the large and important, the simple use of the number of firms in the industry is not sufficient. The way in which this problem has been tackled forms the major topic of Chapter 3 on concentration.

Barriers to entry into an industry comprise all the factors which lead to new entrants into the industry being at a disadvantage *vis-à-vis* the existing firms. One factor is the existence of economies of scale which means that a new entrant would have to produce on a relatively large scale, increasing supply by a significant amount and thereby depressing price by a significant amount. Another factor is the extent of product differentiation and advertising so that a new entrant has to incur costs to overcome the loyalty of consumers to existing products. A third factor is the ability of existing firms to produce and distribute at lower costs than new entrants through, for example, access to cheaper raw materials, accumulated knowledge of the industry, etc. In Chapter 4 we consider the way in which economists have sought to measure economies of scale and the findings of their research. The other elements of barriers to entry which have just been mentioned are discussed in Chapter 5.

The linkage of structure to performance runs through the conduct of the firms in the industry. The conduct of firms can be considered in terms of their objectives. The motivation assumed for firms under both perfect competition and monopoly is short-run profit maximisation, and indeed this motivation is generally retained for the analysis of oligopoly. Some of the alternative objectives of firms are briefly considered in Chapters 5 and 11. One major concern in Chapter 5 is the ways in which firms try to build barriers against entry into their industry in order to protect their future position. Another major concern in that chapter is the possibilities of collusion amongst independent firms. The building of entry barriers and collusion are major examples of the forms of conduct and behaviour which influence directly, or indirectly, industrial performance.

The four elements of industrial performance which we examine in detail are profitability, advertising, technical progress and price change (and pricing in general). In each case it is necessary to look at the ways in which the links between structure and performance have been developed. But in every case there are alternative approaches, and the variants are discussed before a consideration of the empirical evidence.

If the industrial structure determines or influences performance, then governments concerned with aspects of industrial performance (particularly aspects like price changes, technological progress and employment levels) would seem to have a potentially powerful instrument of policy at their disposal. The route by which industrial performance could be improved would then appear to be through making changes to the industrial structure. If, on the other hand, structure has little effect on performance, then there would be little *economic* purpose in seeking to change industrial structure. There may, however, be political reasons, such as a desire to avoid undue concentration of economic decision-making, in seeking to change industrial structure, particularly the reduction of concentration. However, when an oligopolistic structure has become established, the large firms in such a structure may wield considerable political influence and may resist any attempts to change industrial structure which is to their disadvantage. There may be practical difficulties of changing industrial structure which may involve merging firms together or breaking up firms.

Such considerations feed into any discussion of public policy. Difficulties arise because evidence is not available on many key propositions and because there is disagreement over the evidence and its interpretation. Further ideology and political preferences (or value judgements) are almost certain to play a role in any such discussion. Nevertheless such considerations are of relevance and in Chapter 15 we indicate the nature of the empirical results which would be consistent with each of the four basic policy approaches discussed there.

Some Econometric Considerations

Most, though not all, econometric estimation in industrial economics relates to a single equation of the form:

$$y_i = a_0 + a_1 x_{1i} + a_2 x_{2i} + \ldots + a_n x_{ni} + u_i$$

where y is the variable which is being 'explained' and $x_1, x_2, \ldots, x_n$

the variables which are believed to determine y and u is a random variable. The subscript i refers to industry i so that, for example, y_i is the observed value of y for industry i. The presence of the random variable implies that the variables $x_1, x_2, \ldots, x_n$ are not able to predict the value of y exactly. The presence of the random variable can arise from the omission of relevant variables (through problems of measurement, incorrect specifications, etc.), inexact measurement of the variables involved (both the y variable and the x variables) as well as random factors.

The next few paragraphs provide the briefest of introductions to econometrics, and anyone familiar with econometrics should skip on to the next subsection headed Some Problems.[1]

The ordinary least squares estimation of the above equation proceeds by seeking to estimate the values of $a_0, a_1, a_2, \ldots, a_n$ (and we label those estimates $\hat{a}_0, \hat{a}_1, \hat{a}_2, \ldots, \hat{a}_n$) so that the sum of squares $\Sigma(y_i - \hat{y}_i)^2$ is minimised where $\hat{y}_i = \hat{a}_0 + \hat{a}_1 x_{1i} + \hat{a}_2 x_{2i} + \ldots + \hat{a}_n x_{ni}$. Thus $\hat{y}_i$ is the value of y for industry i which would be predicted with the known values of $x_1, x_2, \ldots, x_n$ for industry i and the estimated values of the coefficients $a_0, a_1, \ldots, a_n$. Using the criteria of the squared difference between actual and 'predicted' values of y, this technique seeks to minimise the difference between actual and 'predicted' values. We label this difference $y_1 - \hat{y}_i$ as e_i the residual for industry i.

Regression results generally report the value of R^2 (the square of the correlation coefficient), which is defined as $1 - \Sigma e_i^2 / \Sigma(y_i - \bar{y})^2$ which can also be written as $1 - \Sigma(y_i - \hat{y}_i)^2 / \Sigma(y_i - \bar{y})^2$. Thus R^2 is a measure of the extent to which the predicted values on the y variable ($\hat{y}_i$) lie close to or far away from the y variable (y_i). When the 'distance' of $\hat{y}_i$ from y_i is in total as large as the distance of $\bar{y}$ from y_i, then it can be seen that R^2 will take the value zero (since then $\Sigma e_i^2 = \Sigma(y_i - \bar{y})^2$. When the selected equation is able to predict exactly the values of y_i (i.e. $\hat{y}_i = y_i$), then the value of R^2 is unity. Hence R^2 is commonly used to describe how well the estimated regression line fits the observed data.

If the random term were always zero, then with $n + 1$ observations on y and the x's we would be able to calculate exactly the value of the a's. But the presence of random term means that the estimated values of a's are subject to a range of doubt, and this range of doubt is indicated by the standard error of the estimate.

There is often interest in hypothesis of the form that the value of a_1 is a_1^* (which will often be zero or unity), formally expressed as $H_0: a_1 = a_1^*$. The alternative hypothesis is then $H_A: a_1 \neq a_1^*$. The centre of interest lies in whether the observed difference between a_1 and a_1^* is in some relevant sense significant, and whether a_1 is greater or less than a_1* is not important here. The conventional statistical test which is applied is to look at the ratio $Z = (a_1 - a_1*)/s.e.(a_i)$ where $s.e.$ denotes standard error. This variable has a statistical distribution known as the t-distribution. The exact shape of that distribution depends upon the number of degrees of freedom which is equal to the number of observations minus the number of estimated coefficients. Essentially we form an acceptance region lying between Z_L and Z_H such that if Z lies within that range then a_1 is regarded as being 'close' to a_1*, and H_0 is accepted (more strictly not rejected), whilst if Z falls outside that region, then H_0 is rejected.

The acceptance region of H_0 depends upon the level of statistical significance which is chosen. Taking, for example, the conventional level of 5 per cent, Z_H is fixed by reference to the tables for the t-distribution using the value of t for the relevant degrees of freedom and the $2\frac{1}{2}$ per cent cut-off, and Z_L as the negative of Z_H. This is illustrated in Figure 2.1, with 25 degrees of freedom assumed. This if a_1's true value was a_1*, then from the information available it is estimated that there is a $2\frac{1}{2}$ per cent chance that a value of Z in excess of 2.06 would be observed, and a $2\frac{1}{2}$ per cent chance of a value less than -2.06 and hence a 5 per cent chance that the value of Z falls outside the acceptance region.

However we are often interested in whether a_1 is greater than a_1* (particularly when a_1* is zero), in which case the alternative hypothesis becomes $H_A:a_1 > a_1*$. The acceptance region now becomes $Z > Z'_H$, where again the value of Z'_H is derived from the t-distribution tables. With 25 degrees of freedom and the use of the 5 per cent significance level the value of Z'_H is 1.708.

We report in parenthesis below the estimated coefficients the standard error of the estimate, even where a t-ratio was given in the original source.

Most econometric analysis in industrial economics relates to cross-section observations rather than time series. In other words, the observations are drawn from a number of industries at a specified time rather than from one industry for a number of time periods. This means that many of the problems associated with time series (such as serial correlation) do not generally arise in industrial economics. For this reason statistics like the Durbin-Watson statistic are not generally reported. There are problems such as heteroskedasticity (discussed below) which are more associated with cross-section analysis than time series which do need to be taken into account. Cross-section regression frequently yields R^2 which are much lower than those typically reported in time series.

Figure 2.1: Acceptance and Critical Regions for a t-distribution

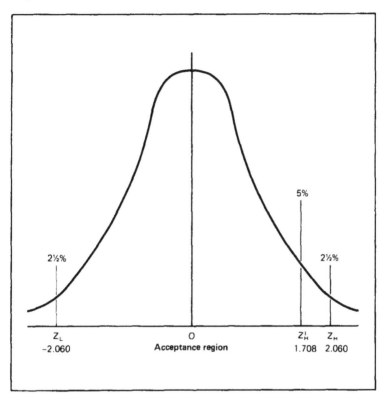

Some Problems

The use of ordinary least squares estimation of a single equation poses a number of problems in the context of industrial economics. The first major problem area is that many variables which the theory indicates should be included are excluded because of lack of data or virtual impossibility of measuring variables. In structure-profitability relationships, for example, variables such as the elasticity of demand and effective competition from imports are thought relevant but are difficult to measure. When a potential explanatory variable is omitted, then a degree of 'explanation' achieved (in terms of R^2) is thereby reduced. Whilst it is annoying that the power of explanation is reduced, that in itself is not crucial. The crucial problem is that the omission of a variable may affect the coefficient and apparent statistical significance of the other variables.

Let us see how these remarks impinge on the structure-profitability relationship where it is generally the case that the elasticity of demand cannot be measured. Above we saw that the elasticity of demand plays an important part in the determination of the mark-up of price over marginal cost and hence of profitability. One partial remedy is to restrict the analysis to those industries which are felt to have roughly the same elasticity of demand: alternatively, if it is acceptable to assume that the elasticity of demand for a product does not change over time, to look at changes in profitability in terms of changes in structure. However, the other elements of structure may be influenced by the omitted elasticity of demand. For it is predicted that the smaller is, in absolute terms, the elasticity of demand, the larger will be the mark-up over marginal costs under monopoly, and hence the greater is the incentive for firms to merge in order to move towards a monopoly situation. Thus profits may be found to be higher under monopoly, but the ultimate reason could be smaller elasticity of demand which induced the formation of a monopoly situation.

A second and related problem is the use of proxy variables, in an attempt to measure a relevant variable. An example of this occurs where the degree of product differentiation is thought to be relevant in the determination of profitability (see pp. 107–11). The precise measurement of product differentiation has so far proved impossible, and a number of attempts have been made to allow for it in the estimated equations. One attempt has been to argue that the level of product differentiation is associated across industries with the ratio of advertising to sales, and that the advertising-sales ratio can be used as a proxy for the degree of product differentiation. This poses two problems. First, there is unlikely to be an exact relationship between product differentiation and the advertising-sales ratio. Second, the interpretation of the estimated coefficient is made difficult since advertising may have a direct effect on profitability.

Another approach is the use of subjective judgement often combined with the use of dummy variables. A dummy variable is a variable which takes on values of zero or unity, and the dummy variable could be assigned the value zero if product differentiation was judged to be low in an industry and the value unity if there was a high degree of product differentiation judged to be present. The use of dummy variables means that there is a sharp distinction made between the two categories (in this case of degree of product differentiation). The problems of using subjective judgements are fairly clear.

A third area of concern is that the theory makes predictions about equilibrium outcomes, but there is no guarantee that the actual

Figure 2.2: Disequilibria and Equilibria Relationships

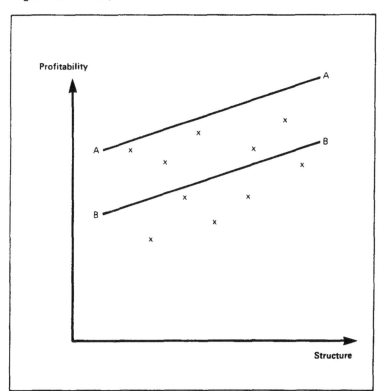

observations relate to a situation of equilibrium. There is the fundamental question of the usefulness of theories which deal with infrequently observed equilibria.

The importance of the disequilibrium situations depends on their relationship to the equilbrium situations. If the observed disequilibrium outcomes are evenly scattered around the equilibrium situations, then in terms of the estimated regression equation this provides a reason for the random terms. In terms of the structure-profitability relationship this would mean that some industries would be earning profits at the equilibrium level and others would have profits below the equilibrium level. The estimated structure-profitability relationship would not be affected, though the random terms will be larger and the R^2 lower than if equilibrium held. However, disequilibrium may be more likely to occur in some types of industries than in others. For example, it could be argued that high-concentration industries adjust to equilibrium more rapidly than low-concentration industries, and hence the departure from equilibrium may be more pronounced in low-concentration industries than in high-concentration industries. This leads in this example to the dispersion of the random terms being larger for low-concentration industries than for high-concentration ones. The general problem when the dispersion of the random terms is related to an independent variable is known as heteroskedasticity, and is discussed below.

Another possibility is that observed disequilibrium tends to lie on one side of equilibrium rather than the other. For example, equilibrium derived from profit maximisation would lead to disequilibria exhibiting profitability below the equilibrium level. The outcome of this is illustrated in Figure 2.2 where *AA* is the equilibrium relationship and *BB* is the estimated equation from observed disequilibria.

The fourth problem area can be described as the question of whether the relationship is continuous or discontinuous. The notion that the relationship is discontinuous could arise from a classification of industries as either basically atomistically competitive or basically monopolistic, with their profitability determined accordingly. Thus although industries vary in their level of concentration and barriers to entry they can be assigned to one or other of the two polar cases. In contrast the idea that the relationship is a continuous one would mean that as industrial structure varies between the atomistically competitive through to monopoly, so profitability gradually changes. These two alternatives are summarised in Figure 2.3, with the curve *AB* indicating a continuous relationship and *CDEF* a discontinuous one. A third variant would correspond to the curve *CDG*, where there is a threshold effect, such that for a range of structure there is no impact of changing structure on performance, but after that there is such an impact.

There is one particular problem of applying the discontinuous approach which is the identification of the 'break-point' (or of the threshold). The data on industrial structure do not reveal any obvious break in the variation from atomistic competition to monopoly so that there has to be experimentation with the data to determine the break-point. The danger is that if a lot of possible break-points are tried, then the chances of finding 'phoney' break-points which reveal apparently significant differences in profitability between the competitive and the monopolistic industries are increased.

Finally, there are two problems of an econometric nature arising from the use of single equation ordinary least squares. The first one is that of heteroskedasticity, which means that the variance of the random variable

Figure 2.3: Continuous and Discontinuous Relationships

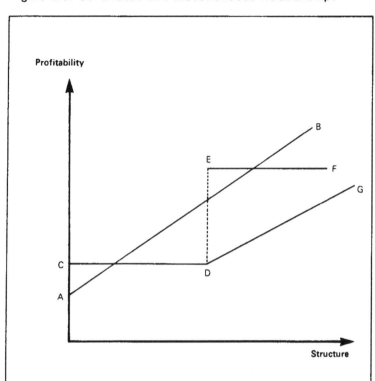

is related to one (or more) of the explanatory variables (in contrast to the assumption used in the derivation of the ordinary least squares estimates that the variance of the random term is constant). This often arises from the dispersion of experience (e.g. profit rates) being found to be smaller for larger firms than for smaller firms, leading to a lower variance of the random term for larger firms than for smaller firms. When size is an explanatory variable, this would lead to the variance of the random term being negatively related to one of the explanatory variables. This leads to the standard error calculated for the ordinary least squares estimate, which does not make any allowance for the heteroskedasticity, being biased upwards giving an acceptance region larger than the correct one. Conversely, when the variance and an explanatory variable are positively related the standard error is biased downwards. More recent econometric estimation tests for heteroskedasticity, makes a correction for it if necessary, as indicated below (particularly Chapters 6 and 12).

The final problem is that, in terms of the above terminology, whilst the x variables influence the y variable, the y variable may in turn influence some of the x variables. In terms of the structure-profitability relationship it is argued, for example, that whilst advertising intensity influences profitability, profitability also influences advertising intensity (see pp. 107–11). When the assumptions underlying the ordinary least squares estimation are satisfied, then the expected value of the estimate of the coefficient is the 'true' value, even though any particular estimate of the coefficient will usually diverge from that 'true' value. But in the presence of simultaneous effects the assumptions of ordinary least squares do not hold, and the estimated coefficients are biased away from their 'true' values (and this bias would not tend to disappear with an increase in sample size).

The equation which is estimated is usually linear, although some of the variables may be non-linear functions of other variables (e.g. some of the y and x variables may be logarithms, squares, etc., of other variables). But the linear form of the equation may be an inadequate representation of the underlying theory, which may indicate a complex functional relationship between the y and the x variables. For example, suppose that the theory indicated that $y = x_1 \cdot (1 + x_2)$, the estimation would be made for an equation of the form $y = a_0 + a_1 x_1 + a_2 x_2$, which may be a poor approximation. The goodness or otherwise of the approximation depends in part on the range over which the variables lie. It is technically possible to make non-linear estimation but it has not generally been pursued within the area of industrial economics.

This discussion indicates that the econometric testing of theories within the sphere of industrial economics is not a straightforward matter. Even when the theory is well-specified, there are numerous problems to be overcome before a satisfactory econometric test can be applied to the theory.

Definitions of Firms and Industries

Much of the theorising within industrial economics relates to concepts of firms, of industries and of markets, and so far we have used those terms without defining them. In the remainder of this chapter we review the way in which firms, markets and industries have been defined and measured.

Much discussion within theories of industry and firms centres around firms which produce a homogeneous product under similar or identical cost conditions. These firms are then grouped together as an industry and as firms which sell in the same market. This is the case with theories of perfect competition, homogeneous oligopoly and monopoly. In these cases, an industry is defined in terms of a product and the producers of that product are members of that industry. Market and industry are very closely related in the case of homogeneous products. It is assumed implicitly that each firm produces only one product, so that there is no problem with allocation of a particular firm to a specific industry in terms of the nature of the firm's output and the product which defined the industry. What happens when a world of differentiated products and of multiproduct firms is considered?

The complication introduced by the existence of differentiated products could be avoided in principle by saying that an industry is defined in terms of the firms who produce goods which are close substitutes in demand. More formally, a group of goods (or services) is considered as close substitutes for each other when the cross-elasticity of demand between any two of those goods (or services) is greater than some preassigned number x. If a high degree of substitutability is required so that the value of x is pitched high, then the resulting groups of goods will tend to be small. Conversely, if a low degree of substitutability is required with a low value of x used, then relatively large groups of goods will be placed together as substitutes. The approach assumes that it is possible to divide products into these groupings such that within each grouping the goods are close substitutes, but between any two goods in different groupings the degree of substitution is low (i.e. the cross-elasticity of demand between them is less than x). In this approach, the industry is defined in terms of demand conditions, and it would be expected that the size of industries would depend on the degree of substitutability used.

This approach focuses on the demand side and does not take account of the supply conditions. Supply-side considerations often come into play when an industry is defined in terms of a common production process or the use of a common major input. In the conventional theory, demand-side considerations and supply-side considerations converge in that firms facing similar demand conditions are assumed to have access to the same cost conditions. In practice, both demand-side and supply-side considerations are used in arriving at statistical definitions of industries. Industry groups such as leather goods and rubber products can be seen as defined by the use of a common major input (leather, rubber) rather than by demand considerations. There are cases where demand considerations and supply considerations clearly conflict with one another. Thus, for example, should leather clothing be classified under leather goods (as using a common major input and perhaps produced in factories producing other leather goods) or under the relevant clothing industries? In this particular case, the British system of classification places leather gloves and clothing under the relevant clothing industries. But the leather goods industry group contains a wide collection of goods (e.g. travel goods, saddlery, leather goods for industrial use) whose common characteristic is the use of leather, but which appear not to be close substitutes on the demand side. However, for each industry, there is a list of products which serves to define the industry, although the links between the goods on the list arise sometimes from demand considerations and sometimes from supply conditions.

Some of the reasons for the use of supply-side considerations arise from the manner in which statistics for the Census of Production are derived (and the Census forms a major source of data used in industrial economics). The basic unit for the collection of statistics is the establishment (approximately, in the case of manufacturing industry, a factory). An establishment is assigned to an industry by reference to the major output of that establishment. When there are establishments which use a common input to produce a variety of products (which are not demand-related), then it is not practical to define an industry from demand-side considerations. For if demand-side considerations were used, then an establishment producing goods from a variety of industries could not be easily assigned to a particular industry. This problem is not entirely avoided by using supply-side considerations (or a mixture of demand- and supply-side considerations). For when establishments produce different ranges of goods, then however an industry is defined, some establishments will be producing goods from more than one industry, and the allocation of such establishments to a particular industry may be difficult. In practice, an establishment is assigned to that industry in which it has the largest part of its output, even if the proportion of the establishment's output in the industry to which it is allocated is relatively low. The specialisation index is defined as the ratio of total sales of principal products of an industry (i.e. the products used to define the industry) by the establishments of that industry to the total sales by those establishments. For the British Census of Production, the specialisation ratio averaged 91.7 per cent (in 1980), and that ratio was above 80 per cent in the vast majority of industries. Definition of an industry, the statistics on any particular industry (relating, for example, to employment, profits) relate to the establishments allocated to that industry, but would include the effects of output in the establishments of that industry of products allocated to other industries. Similarly, some output of products of the industry under consideration will come from establishments allocated to other industries, but this output will not be included under the industry in question.

When establishments are used as the basic unit of analysis, those under common ownership within a particular industry are placed together as a single enterprise. Thus a company with establishments in different industries would be reported in the statistics as a number of separate enterprises operating in each of the industries in which the company had establishments. But in each industry, only those activities within establishments allocated to that industry would be included in the statistics for that industry. Thus, any influence on a company's activities arising from its multi-industry nature is not captured by the statistics nor by any analysis based on those statistics. When the published accounts of companies are used, the whole of a company has in general to be allocated to a single industry even though it may produce goods and services of several industries.

When demand-side considerations were discussed above, it was seen that the size of an average industry would depend upon the closeness of substitution used to define the groups of products. The degree of 'fineness' of industry definition used may have some impact on empirical work. If the way in which industries are defined is such that the typical 'statistical' industry is composed of several 'true' industries, then using statistics on those over-aggregated industries may mean that the underlying relationships between structure and performance are obscured by aggregation. Conversely, if a 'true' industry is subdivided into several 'statistical' industries, again the underlying relationship between structure and performance may well be lost.

A number of levels of aggregation are used in published statistics. We begin with the level of aggregation which is now labelled the group-level in the British Census of Production statistics. It is often referred to as the three-digit level (since three digits are often used to identify an industry) and was previously called the Minimum List Heading (MLH). At that level of aggregation in the 1980 Standard Industrial Classification used in the UK there are 103 industries covering the manufacturing sector and four typical industry groups are steel tubes, paints, varnishes and printing ink, cotton and silk industries, and motor vehicles and their engines. For some purposes, the three-digit level industries are disaggregated into four-digit industries (and occasionally five-digit industries).

In the other direction in terms of aggregation, there is the Class level (previously called the Order level and effectively the two-digit level). At that level, the 103 industry groups are aggregated into 21 classes. The four examples of groups given above are part of metal manufacture, chemical industries, textiles, and manufacture of motor vehicles and parts thereof respectively.

One definition of a firm is a person or group of people who turn inputs into outputs. But this view would include households seen as converting the input of income, household labour, etc. into the output of consumption goods and services. Thus we would wish to restrict this definition of firms to organisations which produce marketable output. Our discussion of firms below will largely be restricted to those organisations operating under private ownership.

This serves to define the functions of a firm, but it still remains to draw the precise boundaries around a firm. One view is based on the contrast between co-ordination of economic activity through a decentralised price mechanism and co-ordination by central decision-making (Coase, 1937). This view of the firm is further discussed in Chapter 12. Within the firm, resources are seen as allocated by the controllers of the firm, though market prices may influence those decisions. In a market-based economy, a firm would be seen as an area of the economy in which the price mechanism does not operate to allocate resources.

In practice the definition of a firm is based on ownership. Thus two organisations which operate for all practical purposes as independent entities but nevertheless are under common ownership (as could happen within a holding company), would be grouped as a single firm when ownership is used as a means of defining a firm. When, as will often be the case for empirical work reported in Part Two, statistics are drawn from company accounts, then the firm is implicitly defined in terms of ownership. But, for much of the work reported in Part One, organisations under the same ownership and operating within the same industry are grouped together, but a business which operates in, say, two industries will effectively be treated as two separate firms.

Notes

1. There are numerous texts on econometrics; see, for example, Allard (1974), Kmenta (1971), Maddala (1977).

3 INDUSTRIAL CONCENTRATION

Introduction

Concentration is regarded as an important element of industrial structure within the context of the structure-conduct-performance approach. Concentration is also an important indicator of the extent of the centralisation of economic activity and power, both within markets and within the whole economy.

The Measurement of Concentration

We begin by looking at some of the problems of measuring industrial concentration. Some basic problems can be illustrated by looking at statistics on firm size, and some relevant statistics for a fairly typical industry are given in Table 3.1. The firms (or enterprises as they are called in the Census of Production) are arranged by size as measured by employment. The first line, for example, refers to firms with between one and 99 employees, of which there were 1155 firms operating between them 1177 establishments (factories), accounting for 13.1 per cent of employment and 12.2 per cent of net output (value added).

The first feature of the figures in Table 3.1 is that whilst there are over 1200 firms in the industry, the largest five firms account for 38 per cent of employment and 42 per cent of output. Small firms (here, as often elsewhere, meaning firms with under 200 employees) are nearly 1200 in number in this industry, but account for around $17\frac{1}{2}$ per cent of employment. A second feature is that there is no clear division between large, medium and small firms. A third feature is that the large firms each operate a number of establishments, which are of above average size. Here, the largest ten firms operate on average six establishments, which employ on average 99 workers as compared with the industry average of 87 workers.

When we try to summarise statistics on firm size in one or two figures, some aspects of the size-distribution will be lost whilst others will tend to be overemphasised. For this reason, it is useful to have some idea of the properties of each measure of concentration, and the aspects of the size-distribution of firms which are overemphasised and those which are

25

Table 3.1: Size-Distribution of Firms in Vehicle Parts
Industry (UK 1981 Class No. 353)

Size-class (number of employees)	Number of enterprises	Number of establishments	Average number of employees	Share of employment (per cent)	Share of net output (per cent)
1—99	1155	1177	13.8	13.1	12.2
100—199	37	45	143	4.4	3.7
200—499	22	29	273	4.9	5.3
500—999	16	28	681	9.0	8.2
1000—1499	11	34	1282	11.9	11.4
1500—1999	5	13	1660	6.8	6.1
over 2000	10	61	6040	49.8	53.0
of which largest five firms	5	33	9260	38.2	42.2

Source: Calculated from Census of Production 1981.

underemphasised.

When concentration is used as a dimension of structure the main requirement is that the measure of concentration is relevant for explaining industrial performance. With a few exceptions indicated below, the theories of structure-performance relationships do not give clear guides to the way in which concentration should be measured. In the Cournot model outlined in the previous chapter, the theory predicted that profitability would rise as the number of equal-sized firms declined (with given elasticity of demand). A glance at Table 3.1 indicates that firms vary in size and it is not usually possible to identify a distinct group of large firms for the variation in size is practically continuous.

The other use which is made of the measures of concentration is to answer questions like has concentration increased, and is it higher in industry A than in industry B? These two questions have a basic identity in that a comparison is being made between two size-distributions of firms, in one case over time and in the other between industries. The nature of the problem is illustrated in Figure 3.1, where the cumulative share curves for three industries (or equivalently for an industry at three different times) are drawn. In a cumulative share curve, firms are ranked in terms of size, with largest first, and the share of the first firm, share of the first two firms, up to the share of all firms (i.e. 100 per cent) plotted. A comparison between industry A and industry B indicates that the share of the largest *n* firms is higher in industry B than in industry A, whatever value of *n* is used. Thus it would be relatively uncontroversial to say that industry B is more concentrated than industry A. But if we wanted to say how much higher in B than in A so as, for example, to predict by how much performance would differ between industry A and

Figure 3.1: Cumulative Share Curve

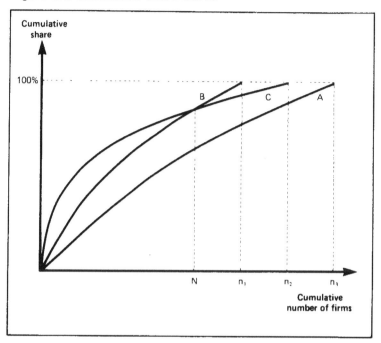

B, then a quantitative measure of concentration would be needed.

When the comparison is made between concentration in industry B and that in industry C then matters are not so straightforward. The share of the largest n firms is higher in industry C than in industry B for values of n less than N. But for values of n greater than N the reverse is the case. Thus the choice of n becomes crucial. Further, within the largest N, the large firms have a greater share in industry C whilst the medium-to-large firms have a greater share in industry B.

Any single measure of concentration will yield an answer to the question of whether industry B is more concentrated than industry C, and also answer the question of how much more concentrated industry B is than industry A. But the answer given may not be the correct one; indeed there may not be a correct answer. Whilst it would be convenient to be able to answer the questions listed in the opening sentence of this paragraph, and to summarise a whole size-distributiuon of firms in a single number, the search for a single ideal measure of concentration may be futile. Opinions differ on the relative importance of different aspects of the size-distribution. Until there is a concensus on that, it will not be possible to devise a measure which reflects that agreement on the relative weight to place on different aspects of the distribution. Here we describe widely-used measures of concentration and indicate some of their properties.

It is first necessary to say a little about the measurement of the size of firms. When concern is with the concentration in a product market, then output or sales in that market would seem a natural measure to use, since both are related to the importance of firms in that market. Similarly, concern with buyer concentration in the labour market would indicate that employment would be the relevant measure. But the ideal is not always available, and alternative measures of size have to be used. It is expected that measures of size such as sales, output, employment and assets would be closely related. It is usually thought that large firms are more capital-intensive than small firms, so that the share of the largest firms in terms of capital assets tends to be higher than the share in terms of output, which in turn tends to be higher than the share in terms of employment.

Measures of Concentration

A large number of possible measures of concentration have been proposed, and only the more widely used measures are discussed here. Curry and George (1983) summarise the ideas which have been put forward on the desirable properties which concentration measures should possess, and after defining a number of measures discuss the relationship between them. Aaronovitch and Sawyer (1975a) provide an extensive list of measures of concentration.

The simplest, and most widely used, measure of concentration is the *concentration ratio*. The n-firm concentration ratio (which we will abbreviate to *CRn*) is defined as the share of the largest n firms in the industry concerned (using whatever measure of size is thought appropriate or is obtainable). This measure can be written formally as $CRn = \sum_{i=1}^{n} s_i$ where s_i is the share of firm i in sales, employment or whatever measure of economic activity is appropriate or available. Firms are identified such that firm 1 is the largest, firm 2 the second largest, etc.

The obvious problem with this measure is the choice of the value of n. Unfortunately, economic theory does not indicate what value n should take. Oligopoly theory is cast in terms of dominance of a few firms, but how many is a few? Clearly when a comparison is made between industries B and C (Figure 3.1) then the choice of n is rather crucial.

Without a great deal of justification, a value of n in the range three to five has been frequently used at the industry level, and an element of concensus has developed that the activities of the largest three to five firms are of considerable importance.

A closely related measure, which poses a similar problem, is one which looks at the number of firms which account for X per cent of the industry, with 80 per cent being a figure often chosen. This measure recognises the importance of the number of firms in the industry, but implicitly says that a tail of smaller firms is largely irrelevant.

A measure of concentration which is increasingly used in empirical work is the Herfindahl index (sometimes called the Herfindahl-Hirschmann index) which we abbreviate to *HI*. This index is defined as $HI = \sum_{i=1}^{T} s_i^2$, where there are T firms in the industry, with the share of each firm (s_i) weighted by itself. Whereas the concentration ratio places a weight of 1 on the share of the largest n firms and zero on the share of the other firms, this index places a weight equal to the share on the share of the firm. This index thereby includes information on all firms and not just the largest n firms. The Herfindahl index can vary between a value of zero (where there are a large number of roughly equally sized firms) and unity (where there is just one firm).[1]

The third measure of concentration is *entropy*, which is used in physics as a measure of disorder. Its use in this context has been justified along the lines that an industry will be more competitive the greater the uncertainty as to which of a given number of firms will secure the business of a buyer chosen at random, and entropy is a measure of this uncertainty (e.g. Horowitz and Horowitz, 1968). Entropy is defined as $E = \sum_{i=1}^{T} s_i \log(1/s_i)$, so that the weight attached to any firm depends upon the logarithm of the firm's share. This is an inverse measure of concentration in that a rise in entropy indicates an increase in competitiveness, and hence a decrease in concentration. In an industry with firms, the value of entropy can vary between $\log T$ (when firms are of an equal size) and close to zero (when one firm controls the vast bulk of the industry).[2]

The measures discussed above are often described as *absolute* measures of concentration since they lay stress on the absolute number of firms and the share of firms. The two measures of concentration which are discussed below are described as *relative* measures and akin to measures of inequality. The sharpest distinction between absolute measures and relative measures can be seen by applying them to an industry dominated

by four firms of roughly equal size. The absolute measures would draw
attention to the fact of four firms, whereas the relative measures would
focus on the equality of size of the firms.

The absolute nature of the above measures can be seen more clearly
by using the concept of 'numbers-equivalent'. The numbers-equivalent
for a particular size-distribution of firms is the number of equal-sized
firms which would generate the same value of the concentration measure
as that derived from the given size-distribution. For example, suppose
that a particular size-distribution of firms produces a value of 0.25 for
the *HI* index. Four equal-sized firms would also generate a value of 0.25
for this index, for with each of the four firms having a share of 0.25,
the index has a value of $(0.25)^2 + (0.25)^2 + (0.25)^2 + (0.25)^2$, which
equals 0.25. In general, a value of the *HI* index of H would have a numbers-
equivalent of $N_h = 1/H$, for the *HI* index for an industry with N_h equally-
sized firms each with a share $1/N_h$ would be $N_h \cdot (1/N_h)^2 = 1/N_h = H$.

For entropy the numbers equivalent N_e for a value of E is anti-log
E. Entropy for an industry with N_e equally-sized firms would be
$N_e(1/N_e) \cdot \log(N_e) = \log N_e = E$. For an n-firm concentration ratio of c
then the average share of these n largest firms is c/n, and n/c equally-
sized firms would generate the same n-firm concentration ratio as that
observed. For example, from a four-firm concentration ratio of 50 per
cent, the average share of these largest firms is 12.5 per cent, then the
numbers equivalent here is 8 (i.e. 1/0.125).

The importance of this numbers-equivalent approach can be seen to
some extent by reference back to the Cournot model in which the number
of firms determined the profitability. Within the context of a particular
measure (and the weights attached to firms of different size implicit in
that measure) the observed size-distribution can be said to be equivalent
to one with the numbers-equivalent of equal-sized firms, and this provides a link between the measure of concentration and profitability.

The first of the relative measures of concentration is the *Gini coefficient*, which can be defined in terms of the Lorenz curve illustrated in Figure
3.2, as the ratio of the shaded area *ABC* to the area *ACD*. The axes for
this figure are the cumulative share of the number of firms and the
cumulative share of those firms. Thus the *x*-axis of this figure differs
from that of Figure 3.1 where the cumulative *absolute* number of firms
was used. There are a number of alternative, but equivalent, formulae
for the Gini coefficient. One of these is $(1/T) \sum_{i=1}^{T} (T - 2i + 1)s_i$ which
indicates the emphasis which this measure places on the rank of a firm.
The value of the Gini coefficient ranges between 0 (complete equality)

Figure 3.2: A Lorenz Curve

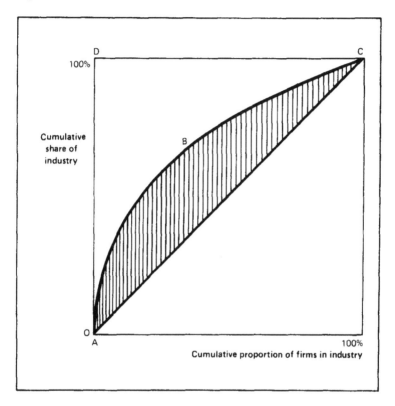

and 1 (complete inequality).

The second measure is the *variance of logarithms*, which is defined as $V = \sum_{i=1}^{T} (\log s_i/\tilde{s})^2/(T-1)$ where $\tilde{s}$ is the geometric mean of s_i's. The major argument for this measure is that if the underlying size-distribution of firms is log-normal, then the variance of logs is the natural measure to use. A log-normal distribution, illustrated in Figure 3.3, is rather bell-shaped when the log of size of firms is used, and whilst there is dispute about how close the size-distribution of firms is to being log-normal, there is little doubt that there is some similarity between the actual size-distribution and a log-normal distribution. If indeed the size-distribution of firms is log-normal, then knowledge of the variance and mean of the logarithm of size is sufficient to enable calculation of many other measures of concentration (Hart, 1975).[3]

Figure 3.3: Log-normal Distribution

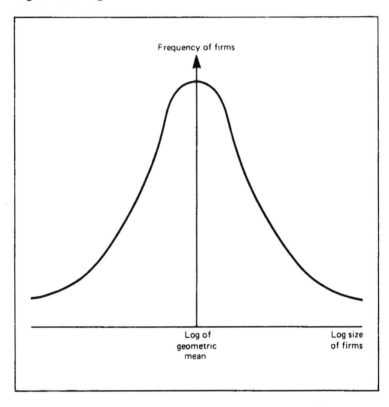

However there is one major problem with the variance of logarithms, which can be illustrated in terms of Figure 3.1; the problem is that there is no guarantee that the variance of logs would rank industry B as more concentrated than industry A, even though most would regard industry B as clearly more concentrated than industry A.[4]

Measures of concentration have often to be calculated from data which do not give information on individual firms but on size-classes of firms. In calculating measures of concentration, the size of firm within a size-class has often been taken as equal to the average for that size-class. In such cases, it means that the calculated measures of concentration (apart from the concentration ratios) tend to understate actual concentration since the inequality within a size-class is omitted from the calculations.

Concentration in Britain and the United States

In this section, we survey information on the level of and recent changes in concentration in Britain and, briefly, in the United States. The position on concentration for EEC countries is discussed in Locksley and Ward (1979) and in the annual reports on competition policy issued by the European Economic Community. The concentration ratio is used throughout this section as the measure of concentration, since most of the statistics are reported in terms of such ratios. When concentration at the industry level is discussed, some figures refer to industries defined at the three-digit level and some to industries defined at the four-digit level. When concentration is measured at the four-digit level, the calculated *CRn* will be considerably higher, *ceteris paribus*, than when concentration is measured at the three-digit level. Unless the level of disaggregation which is being used (i.e. whether it is the three-digit level or the four-digit level) is kept clearly in mind, there is room for confusion and comparison of the incomparable.

We begin by looking at concentration for British manufacturing industry in 1981. The Census of Production for that year provides information at the three-digit level, and the definition of industries used is that of the 1980 Standard Industrial Classification.[5] There are 103 industries and information is available for all but one of them.[6] The largest five firms (ranked by employment) accounted for, on average, 39.6 per cent of employment, 42.5 per cent of net output and 45.9 per cent of sales of the industry.[7] These averages conceal a wide variation from 98.5 per cent of the labour force by the largest five firms in the tobacco industry to 10.2 per cent in the leather goods industry.

Table 3.2: Distribution of Five-Firm Concentration Ratios, UK Manufacturing Industry 1981

Range (per cent)	By employment		By net output	
	Number of industries	Proportion of employment (per cent)	Number of industries	Proportion of net output (per cent)
0– 10	—	—	1	1.7
10– 20	20	31.9	15	19.3
20– 30	13	11.8	13	18.1
30– 40	18	13.6	18	13.1
40– 50	12	11.8	13	10.3
50– 60	15	11.4	14	15.5
60– 70	9	4.1	9	6.4
70– 80	6	6.7	8	7.1
80– 90	5	6.8	5	6.8
90–100	4	1.8	6	2.9

Source: Calculated from Census of Production, 1981.

Table 3.3: Average Five-Firm Concentration Ratios by Broad Industry Category

Industry category (Order)	Number of industries	Employment	Weighted average in terms of Gross output	Net output
22 Metal manufacture	4	61.9	65.2	63.0
23 Extraction of minerals n.e.s.	2	53.5	54.4	51.4
24 Non-metallic mineral products	8	43.9	46.6	48.2
25 Chemical industry	6	42.9	47.8	44.4
26 Production of man-made fibres	1	92.4	91.2	90.3
31 Metal goods n.e.s.	5	17.5	21.7	19.3
32 Mechanical engineering	10	23.0	24.5	22.4
33 Office machinery and data processing equipment	1	49.7	67.5	68.0
34 Electrical and electronic engineering	7	51.8	53.4	54.0
35 Motor vehicles and parts	3	66.1	72.8	69.4
36 Other transport equipment	5	80.0	79.7	76.1
37 Instrument engineering	4	31.8	36.5	31.0
41/2 Food, drink and tobacco	15	52.3	56.9	58.0
43 Textile industry	9	35.4	35.4	34.4
44 Leather and leather goods	2	22.7	27.9	25.4
45 Footwear and clothing	4	17.7	19.8	20.7
46 Timber and wooden furniture	7	14.4	16.4	14.9
47 Paper and paper products, printing and publishing	3	23.1	25.0	25.1
48 Processing of rubber and plastics	2	26.5	28.2	27.2
49 Other manufacturing industries	4	25.8	24.8	26.5

Source: Calculated from Census of Production, 1981.
n.e.s. = not elsewhere specified.
Note: Weighted averages are concentration ratios weighted by employment, gross output and net output respectively.

The variation in the *CR5* is further indicated in Table 3.2 . This shows, for example, that in 20 industries the largest five firms accounted for between 10 per cent and 20 per cent of employment, and that those industries accounted for 31.9 per cent of the total employment in all 102 industries. At the other end of the scale, there are six industries in which the largest five firms (in terms of employment) accounted for more than 90 per cent of net output, and those industries produced 2.9 per cent of the net output of the 102 industries.

The average shares of the largest five firms in employment, gross output and net output within each two-digit industry category are indicated in Table 3.3. The considerable variations in the average level of concentration across various sectors of manufacturing industry can be clearly seen from that table. Thus, in the industry category covering metal manufacture, there are four industries with an average of 61.9 per cent for the share of the largest five firms in employment in the industry. These averages are calculated as weighted averages, using employment, gross output, and net output respectively as weights.

In general, the industries which are generally associated with small-scale production, such as leather and leather goods, footwear and clothing, timber and wooden furniture have low levels of concentration. At the other end of the spectrum, heavy industry and mass production industries, such as metal manufacture and motor vehicles, tend to have high levels of concentration. But some industrial categories, such as food, drink and tobacco, office machinery and data equipment, which are not always thought to exhibit substantial economies of scale, also have above average levels of concentration.

The post-war experience of the British economy in respect of concentration can be divided into two distinct phases. The first phase, which lasted up to the end of the 1960s, saw substantial rises in concentration, whereas the second phase, covering the 1970s and into the 1980s, saw little change in the overall level of concentration. We look first at changes in concentration at the industry level and then at the aggregate level.

The evidence at the industry level for British manufacturing industry is summarised in Table 3.4.[8] The general rise in concentration up to 1968 is clear from that table, as is a broad stability in concentration since 1970. The exact changes between 1968 and 1970 and since 1979 are muddied by changes in the method of data collection. Although not shown in Table 3.4, in the period up to 1968, the number of industries in which concentration was increasing outnumbered those with decreases by at least a margin of two to one.

Whilst concentration at the industry or product level is relevant within

Table 3.4: Changes in Industrial Concentration, 1951–75

Period	Concentration measure	Number of comparable industries	Initial concentration (%)	Final concentration (%)
(a) Three-digit level (employment)				
1951–58	CR3	52	30.7	32.3
1958–63	CR4	117	29.0	32.2
1970–75	CR5	94	44.6	45.5
(b) Four-digit level (sales)				
1958–63	CR5	209	54.4	58.9
1963–68	CR5	297	63.5	69.0
1968–75	CR5	256	63.4	65.1

Source: Aaronovitch and Sawyer (1974) (and sources cited there), Hart and Clarke (1980), and calculations from Census of Production 1970, 1975.

the structure-conduct-performance approach, concentration at the aggregate level is also of interest. Aggregate concentration relates to the centralisation of economic power and decision-making within an economy, and also may give clues to the extent to which firms dominate more than one industry.[9] The share of the largest 100 firms in net output in the manufacturing sector over time is described in Table 3.5. A substantial increase in concentration up to 1968 is again revealed, with the share of the largest 100 firms having increased from 22 per cent in 1949 to 41 per cent in 1968. In the years since 1968, aggregate concentration in manufacturing has barely changed.

Hughes and Kumar (1984a, b) provide a number of calculations on aggregate concentration for the United Kingdom over the period 1968 to 1980. They conclude that '[t]aken as a whole the results suggest that in contrast to Census results for manufacturing alone, aggregate concentration in more widely defined sectors was increasing between 1968 and 1975, but that it has been declining since the mid-1970s'. For example, for the whole economy the largest 100 privately-owned corporations accounted for 25.7 per cent of private employment in 1968, rising to 31.5 per cent in 1975 and then falling to 27.5 per cent in 1980.

Statistics for the manufacturing sector have been more readily available than those for other sectors of the economy. The level of concentration outside the manufacturing sector is discussed in Aaronovitch and Sawyer (1975a), Chapter 5. An indication of concentration in one of those sectors — retail distribution — is given in Table 3.6. Figures for more recent years are not, in general, available. There are considerable variations between different sectors, with concentration higher than average in grocery and retail provision, and clothing and footwear. Hughes and Kumar

Table 3.5: Share of the One Hundred Largest Firms in
Manufacturing Net Output: UK

	%
1909	16[a]
1924	22[a]
1935	24
1949	22
1953	27
1958	32
1963	37
1968[b]	41
1970[c]	39.8
1975	41.7
1978	41.1
1981[d]	40.6

Source: Prais (1976) and calculations for Census of Production (various issues).
a. Approximate figures only.
b. The nationalisation of steel companies in 1967 reduced the increase between 1963 and 1968 by about one percentage point.
c. Improvement in data collection reduces figures calculated for years after 1968 in comparison with those for earlier years.
d. Changes in industrial classification means that the figure for 1981 is not completely comparable with figures for earlier years.

(1984a, b) cover the whole economy in their aggregate concentration calculations for the years 1968, 1975 and 1980, and some representative figures from their study are given in Table 3.6.

The level of concentration in American manufacturing industries is summarised in Table 3.7. In the first half of this century, an upward trend in concentration is clearly visible in those figures. The picture is not clear-cut for the post-war period, with some authors arguing that there has been a rise and some that there has been a decline in concentration. The impression from Table 3.7 is that concentration in the USA has changed only slowly in most of the post-war period. Shepherd (1982) classifies American industries into the four groups of pure monopoly, dominant firm, tight oligopoly, and effectively competitive. He calculates that industries in the last named group accounted for 52 per cent of national income in 1939, rising to 56 per cent in 1958 and to 77 per cent in 1980. The decline in the non-competitive sectors can be attributed in part to rising imports and the deregulation of some industries (e.g. airlines).[10]

The share of the largest 100 firms in manufacturing net output is now considerably below the corresponding figure for Britain. A comparison between concentration at the industry level in the UK and the USA cannot

Table 3.6: Further Data on Concentration in UK

(i) Concentration in Retail Distrubtion in 1971

		Per cent
All retail distribution	CR 25	22.8
	CR100	33.6
Grocery and retail provision	CR 25	29.1
Other food retailers	CR 5	12.7
Confectioners	CR 5	6.8
Clothing and footwear	CR 4	29.0
Household goods	CR 8	13.0
Other non-food	CR 4	22.3
General stores	CR 3	30.5

(ii) Percentage share of the largest 100 firms in

	1968	1975	1980
Whole economy, private	24.7	24.5	25.1
Non-financial, private	24.0	26.5	26.4
Financial (largest 40)	34.9	39.8	35.1

Sources: (i) Calculated from Census of Retail Distribution; (ii) Hughes and Kumar (1984a, b).

be undertaken from the figures given in Table 3.7 and earlier tables. The American figures refer to the four-digit level of industrial classification, whereas the bulk of the British figures relate to the three-digit level.

Multinational Enterprise

The figures discussed above relate to concentration of production within a particular country. A high level of concentration of production within a country may give less cause for concern if there is competition from foreign firms through imports. Many have suggested modifying concentration figures to take account of imports. For example, the largest five firms may account for, say, 75 per cent of domestically produced output sold in the home market, but if imports account for 50 per cent of the total domestic market, then the largest five domestic firms account for only $37\frac{1}{2}$ per cent of that market.[11]

However, a high domestic level of concentration in an industry may cause concern. It means that if that industry is considered to be of some national importance (as, for example, the car industry is often regarded), then the success or failure of the domestic industry lies in the hands of a few firms.

Table 3.7: Concentration in the United States

(a) Average CR4 for 166 industries 1947–70

	Unweighted	Weighted
1947	40.9	38.7
1954	40.6	43.0
1958	40.3	42.1
1963	41.3	42.9
1968	41.4	42.3
1970	42.7	42.6

(b) Unweighted averages for CR4, CR8 for 292 industries 1958–70

	CR4	CR8
1958	39.2	51.6
1970	41.2	54.2

(c) Share of the hundred largest firms in net output (per cent)

1909	22
1935	26
1947	23
1954	30
1958	30
1967	33
1976	34

(d) Share of largest firms in corporate assets (per cent)

	Largest 50	Largest 100
1909	14.0	17.7
1929	19.6	25.5
1948	20.7	26.7
1958	23.1	32.0
1967	24.6	32.0
1974	23.6	30.7

Sources: Mueller and Hamm (1974), Prais (1976), Stonebraker (1979), White (1979).
Notes: For alternative (and slightly different) series comparable with part (a), see Caves and Porter (1979).

Another factor in the interpretation of concentration figures, particularly when modified for international trade, is the extent to which 'domestic' firms and 'foreign' firms are under common ownership, i.e. are part of multinational enterprises. In this section, we first briefly review the evidence on the importance of multinational enterprises, which can be seen as an aspect of concentration at the international economy level. The abbreviation MNE will be used for multinational enterprise. The second aspect which we review is the nature of the industries in which MNEs operate.

The definition of multinational enterprise is not without difficulty. But

Table 3.8: Significance of Foreign Ownership: UK
Manufacturing Industry 1981

Industrial group	Percentage of employment accounted for by foreign enterprises	Percentage of total employment in foreign enterprises in this group
Metal manufacture	11.1	3.1
Extraction of minerals n.e.s.	2.3	0.1
Non-metallic mineral products	7.0	1.8
Chemical industry	30.8	11.4
Man-made fibres	17.1	0.3
Metal goods n.e.s.	8.1	3.8
Mechanical engineering	19.8	18.7
Office machinery, etc.	38.2	1.7
Electrical and electronic engineering	21.4	14.9
Motor vehicles and parts	36.1	15.6
Other transport equipment	1.8	0.8
Instrument engineering	30.8	3.3
Food, drink and tobacco	11.1	8.5
Textile industry	3.9	1.2
Footwear and clothing	2.9	1.1
Timer and wooden furniture	1.4	0.4
Paper, printing and publishing	12.7	7.2
Processing of rubber and plastics	19.7	5.1
Other manufacturing industry	13.2	1.1

Source: Calculated from Census of Production, 1981.

most definitions are along the lines used by Hood and Young (1979) that
'a multinational enterprise is a corporation which owns (in whole or in
part), controls and manages income-generating assets in more than one
country'. This would mean, for example, that a corporation which produced in just one country but exported through agents to other countries
or which had only some minority ownership interest in foreign firms (often
labelled portfolio investments) would not be included as multinational.

The scale of the operations of multinational enterprises can to some
degree be gauged by looking at the worldwide employment of such enterprises. The largest 500 MNEs have been estimated by Stopford and Dunning (1983) to have nearly 26 million employees in 1981, of which over
17 million were in the home country of the enterprises. These figures
can be compared with a total of around 300 million people in employment in OECD countries in 1981.[12]

The significance of foreign-owned firms in different UK manufacturing industries is indicated in Table 3.8. In this table, the operation of UK-
owned MNEs is not included. Around 60 per cent of the total employment

in foreign-owned firms in the UK is accounted for by just four industrial groups (chemical, electrical and electronic engineering, mechanical engineering and motor vehicles). Further, there are four industrial groups where foreign-owned firms account for more than one-quarter of employ- ment (namely, the first two named in the previous list plus instrument engineering and office machinery).

The industries in which foreign ownership is important as indicated by Table 3.8 corresponds with more general findings. First, there is a weak correlation between the level of concentration and the extent of foreign ownership. Caves (1982) concluded that the empirical evidence supports the view that foreign investment and seller concentration are closely associated. He reported on studies that indicate that 'foreign in- vestment is never prominent in unconcentrated industries, whereas it may or may not be in concentrated industries. (Concentration industries lack foreign investment when concentration rests on scale economies in pro- duction that national firms have attained)'.

The figures in Table 3.8 indicate a considerable variation in the in- volvement of foreign-owned MNEs between industries. These variations are not untypical, and not surprisingly economists have sought to explain these variations. Space precludes a full discussion for which the reader is referred to texts on multinationals, e.g. Hood and Young (1979), Caves (1982). Here we can note that links with advertising intensity and with research and development expenditure have often been noted. The latter case is of particular importance. The underlying argument is that firms will seek multinational operations in order to increase the returns generated from inventions arising from their research and development programmes. Hood and Young (1979) conclude that '[t]he impact of variables such as R & D, advertising and capital-intensity is thus clearly established'.

Determinants of Concentration

It has often been argued that the level of concentration in an industry is largely technologically determined, and that increases in concentra- tion reflect the impact of technological advance which increases the desired size of factory or firm. This line of argument can be formalised in an extreme form in the following manner. Suppose that there is a minimum efficient scale of production S such that average costs of production on a scale below S are so much higher than average costs for output greater than S so as to make production at a rate lower than S virtually impossible.

Then if the market size is R there is room in the industry for at most R/S firms. The n-firm concentration ratio would be at least $n.S/R$, where each of the n largest firms has a market share of at least S/R.

Before reviewing the evidence, there are two points which should be made about this proposition that concentration is technologically determined. First, in the form used above, the proposition implies that the size of firms would cluster around the minimum efficient size. In a less extreme form, it would be interpreted as indicating the minimum level of concentration which is compatible with existing economies of scale. Second, in seeking to explain concentration the concern is with the minimum efficiency scale of *firms*. Much discussion on economies of scale, including that in Chapter 4 below, is concerned with how unit costs change as the size of *factory* changes. The minimum efficiency scale (*m.e.s.*) of a plant (i.e. factory) is defined in terms of the scale of output after which unit costs fall, at most, only slightly. But as can be judged from Table 3.1, large firms typically operate a number of plants, so that if concentration is to be explicable in terms of economies of scale then one would have to look to economies arising from multi-plant operation and/or from increasing firm size. Examples of firm-level economies would include economies of scale in raising finance and in marketing. Multi-plant economies would include the lowering of labour costs through drawing on several labour markets.

Two main methods have been used to examine the proposition that technological factors determine the level of concentration in an industry. The first one has been to utilise international comparisons of concentration. The argument is that technological factors are common to most countries, leading to a similarity in the concentration for any given product in different countries. However, countries differ in their size, and hence in terms of the size of markets. This leads to a comparison of the rank ordering of industries in terms of concentration in different countries, rather than a comparison of the actual concentration levels. The second approach has been the direct measurement of the minimum efficient scale of firms, to see whether this can explain the level of concentration. The difficulty is finding estimates of *m.e.s.* which are not influenced by the observed degree of concentration.[13] Often measures of the relative size of factories in operation have been used, and such measures are likely to be related to the relative size of firms, whether or not technological factors are influencing the size of firms. Our earlier discussion on measures of concentration clearly indicates that measures of concentration are calculated from the relative size (i.e. market share) of the firms.

Much of the evidence of the relationships between industrial structure in different countries is surveyed by George and Ward (1975). They conclude that the 'general findings of these studies are that concentration tends to be higher in the UK than the US and that the concentration ranking of industries tends to be similar in both countries'. Extending the evidence to include European countries they conclude that the 'main findings of these studies in comparative industrial structure may be summarised as follows:

A. Concentration

(1) There is a general tendency for concentration to be inversely related to the size of the domestic market.

(2) Concentration tends to be positively related to plant size especially in Western European countries.

(3) The ranking of industries by concentration level tends to be similar in a number of countries.

(4) There is also a similarity in the level of concentration in particular industries in several countries, but with the UK apparently being something of an exception, though the data used are not very satisfactory in this instance . . .'

In their own work George and Ward find that concentration in the early 1960s was substantially higher in the UK than in France, Germany or Italy. For a group of 41 industries in manufacturing which are defined in a comparable manner in the statistics for all four countries, the (weighted) average CR4s were 30 per cent in the UK, 22 per cent in France and 19 per cent in both Germany and Italy. The simple correlation coefficient between concentration in a number of manufacturing industries in pairs of these four countries ranges between 0.56 (between the UK and Germany) and 0.80 (between France and Germany).

Some of the extent of underlying technological forces can, perhaps, be seen from the following remark of George and Ward when they say that 'more striking, however, is that the UK and other EEC countries are more similar with respect to plant concentration levels than with respect to the level of firm concentration'.

The other approach is the more direct one of seeking to relate levels of concentration to the factors which are thought to influence it, usually using cross-section regression analysis. Curry and George (1983) provide a summary of eleven such studies, all of which relate either to the United States or the United Kingdom.[14] Some measure of plant-level scale economies (more fully discussed below, pp. 90–1) was included in ten of the studies, and found to have positive and significant effects in all cases. In the other study (Ornstein *et al.*, 1973) the average firm size was included and again found to have a positive and significant effect on concentration.

There is a general consistency in the results found by the various studies. In the four studies where the plant-firm ratio was included, it was found to have a positive and significant effect. The industry size was found to have a negative effect on concentration (two studies), and the advertising-sales ratio a positive effect (three studies found this and results were mixed in a fourth study).

However, whilst 'there can be little doubt that technical factors, as reflected in optimal plant size, do play an important part in explaining inter-industry differences in the level of concentration . . . [Nevertheless], it is generally agreed that plant scale economies do not, except in a minority of cases, explain high levels of concentration . . . Multi-plant operation is also a feature of leading firms in highly concentrated UK markets'.

In many respects, it might be anticipated that changes in concentration could be explained by changes in the determinants of concentration, and this has been done to some extent. However, rather more emphasis has been placed on the question of whether the rate of growth of an industry has a deconcentrating effect. The basic argument here is that the faster an industry is growing, the more 'room' there is for new entry into the industry, and as new firms enter the industry the level of concentration will decline (*ceteris paribus*). The other variable which has often been included is the initial level of concentration, which enables the proposition that there is some tendency for concentration in highly concentrated industries to decline, to be tested.

Curry and George (1983) provide a summary of 17 studies on the determinants of changes in concentration. In their summary, they report that of the 15 studies where industry growth was included, it was found to have a negative impact on changes in concentration (i.e. faster growth led to lower rises in concentration) in 13 studies (of which seven were found to be statistically significant), and the remaining two studies found a positive but statistically insignificant effect. The initial level of concentration was found to have a negative impact on changes in concentration in nine of the ten studies where it was included.

There may be many other forces besides those discussed above operating on the level of concentration and changes in concentration. The discussion in this chapter has focused on the technological aspects, and has ignored forces such as the motives of the controllers of firms, the striving for growth, monopoly power, prestige, etc. Some of these forces will be discussed in Chapters 12 (stochastic factors) and 13 (acquisitions and mergers).

Notes

1. When there are T firms of an equal size, hence with share $1/T$ each, then $HI = T \cdot (1/T)^2 = 1/T$, and the larger is T the smaller is the index, and would tend to zero as T tends to infinity. With one firm, $s_1 = 1$, and hence $HI = 1$.

2. With T firms of an equal size, $E = T \cdot (1/T) \cdot \log T = \log T$ whereas with one firm with the bulk of the industry (so that s_1 is close to unity) and the other firms having a very small share (so that s_i is close to zero for i not equal to 1), then each of the terms in the entropy formula is close to zero (noting that $\log 1 = 0$).

3. Davies (1979a) argues that most concentration measures can be viewed as being influenced by both the number of firms in an industry and the degree of inequality of firm size. In the context of the log-normal distribution (illustrated in Figure 3.3), Davies maps out iso-concentration curves (i.e. curves along which the given measure of concentration is constant) for combinations of numbers of firms and the variance of log of firm-size (taken as a measure of inequality).

4. The idea that a measure of concentration should rank industry B as more concentrated than industry A is usually discussed under the heading of the measure obeying the 'principle of transfers'. For further discussion on this, see Hannah and Kay (1977), Chapter 2, and Sawyer (1977b); for a defence of the variance of logs see Hart (1971, 1980).

5. This classification replaced the 1968 Standard Industrial Classification, and is intended to be more in harmony with the classifications used within the EEC. The number of industries in manufacturing is now 103, compared with 155 industries used in pre-1980 Census of Production reports. Thus the reported concentration figures are now, *ceteris paribus*, lower than they were under the previous system of classification.

6. The one industry for which the five-firm concentration ratio is not given is sugar. This is because there are very few firms in that industry, and problems of disclosure of individual firm information would arise. Thus the sugar industry has a very high concentration figure.

7. These averages are weighted averages, where the weights are employment, net output and sales respectively. The corresponding unweighted averages are 44.0 per cent (employment), 46.0 per cent (net output) and 45.1 per cent (sales).

8. The details on concentration in manufacturing industries for earlier years are given in Leak and Maizels (1945) (for 1935), Evely and Little (1960) (for 1951), Armstrong and Silberston (1965) (for 1985) and Sawyer (1971) (for 1963). For a more extensive summary see Aaronovitch and Sawyer (1974) and Hart and Clarke (1980).

9. Utton (1979), Chapter 3, discusses the links between aggregate concentration and market concentration, and indicates the extent to which the largest 200 firms within manufacturing industry are the largest firms in the industries in which they operate (see also Utton, 1974a). Clarke and Davies (1983) calculate that over the period 1963 to 1968, the Herfindahl index for aggregate concentration in British manufacturing industries rose by 47 per cent, of which changes in market concentration accounted for a rise of 43 per cent, the remaining increase being accounted for by changes in the extent of multi-industry operations. But over the period 1971 to 1977, the aggregate Herfindahl index declined by 6 per cent, all of which was accounted for by changes in diversification.

10. Shepherd (1982) uses a number of criteria to classify industries into the four groupings he uses. These criteria can be summarised as follows:
(i) Pure Monopoly: market share of one firm approaches 100 per cent, with effectively blockaded entry and evidence of monopoly control over prices;
(ii) Dominant Firms: market share of largest firm over 50 per cent, with no close rival and high entry barriers and ability of largest firm to control prices;
(iii) Tight Oligopoly: Four-firm concentration ratio above 60 per cent, with stable market shares, medium to high entry barriers and ability of largest firms to control prices;
(iv) Effectively Competitive: Four-firm concentration ratio below 40 per cent, with unstable market shares, flexible prices and low entry barriers.

11. Adams (1980) provides examples of the differences between seller concentration and producer concentration in the market for passenger cars for each of ten countries. For example, in the UK for 1977, the largest four car firms accounted for 67 per cent of sales but 99 per cent of domestic production.

12. The two sets of employment figures are not exactly comparable in that some rather small part of employment by MNEs is outside the OECD area and the total OECD employment figures include public sector employment.

13. See Davies (1980) for a strong argument that studies on the determinants of concentration which use measures of minimum efficient scale based on actual plant size in operation are flawed.

14. Ornstein *et al.* (1973) provide an earlier summary of eight studies. The four of those studies relevant to our discussion here are also covered by Curry and George (1983). Two others, mainly interested in the impact of advertising on concentration, are discussed in Chapter 7.

4 COST CONDITIONS AND ECONOMIES OF SCALE

Introduction

The way in which unit costs change with the scale of production is of considerable importance. The impact of economies of scale on concentration was discussed at the end of the previous chapter, and their impact on the ease of entry into an industry is considered in the next chapter. When public policy favours active industrial intervention to change industrial structure, some indication is required as to whether the minimum efficient scale is small or large relative to the total market. In the former case a policy favouring small units would be indicated, whereas in the latter case large units may be favoured. In this chapter, the way in which the nature of the cost conditions under which firms operate has been estimated is the major topic. We also summarise the results of some of these estimations of cost conditions, and look at some possible sources of economies of scale.

The unit cost curve drawn in the first frame of Figure 4.1 relates to long-run costs and exhibits decreasing unit costs up to output of q_0 per period, and increasing unit costs thereafter. In an industry where all firms operated along such a cost curve, it would be easy to define the minimum efficient scale (m.e.s.) of production as q_0. However, it has often been argued that cost curves are typically more like the one drawn in the second frame of Figure 4.1. Here unit costs continue to decline (or at least do not increase) as the scale of output is increased. In this context the m.e.s. is defined as the level of output q_1 before which unit costs decline fairly rapidly and after which unit costs decrease slowly.

Increasing returns to scale (and economies of scale) are usually defined as a situation where when all inputs into the productive process are increased in the same proportion the volume of output increases in a greater proportion. Conversely, decreasing returns would generate smaller increases in output than the increase in inputs. However, when the scale of output is changed the nature and relative use of the inputs is likely to change. It may be expected, for example, that as the scale of output increases the degree of capital intensity rises. But within that change the type of the capital equipment is likely to be varied. Further, the balance between skilled and unskilled or between manual and non-manual labour

Figure 4.1: Illustrative Cost Curves

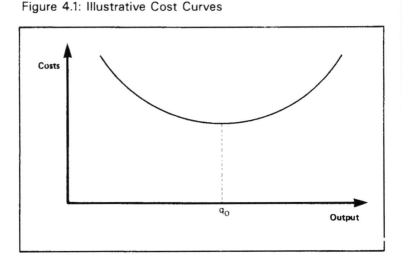

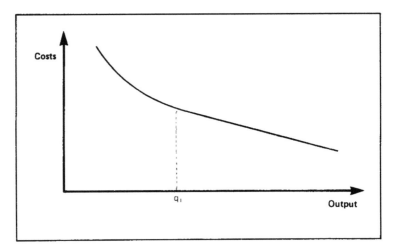

may change. Thus it is necessary to adopt a broader view of increasing and decreasing returns. The definition of increasing returns to scale becomes the situation of unit costs of output declining with increased output. This must refer to all costs (including capital costs), and can only relate to a particular set of relative prices for inputs from which the unit costs are calculated. It would include any change in the price of inputs which results from a change in the level of input usage. Thus if a firm had to pay more wages as its use of labour increased, that would have to be included. It is generally assumed that, for any scale of output, the firm is combining the inputs in an efficient manner. This effiency includes economic efficiency (choosing the least cost combinations of inputs) and technical efficiency (producing the maximum feasible output from given inputs). The definition for decreasing returns is analogous. The measurement of returns to scale under this definition may be only relevant to a particular economy, as it depends upon the particular relative prices used.

When discussing the relationship of costs and output, the emphasis will be on private costs for the firm. For policy purposes social costs are more relevant so that any conclusions arising from our discussion on the relationship between private costs and output may require modification before use in policy discussion. It is then useful to look at how different cost elements vary with output so that some assessment can be made as to whether a reduction in private costs with increased output is paralleled by a reduction in social costs. It is sometimes useful to distinguish between pecuniary and non-pecuniary economies. The former arise from changes in the price paid for inputs, whereas the latter arises from a change in the output/input ratio. Many, but not all, of the former are not changes in social costs though they are changes in private costs. This could arise, for example, from a reduction in the effective price of an input as the volume of purchase increased arising from an increase in monopsony power.

Sources of Economies of Scale

Some authors (for example, Florence, 1972; Pratten, 1971; Robinson, 1958) have argued that there are many sources of unit cost reductions as output expands. Here we mention four of the sources which have been discussed. The first has been labelled the 'principle of bulk transactions' (Florence, 1972). The essential idea is that the costs associated with making a purchase or a sale do not rise proportionately with the scale of the transaction. The second draws upon the gains from specialisation and from further division of labour. This has a number of aspects. Employees can be used for the tasks for which they are best equipped, and can concentrate on a narrower range of tasks as the scale of operations expands. When specialised factors are only available in some minimum quantity, then these factors can be more intensively employed as the scale of operations expands.

The third source arises from the relationship between area and volume. It is argued that for many productive processes the throughput depends upon the volume of the pipes, tanks, etc. But the costs of these pipes, tanks, etc., depend upon the area of material used in their production. This leads to a fall in unit cost as the output increases with the cube of the dimension of the pipes, etc., whereas the cost increases with the square of the dimensions.[1]

The final source arises from the response of firms to risk and the operation of large numbers, labelled by Haldi and Whitcomb (1967) as stochastic increasing returns. Suppose that a firm wishes to hold spare parts for machinery in order to reduce the frequency of a breakdown occurring, which cannot be immediately repaired to a given level.[2] The 'optimal' frequency of unrepaired breakdown may upon the probability of machine breakdown, the costs of breakdown etc. In the present context, with breakdown taken to be a random event, then the number of spare parts which the firm needs to hold to reduce the frequency of unrepaired breakdown to the chosen level, declines as the number of machines increases.

This discussion indicates several sources of decreasing unit costs as the scale of production increases. Are there any off-setting forces which prevent unit costs actually declining (as the scale of operation expands)?

A general source of diseconomies of scale is often seen as management. The emphasis may be on the problems of transmitting accurate information through successive layers of administration to the decision-makers which become progressively more difficult as the scale of the firm increases. Additionally, it may become more difficult for the controllers to ensure that their decisions are put into effect.[3] A related source may be that industrial relations become more difficult as the scale of operation (particularly the scale of plant) increases. Some have argued, for example, that strikes increase with the size of plant. There is also substantial evidence (summarised by George *et al.* 1977) that wages increase with plant size. Whilst it is difficult to establish why this happens, we can note here that if it reflects payment to overcome workers' dislike of working in a large factory, then this constitutes a source of diseconomies of scale.[4]

It is often useful to distinguish between plant-level returns to scale and firm-level returns to scale. Plant-level increasing returns to scale, for example, would arise if unit costs declined as the size of plant increased. These would be mainly increasing returns arising from production economies of scale. Firm-level returns to scale are those associated with a change in the size of firm, whether arising from a change in the average plant size or from a change in the number of plants operated by the firm.

Clearly for a firm operating one plant there is no distinction between plant-level and firm-level returns to scale. For large firms operating many plants, not only is there a distinction but in seeking to explain the emergence of multi-plant firms one would need to look to firm-level increasing returns rather than plant-level increasing returns. Much of the discussion in this chapter focuses on plant-level returns to scale, but we outline some aspects of firm-level economies of scale.

Estimation of Cost Conditions

We now examine three approaches to the estimation of cost conditions which have been proposed and used by industrial economists, and look at the problems which they raise. The approach of the econometric estimation of production functions is not discussed for reasons of space. The reader is referred to Walters (1963), Wallis (1973) and Johansen (1972) for discussion of the estimation of production functions. Our main concern in this section is with the estimation of the long-run relationship between average costs and the scale of output. However, one of the approaches (statistical cost curves) has been applied to the estimation of both short-run and long-run cost conditions, so that discussion of that approach deals with both the short-run and long-run cost curves. Later, we briefly discuss the possible dynamic relationship between unit costs and cumulative output under the heading of learning or experience curves.

Statistical Cost Curves

This approach is based on the idea of estimating an equation of the form $A.C. = f(q)$, where $A.C.$ is average costs, and q the rate of output, by means of regression analysis. The function f may be linear (indicating unit costs always increasing or decreasing with output), quadratic (so that the returns to scale can vary) or more complex. The observations on $(A.C., q)$ are obtained from existing firms. Thus in terms of Figure 4.2, from the scatter of observations on $(A.C., q)$ for firms, a 'best fit' line such as CC is estimated.

One of the advantages of this approach is that it utilises standard statistical techniques which makes it easier to evaluate the statistical significance of the results obtained, in contrast to the other two methods discussed. A second advantage is that it draws upon the actual operating experience of firms.

Figure 4.2: Estimation of Statistical Cost Curves

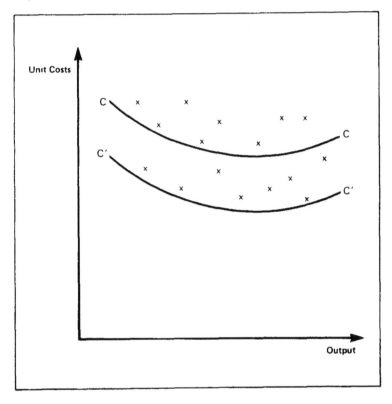

There are, however, some formidable drawbacks. The first one is that the observations on $(A.C., q)$ should be drawn from firms producing the same product. In principle, output is measured in physical units. But in general the nature of the product varies across firms. Output has then to be measured in money terms, and effects of market power influencing price show up in the measure of output. The firm itself is interested in the behaviour of *private* costs as output changes, no matter what the source or reason for the change in private costs, and this point becomes important if a translation from private to social costs is required. Because of the problem with heterogeneous products, one of the major studies (Johnston, 1960) on statistical cost curves is restricted in the main to industries which produce a homogeneous product.

A second drawback is that the cost curve (CC) identified by this method is not the cost curve about which economists generally talk, which would

Figure 4.3: Average Cost Curve

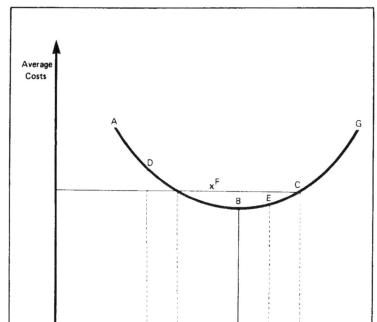

be the curve *C'C'* in Figure 4.2. This relates to costs when output is produced under full technical efficiency. The *CC* curve, being a 'best fit'
curve, will have some firms with costs below the curve and others with
costs above the curve. The *CC* curve cannot be a full technical efficiency
cost curve for such a curve would not have firms operating with lower
costs. However, if our main interest is to identify the *m.e.s.*, then the
m.e.s. derived from the observed *CC* curve may provide a reasonable
guide to the *m.e.s.* for the *C'C'* curve. This would result if the degree
of technical efficiency is roughly the same for all output levels.

The third and fourth drawbacks are based on a view of how the market
works. The third drawback argues that the output of firms results from
attempts to minimise costs, so that in terms of Figure 4.3 firms would
want to produce around point *B*. Small firms producing less than Q_m
have to operate along the section *AB* if they are to operate at all. But
larger firms do not have to operate along *BG*. An option available to these

firms is to operate another plant. In particular, a firm wanting to produce output of more than $2q^*$ would find it cheaper to operate two plants
(provided that there were not offsetting costs arising from co-ordination
of the plants). Thus it would be anticipated that few firms would locate
in the position of the curve labelled *CG*. Hence most observations on
costs and output would be drawn from the range *AC* with few from the
range *CG*. Thus a predominantly downward sloping unit cost curve may
be observed, but this does not necessarily imply that unit costs would
continue to fall if plants were larger than those currently in use.

A fourth drawback arises from the problem of measuring costs. The
centre of interest lies with average total costs including capital costs. We
take the case of an industry which produces an homogeneous product
and in which common price p prevails.

**Figure 4.4: Illustration of Impact of Revaluation of Capital on Cost
Curves**

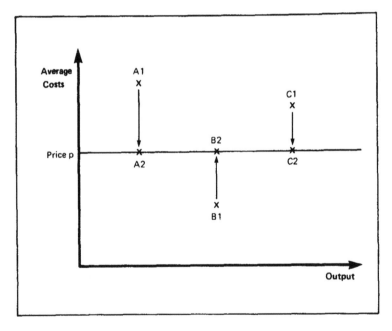

Three plants *A*, *B* and *C* (see Figure 4.4) are assumed to have a fixed output, and initially produce with unit costs *A*1, *B*1 and *C*1, respectively. From that figure it can be seen that plants *A* and *C* would make subnormal profits and plant *B* super-normal profits, when capital costs are based on the historic cost of the plant. Now the capital values of plants *A* and *C* are, it is argued, likely to fall and that of plant *B* to rise, for the amount which another firm would be prepared to pay for a plant will reflect its profit prospects. If the decline in capital value fully reflects the initial deviations for normal profits, unit costs shift to *A*2, *B*2 and *C*2 respectively. Thus there is a tendency at work towards constant unit costs being observed. How far this tendency operates depends upon the basis on which firms value their assets. When the value is based on historic cost, the tendency does not operate. But the tendency does operate when the value is based in some way on the assets' profit prospects.

The next observation arises from the view that firms build plants of a particular size, but that in the short run with the capital equipment fixed in amount and nature, firms operate along short-run cost curves. Short-run average cost curves touch or lie above comparable long-run average cost curves. Hence observations on average costs and output drawn from short-run cost curves lie on or above long-run cost curves. Firms will often be unable to operate their plants at the desired or optimal level of capacity (because of, for example, demand fluctuations). In particular, plants currently producing at below designed capacity are likely to combine relative high average total costs (since the fixed capital costs are spread over a small output) and low output. Those plants producing at or above planned capacity would combine relatively low average costs with high output. If such observations are combined, then an apparently downward-sloping average cost curve would be observed.

When statistical cost curves are used to derive short-run cost conditions, there is a possible averaging process which would tend to produce a 'flattish' cost curve. This can be illustrated by using Figure 4.3, treating the average cost curve as a short-run cost curve. Suppose, for example, that output in one week was Q_1 and in another week Q_2. Further, suppose that observations on costs and output are made for periods of a fortnight. Then the recorded observation would be point F in Figure 4.3 rather than the two points D and E, producing a tendency towards removing part of the curvature of the cost curve.

The data used in other estimation of statistical cost curves are historical, usually accounting, data in the sense of recording events (average costs, output) which have occurred and using accountants' ideas on costs. Decision-making in economic theory is often analysed in terms of opportunity costs, which are perceived future costs (of taking one course of action rather than another). The two questions of interest which arise here are, first, to what extent do costs recorded after the event (in this case production) correspond to costs as perceived before the event? Second, to what degree do accounting costs correspond with economists' notion of costs?

Engineering Approach

The method described as the engineering approach is based on the idea of breaking down a productive process into its component parts, and seeking to estimate the cost conditions for each part of the process. But, further, that estimation of cost conditions is derived from either the operation of scientific laws or engineering principles (as in the pioneering study of Chenery, 1949) or on the knowledge of current practitioners (Bain, 1956). A recent survey of this area summarised the engineering approach as the construction of 'hypothetical production data by utilizing direct technological information: reading blueprints, talking to engineers, using engineering theory and so forth' (Wibe, 1984).

This method has the advantage that the assumptions underlying the calculation of costs are set out and can be varied as and when required. Further, it can incorporate the costs arising from the operation of the currently 'best practice' technique, and thus yield estimates of the cost conditions for new plants. The other approaches discussed in this chapter draw upon the experience of plants in operation, which may utilise a range of production techniques of different vintages. In contrast the engineering approach deals with hypothetical production and cost data.

The proportions in which the various parts of the productive process are combined is a decision which is taken by the firm concerned. But, using the engineering approach, the investigator has to combine the costs of each part in some way, which may nor may not correspond with the proportions which would be chosen by firms. The seriousness of this problem depends upon the extent to which it is feasible in practice to vary the proportions in which the various production processes are used.

This approach is rather time-intensive to apply. The assessment of the costs of each part of a productive process is likely to take much longer than the estimation of a regression equation for the statistical cost curve estimation or the application of the survivor technique (which follows). As a partial consequence of this, there may be a tendency to focus on those parts of the productive process which are the more easily assessed, and functions which are difficult to assess, like management, raising of finance and advertising, will tend to be left out. In those parts of the productive process where the relationship between inputs and outputs is dictated by technological factors, then it would be relatively straightforward to estimate the cost conditions of this part of the process. But in those part of the process where, for example, the intensity and efficiency of labour can vary there will be considerable difficulties in establishing the relationship between inputs and outputs, and hence between unit costs and output. For example, it may be possible for a person working flat out to produce, say, 100 units in an hour. But there are many reasons why 100 units are not produced every hour.

The more recent work using the engineering approach (in particular Bain, 1956 and Pratten, 1971) has relied more on the knowledge of current practitioners (gained through questionnaire interview or the work of other investigators) than on the operation of scientific laws. To the extent to which the use of the engineering approach makes use of interviews, the difficulties which can arise with such use could operate. Thus, for example, there may be problems in ensuring that those managers and others who co-operate in responding to requests for interviews are a representative sample. Further, words such as costs and profits have specific meanings attached to them by economists which may not correspond to everyday usage, with possible subsequent confusion.

There may be some general tendency towards finding increasing returns to scale. First, certain types of costs are likely to be omitted or understated because they are difficult to measure. The nature of the functions to which these costs relate suggests that they are more likely to suffer from increasing unit costs than those types of costs which are included. Second, there may be a bias towards interviewing the 'better' managers, who have a natural optimism on the gains which would accrue from larger operations and a tendency to neglect the losses. This point is reinforced if the scale of operations being considered is above anything so far experienced. Under such circumstances, which apply in a number of industries investigated by Pratten (1971), it is reasonable to ask why firms do not operate at a larger scale when it is reported that such a scale would yield lower unit costs.

Survivor Technique

In a number of ways the survivor technique, advocated by Stigler (1958), is the polar extreme to the engineering approach. The engineering approach relied on the technical assessment of costs, and was not directly using the actual market experience of firms. The survivor technique in contrast places total reliance on the market experience of firms, and none on the technical appraisal of the productive process.

The essential idea behind the survivor technique is that evidence on cost conditions, particularly in respect of the efficient plant (or firm) size in an industry, can be inferred from an inspection of the changes in the size distribution of plants (or firms) within an industry. Thus if plants of a particular size are seen to be increasing in number and in market share, then that is taken as an indication that the size-class in question is well-adapted to the current economic environment. Thus the survivor technique draws upon the notion of survival of the fittest in a competitive environment. The survival of particular size-classes may arise from the deliberate decisions of firms when building new factories, or from the enhanced profitability of the firms owning plants of the efficient size, and the demise of some other firms.

The advantage of this technique is that the full range of functions performed by firms is taken into account, provided that the effect of those functions is reflected in the firms' profits. The survivor technique reflects firms' reactions to the private costs and benefits generated by the economic environment in which the firms operate. So functions, such as management, which pose great measurement problems in the other techniques, are capatured by this technique.

The survivor technique can be applied to plants or to firms, though is usually thought to be more applicable to plants than to firms. Within an oligopoly situation, the size of form which survives may reflect, in part, private advantages arising from market power. Then survival may reflect little about the underlying cost conditions. It can be argued that an oligopolist will be interested in minimising costs of any given level of output in its pursuit of profits (or other objectives), so that an oligopolist would tend to build plants of an efficient size to yield minimum cost units. But an oligopolist seeking to supply the national market would, *ceteris paribus*, have more smaller plants when transport costs are higher.

A further advantage of the survivor technique is that it can be quickly applied to a large range of industries, with the only data requirements being that statistics on number of plants and share of output are available for each size-class.

The survivor technique can only indicate a range of size of plant within which the efficient size of plant is to be found. It cannot indicate the extent by which unit costs of plants of the efficient size are below unit costs of other plants. Indeed, this technique has been largely used to provide estimates of the *m.e.s.*, which are expressed in terms of either the lower bound of the size-classes which are thought to contain the efficient size

or the average size of plants operating within the range containing the
m.e.s.

Finally, it should be noted that this technique must assume that all
plants operate within a common environment, so that the pressures on
the plants which lead to some prospering and some declining operate
across the board. Otherwise a variety of size-classes may prosper, reflecting the different environments within which the various plants operate.

There are a number of drawbacks in using this technique. Since plants
are usually in operation over long periods of time, the effect of the lower
costs of some plants' sizes may take a long time to have an effect on the
size distribution of plants requiring consistent data over a long period
of time. Technical change may mean that the efficient size of plant is
constantly changing. Plants of a sub-optimal size may be able to continue in existence for a considerable time since continued operation is
likely to depend upon the excess of revenue over variable costs, rather
than excess over total costs. Bain (1969) gives a number of ways in which
firms of a non-optimal size can survive.

It has often proved difficult to obtain results from the application of
the survivor technique, possibly for some of the reasons indicated above.
The results from different time periods can often conflict, as shown by
Shepherd (1967) (and to a lesser extent by Rees, 1973). It sometimes leads
to more than one efficient size-class being reported, and the implication
that the cost curve is like that illustrated in Figure 4.5.

The size of a plant has to be measured in terms of some relevant
economic variable. Employment is often used as it is readily available
but may not be an appropriate measure in a capital-intensive industry.
Output may be inappropriate when technical progress and learning-by-
doing leads to an existing plant increasing the volume of output over time.

Some changes in the share of output of size-classes will be small and
the investigator would want to discount such changes. Small changes need
to be filtered out by the use of some rule of thumb as to what changes
are small. However, this may not be sufficient as for the larger size classes
the number of plants can be small (say three or four). Thus a small change
in the size of one plant may take it into another size-class and increase
considerably the number of plants and the share in output of the receiv-
ing size-class.

The survivor technique focuses on changes in the size-distribution
rather than the distribution itself. Thus the dominance of a particular
size-class would be ignored but relatively small changes in the share of
another size-class would be reflected in the results reported. An approach
has been suggested by Lyons (1980) which focuses on an aspect of the

Figure 4.5: Possible Cost Curve from Survivor Technique
Estimation

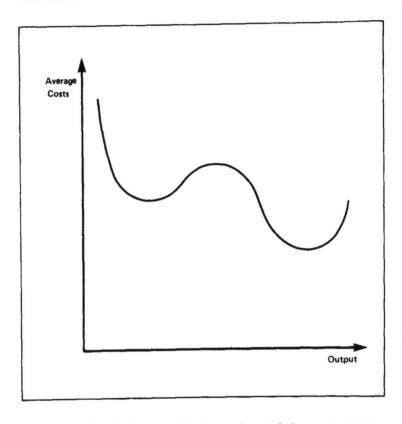

existing size-distribution, and like the survivor technique uses assumptions about the motivation of firms. The basis of Lyons' argument is that
the *m.e.s.* of plants can be inferred by examining the size of firms which
appear to be indifferent between operating one plant or two plants. This
border of indifference is taken to occur at that size of firm which operates,
on average, 1.5 plants, indicating that half of the firms of that size use
one plant and the other half two plants.[5] The plant-firm ratio in general
rises with the size of firm so that technique looks for the size-class for
which the plant-firm ratio is 1.5.

The survivor technique, in contrast to the engineering approach, must
always find that the 'efficient' plant size is within the range of plant sizes
currently in operation. Only some size-classes can be increasing their

share of the market and thus at any time the other size-classes would be regarded as sub-optimal.

Estimates of Cost Conditions

There have been numerous studies of the cost conditions under which industries operate using a variety of techniques and definitions. We report briefly on these studies, grouping them in terms of the three techniques discussed above.

Statistical Cost Curves

Wiles (1956), summarising 44 sets of data on long-run cost-output relationships, concludes that in general:

> [Average costs] descends like the left hand branch of a capital U, swiftly at first and then more gently. Decreasing costs with size are almost universal. But the U seldom turns up again. *Sharply increasing costs with size are practically unknown, and even slight increases are rare.* Sixty per cent of the example obey what we may call the *law of the L-shaped curves.* Another 31 per cent show a slight increase of costs in the largest size class. Most — but by no means all — of these slight increases are all within the expected margin of error that any empirical correlation should show. (Italics in original.)

Johnston (1960) summaries another set of estimates, which do not overlap with those summarised by Wiles (though not quite all utilise the statistical cost curve technique). He concludes that 'the preponderance of the L-shaped pattern of long-run average cost that emerges so frequently from the various long-run analyses' is one of the major impressions to be gained from his survey.

Haldi and Whitcomb (1967) seek to summarise a large number of studies on cost conditions in terms of a coefficient b in an equation of the form: costs $= aq^b$ (q is output). Based on costs of operation of a large assortment of common industrial equipment, Haldi and Whitcomb report that of 687 studies, 618 (90 per cent) show increasing returns, 50 show constant returns (defined as a value of b between 0.9 and 1.1), and the remaining 19 show decreasing returns. They argue that studies of investment costs and of plant operating costs show similar results.

Engineering Approach

Bain (1956) drew upon responses to questionnaires and follow-up interviews of managers of firms in 20 American industries, and the information obtained refers to 1951 or thereabouts. He sought opinions of managers on the efficient plant scale in their industry, which was then related to the current industry capacity. A summary of the results is given in Table 4.1, and it can be seen that for the majority of industries the efficient scale accounts for less than $2\frac{1}{4}$ per cent of the total industry capacity. The 'industries with slight economies of scale of plant are engaged in the processing of agricultural or mineral materials, whereas greater plant economies are frequently encountered in industries making mechanical devices' (Bain, 1956, p. 73). The smallest *m.e.s.* (relative to industry size) occurred in fresh meat packing (in the range 1/50 to 1/5 of a per cent) and flour milling (1/10 to 1/2 per cent) and the largest *m.e.s.* in tractors (10 to 15 per cent) and typewriters (10 to 30 per cent). These figures may understate the barrier to entry posed by economies of scale because they relate *m.e.s.* to national market size, whereas for many industries there were a number of regional markets (arising partly because of transport costs). Bain calculates that, for example, relative to the capacity supplying the smallest recognised sub-market in each industry, for six industries (out of the sample of 20) the *m.e.s.* was greater than 25 per cent.

The slope of the cost curve up to the *m.e.s.* is also of significance, as will become more apparent in the next chapter. Bain is not always able to quantify the cost advantage of a plant of *m.e.s.* over smaller plants. For his sample, he tentatively concludes:

> There is a substantial share of manufacturing industries in which operation at one-half of the designated optimal plant scale imposes very slight total unit cost disadvantages, whereas operation at one-fourth of optimal scale may in the same cases impose unit cost disadvantages of five per cent or less. On the other hand, there appears to be at least a minority of industries in which movement back to one-half of minimum optimal scale imposes a moderate and perhaps quite significant cost disadvantage, and in which operation at a quarter of optimal scale imposes a severe cost advantage (Bain, 1956, p. 81).

Pratten (1971) performed a similar exercise for British industry in the 1960s, and a summary of his results is given in Table 4.2. These estimates clearly indicate that the minimum efficient scale of plants is substantial (relative to the British economy) in many industries. The calculated *m.e.s.*

Table 4.1: Distribution of *m.e.s.* of Plants (as Proportion of Market): USA

Proportion of market (%)	Number of industries
0 – 2½	11
2½– 5	1
5 – 7½	3
7½–10	2
10 –15	2
15 –25	1
	20

Source: Bain (1956).

Table 4.2: Distribution of *m.e.s.* of Plants (as Proportion of Market): United Kingdom

Proportion of market (%)	Number of industries
Under 1	4
1– 5	7
10– 25	7
25– 50	6
50–100	3
Over 100	8
	35

Source: Silberston (1972), based on Pratten (1971).

is well above the current scale of operation, and for nearly a quarter of industries the *m.e.s.* is greater than the total market size (which includes domestic sales and exports).

The results of Bain and of Pratten are not directly comparable for they relate to different samples of industries and to different time periods. However, the results of Pratten indicate much more substantial economies of scale than do the results of Bain. This difference may be partially, but not completely, explained by differences in the size of the American and British markets.

Wibe (1984) provides a summary of 19 papers (which do not include those of Bain or Pratten discussed above), covering 28 industries between them, of which studies on 18 industries were usable from Wibe's standpoint. His conclusions on three aspects of the results of applying

Table 4.3: Estimates of *m.e.s.* Using Survivor Technique: USA

m.e.s. as per cent of industry	Mean *m.e.s.* (per cent of industries)	Minimum *m.e.s.* (per cent of industries)
0 -0.9	55.1	71.9
1.0-1.9	22.4	16.9
2.0-4.9	15.8	6.7
5.0-9.9	4.5	2.3
10 and over	2.2	2.2

Source: Saving (1961).

Table 4.4: Estimates of *m.e.s.* Using Survivor Technique: UK

m.e.s. as per cent of industry	Mean *m.e.s.* (per cent of industries)	Minimum *m.e.s.* per cent of industries)
0 -0.9	36.7	53.3
1.0-1.9	30.0	33.3
2.0-4.9	20.0	10.0
5.0-9.9	10.0	3.3
10 and over	3.3	0.0

Source: Rees (1973).

the engineering approach are of interest here. These are first that 'the overall impression is thus that the [elasticity of substitution] between capital and labour varies greatly, but with [that elasticity as unity] as an approximate average, whereas [the elasticity of substitution] between other factors is far below 1'. Second, economies of scale were generally reported in these studies. However, third, a change of scale generally involves changes of factor proportions even if factor prices do not change.

Survivor Technique

Despite the apparent ease of applying the survivor technique, there have been relatively few such applications. In Tables 4.3 and 4.4, we summarise the two such studies. The first one (Saving, 1961) draws on the experience of American industry over the period 1947 to 1954, and the second (Rees, 1973) on the experience of British industry over the period 1954 to 1968. The study of Saving (1961) started with 200 industries, of which 68 could not be used because of data problems, and a further 43 did not yield usable results. Similarly the study of Rees (1973) found that the estimates for some industries yielded multiple *m.e.s.* and for some others were inconsistent for different periods. His results are for 30 industries. The results are given for the lower bound of the size-classes which are identified as containing the *m.e.s.* and the average size of plants which are found within the size-classes containing the *m.e.s.* In the presentation of data, the Census of Production (which is the usual source of data for survivor technique estimates) uses size-classes which contain at least three or four plants to avoid the possibility on any single plant being calculated. This means that it is difficult to find an *m.e.s.* which is equivalent to more than 25 per cent of the industry.

Both sets of results imply that the bulk of industries have an *m.e.s.* which is less than 5 per cent of the output of the relevant industry. The results of Lyons (1980), using his technique outlined above, point to even smaller values of *m.e.s.* There were no cases (out of a total of 115 industries) where the *m.e.s.* exceeded 5 per cent of the industry's output, and for 82½ per cent of cases the *m.e.s.* was less than 1 per cent of output.

Short-run Cost Conditions

The importance of the nature of short-run conditions arises from two considerations. First, as will be seen in Chapter 9, prices are often seen as linked to average costs, and hence how prices vary as demand changes could depend on how unit costs vary as the level of output changes. Second, a conventional U-shaped cost curve indicates that a major constraint on the expansion of output arises from increasing average and marginal costs. In constrast, a 'flattish' average cost curve would imply that there were not major cost constraints on the expansion of output (over the range for which average costs are approximately constant).

The statistical cost curve approach can be used to estimate either short-run or long-run cost conditions, whereas the other two are mainly applicable to the estimation of long-run conditions. Our discussion on the statistical cost curve technique indicated that there were difficulties in its application to the estimation of short-run cost conditions. The survey by Johnston (1960) on the results of the application of statistical cost curves concludes, in respect of short-run cost curves, that 'the various short-run studies more often than not indicate constant marginal cost and declining average cost as the pattern that best seems to describe the data that have been analysed'.

Firm-level Economies

Most of the above discussion has been with production costs. Whilst these are important in looking at plant-level returns to scale, important firm-level costs are ignored. In this section we discuss one type of firm-level costs, namely finance, and indicate how these costs might vary with the scale of operation of the firm. Advertising expenditure is a cost of this type, and that is discussed in Chapter 7 (pp. 108–10), and research and development is another and is discussed in Chapter 8 (pp. 130–3).

Two aspects of the cost structure of finance concern us here. First, for a given size of firm, does the cost of finance decline as the volume of finance increases? Second, for a given relationship of finance required to size of firm, does the cost of finance depend upon the size of the firm?

The cost of finance to a firm includes not only the interest payment but also the costs of negotiating a loan or the costs of bond issue, etc. These transactions costs are unlikely to increase much with changes in the size of the loan and this injects a decreasing unit cost element into the cost structure. But eventually this effect is likely to be offset by higher interest charges, reflecting the higher risk which is perceived by the lender as the loan increases.

The transactions costs also point to lower costs of finance for larger firms in that the absolute size of loans will tend to be larger. But in addition to that, larger firms may face lower interest rates than smaller firms. Larger firms are more widely known than smaller firms, have lower bankruptcy and failure rates, and these factors lead lenders to perceive larger firms as better risks than smaller firms, reflected in lower risk premiums being added to arrive at interest charges.

Prais (1976) concludes that

> various studies of prospectuses of quoted companies have indicated that issue costs fall substantially with the size of issues; they range from 10–15 per cent of the sum raised when that sum is at the lower end of what is regarded as practical to raise by means of public issue (say, £¼ million in 1970) to some 3–5 per cent when the sum raised exceeds, say, £1 million.

Another source of finance for a quoted company is the issue of new shares. The cost of finance obtained in this way for the firm is related to the price-earnings ratio. The price-earnings ratio is the ratio of the share price of the firm to the earnings (i.e. post-tax profits) of the firm per share. The higher the price-earnings ratio, the more money the firm can raise from the issue of shares per pound of profits. Suppose that the firm earns £10 per share and has a price-earnings ratio of 10, then the share price of £100. Besides raising more money per pound of profits, a higher price-earnings ratio means that the amount of profits which needs to be earned from the use of the money raised through a new share issue is lower (per pound of finance raised).

There is evidence which suggests that the capital market prefers larger companies to small ones in the sense that the price-earnings ratio of the former are, on average, higher than the ratio for the latter. This may arise from the lower variability of profits, and also from the 'wider' market and easier saleability of shares in larger companies.

Prais (1976), summing up his survey of a number of British and American studies, says that '[t]here is thus an exceptional consistency in the results . . . all pointing to a falling cost of equity capital as size of firm increases . . .'

This discussion has only been concerned with the variation in unit *private* costs as the scale of output changes. Thus even if it were concluded that there were increasing returns to scale when private costs are concerned, this may not lead us to conclude that larger firms are preferable. For apart from any concern with market power, there would also be concern in what happens to social costs as the scale of operation varied.

Learning-by-doing

The discussion so far has been concerned with differences in average costs between different levels of output per period of time. But some have argued that the cumulative amount of output which has been produced by a particular factory or industry and the length of time for which a particular product has been produced may also be relevant. The general notion here is often described as learning-by-doing. Thus as experience of a particular production process builds up, ways of improving the production process are gradually discovered and put into operation. Debate has surrounded the question of whether experience is better measured by the amount of (cumulative) output produced or by the length of time during which the process has been used.

In respect of the cumulative output view, it has usually been argued that many of the learning or experience effects can be summarised by an equation of the form $\log UC = a + b \log Q$, where UC is the unit cost (of output produced to date) and Q the cumulative output, and b expected to be negative. Thus each successive proportionate increase of output has the same proportionate effect on unit costs. For example, a value of $b = -0.32$ indicates that for each doubling of output unit costs decline by 20 per cent.[6]

The Review of Monopolies and Mergers Policy (1978) summarises work undertaken on learning effects. They report that these effects have been found for a large range of industries. The learning effect was found to be roughly twice as large in assembly (with a cost reduction of 25 per cent for a doubling of output) as in machining (14 per cent reduction). Work by Nadler and Smith (1963) indicates that the learning effect is related to the proportion of manual to mechanical effort in a given operation. It has also been found that the contribution of individuals is of some importance. One study (Harvey, 1976) indicated that if all workers remained on a particular complex task without interruption there would be a 25 per cent reduction in unit labour costs for a doubling of output, but when the same firm opened a new assembly line with new workers the reduction was 16 per cent for an output doubling.

Lieberman (1984) also surveys a number of studies on learning effects. In his own work connected with 37 different products in the chemical industries, he concluded that '(t)he learning curve appears to be a function of cumulated output and cumulated investment rather than calendar time, and it is distinct from standard economies of scale'.[7]

Some of the learning effects are related to the cumulative output in an industry, and thus all firms in that industry benefit together. But other learning effects relate to the individual companies. When this occurs the larger firms have an advantage over smaller firms in general (unless the smaller ones have been in production substantially longer than the larger firms). Further, the experience effects give existing firms cost advantages over potential entrants. This provides a source of barriers to entry into an industry, which are more extensively discussed in the next chapter.

Conclusions

It is clear that the proposed methods of measuring cost conditions under which firms operate are surrounded with difficulties, and that methods produce divergent results.

Notes

1. Consider, for example, two spherical containers. The volume and throughput are proportionate to $(4/3)r^3$, where r is the radius, and we put throughput equal to $d.(4/3)r^3$, where d is a constant. The surface area and cost of materials are proportionate to $4r^2$, and we put the cost equal to $4cr^2$. Total costs can then be written as $a.(4dr^3/3)^{2/3}$ where a is a suitable constant, and thus costs equals $a.X^{2/3}$, where X is the level of output. Thus

costs rise with the power two-thirds of output, yielding increasing returns. This result is sometimes referred to as the '0.6 rule', for it implies that a doubling of output leads to an increase in costs of approximately 0.6. The precise figures are that a doubling of output would increase costs by 58.7 per cent.

2. With a given stock of spare parts, a run of sufficiently bad luck will exhaust stock. The greater the stock of spare parts, the worse the luck has to be before the stock of spare parts is exhausted.

3. If it is considered that in all organisations there is a single 'top' controller, then the capacity of that top controller is likely to create the ultimate source of diseconomies of scale. For a formal model see Williamson (1967).

4. But the higher wages could reflect the higher skill or labour quality requirement of larger factories, so that labour costs per 'effective' labour unit may not increase with factory size.

5. A number of supplementary assumptions are required which are detailed in Lyons (1980). The most important is that the cost surves for a plant slope downwards for output up to the *m.e.s.*, say, S and then is horizontal up to output S^*, which is at least twice the value of S, and thereafter the cost curve slopes upwards.

6. At output Q_1, we have log $UC_1 = a + b$ log Q_1, and at output $2Q_1$ we have log $UC_2 = a + b$ log $2Q_1$. Thus log UC_2 − log $UC_1 = b$ log 2, from which we have $UC_2 = 2bUC_1$. With $b = -0.32$, $UC_2 = .8UC_1$ and hence cumulative unit costs fall by 20 per cent.

7. See Baden-Fuller (1983) for an opposing view to that expressed by Lieberman.

5 CONDUCT AND BEHAVIOUR

Industrial structure forms the backcloth against which firms operate. A major determinant of the outcome from a particular structure is likely to be the objectives of the firms concerned. This chapter begins by briefly looking at the objectives of firms. It then moves to a consideration of barriers against new entry into an industry, and how such barriers may affect the existing firms, particularly in terms of prices and profits. The existing firms may compete to a greater or lesser extent with each other, and collusion is the third main topic of this chapter.

Objectives of the Firms

A long discussion on the objectives of firms is outside the scope of this book. Instead we make a few pertinent remarks. The usual assumption about the objectives of firms made by economists is that firms seek to maximise profits. This means that firms feel that they are protected against the possibility of new entrants, and proceed to maximise short-run profits. Firms feel that the barriers against new entrants ensures that their profits will not induce new firms to enter the industry. Alternatively firms are seen as interested in long-run profits, and pursuit of long-run profits requires that entry into the industry should be restricted. This may lead to a price being set such that entry into the industry is discouraged — in other words limit-pricing is practised. It may also take the form of erecting barriers to entry. It is implicitly assumed that the costs of preventing entry (whether arising from charging a limit-price, less than the short-run profit maximising one, or from the costs of erecting entry barriers) are outweighed by the enhanced profits which result from the absence of entry. The erection of entry barriers and limit-pricing may be practised because it is thought that new entrants in an industry would upset collusive understanding between the existing firms. The models of short-run profit maximisation and of limit-pricing are discussed elsewhere (pp. 9–10 and p. 72 respectively), and will be further discussed in Chapter 6 (pp. 81–4).

A major challenge to the profit maximisation objective has come from proponents of the view that modern larger corporations are under a managerial control, which it is argued leads to the pursuit of other objectives such as growth. These theories are extensively discussed in text-books on the theories of the firm (e.g. Sawyer, 1979a; Wildsmith, 1973). Some managerial theories are briefly outlined in Chapter 11, where some of the relevant evidence is examined. However, within the context of industrial economics, these theories have not had much impact. This is largely because managerial theories are firm-centred and give little, if any, role to competition between firms or to the impact of industrial structure on firm performance. Further, these theories have little to say on matters like advertising and research and development, which are important topics within industrial economics.

The pursuit of non-profit objectives is not unique to managerial-controlled firms, although the growth of such firms and of theories about them have emphasised these types of objectives. Another view has focused on the controllers of the firm, whether owners or managers, having a wider range of objectives and that the achievement of profit maximisation and the concomitant cost minimisation requires considerable time and effort by the controllers. Thus the controllers have incentives to forgo profit maximisation, unless they are forced to do so. A perfectly competitive market in equilibrium would force a firm to maximise profits if it wants to survive. But outside that situation firms have some leeway as to whether they do maximise profits. Under oligopoly, firms can earn profits above the normal level. They may charge a profit maximising price, but actual reported profits may be less than potential profits. This could arise from technical inefficiency (often labelled in this context as *X*-inefficiency) or from higher than necessary payments to the factors of production. The technical inefficiency can arise since it takes effort by the controllers to reach full efficiency and they may be willing to make the necessary effort. The higher payments can involve higher salaries to the controllers of the firm.[1] For either reason, reported profits fall below 'true' profits of the firm, with the difference used to finance inefficiency and higher factor payments.

Impact of Economies of Scale on Price

There are a variety of routes through which economies of scale can influence the mark-up of price over costs. The indirect route (pp. 41–4) runs through increasing returns to higher levels of concentration, and then as indicated in Chapter 2, on to larger price-cost margins. A more direct route arises from the theory of limit-price (see, for example, Sawyer, 1979a, Ch. 5). The essence of this theory is that when there are increasing returns to scale up to a level of output which is significant relative to the total market size, then the entry of new firms into the industry adds significantly to total supply. This increase in output would have a depressant effect on prices and profits. Thus a potential entrant must look to an estimate of post-entry profit rather than to existing profit levels before deciding whether to enter the industry. Existing firms can earn a profit above the normal level without inducing entry into the industry, provided that potential entrants believe that post-entry profits would be, at most, at the normal level.

We consider (following Modigliani, 1958) the case where existing firms anticipate that potential entrants believe that the existing firms will maintain output at the pre-entry level after any entry into the industry. This anticipation is pessimistic from the viewpoint of the existing firms, but optimistic for the potential entrants. We can make the case a little more concrete by considering the case where there are sharply declining costs over a range of output such that new entrants must enter the industry at a scale of output of at least q_0. After that scale of output, unit costs are taken as constant and equal to k. Thus, under zero barriers to entry, price would be bid down to a level $p_c = k$, which could be described as the competitive level (with price equal to average cost and to marginal cost). At that competitive price, the competitive output level, labelled q_c, would be given as $q_c = D(p_c)$ where $D(\ )$ is the demand function. Define $s = q_c/q_0$, which is an inverse measure of the minimum scale (q_0) relative to the competitive output level. The smallest output which the existing firms can produce without inducing entry into the industry is $q_l = q_c - q_0$. If the existing firms produce less than q_l, then they leave an unsatisfied demand of more than q_0, which can be met by a new firm coming into the industry. Then, with an elasticity of demand of e in the region of p_c, the limit price under this set of assumptions becomes $p_l = p_c (1 + 1/es)$.[2] Thus the mark-up of price over its competitive level, and hence over costs, depends upon the elasticity of demand and the minimum feasible scale.

This provides an initial indication of how economies of scale create an impediment for new entrants into an industry. Bain (1956), in his study of barriers to entry, identified two further major barriers. These were product differentiation and absolute cost advantage, and we look now at these in turn.

Product Differentiation

Product differentiation makes entry into an industry more difficult when there are significant buyer preferences for the established products over the products of new entrants. In order to break into a market a new entrant will then have to charge a lower price or incur higher selling costs (than otherwise). Existing firms can try to enhance the advantages of product differentiation to them by a range of activities. Foremost amongst these activities is sales promotion, particularly advertising (more fully discussed in Chapter 7). Influence or control over the distribution network for the product is another way in which entry is made more difficult, and which arises from the existence of product differentiation.

Bain (1956) indicates (pp. 128–9) that brand allegiance based on advertising and an established dealer system are the main basis of prospective entrants' disadvantages. Others arise from product reputations (for the existing products), conspicuous consumption motives (which favour the established over the unestablished) and lower trade-in values of second-hand products of entrants (particularly in the car market).

For some products differentiation is virtually inherent in the product. Cars, for example, do not have a common prototype and each manufacturer must design its particular model. In contrast, for a product like sugar there is a common prototype, and differentiation through branding is within the discretion of the firms involved. Thus for some goods product differentiation may be intrinsic whereas for other goods differentiation is not inevitable. But in all cases the extent of product differentiation depends upon the activities of the firms involved, although the costs and benefits (to the existing firms) varies between products. However, the height of the barrier to entry erected by product differentiation is likely to be influenced by the behaviour of the firms involved, and thus in this case there is an element of behaviour influencing structure.

Absolute Cost Advantage

The third source of barriers to entry identified by Bain was any absolute cost advantage held by the established firms over potential entrants. Established firms can then charge a price up to the unit costs of potential entrants and earn supernormal profits without inducing entry into the industry.

The absolute cost advantages can arise from the use of production techniques superior to those available to new firms. The main way in which this could arise would be through the development of production techniques by the established firms which are subject to patents or commercial secrecy. These cost advantages could also arise from 'learning-by-doing' (see pp. 67–8).

Cost advantages can also arise from the price of the factors of production. One source comes from a rising supply curve for a key input. A new entrant by increasing the demand for the input would bid up the price. The advantage for established firms is that the profits which they can earn without attracting entry are enhanced. A related source of cost advantage arises from the effective control (e.g. through ownership or long-term contract) by the established firms over key inputs, so that new firms could be denied access to these inputs (or only at prices determined by the established firms), or would need to turn to inferior inputs.

Another source of cost advantage for established firms can arise from the capital market, where higher interest charges may face new firms. These higher charges could arise, for example, when banks and other lenders perceive new firms to be riskier undertakings than established firms. The barrier formed by the capital market may be heightened when new firms need to undertake investment in advertising, research and development, etc., to be able to compete with existing firms. These forms of investment are seen as particularly risky and liable to failure, and do not lead to the creation of tangible assets which could be claimed in settlement of a loan in the event of failure by the new firm.

The quantitative importance of some of these sources of barriers to entry depends upon the nature of the potential entrants. For example, a firm already established in one industry contemplating entry into another industry is unlikely to face problems of raising capital. An international firm entering the market in another country would be unlikely to suffer from absolute cost advantages. The ease, or otherwise, of entry by already established firms is further discussed by Hines (1957).

The existence of barriers to entry is crucial for existing firms to be able to charge prices above the competitive level to gain monopoly profits. The absence of barriers to entry would lead to firms entering an industry until profits are bid down to the competitive level.

When there are some barriers to entry, but these are not high enough to blockade entry completely, then existing firms face a choice. One alternative is to charge the highest price which does not induce entry, and the other is to charge a monopoly price in the short term which induces entry and consequent lower future prices. This indicates the potentially central role of barriers to entry in determining profits and also in influencing views about how industry operates. In Chapter 6, the relationship

between structure (including barriers to entry) and profitability is discussed in detail. In Chapter 15, the discussion will draw out how the belief
in the existence or otherwise of significant barriers to entry influences
the debate on public policy towards industry.

Impediments Against New Entry

The activities undertaken by existing firms to help secure their own positions can be analysed under the heading of conduct and behaviour, though
the intention of such activities could be seen to make industrial structure
different from what it would otherwise be. For example, if an existing
firm prices to avoid other firms entering the industry, then the structure
would be different from that which would result from other pricing decisions. In addition, established firms may respond to new entrants in order
to make life difficult for those entrants and to discourage others. Thus
the general proposition would be that existing firms would seek to mould
industrial structure and to influence the behaviour of others by their own
conduct. This would be subject to the proviso that such activities are
believed by the existing firms to be profitable for themselves.

There are a number of tactics which firms can use *vis-à-vis* (retail
and wholesale) distributors which have the effect of making it more difficult for the distributor to switch to another supplier. This may have the
effect of enhancing the position of some existing firms relative to others,
and of existing firms relative to potential entrants. One is for the manufacturer only to supply goods if the distributor agrees not to stock the products of other manufacturers.[3] This may be reinforced by the supply of
necessary equipment by the manufacturer to the distributor, conditional
on the equipment only being used with that manufacturer's goods. Another
tactic is the use of cumulative discounts, so that the discount received
by a distributor depends on the total purchased from the manufacturer
over a stated period of time (like a year). A firm may use its power in
one market to influence operations in another market. For example, it
may use 'tie-in' sales, whereby purchase of one good is made conditional
on purchase of another.[4] Reports of the British Monopolies and Mergers
Commission (cf. pp. 277–8 below) provide examples of these types of
activities which established firms can use to seek to reduce new entry
into their industry. Reports of the Monopolies and Mergers Commission
(1981a, 1981b) into full-line forcing and tie-in sales and into discount to
retailers provide extensive illustration of these activities, as well as discussion of the relationship between those activities and the 'public interest'.

The Commission suggests four main types of full-line forcing and tie-in sales, namely where:

(1) The supplier's monopoly power in the market for product A can be extended to the market for product B by tying the supply of good B to that of good A.

(2) The supplier can effectively charge different consumers different prices for good A on the basis of their use of the tied good B.

(3) The supplier can ensure a standard of performance of good A, thus maintaining consumer goodwill, by insisting that it is only to be used in conjunction with the tied good B.

(4) The supplier can supply good B at a lower price than he otherwise could because, by tying its supply to that of good A, economies of scale can be realised. (Monopolies and Mergers Commission, 1981a.)

Barriers against new entry can be seen to play a crucial part in determining the profits of the existing firms. When there are barriers to entry, then the existing firms can raise, to some degree, their profits above the average level without inducing new entry into the industry. In contrast, the absence of barriers to entry would be seen to lead existing firms unable to gain profits above the 'normal' level. The assumption of the absence of barriers to entry is an important part of the theory of contestable markets discussed below (pp. 250–2).

Discussion in other chapters provides indications of ways by which firms influence, deliberately or otherwise, the nature of the structure of the industry in which they operate. Advertising expenditure may create barriers to entry (Chapter 7) and the search for technical advance may change the efficient scale of operation and provide knowledge for existing firms which is not readily available to new firms (Chapter 8). The more direct influence on industrial structure comes through acquisitions and mergers, which are discussed in Chapter 13.

Collusion and Restrictive Practices

There are many linkages between firms which can lead them to some co-ordination of their behaviour, particularly on pricing and production decisions. These linkages may be formalised through interlocking directorships, through trade associations, or they may operate informally through tacit agreements and acknowledgement of mutual interests. Our concern in this section is the operation of agreements, whether formal or informal, explicit or tacit, between firms. Where formal arrangements between firms operate, the group of firms will be described as a cartel. The agreements between firms, whether formal or informal, will be described as a restrictive practice or agreement, and we will talk generally of collusion between the firms.

The profit maximisation model of oligopoly discussed in Chapter 2 yielded the result that the mark-up of price over (marginal) cost

$$\frac{(p - c)}{p} = \frac{\Sigma s_i^2 (1 + a_i)}{e}$$

where s_i was share of firm i, e the elasticity of demand and a_i was the response by other firms' output to change in firm i's output, can be seen as a measure of effective collusion. When there is no co-ordination so that $a_i = 0$, then $(p - c)/p = (\Sigma s_i^2)/e$, whereas when there is co-ordination such that $a_i = (\partial Q_i/\partial q_i) = (Q_i/q_i)$ (which means that all firms change their output proportionately) then $(p - c)/p = (1/e)$, which is the mark-up achieved under monopoly, and this 'co-ordination' solution is a joint profit-maximising one. The important implication is that, in general, co-ordination between firms increases total profits, providing a powerful incentive towards collusion. This incentive can be restricted by legislation again collusion and restrictive trade practices amongst firms. The climate amongst politicians and business may sometimes favour competition and at others favour collusion, and this will have an influence on behaviour.[5] However, the extent of collusion may be held back by the feeling by the stronger firms that they are forgoing output and, more importantly, profits in the interests of protecting the weaker firms. Collusion is likely to increase total profits of the firms in the industry, but the profits of some firms may be held back by collusion. When there are agreements on prices between the firms, each firm may be able to expand its own business by 'price shading', offering its output at just below the agreed price. Thus there are incentives to form a cartel, but also incentives for firms to break agreements. The difficulties of holding together a cartel are likely to depend upon legislation, climate of opinion, level of demand and chances of detection, and this forms the basis of some theories of oligopoly, e.g. Stigler (1964).

The above analysis was based on the assumption of a homogeneous product, with firms deciding the level of output, and then given the conditions of demand the price is determined. The analysis for firms fixing prices for heterogeneous products (which is sketched in Chapter 9) is essentially similar, and does not change the tone of the analysis.

It has often been suggested that the degree of effective collusion will be positively associated with the degree of concentration. The basis of this is the simple idea that the organisation of a cartel and of collusion will be easier the smaller the number of firms involved. Further, detection of 'price shading' is likely to be easier with a smaller number of firms. This view is generally supported by the findings of Fraas and Greer (1977) in their work on over 600 anti-trust cases brought by the Department of Justice during the period 1910 to 1972 which involved elements of price-fixing. They conclude that 'the structural conditions most favourable to tactic cooperation are a relatively small number of rival firms and a market setting relatively free of complications'. However, it should be noted that some of the apparently effective cartels in the UK in the era prior to legislation against restrictive practices involved large numbers of firms.[6]

The nature of the product and of the elasticity of demand are structural features likely to influence the degree of collusion. Industries where the products of the firms are regarded as very close substitutes by buyers are likely to be more prone to collusion than other industries. This arises firstly because the fewer the number of prices involved the easier it is to make agreements. In industries where the products of the firms are distinct in the eyes of buyers, it is difficult to conceive of agreements about prices amongst the producers (although a consensus may emerge about profit margins). Secondly, with very close substitutes, buyers are willing to switch from one product to another for relatively small changes in prices (by definition of close substitute), and hence firms are likely to match any price reductions of other firms. This would be exacerbated when the overall elasticity of demand for the products of the industry is low. Then an individual firm is likely to gain by a price reduction provided that it is not followed by other firms. But there would be losses for the firms as a whole arising from price reductions by all.

Agreements between firms often centre on prices. The Registrar of Restrictive Practices reported that 730 of the 970 nationwide agreements reported to him covered prices, although the proportion of local agreements covering prices appears somewhat lower (Gribbin, 1978). When the parties to the agreement still wish to increase their own share of the market, they begin to compete through other means.

The nature of the product which firms offer can be changed so that it is more attractive to potential buyers. Changes in the product can include physical changes in the product concerned, in credit terms and in services provided with the product. Thus agreements may escalate to cover the nature of the product and associated services offered. The virtual banning of restrictive agreements between firms is likely to affect these non-price aspects particularly. The price of a good is an easily communicated feature which is often widely known, whereas the non-price features may be very complex.

With the introduction in many countries of legislation hostile to restrictive agreements, it may be asked whether this discussion is of historic interest only.[7] There are inevitably difficulties in obtaining information on the extent of illegal activities. But there is evidence for the United Kingdom (e.g. Swann *et al.* 1974) of a continuation of restrictive agreements, though of a less formal nature than previously. Trade associations continue to operate, and through them information can be exchanged. Whilst legislation can seek to control restrictive agremeents, it cannot force the firms to compete. There are generally ways of avoiding competition if firms do not want to compete. Price leadership, where it is tacitly agreed that the price decisions of one firm will be followed by the other firms, is one possible device. More generally, parallel pricing, where sellers tend to change prices around the same time and for similar amounts, can emerge. Monopolies Commission (1973) has an extensive discussion of this. It is difficult to distinguish between tacit collusion which leads to a common timing of similar price rises, or the necessity for firms to match other firms' price changes.

There may be an asymmetry between price decreases and price increases. Firms may be virtually forced to follow a price decrease, but not a price increase. The view underlies the kinked demand curve theory (Sweezy, 1939, and pp. 143–4 below).

For a cartel of firms the maintenance of the higher price requires a successful reduction in output. It then becomes necessary to share out the reduction in production amongst the member firms to ensure the maintenance of the higher price. Thus price-fixing is likely to evolve into quotas on the output of the firms it if is to be successfully maintained (Allen, 1968, p. 38).

An effective cartel raises price, and this leads to a combination of higher profits and the survival of high-cost firms. The higher price acts as an attraction for entrants into the industry. This, in turn, may lead the cartel to strive to create impediments against such entry.

Conclusion

This chapter has briefly surveyed the behaviour and conduct of firms. It is clear that, at least potentially, firms have considerable discretion over their actions, and that industrial structure may have only a limited influence on the behaviour and hence performance of firms. The behaviour of firms may be influenced by the history of the industry (degree of collusion and competition in the past and its results), on legislative and political attitudes to collusion and the motivation of the firms.

Notes

1. The view that managers seek to maximise a utility function which has managers' emoluments as one of its arguments is contained in the theory of Williamson (1964). Leibenstein (1966) (1975) argues that firms are not typically technically efficient, and Crew, Jones-Lee and Rowley (1971) link the degree of inefficiency with the degree of monopoly.

2. From $q_1 = q_c - q_0 = q_c (1 - q_0/q_c) = q_c (1 - 1/s)$, we have that $(q_1 - q_c)/q_c = -1/s$. Then from the approximation for $e = -(p_c/q_c) (\Delta q/\Delta p)$, we have $(p_1 - p_c)/p_c = 1/es$, and then $p_1 = p_c(1 + 1/es)$.

3. See, for example, Monopolies Commission Reports on petrol (Monopolies Commission, 1965) and on ice cream (Monopolies and Mergers Commission, 1979).

4. The best-known example is probably the attempt by IBM to make leasing of certain machines conditional on purchase of IBM punch cards.

5. Allen (1968, Ch. 4), Swann *et al.* (1974, Ch. 1) provide an historical survey of cartels, and particularly the government encouragement of cartels during the 1930s and 1940s. Whilst legislation has been largely hostile to cartels and restrictive practices agreements since 1956, there has been official encouragement of co-operation between firms operating via, for example, the activities of the National Economic Development Office.

6. This is indicated by some of the reports of the British Monopolies and Restrictive Practices Court during the period 1948 to 1956. These are summarised in Elliot and Gribbin (1977).

7 Legislation on restrictive practices is discussed in Chapter 16. For an outline of policies in a number of countries see Review of Restrictive Trade Practices Policy (1979).

6 INDUSTRIAL STRUCTURE AND PROFITABILITY

Profits play a key role in any discussion on the workings of the private enterprise system. The pursuit of profits is often regarded as the main motive of firms. A tendency towards the equalisation of profits in all lines of production is a major requirement for the efficient allocation of resources. The major theme of this chapter is the question of whether structural features of an industry, particularly the level of concentration, enable the firms in that industry to earn above average profits.

Links between Concentration and Profitability

In our preliminary discussion in Chapter 2 of some of the problems of formulating the structure-conduct-performance relationships, we used the links between concentration and profitability as our example. It is useful to summarise the results of that discussion. In a general model of oligopoly with firms seeking to maximise short-run profits the mark-up of price (p) over marginal cost (c) was determined by the elasticity of demand (e), the degree of concentration as measured by the Herfindahl index (Σs_i^2) and the firms' perceptions of their rivals' reactions (a_i). In particular, we derived

$$(p - c)/p = \Sigma_i s_i^2 \, (1 + a_i)/e$$

Writing ac for average costs, we can rewrite this equation as

$$(p - ac)/p = \Sigma_i s_i^2 \, (1 + a_i)/e + (c - ac)/p$$

The left-hand side is the profit-sales ratio (multiply numerator and denominator by output), often labelled the profit margin. In much empirical work in this area the second term on the right-hand side is taken as zero, from an assumption of constant costs (so that marginal costs and average costs are equal, i.e. $ac = c$). The above equation involves the somewhat paradoxical result that the profit margin is, *ceteris paribus*, lower when there are decreasing costs (for then $ac > c$) than when there are constant costs (so that $ac = c$). But in this case, the *ceteris paribus* conditions include the same level of price, output and marginal costs, and with given marginal costs the industry with decreasing costs has average costs higher than the industry with constant costs. This is illustrated in Figure 6.1, where subscript 1 refers to the constant cost industry and subscript 2 to decreasing costs industry.

Figure 6.1: Difference between Constant Cost and Decreasing Cost Industries

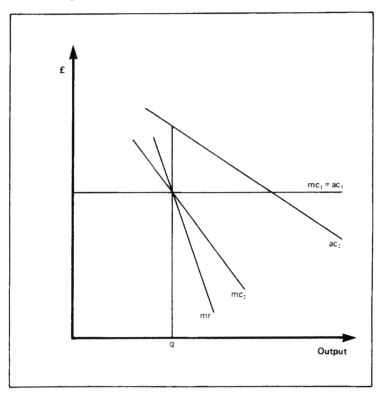

The term a_i, defined as $\partial Q_i/\partial q_i$, is the perceived response of firms other than firm i to a change in the output of firm i. Under a situation of firms effectively operating in ignorance of each other (the Cournot solution), $a_i = 0$; whereas under effectively joint profit maximisation, $a_i = Q_i/q_i$. These indicate the outer limits of a_i. Now if, as would appear reasonable, the degree of effective collusion (whether open or tacit) increases as the effective number of firms decreases and as concentration increases, then the effect of concentration on increasing the profit margin is enhanced.

The equation above for the price-cost margin indicates that the Herfindahl index is an appropriate index of concentration to be included in an explanation of the price-cost margin. A similar conclusion is reached by Stigler (1964) using a different approach to the determination of price-cost margins in terms of the problems of cartelisation. However, other measures of concentration may be appropriate as well. The term a_i may be a function of the level of concentration, but the theory gives no clear indication of which measures of concentration may be appropriate. Further, 'threshold effects' may be involved. This would mean that only when concentration exceeded some critical level would any effective collusion become possible.

The background to this model is the existence of effective barriers to entry into the industry, so that the existing firms do not concern themselves with the effect of their current profitability on entry and future profitability. The two key factors determinining profitability are seen to be concentration and the elasticity of demand. Factors which influence concentration or the elasticity of demand will then indirectly influence profitability. In Chapter 3 we briefly reported on some influences on the level of concentration. In general, elasticity of demand presents a considerable problem in the estimation of the structure-profitability relationship, with direct estimates of the elasticity of demand not generally available. Further, in the general heterogeneous product case, there are intense problems of defining industry-level elasticities of demand. There have been four responses to the problem raised by the elasticity of demand. The first has been to ignore it. The second has been to restrict the sample of industries to those which can be regarded as having similar elasticities of demand, and thereafter to ignore the elasticity of demand. A frequent device has been to divide industries which produce consumer goods from those which make producer goods and to estimate separately for the two groups. In this way it is hoped that the problem caused by the omission of elasticity is contained.

A third way has been to introduce other variables which are thought to influence the elasticity of demand facing the firms. For example, the advertising-sales ratio is sometimes included on the grounds that a high ratio would be associated with a high degree of product differentiation which, in turn, would be associated with a low demand elasticity. Some measures of import penetration can be seen as indicating a high elasticity of demand facing domestic producers, since consumers can switch relatively easily between domestic products and imported goods, when imports are well established in a market.

A fourth alternative adopted by for example, Cowling and Waterson (1976), is the elimination of the elasticity of demand by looking at the relationship between the profit margin in two periods. Writing M for profit margin and $Z = \Sigma s_i^2 (1 + a_i)$, we have $M^j = Z^j/e^j$ ($j = 1, 2$) where the suffixes relate to periods 1 and 2. Then, by division, we obtain $M^2/M^1 = Z^2/Z^1$ when $e^2 = e^1$ is assumed.

The other major approach to the relationship between industry structure and profitability focuses on the role of barriers to entry. In Chapter 5 we explored the influence of economies of scale and other barriers to entry on the limit price. In the context of economies of scale, we derived that the limit price $p_l = p_c (1 + 1/es)$, where e is the elasticity of demand and s the reciprocal of the minimum feasible scale of operation relative to total output. The profit margin is then $(p - c)/p = 1/(1 + es)$, when the limit price is changed and assuming that average costs provides a good approximation for the competitive price (p_c).

Firms contemplating entry into an industry are likely to be encouraged by high levels of profitability, but discourged by the difficulties surrounding entry. Let us label the various impediments to entry as a vector X, where $X = (x_1, x_2, \ldots, x_n)$ when there are n types of entry barriers and x_1 is the measure of the height of barrier 1 (say advertising), x_2 a measure of the height of barrier 2 (say control of retail outlets), etc. The barriers which could be included in such a vector have been discussed in Chapter 5 (pp. 71–5). We label the measure of profitability which is regarded as relevant by potential entrants as P. It is convenient to talk in terms of any entry function $E(P, X)$ which indicates the number of firms who would enter an industry for given level of profitability and height of barriers to entry. The exact nature of this entry function will depend upon factors like the way in which potential entrants believe the existing firms and fellow entrants will react to entry. When existing firms blockade entry into the industry, they implicitly set P and X at levels P^*, X^*, such that $E(P^*, X^*) = 0$, i.e. so that no entry occurs. Solving this for P^* in terms of X^* indicates the entry prevention relationship between profitability and barriers to entry, i.e. $P^* = f(X^*)$.

Impediments on entry into an industry can arise from factors specific to the industry concerned and from factors arising in the capital market. For example, an entry barrier which arose from advertising intensity which increased the degree of product differentiation would be a factor specific to the industry/market concerned, whereas if the barrier arose because new firms found it difficult to raise finance for advertising then this would be a factor arising from the capital market. Similarly, the entry barrier arising from the degree of economies of scale *relative* to the market size, as in the limit-price theory of Modigliani (1958), is an industry-specific factor. The barrier arising from the *absolute* size of the plant size necessary for entry leads to an absolute capital requirement for entry and this is a capital market factor. In these examples, advertising and economies of scale may influence entry and thereby profitability through two distinct routes. In each case, one route is through the product market and the other through the capital market. The measurement of advertising intensity and economies of scale should reflect the routes through which it is thought that they influence entry and profitability.

In the theory of limit-pricing, concentration has a more limited role to play than under the profit-maximisation approach. This arises in part because the theory of limit-pricing focuses on the relationship between one existing firm and potential entrants. Concentration may operate as a barrier against new entry in at least two ways. First, in a high level of concentration which may reflect a high degree of *firm-level* economies of scale. Thus concentration operates as a proxy for *firm-level* economies of scale. Second, potential entrants may regard a highly concentrated industry more likely to take concerted action against entry than a low-concentration industry would.

The major dimension of barriers to entry which are considered in structure-profitability studies are advertising intensity, concentration and economies of scale, expressed either relative to industry size or as an absolute capital entry requirement.

The measure of profitability which appears appropriate for the profit-maximisation model is the price-cost margin, which is equivalent to the profit-sales ratio (π/S). In the blockaded entry case, measures of profitability like profit-net output ratio and the profit-capital (i.e. rate of return) ratio may be the appropriate measures of profitability which influence the decisions of potential entrants.

The profit-sales and the profit-net output ratios will not vary together because of differences in the degree of vertical integration, reflected in the net output/sales ratio. Industries near the beginning of the production chain will tend to have a higher net output/sales ratio than those industries near the end of the chain. In other words, producer goods industries will tend to have a higher ratio than consumer goods industries. Some industries (like tobacco) will have particularly low net output/sales ratio because of the excise duties charged on their inputs. The profit-sales and profit-capital ratio will reflect, *inter alia*, differences in the degree of capital-intensity as reflected in the sales/capital ratio.

We could broadly summarise the above discussion by identifying two views. In the first, above average profit rates arise from market power, which is often proxied by measures such as concentration. In the second, it is the existence of barriers to entry (economies of scale, cost advantages, etc.) which permit higher levels of profitability. Concentration may enter this explanation, but often as a proxy for or related to economies of scale.

There is, however, a school of thought which puts quite a different interpretation on any links between concentration and profitability. Demsetz (1973, 1974), Peltzman (1977) and others have argued that firms with superior efficiency will have both high market shares and high profitability. Thus there could be an observed association between market shares and profitability, but there would not be an underlying causal link between those two variables. Instead, the association between the two would be seen as arising from a common link of market shares and profitability with superior efficiency. Demsetz argues that above-average profits of large firms could arise either from superior efficiency or from successful collusion (as in the model of oligopoly discussed above, pp. 9–10). However, if the profit sales arise from collusion, Demsetz argues that this leads to a higher price from which both small firms and large firms benefit. Thus in a concentrated industry, the superior efficiency of large firms argument would predict that large firms gained larger profit margins than small firms, whereas the collusion argument would predict that both small and large firms would gain higher profit margins (than in an unconcentrated industry). It is this proposition which Demsetz tests. In the profit-maximising model used above, one consequence of the way the model is constructed is that little is said about the profitability of large firms relative to small firms. But, taking into account possible economies of scale and that part of the market power of larger firms may be the ability to squeeze smaller firms, then it could still be the case that larger firms obtained higher profitability than smaller firms, combined with a finding that more concentrated industries have higher profitability than less concentrated ones. Clarke *et al.* (1984) provide extensive discussion on these arguments, as well as some empirical testing for the UK (discussed below).

Some Further Considerations

Studies which have related profitability to the industry structure variables just discussed, have included other variables as well. Sometimes these additional variables have been included as 'control' variables, in order to try to allow for influences other than structural characteristics. In a few cases, the other variables have been the centre of the study, and the structural variables are cast in the role of 'control' variables.

A growth variable (usually relating to growth of sales in nominal terms) is often included in the belief that fast growth of sales reflects a fast growth in demand, which tends to favour higher profit levels. A measure of capital intensity, like capital-output or capital-labour ratio, is often included under the argument that the higher the capital intensity, the higher will be the profits required to cover the opportunity cost of the capital, and hence, *ceteris paribus*, the higher profits will be. A distinction is sometimes made between consumer goods and producer goods, either by the inclusion of a dummy variable or by separate estimation of the profitability equation for the two groups of goods. The rationale for making the distinction between consumer and producer goods is that this makes some allowance for differences in the elasticity of demand which may be particularly marked between the two groups, and for different impacts of advertising on demand for the two groups. Alternatively, buyer concentration may be more substantial for producer goods than for consumer goods, although this argument neglects the role of concentration in the wholesale and retail distribution sectors.

In an open economy, such as the United Kingdom, foreign competition can be a constraining influence on domestic firms and their ability to raise prices above costs. Further, the profit and sales figures reflect both domestic activity as well as exports. Allowance for the role of foreign competition is usually made by the inclusion of variables like import-sales and export-sales ratio. But these are likely to be rather imperfect measures. They do not, for example, directly reflect any comparative cost advantage or disadvantage possessed by domestic firms *vis-à-vis* their foreign rivals, nor do they take account of the activities of multi-national firms. One study (Hitiris, 1978) have moved a stage further by incorporating the effective degree of protection offered to domestic producers by tariffs in the profitability equation.

Variables which seek to measure aspects of regional dispersion have often been included in American studies. These have taken the form of adjusting the concentration ratios to reflect regional rather than national market concentration, or including dummy variables which have value of unity for industries where there are significant regional markets and zero otherwise.

There are a number of ways in which monopoly profits could evaporate, though their significance is rather different. We look at three possible ways. First, above-average profits may reflect a position of disequilibrium rather than one of monopoly. Such profits would decline as the industry moves towards equilibrium, during which new firms enter the industry and existing firms expand. Barriers to entry are of very limited importance, and do not serve to protect the existing firms and their profits. This view is discussed more fully in Chapter 15 (pp. 256–9). The second way is that potential monopoly profits do not show up as reported profits but rather tend to disappear through higher costs. These higher costs are often labelled X-inefficiency, and may arise from inefficiencies and from higher payments (in money and in kind) to managers and workers. The third way arises from the measurement of the capital stock of firms. In Chapter 4 (pp. 54–5) it was seen that when the capital stock was valued in terms of potential profits there was a tendency towards the finding of constant costs. The counterpart of that conclusion in this context is a tendency for profitability to move towards the average level. This can be most easily illustrated for the profit-capital ratio, when capital is measured by discounted future profits. Then we have the capital value

of firm $V = \sum_{t=0}^{\infty} \pi_t^e /(1 + i)^t$, where i is the rate of discount, π_t^e is

expected profits in time t, and the (current) profit-capital ratio is π_0/V. When π_t^e is expected to be constant in the future, V is equal to π_0/i, and hence the profit-capital ratio becomes i.

The significance of these remarks depends upon the way in which the capital stock is measured in practice. If the capital stock is taken to be the stock market valuation of a firm, then it could be anticipated that expected future profits will have a strong influence on that valuation. Consequently, expected monopoly profits would become capitalised into the valuation of the firm, and the rate of return on the stock market valuation is pushed toward the average level. However, if the capital stock is measured by the book value of the firm, based on the machinery, land, etc., owned by the firm, this capitalisation effect may be quite small.

There are two frequently discussed aspects of the estimation of structure-profitability relationships which are referred to elsewhere in this book. The first one is the question of whether the relationship between structure (particularly concentration) and profitability is continuous or discontinuous (pp. 18–9). One view is that industries can be categorised as either essentially monopolistic with high levels of concentration and relatively high rates of profits predicted, or essentially competitive with low levels of concentration and relatively low rates of profits predicted. The other view that profitability is expected to rise continuously with the level of concentration.

The second aspect is the question of whether a single equation linking structure and profitability can be estimated by itself or whether it is one equation amongst a number of equations which need to be estimated together (p. 20). In the preceding discussion, the possible impact of advertising on profitability was indicated. In Chapter 7 on advertising, the impact of profitability on the advertising-sales ratio will be outlined. Thus there are arguments which indicate that advertising influences profitability and that profitability influences advertising, an example of the well-known simultaneous equation problem, and this is discussed more fully in Chapter 7. However, of the very large numbers of studies on structure-profitability, only three have not been confined to a single-equation approach.

It has been usual to estimate a linear relationship between profitability and concentration, e.g. $\pi/S = b_0 + b_1 \cdot CR + b_2 \cdot Z$, where CR is some measure of concentration and Z represents other variables included in the regression. The estimation of this equation imposes the view that the effect of a one-unit difference in concentration on profitability is the same regardless of the level of concentration. Thus if CR were taken as the five-firm concentration ratio, then a 1 per cent difference in concentration ratio would be predicted to lead to a difference of b_1 in the profit-sales ratio. However, it could be the case that the effect of differences in concentration varies with the level of concentration, e.g. the value of b_1 is different for low and for high levels of concentration (e.g. Geroski, 1981). Further, the underlying relationship may not be linear (and there is little in the theory to indicate that it would be linear). For example, the underlying relationship might be log-linear ($\pi/S = b_0 + b_1 \log CR + b_2 Z$) or quadratic ($\pi/S = b_0 + b_1 CR + b_2 CR^2 + b_3 Z$).

There is one further econometric problem — that of heteroskedasticity — which should be noted. Those studies which have tested to see whether the variance of the residuals varies systematically with the level of concentration have concluded that they do. It might be expected, *a priori*, that the variability of profitability would tend to decline with increased concentration, with one of the gains by firms in highly concentrated industries being a less variable profit record. This would tend to lead to a negative relationship between the variance of the residuals and the measure of concentration. However, studies have generally found a positive relationship between the variance of residuals and concentration, although a negative one between the variance of residuals and average firm size.

Measurement of Variables

Some attention needs to be paid to the measurement of the variables involved. We have already indicated that three measures of profitability have been used, namely profit-sales, profit-net output and profit-capital ratios. The degree to which costs are deducted from the sales revenue before arriving at profits varies and may influence the results. Of particular note is whether advertising expenditure is regarded as a cost. If advertising is *not* included as part of costs, then it would be expected that advertising has a significant impact measured on profitability, and allowance must be made when interpreting the estimated coefficient on the advertising variable. The clearest example of this arises when the profitability measure π/S is (sales revenue minus non-advertising costs)/sales revenue, and the advertising intensity measure is advertising-sales ratio. Then the estimated equation is often of the form $\pi/S = \alpha_0 + \alpha_1 A/S + \alpha_2 Z$ where Z is a vector of the other variables included. When the extra revenue generated by advertising balances the extra cost of advertising, the value of the coefficient α_1 would be unity. Super-normal profits generated by advertising would, in this instance, require a value of α_1 in excess of unity. In reporting the structure-profitability results in Table 6.2 allowance has been made for whether advertising expenditure has been included as a cost in arriving at profits so that a judgement can be made as to whether advertising yields super-normal profits.

Concentration has usually been measured by a concentration ratio or the Herfindahl index (see pp. 28–9). For the British results, a number of investigators have used a weighted average of the four-digit level five-firm concentration ratios, whereas the other data refer to the three-digit level.[1] This measure of concentration is deficient in two respects. First, there is less than complete coverage of data at the four-digit level and the extent of coverage varies between three-digit industries considerably. Second, the average of the four-digit concentration figures may be a poor guide to the three-digit level figures, since the picture at three-digit level will be influenced not only by the concentration with each component four-digit industry but also by the extent to which firms operate in the compontent industries.

The barrier to entry posed by economies of scale can arise from the minimum efficient scale either in absolute terms or relative to the size of the industry. Essentially three approaches have been used to estimate the efficient scale of production. The first method has been to draw upon the work on the estimation of economies of scale. The results of applying the survivor technique have been the main ones used, though as indicated above (pp. 57–60) such estimates usually only cover a relatively small number of industries.

The second and third approaches do not attempt to make direct estimates of the efficient scale. Instead they argue that there is a strong relationship across industries between the efficient scale and some measure of some or all of the plants in use. The second approach uses the average size of plant in use in an industry, where the average can be the mean, median, weighted mean or weighted median.[2] However, particularly when the simple mean or median plant size is used, this type of measure is often felt to be over-influenced by the number of smaller plants, who may be operating on the fringe of the industry. The third approach seeks to overcome that criticism by taking the average size of only some of the plants in an industry. Some authors have divided plants into larger ones and smaller ones such that each group is responsible for half of the industry's output or employment, and then calculated and used the average size of the larger plants. Here again the average may be mean, median, etc. Other authors have used the average size of plants on the borderline between the larger and smaller plants.

The third approach incorporates the implicit assumption that the experience of the larger plants is relevant for the assessment of the efficient scale of production. Further, the degree of advantage of the efficient scale over other scales of plant is important in determining the height of the barriers facing new entrants. For these reasons, Caves *et al.* (1975) and Khalilzadeh-Shirazi (1974) have used a cost disadvantage ratio (*CDR*). This is defined as the ratio of the value added per worker in the smaller plants, to the value added per worker in the larger plants. These authors argue that unless the *CDR* lies below some critical value (0.8 and 0.9 were used) then the barrier presented by economies of scale is ineffectual. They form a new variable which takes the value of the estimated efficient scale if the *CDR* is below the critical value and zero otherwise.

The intensity of advertising is typically measured by the ratio of advertising expenditure to sales or to net output. The figures on advertising expenditure exclude 'in-house' advertising expenditure, and only include expenditure on advertising made outside of the firm concerned. The possible deficiencies of this type of measure of advertising intensity are discussed in the next chapter (p. 114).

Table 6.1: Summary of Measurement of Certain Variables in Estimated Structure-Profitability Equations: United Kingdom

Authors	Measure of profitability	Measure of concentration	Measure of economies of scale as barriers to entry	Nature of regression
Cowling and Waterson (1976)	$(N.O. - W)/N.O.$	CR4, HI	n. inc.	Ratio of levels in two years
Waterson (1980)	$(N.O. - W)/S$	HI	n. inc.	Ratio of levels in two years
Caves et al. (1975)	$(N.O. - W - A - O.C.)/S$	Weighted average of four-digit CR5	Interaction of − (i) minimum efficient plant size in 'median' size-class divided by total output; (ii) cost disadvantage ratio = value added per worker in smaller plants to that ratio in larger plants	Linear
Hart and Morgan (1977)	$(N.O. - W)/N.O.$	CR5 (three-digit level)	Median enterprise size	Log linear
Hitiris (1978)	pre-tax profits/sales	CR5 (three-digit level)	n. inc.	Linear
Holtermann (1973)	(i) $(N.O. - W - O.C.)/S$ (ii) $(N.O. - W - A)/S$	Weighted average of four-digit CR5	Average size of the larger plants which account for 50 per cent of employment	Linear
Khalilzadeh-Shirazi (1974)		As Caves et al. (1975) above		Linear
Khalilzadeh-Shirazi (1976)		As Caves et al. (1975) above		Linear

	Ratio of price of own brand to price of proprietary brand[a]	Herfindahl index and CR5 (three-digit level)	Minimum efficient size (estimated by survivor technique) as percentage of industry size	Linear
Nickell and Metcalf (1978)				
Phillips (1972)	$(N.O. - W)/S$	CR3	Average plant size	Linear
Shepherd (1972)	Not defined but assumed to be $(N.O. - W)/S$	Weighted average of four-digit CR5	n. inc.	Linear

Abbreviations

n. inc.	not included
N.O.	net output
S	gross output or sales
W	wages and salaries
A	advertising
O.C.	other costs (which include expenditure on repairs and maintenance, insurance, rates etc.)
CRn	n-firm concentration ratio
Note:	(a) The own-brand price is taken as an indication of the competitive price.

British Studies

The manner in which profitability, concentration and the economies of scale barrier have been measured for British structure-profitability studies is summarised in Table 6.1. The measure of profitability is always the ratio of profits to either gross output or net output. A wide variety of measures of concentration and of economies of scale as a barrier to entry have been used, which makes precise comparisons between different studies difficult.

The results for the British structure-profitability are presented in very summary form in Table 6.2. Authors often report a number of regression results (and leave a large number unreported), and the sign and significance of the estimated coefficients of variables often vary between different regressions. This variation appears to be a particular problem in structure-profitability relationships, with the significance of a variable sometimes depending on the absence or presence of other variables in the regression (as, for example, in the study of Hart and Morgan (1977); see their Table I and the significance of the concentration term). This condensed summary consequently contains our assessment of the balance of results in each study.

The studies of Cowling and Waterson (1976) and Waterson (1980) are explicitly designed to test a profit-maximising model, similar to that outlined above (pp. 9–10). Cowling and Waterson argue that the elasticity of demand is an important variable for which there is little information. But the elasticity of demand in a particular industry is not likely to change substantially over a relatively short period. By looking at changes, rather than levels, they can obtain an equation which links changes in the profit margin with changes in industrial concentration, with the no change in the elasticity of demand assumed. They find that changes in concentration (as measured by the Herfindahl index) over the period 1958–63 had a significant positive influence on changes in profit margin over the period 1963–8, arguing that changes in structure only lead to a change in the profit margin with a time lag. Waterson (1980) extends the analysis to deal with the power of producers in related markets and the market power of the buyers. He finds that producer power in related markets has a positive and buyer concentration a negative impact on the profit margin of the producers, and both impacts are statistically significant. Nickell and Metcalf used a model similar to that of Cowling and Waterson and were able for a range of products investigated (those sold through grocery outlets) to find estimates for the elasticity of demand, albeit often relating to a higher level of aggregation than the other variables. However, they

Table 6.2: Summary of Results for Estimated Structure-Profitability Equations: United Kingdom

Authors	Concentration	Economies of scale entry barrier	Advertising
Cowling and Waterson (1976)	+	*n. inc.*	*n. inc.*
Waterson (1980)	+	*n. inc.*	*n. inc.*
Caves *et al.* (1975)	+	+	+[a]
Hart and Morgan (1977)	[b]	(−)	+[c]
Hitiris (1978)	+	*n. inc.*	(−)
Holtermann (1973)	(−)	(−)	(+)[d]
Khalilzadeh-Shirazi (1974)	(+)	+[e]	(+)[a]
Khalilzadeh-Shirazi (1976)	+	+	+[a]
Nickell and Metcalf (1978)[f]	+	(−)	(+)[g]
Phillips (1972)	+[h]	−	+[h]
Shepherd (1972)	+	*n. inc.*	*n. inc.*

n. inc.   not included.

Notes: Sign indicates the sign of the relevant estimated coefficient generally found in the study. Where not in parenthesis the coefficient is generally statistically significant in that study at the 5 per cent level using a one-tailed test. Often a number of equations are reported, and there may be differences in sign and/or significance between the various reported regressions.

a   References to estimated coefficient for a product differentiation dummy, which takes value 1 if advertising-sales ratio exceeds 1 per cent; 0 otherwise.

b   Coefficient on concentration term is always positive; coefficient is statistically significant in absence of the ratio of gross capital expenditure to labour, but insignificant in its presence.

c   Advertising expenditure is not deducted from costs in measuring profits, which leads to a larger coefficient on the advertising-sales ratio than otherwise. In this case it is not possible to judge whether advertising-sales ratio would be significant if advertising expenditure included in costs.

d   Refers to regression when advertising expenditure was included as part of costs in measuring profit.

e   The significance of the coefficient depends on the omission of one outlying observation.

f   The equations reported by Nickell and Metcalf use the cost-price ratio as the dependent variable. The signs reported in this table are the opposite of those reported by the authors so that their results can be easily compared with the other results. In their regression, the elasticity of demand is included.

g   Coefficient is not statistically different from the value predicted if advertising has no impact on profits.

h   A term involving the interaction of advertising-sales ratio and concentration is also included, which has an insignificant negative coefficient.

found that elasticity was not statistically significant. In that study, the comparison was made between the price of advertised branded goods and the grocery outlets' 'own brands' on the basis that the price of 'own-brand' goods is a reflection of the long-run average cost of production.

The other studies for Britain have been in the limiting-pricing tradition. Most of the studies find that the estimated coefficient of the concentration variable is positive, and has usually been significantly so. But the more recent studies reported in the table tend to produce a mixture of positive and negative coefficients, in contrast to the earlier studies which produced more of predominance of positive coefficients. The economies of scale, which have been measured in many different ways, are only found to have a positive effect in the three connected studies of Khalilzadeh-Shirazi (1974) and (1976) and Caves *et al.* (1975), with the differences between those studies arising from the inclusion or exclusion of variables relating to foreign trade and from differences in sample definition. There are clearly a lot of measurement difficulties in this area, and the apparent rejection of the view that economies of scale raise profitability may arise from poor measurement of minimum efficient scale. Finally, advertising is found to have an apparently positive effect on profitability. But, as noted above, the frequent exclusion of advertising expenditure from costs in the calculation of profits means that the interpretation of the coefficient of advertising intensity is not always straightforward.

The three most recent studies cited in Tables 6.1 and 6.2 have sought to discuss issues additional to those covered by earlier studies. Geroski (1981) investigated the question of whether the impact of a difference in concentration on profitability varies at different levels of concentration. He found that for some ranges of concentration, higher levels of concentration led to lower levels of profitability, although over most ranges the relationship between concentration and profitability was a positive one. Geroski (1982) presents some further results using the same data set. Clarke (1984) estimated an equation of the form $\pi_{jt} = a_j + b_j.t$ for each industry over the period 1970 to 1976, where π_{jt} is the profit margin in industry j at time t. The results in Table 6.2 relate to using the estimated value of each a_j regressed against structural variables such as concentration and advertising. Further, he was also able to make estimates of the variability of profitability by the ratio of the standard error of the above regression to the value of a_j. He finds that 'profit margins were clearly more volatile in more concentrated industries'. This finding has been found elsewhere (cf. pp. 151–2), but does not run counter to the often expressed view that prices tend to be less flexible in concentrated industries or that one of the benefits of concentration to the firms involved is the reduction of the volatility of profit margins.

The study of Clarke *et al.* (1984) seeks to contrast the views of Demsetz (1973, 1974) and others that profitability and concentration can be associated through the impact of different levels of efficiency on both (cf. p. 86 above) and the market power view of profit margin determination. Their empirical work relates to UK manufacturing industries in 1971 and 1977. In their comparisons of the profit-net output and profit-sales ratios of the largest five firms with the margins of other firms, they find that only in the case of the profit-net output ratio in industries of above average concentration was the profitability of the largest firms significantly above that of the smaller firms. Further, they seek to estimate for each industry the relationship within the industry between price-cost margin and market share. In those industries where a relationship was discovered, there is a mixture of positive linear (i.e. profit margins rise with market shares), negative linear, inverted U-shaped and U-shaped.

The growth of demand has generally been found to have a positive and significant effect on profitability.[3] Import penetration, as measured by the import-sales ratio, has been included in four of the studies and only in Geroski (1981) is that ratio reported to have a statistically significant (and negative) effect on profitability (see also Geroski, 1982). Hitiris (1978) finds that the degree of tariff protection raises profitability.

American Results

The first empirical study of the relationship between structure and profitability was Bain (1951), which compared the rate of return over the period 1936–40 in 42 industries with the eight-firm concentration ratios in those industries. The correlation between the rate of return and concentration was significant at the 5 per cent level but inspection of the data revealed that high- and low-concentration industries had a higher rate of return than middle-concentration industries. However, when industries were divided into two groups according to whether their CR8 was greater or less than 70 per cent, the high-concentration group (of 22 industries) had an average rate of return of 11.8 per cent which was statistically significantly higher than the average rate of 7.5 per cent recorded by the low-concentration group of 20 industries. Weiss (1971) surveyed most of the subsequent investigations into the structure-profitability relationship. He concluded that '[a]lmost all of the 32 concentration profits studies except Stigler's have yielded significant positive relationships for years of prosperity or recession, though they have depended on a wide

Table 6.3: Summary of some (post-1970) American Studies on Structure-Profitability Relationships

Author	Profitability measure	Concentration measure	Comments on sample and results
Bradburd and Caves (1982)	π/S	CR4 (adjusted for import share)	Covers 77 US industries for 1972. Their regression results indicate that four-firm adjusted concentration ratio, advertising-sales ratio and capital-ouput ratio all tend to raise the price-cost margin
Caves et al. (1975)	π/S	CR8	Concentration has negative and significant effect whilst advertising-sales ratio and absolute capital requirement have positive significant impact on profitability
Dalton and Penn (1976)	Rate of return on owners' equity	CR4 CR8	Study based on 97 food manufacturing firms. Find evidence for a critical level of concentration (for CR4 45 per cent), and high concentration leading to high profits. Find profit rate of larger firms less variable than for smaller firms, and adjust for this heteroskedasticity by weighting by assets raised to power ¼
Espositio and Espositio (1971)	Post-tax profits to net worth	Dummy with value 0,1 as CR8 <, > 70 per cent	Equations estimated by ordinary least squares and with allowance for heteroskedasticity. Effect of concentration on profitability depends on whether a measure of m.e.s. is included, but generally effect positive. Absolute capital requirement has positive and usually significant effect, and a measure of m.e.s. negative effect on profitability
Jones et al. (1977)	Profits plus interest to total assets	CR4 CR8	Concentration has positive, significant minimum efficient scale relative to industry size, a negative non-significant effect on profitability
Khalilzadeh-Shirazi (1976)	π/S	CR5	Concentration, economies of scale, product differentiation, growth and capital-output ratio all have positive impact on profitability. Although only the last two mentioned have a significant impact

...(1975a)	π/S	CR4	investigation of influences of buyer concentration. Finds that profitability affected positively by producer concentration and negatively by buyer concentration, with both effects statistically significant
Martin (1979)	π/S	CR4	Estimates a three-equation model, with profitability-advertising-sales ratio and concentration as the dependent variables. Estimation is by three-stage least squares, for consumer goods and producer goods industries separately. In both cases, concentration has a positive non-significant impact on profitability
Meehan and Duchesneau (1973)	Rate of return on assets	CR4 CR8	Investigate whether the profitability-concentration relationship is continuous or discontinuous, and conclude for the latter with threshold for CR4 of 55 per cent, and of 70 per cent for CR8. Finds variance greater in high-concentration groups than in low-concentration group, and makes correction for heteroskedasticity
Ravenscraft (1983)	π/S	CR4	Regressions estimated at firm level using structural variables for the industries in which firm operates. Differences in results between 'line of business' level and four-digit level. Buyer concentration and $m.e.s.$ significant at former level but not at latter level. Concentration not significant but market share of firm at 'line of business' level positively related to profitability. See text for further discussion
Rhoades and Cleaver (1973)	π/S	CR4	Investigates whether there is a continuous or discontinuous relationship between profitability and concentration. Finds a critical CR4 of 51 per cent, with no systematic relationship between profitability and concentration for low-concentration industries and a strong linear relationship for high-concentration industries
Strickland and Weiss (1976)	π/S	CR4	Estimate three-equation model, using both ordinary least squares and two-stage least squares. Concentration, growth, advertising-sales ratio, minimum efficient scale relative to industry size, capital-sales ratio have positive impact on profitability. The $m.e.s.$ effect is non-significant as is the concentration effect in the two-stage estimation

Notes: Abbreviations as Table 6.1.
π: Profits (various measures).

variety of data and methods. I think that practically all observers are now convinced that there is something in the traditional hypothesis (that high concentration raises profits)'[4] (text in parenthesis added).

This broad consensus was challenged by Brozen (1970, 1971, 1974). Brozen's challenge had two major points. First, he argued that if the high profits of the high-concentration industries represented equilibrium monopoly profits, then these high rates of profit would persist through time. If they did not persist, then there was no cause for concern arising from those high profits.[5] Brozen (1970) reported that in the period 1953–7 the high-concentration industries in Bain's sample had a rate of return which was 1.1 per cent higher than that for low-concentration industries, and this difference was not statistically significant. Thus, he argued, there was not the persistence of high profitability. The second part of Brozen's challenge was derived from the relatively small sample used by Bain. His sample was restricted to industries which corresponded to well-defined national markets, and was further confined by data availability, which led to a sample of only 42 industries out of a possible 340. Brozen (1974) was able to extend the sample to 98 industries, and in that sample the low-concentration industries have a marginally higher rate of return (0.2 per cent) than the high-concentration industries.

Many of the American studies published since 1970 (and hence not covered by Weiss's study) are summarised in Table 6.3. In contrast to the British studies, the American studies have made considerable use of the rate of return on capital assets as a measure of profitability. The tone of the results of these studies is that concentration has some, albeit not substantial, positive impact on profitability. Nine of the eleven studies summarised find a positive effect, of which six are statistically significant. However, the study of Ravenscraft (1983) concludes that 'the profit-concentration relationship in industry regressions almost surely reflects advantages that larger sellers enjoy relative to small rivals', based on his finding that a firm's market share influenced its profitability but the concentration ratio of the industry in which it operated did not.

The results for the economies of scale barrier are much more mixed. Economies of scale sometimes refer to a relative measure and sometimes to an absolute measure; sometimes both are included and sometimes neither. In the two studies where an absolute capital requirement is included, it has a positive and significant impact on profitability. A relative measure of minimum efficient scale (*m.e.s.*) is included in seven of the studies. In two of these, the relative *m.e.s.* has a non-significant negative effect, in three a non-significant positive effect, and in one a positive and significant effect. The remaining study found a positive significant effect in consumer goods industries and a negative non-significant effect in the producer goods industries.

The picture on advertising intensity is more consistent. It is included in nine of the eleven studies, and has a positive effect on profitability in all but one of them, and a statistically significant effect in five-and-a-half cases. The one case where advertising intensity was not statistically significant was Ravenscroft (1983), but here the absolute industry advertising level had a positive and significant impact on profitability. The half case reported above arises from Martin (1979), where the effect is non-significant in the consumer goods industries but significant in the producer goods industries.

Bradburd and Caves (1982) is mainly focused on the effects of market growth on profitability. Their conclusion on that aspect is that 'unexpected growth is positively related to the price-cost margin, although the effect is significantly smaller in concentrated industries . . . By contrast, expected growth wields a positive influence on profits only in the more concentrated industries'.

Canadian Studies

Three studies for Canadian industries give a broadly similar picture. McFetridge (1973) reports positive and significant effect of concentration (with the square of the Herfindahl index as the preferred measure of concentration) on profitability (measured by the ratio of profits to net output). His measure of the relative *m.e.s.* has a negative effect, but advertising-net output ratio a positive effect on profitability, but in neither case is it significant.[6]

Two studies by Jones *et al.* (1973, 1977), which overlap to a considerable extent, use the ratio of post-tax profits plus interest payments to total assets as their preferred measure of profitability. In both studies they find that concentration has a positive non-significant, relative *m.e.s.* a negative non-significant, the absolute capital requirement a positive non-significant and advertising-sales ratio a positive and significant effect on profitability.

Conclusion

The broad consensus from the large number of studies surveyed is that concentration generally has a positive effect on profitability. In many of the individual studies this effect was not regarded as particularly

102 Industrial Structure and Profitability

significant, but the totality of the results suggest that the effect is significant. Economies of scale entry barriers produced a mixed pattern of results, with nearly as many negative impacts on profitability as positive ones found. This may, of course, reflect the acute problems of measuring minimum efficient scale. Finally, advertising intensity (often measured by the advertising-sales ratio) generally had a positive, though not always statistically significant, effect on profitability.

Notes

1. For definition of three- and four-digit levels see pp. 23–4.
2. The weighted mean would be $\Sigma w_i^2 / \Sigma w_i$ where w_i is a measure of size of plant, which would correspond to the size of plant of the 'average' worker. The weighted median is that plant size such that half of the work force in the industry works in larger plants, and half works in smaller plants.
3. Of the studies which have included a measure of growth, only Hart and Morgan (1977) (with a positive non-significant effect) and Phillips (1972) (with a negative non-signigicant effect) did not find a positive and significant impact of growth on profitability. Some (e.g. Geroski, 1981) find a positive impact which is significant in some regressions but not in others. Clarke (1984) finds a positive effect of growth on the trend in profitability.
4. The study referred to by Weiss is Stigler (1963). A further partial exception indicated by Weiss is that Comanor and Wilson (1967) find that concentration does not have a significant impact on profitability when entry barriers are included in the regressions.
5. It can be argued that high profits do not persist because of the threat of entry or actual entry removes the possibility of above-average profits. The precise mechanism is not important in this context. However, if profits do not persist because firms can 'hide' them in higher costs or through the capitalisation of monopoly profits (see p. 88), then in a sense monopoly profits do persist but do not appear in the statistics.
6. Advertising undertaken outside the firm is not counted as part of costs and McFetridge argues that since only 10 per cent of advertising is undertaken within the firm a coefficient on the advertising-sales ratio of more than 0.9 is anticipated if advertising raises profits. The coefficient is generally above 0.9 but not to a significant extent.

7 ADVERTISING

Advertising is a subject on which people tend to hold strong and often opposing views, and economists are not exceptions to this. Some economists regard advertising as one means by which firms mould tastes and opinions in the direction of their products and also more generally in favour of private consumption. Other economists see advertising as an efficient way by which firms supply information to potential consumers. Some economists see advertising as a barrier inhibiting new entrants into an industry thereby enabling the established firms to reap high profits, whilst others see advertising as evidence of competition and an aid to new entrants in establishing themselves. Thus a number of conflicting approaches must be discussed in this chapter, and readers are left to assess the arguments themselves. There are also disputes over the conclusions to be drawn from empirical evidence on the effects of advertising. Even in areas where it would appear that conflicting approaches could be resolved by an appeal to the evidence, this has not generally proved possible, as will be well illustrated below.

We begin by looking briefly at the quantitative importance of advertising. In the United Kingdom, advertising expenditure expressed relative to consumer expenditure varied during the period 1970 to 1983 within the range 1.50 per cent to 1.96 per cent and relative to GNP varied in the range 1.03 per cent to 1.39 per cent.[1] However, advertising expenditure covers advertising by government and by savings institutions, so a comparison with consumer expenditure is not entirely satisfactory. Some parts of advertising expenditure correspond to real resource costs (e.g. filming adverts for television) whilst other parts correspond to a transfer payment with little or no resource usage involved (e.g. hire of television time).

Advertising relative to sales varies considerably between industries. Drawing on a different data source, and a slightly different definition of advertising, the ratio of advertising to sales in manufacturing industries in 1968 varied from over 15 per cent in the toilet preparations industry to over 10 per cent in the soap and detergents industry to near zero in a number of producer goods industries.[2] The figure for all manufacturing industries was 1.09 per cent.

A distinction is frequently made between informative and persuasive advertising, and it is often suggested that some forms of advertising (such

Table 7.1: Distribution of Advertising Expenditure by Media: UK, 1983

Media	Percentage of expenditure
Press	62.5
of which display advertising	40.1
classified adverts.	22.4
Television	31.0
Posters and transport	3.8
Cinema	0.4
Radio	2.2

Source: Advertising Association press release.

as classified ads, advertising in trade and technical journals) are likely to have more informative content than other forms (such as television advertising). As a preliminary to that discussion, the distribution of advertising expenditure by media is given in Table 7.1.

Advertising as a Decision Variable

We begin by treating advertising as a decision variable of the firm. The particular feature of advertising, which enters this analysis and which distinguishes it from many other inputs, is that advertising is modelled as influencing both the demand conditions and the cost conditions facing the firm. Let us start with the simple case where the firm is considered in isolation from its rivals, and when the effect of advertising on demand occurs only in the time period in which the advertising takes place. Then profits $\pi = p.q(p, A) - C(q) - A$, where $C(q)$ is production costs, A is the level of advertising measured so that it has a price of unity, and $q(p, A)$ is the demand function facing the firm which indicates that price and advertising affect demand. The decision variables for the firm are p and A and the first-order conditions for profit maximisation become:

$$\frac{\partial \pi}{\partial A} = p \frac{\partial q}{\partial A} - \frac{\partial C}{\partial q} \cdot \frac{\partial q}{\partial A} - 1 = 0$$

$$\frac{\partial \pi}{\partial p} = p \frac{\partial q}{\partial p} + q - \frac{\partial C}{\partial q} \cdot \frac{\partial q}{\partial p} = 0$$

and then

$$\left(p - \frac{\partial C}{\partial q} \right) \cdot \frac{\partial C}{\partial A} = 1 \qquad (1)$$

$$\left(p - \frac{\partial C}{\partial q} \right) \cdot \frac{\partial q}{\partial p} = -q \qquad (2)$$

and so

$$\frac{\partial q}{\partial A} \bigg/ \frac{\partial q}{\partial p} = -1/q$$

which can be manipulated to yield

$$\frac{A/q \cdot \partial q/\partial A}{p/q \cdot \partial q/\partial p} = -\frac{A}{pq}, \text{ i.e. } A/S = e_A/e$$

where e is the absolute value of the price-elasticity of demand and e_A the advertising-elasticity of demand. This result is often labelled the Dorfman-Steiner condition after the first authors to derive it (Dorfman and Steiner, 1954).

It is often suggested that advertising is akin to investment in capital asset and provides profits for the firm in the future as well as the present. Nerlove and Arrow (1962) have shown that when advertising is treated as a capital input rather than a current input that the Dorfman-Steiner condition is modified to read $G/S = e_g/e \, (d + i)$, where G is 'goodwill', e_g is the elasticity of demand with respect to 'goodwill', e the price elasticity of demand, d the rate of depreciation of 'goodwill' and i is the rate of discount.

Advertising is seen as creating consumer preference for the advertised good, and the capitalised monetary value of these preferences are assumed to decay over time leading to a depreciation of 'goodwill'.

Information or Persuasion

There are numerous aspects of the above approach which can be questioned. Let us begin by asking the simple question of what is the role of advertising in the demand function? One response is that a firm can sell more of its product because consumers have more information on that product. The information may relate to its existence, price, quality, etc. Thus advertising is seen as essentially supplying information to consumers (Nelson, 1974). Further, information yields benefits to the consumer and like other goods involves costs, in this case costs of dissemination. In most of conventional theory perfect information is assumed, which is equivalent to saying that information is costlessly available to all.

When information and its dissemination is valuable to both consumers and producers, the question arises of who pays for the advertising. In the first instance the producer pays, although the utlimate cost may be partially or completely borne by the consumer through higher prices. The consumer will have benefited from being able to make better-informed decisions because of the information supplied by advertising. The producer is, generally, the initiator in the advertising process simply because it has a particular product to sell which it knows about and seeks to inform a large number of consumers. The alternative would be for each consumer, relatively uninformed about the exact nature of the products which he wishes to purchase, advertising his demand for various products (Telser, 1966).

The other response is that advertising seeks to persuade consumers to purchase the advertised products by appeals to snobbery, associations of the product with favoured people or situations, repetition of the same message and so on. Thus advertising seeks to mould tastes rather than to inform. One firm's advertising may not be successful through misjudgement by that firm and its advertisers or because of the impact of the advertising of other firms. Further, advertising is only one aspect of marketing and is regarded as such by the firm, and other forms of marketing (such as 'free gifts', sports sponsorship, etc.) cannot be easily regarded as supplying genuine information.[3]

The difference between the two responses can be put in terms of the conventional utility maximisation approach to consumer demand theory. The first response regards consumers' tastes (i.e. the utility function) as fixed, and advertising informs the consumer about availability, price, etc., so that the utility maximising process can take place more effectively. The second response regards advertising as seeking to mould consumers' tastes and change the consumers' utility function in a manner favourable to the advertiser.

This information-persuasion dichotomy has been frequently applied to advertising with the persuasive advertising generally frowned upon by economists. Different types of advertising have been seen as containing information and persuasion in varying proportions, and thereby varying in the degree of desirability. But for the firm the intention is to sell its products, and it will present any information in a way which seeks to influence the consumer to purchase its products.

Utility maximisation by well-informed individuals plays a central role in conventional micro-economics. Advertising provides a subject on which the conventional approach and opposition to that approach meet head-on. Thus if the empirical work on advertising could resolve the debate over whether advertising is basically informative or persuasive, it would have considerable implications for the whole of micro-economics. For the basic foundations of conventional micro-economics would either be vindicated or condemned.

Advertising plays an uncomfortable role within the structure-conduct-performance approach, partly reflecting the controversy over the role of advertising. It can be seen as an element of industrial structure, operating as a barrier to entry, and thereby influencing performance (specifically profitability). Advertising can be a part of the conduct of firms in that firms use advertising amongst many other things to seek to increase profits (or whatever their objective is). Finally, advertising can be a part of performance, influenced by industrial structure. Whilst not everything written about the role of advertising within industrial economics can be placed under one of those three heads, it is useful to utilise this three-way division.

Advertising and Profitability

There are two routes through which advertising is thought to create barriers to entry, and another line of argument suggests that advertising is indicative of a barrier to entry. We tackle the last point first.

Industries may differ in the suitability of their products for effective advertising — in their 'advertisability'. It can be argued, for example, that highly differentiated products are more suitable for advertising than undifferentiated ones. This argument would indicate that advertising is a sign rather than a cause of product differentiation, and differentiation may itself be the barrier to entry.

The first direct route by which advertising creates barriers to entry is that advertising raises the capital requirements for entry into the industry. First, costs of production, distribution and marketing are raised, so that a new entrant is faced with higher initial outlays than otherwise. Second, advertising may create 'goodwill' for the firm and the current amount of 'goodwill' depends on past investment.

There has been some dispute over whether current advertising does influence future demand, and thus create a capital asset of 'goodwill'. But the general view is that there is a future demand effect of advertising and the evidence for this is summarised in Ferguson (1974) and Cowling *et al.* (1975). However, some of the studies summarised by Ferguson find evidence that for some products there was *no* influence of advertising on future demand.

Existing firms benefit from their past investment in advertising and new entrants have to overcome those advantages. The barrier to entry created by advertising may draw on imperfections in the capital market. Existing firms have financed (by their own funds or borrowing) their past investment in advertising. If new firms could raise any necessary finance at the going rate of interest to undertake advertising to match that (past and present) of existing firms, then the capital market would not aid the entry barrier formed by advertising. But if the capital market is reluctant to lend, whether because a larger capital outlay is required than otherwise or because advertising is at best a risky and nebulous investment, then it adds to the advertising entry barriers.

Comanor and Wilson (1979) argue that the barrier to entry created by advertising arises from 'asymmetries in demand functions', whereby other things including advertising being equal, consumers prefer the established products to the unestablished. This is close to saying that established firms have acquired 'goodwill' in the past, partly through advertising and partly by being known and used.

If advertising is a profitable activity for firms to undertake then the question arises as to why other firms do not follow suit. If other firms (possibly including new entrants) did follow suit then the returns to advertising are likely to be reduced. In other words, the traditional argument is applied that when there are above-average profits (in this case arising from advertising), firms move into the activity generating above-average profits, and as a consequence those profits are reduced. The returns to advertising could be maintained because of the nature of advertising. This could include capital market difficulties in new firms raising funds for advertising (as discussed above). Further, even though advertising by existing firms may raise their profits, it may not necessarily raise the expected profits which new entrants believe they could gain after entry

Figure 7.1: Possible Effect of Advertising on Cost Curve

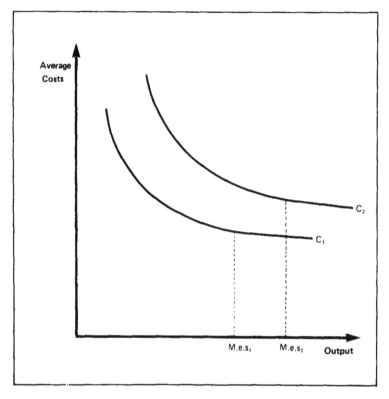

(cf. Cubbin, 1981).

The second possible direct effect of advertising is on the minimum efficient scale (*m.e.s.*) of operation (see pp. 47–8). If advertising is subject to increasing returns up to a scale which is larger than the minimum efficient scale based on production costs, then advertising shifts the ove.all *m.e.s.* to a higher level, thereby raising the barrier to entry formed by economies of scale (pp. 71–2). This is illustrated in Figure 7.1. Of course if advertising is subject to decreasing returns then the *m.e.s.* would be reduced under the impact of advertising.

It is useful to discuss the returns to advertising in terms of the returns (in increased sales) per advertising message and the cost of delivering an advertising message. Increasing returns would occur from a message if repeated showing of a particular advertisement led to the product demand increasing at an increasing rate. Thus if product demand per unit of time $D = f(AM)$ where AM is the number of advertising messages per unit of time, then increasing returns would require the first and second derivatives of the function f to be both positive. Increasing returns arising from reduced unit cost of an advertising message could arise through the spreading of the advertisement's production costs as it is more widely shown (say by advertising nationally rather than regionally), and through the advertising rate structure charged by the media. Thus Comanor and Wilson (1967) argue that 'an increased use of some forms of advertising leads to a lower cost per message, and available evidence suggests that this is very important for advertising on national television and in national magazines'. Arndt and Simon (1983) also find 'some indirect evidence of scale of economies for large advertiser (*sic*) in terms of media discounts and opportunities to use network television, which seems to be more cost efficient'. However, Ferguson (1974) reviews the evidence on increasing returns to advertising and concludes that 'there is no reliable evidence of increasing returns to advertising expenditure'. Similarly Arndt and Simon (1983) conclude that 'there is little conceptual or empirical evidence supporting the *myth* of substantial returns to scale for advertising' (italics added).

The implications of any increasing returns to advertising may depend upon whether the increasing returns operate for advertising of a single product or for advertising of a number of products. Increasing returns from advertising of a single product, or group of products made in the same factory, would affect the *m.e.s.* within that particular industry. But increasing returns from advertising a number of products would encourage the emergence of diversified firms, without any direct impact on *m.e.s.* within a particular industry.

It is unlikely that incrasing returns to advertising could operate forever, but the important question is whether there are increasing returns to advertising over a range such that the *m.e.s.* of firms in an industry is raised. The only current evidence appears to be that of Cowling *et al.* (1975) who find that 'the influence of heavy advertising expenditure . . . increase the minimum efficient size of firms', although that conclusion is heavily qualified.

When advertising creates barriers to entry, then following the analysis in Chapter 6, the limit-price is raised and thereby the profitability of firms within the industry. But there is another channel through which advertising can influence profitability. When firms maximise profits, profitability depends upon the elasticity of demand. If advertising increases the degree of product differentiation, that leads to a decrease in the absolute value of the elasticity of demand, and through that channel advertising would lead to a rise in profit margins. When successful advertising is mainly persuasive in character, it leads to the demand for products becoming less price-elastic as the perceived degree of product differentiation is increased. In contrast when advertising is mainly informative it would lead to a more price-elastic demand for the products as knowledge of products and their properties becomes more widespread. Thus the demand for a product may be relatively inelastic but when close substitutes are discovered by the consumers following informative advertising, the elasticity would increase since now a rise in price of one good can easily be offset by switching to the close substitutes.[4]

Although there is a basic similarity in many of the above arguments in that advertising is predicted to raise profitability, nevertheless the precise nature of the relationship varies. Under the hypothesis that advertising creates barriers to entry through raising the capital requirements for entry, the relevant measure of advertising is the amount required to overcome the cumulative impact of past advertising (with allowance for depreciation). In that case, it is an *absolute* measure of advertising which is relevant. But the advertising required for entry is not directly measurable, and the advertising per firm (current and/or cumulative past advertising) of existing firms has been used as a proxy.[5] When advertising is seen as yielding increasing returns, the important feature is the extent to which the *m.e.s.* is increased (and similarly if there are decreasing returns to advertising). But here it is difficult to isolate the effect of advertising, since it is the overall level of *m.e.s.* which, via the limit-price, influences profitability. Finally if advertising changes the elasticity of demand the relevant measure of advertising may be advertising-sales ratio since that indicates the intensity of advertising on consumer demand.

In the model of firm behaviour discussed at the beginning of this chapter, advertising and price were the decision variables of the firm. Thus advertising and price are jointly determined by the firm. A positive non-causal relationship between the profit margin and advertising-sales ratio can be anticipated. This follows from taking unit costs as approximately constant, so that $p - \partial C/\partial q$ is unit profit on production costs and we write $M = (p - \partial C/\partial q)/p$. Then rewriting equation 1 from p. 105 as $(p - \partial C/\partial q)/(p \cdot q) \cdot A(\partial q/\partial A) = A/S$ and making substitution for M and e_A leads to $M \cdot e_A = A/S$. This positive relationship between the profit margin and advertising intensity does not imply that one causes the other. It means that one would expect to find profit margin and advertising to be positively associated, but with both margin and ratio an outcome of the profit maximisation by the firm. This non-causal linkage creates problems for interpretation of empirical work.

Advertising as Behaviour

Advertising is an element of behaviour in the sense that it is one of the many activities undertaken by firms in order to achieve their objectives (profits, sales or whatever). The act of advertising can be an element of behaviour, but the outcome in terms of the 'goodwill' created is an element of structure. But 'goodwill' as a barrier to entry limits the number of firms in the industry. Thus an association between 'goodwill' (labelled now as G) and concentration can be anticipated. When an industry is in a situation of balance, current advertising will be replacing the loss of 'goodwill' through depreciation so that $A = d \cdot G$, where d is the rate of depreciation of 'goodwill'. From this, an association between advertising and concentration is hypothesised, with the causation running from advertising to concentration.

An alternative view, based on advertising as current expenditure, sees advertising leading to changes in the level of concentration. But in which direction is advertising thought to change concentration? One school of thought places emphasis on existing firms using advertising to enhance their position through the creation of barriers to entry and the raising of *m.e.s.* Thus advertising is seen as increasing concentration or preventing it from falling (Kaldor, 1950). Overall, advertising and changes in concentration are postulated as being positively related. The other school of through focuses on the role of advertising as the means by which new entrants inform consumers of their existence (Telser, 1964). Thus advertising eases entry into the industry, and is negatively related to changes in concentration.

Advertising as Performance

Advertising is part of industrial performance in that it is a part of selling costs, and affects prices and profits (directly or indirectly). But will industrial structure have an effect on the level of advertising? Above we derived the relationship $A/S = e_A/e$, for a profit-maximising firm. The elasticities involved are those perceived by the firm when it makes its decisions, taking into account the reaction of rivals. Thus these elasticities are compounded of two factors — the nature of the product and the industrial structure. This can be seen more clearly if, following Lambin (1970), this condition is written in full for the oligopolistic firm, then

$$A/S = e_A/e \text{ with} \qquad e_A = \left\{ \frac{A_1}{q} \left(\frac{\partial q}{\partial A_1} + \frac{\partial q}{\partial A_2} \cdot \frac{\partial A_2}{\partial A_1} \right) \right\} \text{ and}$$

$$e = \left\{ \frac{p_1}{q} \left(\frac{\partial q}{\partial p_1} + \frac{\partial q}{\partial p_2} \cdot \frac{\partial p_2}{\partial p_1} \right) \right\}$$

where subscript 1 refers to the firm itself and subscript 2 refers to the firm's rivals. The terms $(\partial q/\partial A_1)$, $(\partial q/\partial p_1)$ capture the initial response of demand to own advertising and price. Cable (1972) argues that:

$(\partial q/\partial A_1)$ will typically be higher for the oligopolist [than for the monopolist], since it registers consumers switching brands as well as the total market response. There seems a little *a priori* reason to suppose that $(\partial q/\partial A_1)$ will be any higher or lower at lower concentration levels than in the oligopolistic range, as long as there is sufficient product differentiation for individual brands to be identified by consumers. The absolute value of the term $(\partial q/\partial p_1)$ in the price elasticity will decrease monotonically as concentration increases . . . [But this will] have to be modified if there is recognised interdependence or collusion in the oligopolistic range. With recognized interdependence, the terms $(\partial A_2/\partial A_1)$ and $(\partial p_2/\partial p_1)$ arguably increase with concentration . . . [But] there is strictly no unequivocal theoretical prediction about the relationship between advertising and concentration. It depends upon firms' behavioural reactions and, in particular, on the patterns of interacting behaviour over price and advertising and on whether collusion takes place. On foregoing arguments there seem to be two main possibilities, either no systematic relationship, or an inverted-U shaped relationship, when concentration is measured by the Herfindahl index [text in brackets added].

Summary of Propositions

This discussion leads to four propositions for which the evidence will be summarised below. First, the level of concentration influences the advertising intensity (as measured by the advertising-sales ratio). Second, the advertising intensity influences the level of concentration, and third it influences changes in concentration. Finally, profitability is influenced by advertising. This last proposition has two main variants. It can be the absolute scale of advertising, acting as a barrier to entry because of imperfections in the capital market, or the ratio of advertising to sales by changing the extent of product differentiation and/or the price-elasticity of demand which influences profitability.

Before surveying the empirical work on these propositions, we review some of the difficulties which arise. First, products differ in their 'advertisability'. It could be expected, for example, that goods sold directly to consumers would tend to be advertised more than goods sold to producers. There may be differences which arise from the frequency with which a good is bought by consumers. Further, goods which are sold in relatively small quantities at one time (e.g. tea) and those which are sold in relatively large quantities at one time (e.g. cars) are also likely to have different advertising-sales ratios arising from differences in typical size of purchase. Some of these factors can be controlled by, for example, restricting the sample to industries which produce only consumer goods. But other factors are much more difficult to allow for. An example of this would be the belief that some products (such as cosmetics, alcohol) can be more easily glamorised through advertising than others (for example, sugar) (Cable, 1972).

A second and related problem is that advertising is only one form of marketing. Industries are likely to vary in the extent to which advertising is an effective marketing tool in comparison with other forms of sales promotion. Focusing on advertising may be selecting an arbitrary portion of a firm's marketing budget for investigation.

A third problem arises from the tendency for advertising to influence both current and future demand, and so to have some of the attributes of a capital good. In usual accounting practice, advertising is treated as current expenditure and so is deducted with other costs from revenue before arriving at profits. The treatment of advertising as an investment would lead to advertising expenditure not being deducted from revenue with other costs, but the depreciation on past advertising being deducted to arrive at net (of depreciation) profits. Further, when calculating the rate of profit, the capital assets of the firm would have to be adjusted to include the 'goodwill' of past advertising.

There are further complications. For example, treating advertising as a capital input led above to the profit-maximisation condition that $G/S = e_A/e$, and by extention of the argument above (following Cable, 1972) the dependence of G/S on the level of concentration would be predicted. This would yield a dependence of A/S on the level of concentration only if the current level of advertising is proportional to the level of goodwill. This would occur if, for example, the firms are in a steady-state equilibrium so that current advertising is only replacing depreciation on 'goodwill'.

Finally there are problems of a simultaneous equation nature, which means that X is believed to influence Y as well as Y to influence X. This arises in two respects here. The two propositions outlined above create this type of problem in that advertising intensity and concentration are postulated to influence each other. Further, the fourth proposition outlined above indicates that advertising is postulated to influence profitability. But when advertising is treated as a decision variable, the advertising and price are chosen by a firm at the same time, and that leads to a relationship of association between advertising and the profit margin (arising from the price decision). This was shown above (p. 111) where the equation $M \cdot e_A = A/S$ was derived.

Advertising and Concentration

The first proposition to be examined is that more concentrated industries tend to advertise more (than less concentrated ones). This has generally been examined in terms of $A/S = F(CR)$, and there has been some debate as to whether the function F is linear or quadratic. There are published results to support three views — no relationship, a linear one and a quadratic one! Reekie (1975) using highly disaggregated data for the UK finds 'no evidence . . . to indicate that market structure and advertising are associated either in a linear or in a curvilinear fashion'. Ornstein (1976) finds that his data, covering 328 4-digit American industries, favours a linear rather than a quadratic relationship. Although the relationship is statistically significant, the R^2 is generally low and the quantitative impact of increased concentration on raising advertising is small. For example, he reports

$$A/S = 0.7881 + 0.0225 \, CR4 \quad R^2 = 0.03$$
$$(0.0075)$$

so that a 1 percentage point increase in concentration is associated with a 0.0225 percentage point rise in advertising intensity (compared with an average of the order of $2\frac{1}{2}$ per cent). Rees (1975), challenging the results of Sutton (1974) reported below, finds that although a linear and a quadratic relationship are both statistically significant, the linear version is to be preferred.

Brush (1976) also reports a preference for the linear over the quadratic version, and when other factors are allowed for (such as growth, size of market and durable/non-durable character of product) concentration just loses its statistical significance.

Cable (1972) argues in favour of a quadratic relationship between advertising and concentration, with concentration measured by the Herfindahl index (*HI*). He restricts his sample to 26 non-durable consumer goods, and finds that, within that sample, allowance has to be made for four products 'close to sensitive psychological drives' (toothpaste, lipstick, face powder and toilet soap). For both the ratio of 'goodwill' to sales and advertising to sales, Cable finds strong support for the quadratic relationship. The impact of a change in concentration on advertising intensity can be seen as substantial, with an industry with *HI* = 0.05 having a predicted *A/S* of 3.62 per cent whilst one with *HI* = 0.403 (where the impact of concentration reaches a maximum) has a predicted *A/S* of 15.57 per cent.

Sutton (1974, 1975) also finds support for a quadratic relationship for 25 UK consumer goods 3-digit industries in 1963, and reports, for example, the regression

$$A/S = -3.1545 + 0.1914 \ CR \ -0.0015 \ CR^2 \quad R^2 = 0.39$$
$$\quad\quad\quad (1.3366) \quad (0.0516) \quad\quad (0.0004)$$

where *CR* is measured by a weighted average of *CR5* in terms of sales in sub-industries which compose the industry.[6] The figures in parenthesis, here as elsewhere, refer to standard errors. This equation predicts that the maximum intensity of advertising would occur for *CR5* of 63.5 per cent which is close to the observed median value.

Buxton *et al.* (1984) also find evidence that the relationship between advertising-sales ratio and concentration is a quadratic one. For example, they report:

$$A/S = -1.8975 + 7.6578 \ P + 0.1187 \ \pi/S + 0.1795 \ (S_c/S) \cdot CR5$$
$$\quad\quad (-2.3532) \quad (6.3064) \quad\quad (3.0075) \quad\quad\quad (5.2121)$$

$$-0.0014 \ (S_c) \cdot CR5^2 \quad R^2 = 0.746$$
$$(-3.5334)$$

where *P* is a personal goods dummy (see below), S_c is sales to consumers, *S* total sales, π profits and *CR5* concentration ratio. They find that a distinction should be made between consumer sales and producer sales. There is an impact of the profit-sales ratio on advertising intensity, which remains even when allowance is made for possible simultaneity effects (i.e. advertising intensity influences profit rate and vice versa). The rate of sales growth did not appear to affect significantly advertising intensity, but 'personal' goods (pharmaceuticals, toilet preparations) had a much higher advertising intensity than other goods. In this study, as in others which find support for a quadratic function, the nature of that relationship is that for low to medium levels of concentration, advertising intensity and concentration are positively related whilst at high levels of concentration they are negatively related. For example, in the equation reported in this paragraph, for a given ratio of consumer goods sales to the total sales, the highest advertising to sales ratio would be predicted to arise when the concentration ratio was 64 per cent.

Greer (1971) seeks to take into account the two-way relationship between advertising intensity and concentration (indicated by the first two propositions given above). We defer consideration of his work until later, but note that he finds support for a quadratic relationship between advertising and concentration.

Whilst we have not surveyed everything published on this subject, these results give a flavour of the general run of results. The balance of evidence is that there is a relationship between advertising and concentration with the implied causation running from concentration to advertising intensity.

Concentration and Advertising

The second proposition is that advertising supports the position of the existing oligopolists, and hence that a high level of advertising leads to a high level of concentration. Thus again a relationship between advertising intensity and concentration is postulated, but this time the causation runs from advertising to concentration.

Telser (1964) used data for 42 three-digit consumer goods industries for 1947, 1954 and 1958 and concludes that the 'correlation between concentration and advertising is unimpressive' and indeed is not statistically significant. Mann *et al.* (1967) challenged this view, and found a substantial relationship, for example:

$$CR4 = 35.87 + 9.64 \, A/S \quad r = 0.68 \quad R^2 = 0.46$$
$$(3.17)$$

drawing upon the data of 42 firms, which could be assigned to one of 14 four-digit industries. However, Ekelund and Maurice (1969) pointed out that these data were drawn from the firms who were the hundred largest advertisers. They also argue that to overcome some of the problems arising from omitted variables (such as 'advertisability') the regression should be estimated in change form. Thus there may be some variables, which we will label as a vector Z, which influence the level of concentration. Then the equation reads $CR4 = a + b\,(A/S) + cZ$, but Z cannot be measured. However, taking changes in the variables over a specified period leads to the equation $\Delta CR4 = b\,\Delta(A/S) + c\Delta Z$, where Δ before a variable means changes in that variable. Then, if $\Delta Z = 0$, it drops out of the equation.[7] Characteristics of products such as 'advertisability' may change a little so that $\Delta Z = 0$ can be assumed. When estimated in change form Ekelund and Maurice find that in 'no case was significant correlation indicated'. Telser (1969) also challenges the results of Mann *et al.* (1967) and by extending their sample finds little correlation (but also see the replies of Mann *et al.*, 1969a, 1969b).

Greer (1971) attempts to take account of the argument that the relationship between advertising and concentration is two-way, and also introduces growth as an influence on advertising and concentration and as itself influenced by advertising. He also postulates that the effect of concentration on advertising is quadratic rather than linear. Greer's three equation model is

$$A/S = a_1 + a_2 \cdot CR4 + a_3 \cdot (CR4)^2 + a_4 \cdot G$$
$$CR4 = b_1 + b_2 \cdot A/S + b_3 \cdot G + b_4 \cdot X$$
$$G = c_1 + c_2 \cdot A/S + c_3 \cdot Y$$

where G is the growth rate and X, Y represent other variables used by Greer, which do not directly concern us here. Greer estimates this model using the technique of two-stage least squares which makes some allowance for the simultaneous nature of the model. Combining observations for three years, the estimation is undertaken for three samples of consumer goods industries, with the samples distinguished by the types of goods produced by the industries. Advertising intensity is found to have a significant impact on the level of concentration. Growth tends to lead to lower concentration and advertising intensity, and from the third equation there is no significant impact of advertising on the growth of sales.

Martin (1979) and Strickland and Weiss (1976) investigated a three-equation model in which profitability, concentration and advertising intensity are all inter-related, and we have already reported on their profitability equations in the previous chapter. In both papers the ratio of advertising to sales is found to be a quadratic function of concentration and to depend positively on the profit margin. Concentration is itself found to be positively related to the advertising-sales ratio. Thus in these studies concentration is found to influence the intensity of advertising and advertising influences the level of concentration.

However, there are only small differences reported between the results of estimation by two-stage least squares and those from estimation by ordinary least squares. The latter does not make allowance for any simultaneous effects with each of the three equations taken in isolation. This provides the hope that the previous results given here which are based on estimation by ordinary least squares may not be too far adrift.

Advertising and Changes in Concentration

For the third proposition there are three studies which look at the question of whether advertising leads to changes in concentration. Marcus (1969) divides industries into low, medium and high degree of product differentiation, based upon the intensity of advertising. Based on a sample of 78 consumer goods industries Marcus concludes that 'our main finding is that advertising can be expected to lead to substantial rises in industrial concentration'. Over the longest period which he considers, 1947 to 1963, *CR*8 in medium-differentiation industries is indicated to have increased by over 8 percentage points more than the low-differentiation industries, and by over 17 percentage points more in the high-differentiation industries.

The results reported for the United Kingdom by Gratton and Kemp (1977) contradict the results of Marcus (which were for the United States). They also classify industries as having low, medium or high degrees of product differentiation, based on the intensity of advertising. The effect of a medium or high degree of product differentiation, as compared with a low degree, is to reduce the level of concentration.

Hart and Clarke (1980) find for a sample of 76 UK manufacturing industries that over the period 1958 to 1968 there was no significant impact of advertising-sales ratio on changes in concentration.

Hirchey (1981) examines the question of whether advertising intensity influences the mobility of firms, in which he includes entry, growth of leading firms and growth of the non-leading firms. Using a sample of 87 American industries over the number of sub-periods within the period 1947 to 1972, he concludes that his 'analysis reveals that the mobility effect of advertising is to upset rather than reinforce the market share stability of established firms'. In particular, he finds that advertising growth has no significant effect on growth of leading firms, but in two (out of three) sub-periods has a significant positive effect on growth of non-leading firms with the effect negative and significant in the third sub-period.

Advertising and Profitability

The final postulate is that advertising enhances profitability. Some of the evidence of the impact of advertising on profitability has been reviewed in Chapter 6. The results summarised in Tables 6.2 and 6.3 indicate that there is some support for the view that advertising enhances profitability. We now look at some studies which have given advertising a central role.

Comanor and Wilson (1967) examine the role of advertising both in terms of an indicator of product differentiation, of raising the *m.e.s.* and as a general barrier to entry. Their sample consists of 41 industries, and they allow for the impacts of concentration, growth of demand and other entry barriers on profitability. They examine the role of the advertising to sales ratio and of the advertising barrier to entry. The latter variable is a discontinuous one, and an industry either has a high or a moderate advertising entry barrier. They conclude that 'industries with high advertising outlays earn, on average, at a profit rate which exceeds that of other industries by nearly four percentage points. This differential represents a 50 per cent increase in profit rates. It is likely, moreover, that much of this profit rate differential is accounted for by the entry barriers created by advertising expenditures and by the resulting achievement of market power'.

Whereas Comanor and Wilson study the effect of advertising on the rate of return, Cowling *et al.* (1975) study its effect on the profit-sales ratio at the firm level. They argue that the absolute level of advertising of the firm itself and the level of advertising of its rivals are the relevant measures of the impact of advertising. Cowling *et al.* find that 'advertising has had a significant impact on the market power of the firm in question and advertising at the market level seems also to have had a significant effect as a barrier to entry of new firms'. They find that the variability of the profit margin tends to fall as the net assets (K) of the firm increases, and a correction for this heteroskedasticity is made by estimating a weighted regression with weights $K^{1/4}$. A typical regression is

$$\pi/S = -0.6765 + 0.002322A - 0.4458 \times 10^{-6} A^2$$
$$(0.000913) \qquad (0.2417 \times 10^{-6})$$

$$+ 0.001062 (A/S)_r + 0.1932 \ CR4 - 0.002417 (CR4)^2$$
$$(0.000347) \qquad (0.0672) \qquad (0.000849)$$

$$+ 0.0005894 \ K \qquad \bar{R}^2 = 0.342$$
$$(0.007755)$$

where $(A/S)_r$ is the advertising-sales ratio (expressed as a percentage) of rivals, A is advertising measured in thousands of pounds and K is the net assets of the firm measured in millions of pounds. The absolute scale of advertising by a firm influences the profit margin, but this influence reaches a peak at an advertising level of £26,000. However, the advertising by a firm's rivals enhances a firm's profits, and the effect at work here is presumably that the barriers to entry into an industry (particularly through product differentiation) are created by the advertising of all the firms, and all benefit through higher profits.

Miller (1969) investigates the determinants of the rate of return in 106 'minor' industries over the period 1958–9 and 1961–2 and concludes that 'the profit rates . . . are positively related to the four-firm concentration ratio, the percentage of sales revenue devoted to advertising and (to some extent) the degree to which companies are diversified into industries other than their own'.

Imel and Helmberger (1971) focus on the profit-sales ratio in 99 companies operating in the food sector. They find that whilst the precise measured impact varies (depending on the sample used), nevertheless the impact of the advertising-sales ratio is always positive and usually significant.

We indicated above (p. 114) the problem which could arise from treating advertising expenditure as a current expenditure if it is really a capital expenditure. Bloch (1974) argues that after making adjustments to measured profit rates to take account of the capital investment aspect of advertising, there is no significant relationship between profit rate and market structure and advertising.

However, this has to be set against the finding of Comanor and Wilson (1974), who find that 'these results indicate that the conclusion that advertising affects profit rates does not merely reflect inappropriate accounting procedures. The available evidence is therefore consistent with the view that intensive advertising in an industry permits firms to set higher price-cost margins, thereby yielding rates of return higher than those in other industries where advertising is less important'. (See also Comanor and Wilson, 1979.)

Thus the evidence points towards some significant influence of advertising intensity on profitability. However in interpreting this evidence three considerations stand out. First, there is the two-way nature of the advertising-profitability relationship, for as we saw above profitability and advertising may go together without any implication that advertising enhances profitability. Second, as Bloch (1974) has argued, the investment (as far as the firm is concerned) nature of advertising has not generally been taken into account. Finally, in some studies even with advertising treated as current expenditure, the cost of advertising is not deducted from revenue when profits are calculated, and thus in effect profits plus advertising is being regressed on advertising leading almost inevitably to the finding of a significant relationship between profitability and advertising (see p. 91). Ayanian (1983) reworks some of the data of Comanor and Wilson seeking to make allowance for the capital investment nature of advertising. He concludes that advertising has a long-lived effect and when allowance is made for that the excess return to advertising is eliminated.

Conclusions

It is a disappointment to have to record that the empirical evidence has not been able to settle the issues thrown up by the debate over the role of advertising. The linkages between advertising, concentration and profitability are many and probably not very strong. Thus the formulation of the linkages to be examined and the manner in which the sample and data are constructed may be of crucial importance. A reading of the literature discussed above will reveal that much of the argument is over the appropriate samples and measurement of variables. The conflicting and often weak conclusions may also reflect the difficulties of isolating the impact of one variable (in this case advertising), when it is interacting with many other variables.

Notes

1. The source of these figures is a press release from the Advertising Association.
2. The lowest ratio was recorded by Insulated Wires and Cables at just over 0.1 per cent. It may be more appropriate to measure advertising relative to net output, and the ratio of advertising to net output rises to over 25 per cent for the toilet preparations and

soap detergents industries. Source: Census of Production, 1968.

3. Well-known proponents of the view that advertising supplies little information and is essentially persuasive include Baran and Sweezy (1967), Galbraith (1969) and Packard (1957).

4. 'Advertising can increase sales either by changing tastes or by providing information . . . The crucial difference between the two views of the role of advertising is that in the change-in-taste approach, advertising increases product differentiation, makes demand curves *less* elastic, and leads to *higher* prices; while in the information approach, advertising makes demand curves *more* elastic and leads to *lower* prices' (Ferguson, 1974, p. 28).

5. Whilst the advertising of one firm may enhance that firm's sales, it may reduce the sales of other firms. Thus some, if not all, of the advertising by firms may be offsetting, and so the task facing the potential entrant may be less than would appear.

6. There are some problems with using this measure, and one of these is that the CR5s are not available for all the sub-industries. For further discussion in this context, see Rees (1975) and p. 90 of this volume.

7. It should be noted that the equation to be estimated should be $\Delta CR4 = b . \Delta(A/S)$, i.e. the constant term is hypothesised to be zero, but Ekelund and Maurice include a constant term, though it is not possible from the results which they report to judge whether the estimated constant term is significantly different from zero.

8 INNOVATION, INVENTION AND INDUSTRIAL STRUCTURE

Introduction

This chapter examines the possible impact of industrial structure and firm size on the level of invention and rate of innovation. There are two basic ways in which economists have approached inventions and innovations and the associated technical advance. The first, widely used in macroeconomic growth models, treats inventions and innovations as occurring such that technical progress (defined in terms of higher output for given inputs of labour, capital equipment, etc.) proceeds at an exogenously determined and often constant rate. The second treats invention and innovation as the production of new knowledge which can be analysed in a way similar to that applied to the production of goods and services with some account taken of the special features of the product knowledge. It is not surprising that industrial economists have tended to emphasise the second approach. But the exogenous nature of some technological advance so far as the industrial sector is concerned often needs to be taken into account. One aspect of this arises from technological advance derived from the non-profit sector such as universities and government-sponsored research. But even here the advance has to be introduced into the production of goods and services, and industrial economists have sought to identify the factors which determine whether and how quickly new ideas are introduced. Another aspect of this is that technical advance may be, in some relevant sense, easier in some sectors of the economy than in others.

A distinction has often been drawn (e.g. Freeman (1982), Kamien and Schwartz (1982)) between 'science push' and 'demand pull' approaches to invention and innovation. The 'science push' approach stresses the role of original research and invention, with the uses, if any, of the outcome of that research being sought afterwards. The 'demand pull' approach stresses the role of the demand side such that research effort is invested to find ways of satisfying particular demands. Freeman (1982) argues that the two ways may not be exclusive but rather complementary. Thus there are examples of inventions arising from the pursuit of scientific curiosity without any thought being given to any practical use and there are examples of research directed to the solution of specific problems (for examples, see Freeman (1982), pp. 109–10). Our main concern here is with the influence of industrial structure on the rate of technical advance and the nature of that advance. This leads to a stress on the costs and benefits of research and development as influencing the pace and direction of that research and development. The 'science push' elements are not considered as central in this approach, though the work undertaken (e.g. in universities) in pursuit of scientific knowledge for the sake of knowledge will have an influence on the costs and benefits of research and development undertaken by firms. Further, 'science push' aspects are relevant when evaluating empirical evidence on the various theories put forward on the influence of industrial structure and firm size on technological advance.

Before the main discussion, it is useful to make a number of introductory distinctions. First, it is necessary to distinguish between invention and innovation. Freeman (1982) defines invention as 'an idea, a sketch or a model for a new or improved device, product, process or system', and states that 'an innovation in the economic sense is accomplished only with the first *commercial* transaction involving the new product, process, system or device, although the word is used also to describe the whole process'. It is suggested that not only is innovation more likely to be susceptible to economic analysis than invention, but also that the costs of innovation are much larger than those of invention. Lloyd (1970) indicates that costs associated with invention are only of the order of 10 per cent of the total costs of innovation and invention. With a new process of production or a new product we may also be interested in identifying which types of firms are first to innovate, and then further to investigate the factors which influence the speed with which other firms follow suit.

A second distinction is between an invention which reduces production costs and one which introduces a new product. The former may provide opportunities for increased profits for those who adopt it (depending upon the costs of adoption) and a loss of profit for those who do not adopt it. But the latter may have a much greater effect by rendering previous products obsolete, so that a firm which does not innovate may find that the demand for its product has virtually disappeared. Thus the pressures on firms to innovate may be significantly different in the two categories. An innovation of a new producer good (e.g. new type of machine) may also involve innovation of a new process by the firms which utilise that new good. Further, the introduction of a new process or a new product may often involve investment in new capital equipment, and hence involve investment decisions.

A particularly important characteristic of the knowledge arising from an invention is that the initial costs of making the invention are usually very large in comparison with the costs of spreading the knowledge gained (although the costs of using the knowledge may be large). Indeed, it is often assumed for convenience that the cost of spreading that knowledge is zero. Further, it may be difficult for the originators of new knowledge to prevent the spread of that knowledge, once it has been passed to a few people other than the originator or when it has been embedded in a new product. Thus knowledge has some characteristics of 'public goods' with costs of provision near to zero (once a discovery has been made), difficulties of preventing access to the knowledge and non-rivalrous in use. The last point means that one firm's use of knowledge does not directly limit the use of that knowledge by other firms, though the benefits gained by the use of the knowledge by one firm may well depend on how many other firms are also using it.

Once knowledge has been discovered, the low (or zero) marginal cost of further provision of that knowledge points to a low (or zero) price for that knowledge being required for efficiency purposes. But the costs of discovery point to a higher price to encourage further discoveries. These contrary requirements lie behind patent laws which give inventors certain rights over the use of their invention for a specified period. The rights assigned to inventors and the length of time for which the patent is granted vary between countries. In the United Kingdom the period is generally 16 years (extendable up to 26 years is exceptional circumstances), and the patent holder can be compelled to grant licences for the use of the invention if the patentee is abusing the monopoly position by, for example, not working the invention commercially. The patent system in operation is likely to have some impact on the speed and nature of invention and innovation. Taylor and Silberston (1973) provide a detailed examination of this issue for the British patent system (compared with an alternative of worldwide compulsory licensing). One of their conclusions is that the impact of the patent system varies considerably between industries, being important in, for example, pharmaceuticals and crop chemicals but unimportant in basic chemicals and oil refining. It could be anticipated that patents would be important where the incorporation of a new idea in a new product would allow other firms to easily discover that idea. Chapter 14 provides a summary of their findings. Since our central purpose is to investigate the effect of industrial structure on the level of invention and innovation within the existing legal framework, we will not be dealing directly with the patent system.[1]

We begin with an analysis based on Arrow (1962), which relates to the incentives for invention of the type which leads to a reduction in production costs. The incentives when the industry which makes use of the invention is monopolised are compared with those where that industry

Figure 8.1: Comparison of Costs and Profits of Innovation under Perfect Competition and under Monopoly

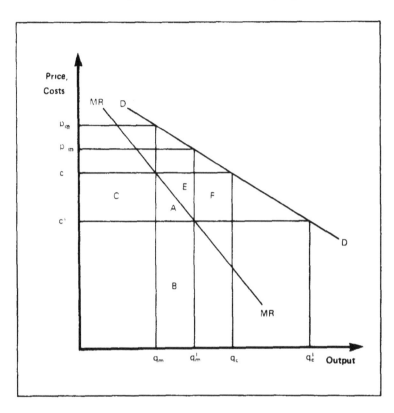

is perfectly competitive. In Figure 8.1 the demand curve facing the industry is D, the marginal revenue MR, unit costs (which are assumed constant) are c prior to the introduction of the invention, and c' after its introduction. Under monopoly, the price is p_m prior to the introduction and p'_m after, whilst under perfect competition the price is c and c', respectively (since zero profits apply there).

In moving from output q_m to q'_m, the monopolist increases its revenue by an amount equivalent to the area $A + B$, and its costs change by $-C + B$ (the first part from the fall in unit costs, and the second from an increase in production), to leave a profit gain of $A + C$. This is the maximum amount (per period) which a monopolist would pay for a cost-reducing invention. The maximum amount which the competitive firms would be able to pay for the cost-reducing invention is $A + C + E + F$, for if more is paid the increased profit would be eaten up by the royalties. Thus the maximum potential payments for the information is lower under monopoly than under perfect competition.

This analysis can illustrate further features of the problem. First, although the unit total costs of the new technique may be lower than the unit total costs of the old technique, a firm with investment in the machinery suitable for the old technique would be comparing the unit *variable* costs of the old technique with the unit *total* costs of the new technique. Whilst the machinery for the old technique remains usable, it may be more profitable to continue to use the old technique and only make the switch when the machinery needs replacement. Second, the pressures on the monopolist to innovate may differ from those on the competitive firms. The monopolist is already making super-normal profits, and whilst it would be profitable for the monopoly to innovate if the costs are less than $A + C$, there may be little market pressure to do so. Under perfect competition, the market price starts at c and if the information is freely available the price would tend to fall towards c'. This puts pressure on firms to innovate, and those that did not would suffer losses of up to $c - c'$ per unit of output. On the other hand, if the royalty charged for the information is near to $c - c'$, then the costs with the information are close to c, and thus there is little downward pressure on price, and little pressure on firms to innovate.

A third aspect is that it is likely to be easier for the inventor to prevent the 'leakage' of information under monopoly than under perfect competition. Under monopoly there are no other firms to which the existing firm could sell the information. Further the monopoly would have the incentive to keep the knowledge to itself in order to reduce the possibility of entry. Under perfect competition, with a large number of firms, a firm which acquires the information has incentives to pass on the information (at a price) to other firms.

This analysis would, on the whole, indicate it was potentially more profitable for an inventor to make advances which were usable in a competitive industry than in a monopolistic industry. Further, there may be more pressure on the competitive firms to introduce the innovation. It could be argued that this overlooks two important aspects of research and development. The first is that invention and innovation are risky undertakings, and the second is that the firms often undertake their own research and development rather than buy it from other firms. These facets led Schumpeter (1954) and Galbraith (1952) to agree that monopoly positions and large firm size favour research and development.

Schumpeter argued that a monopoly position often arose out of a successful research programme and the discovery of new products, and hence monopoly profits were often the return to previous research and development. But, in turn, those profits provide a major source of funds for further investment in research and development. A monopoly position may help to reduce the risks involved to the firm, and that may aid research and development. For 'long-range investment under rapidly changing conditions, especially under conditions that change or may change at any moment under the impact of new commodities and technologies, is like shooting at a target that is not only indistinct but moving — and moving jerkily at that. Hence it becomes nessary to resort to such protecting devices as patents or temporary secrecy of processes or, in some cases, long-period contracts secured in advance' (Schumpter, 1954).

Thus, Schumpeter contends, invention and innovation is higher under monopoly than under atomistic competition. However, the high profits do not last for ever for there is a 'perennial gale of creative destruction' which threatens the monopolist's position. Schumpeter's view is often seen as stressing the benefits of monopoly. But Schumpeter saw the monopolist's position as insecure, continually threatened by the development of new products. He also suggested that these benefits of monopoly in respect of technical advance have to be weighed against the short-run costs of monopoly arising from higher prices and lower output (as compared with a hypothetical perfect competitive alternative (cf. Chapter 14).

Galbraith (1952) arrives at similar conclusions, although his line of reasoning is different from that of Schumpeter. Galbraith argues that 'modern industry of a few large firms [is] an excellent instrument for inducing technical change'. This is because the firms are 'admirably equipped for financing technical development' and because 'development is costly'. The nature of modern technical advance requiring the employment of scientists and engineers working on projects which are subject to considerable risks, favours the large firm. A large firm can hope to finance a number of projects and thereby reduce the overall risk with the successes and failures in some sense averaging out. Further Galbraith indicates that patents and secrecy are not sufficient to prevent innovation being followed. The smaller the share which a firm has in a market, the smaller will be that firm's share of any benefits from an innovation, and so the less likely is the firm to undertake costly research and development. Finally, we note that Galbraith argues that it is oligopoly rather than monopoly which provides these benefits.

Much empirical work within industrial economics has investigated the influence of firm size rather than industrial structure on inventive and innovative activity. A major reason for this is that firm size within an industry can be considered and in this way technological opportunities held roughly constant, whereas between industries those opportunities vary considerably. However, when the speed with which an innovation has been introduced is investigated, differences in technological opportunity do not enter the picture in that the relevant invention has already occurred, and it is the process of innovation which is investigated.

The questions which we hope the empirical evidence can answer are:

(a) How does research activity (both in terms of input and output) vary with firm size?
(b) How does the efficiency of research programmes (i.e. ratio of outputs to inputs) vary with firm size, and with size of the research programme?
(c) How does the rate of innovation vary with firm size?
(d) Questions (a) to (c) above but with 'industrial structure' replacing 'firm size'.

In seeking to answer these questions, we first summarise the measurement problems, indicate the relevance of each question to the earlier discussion and then summarise the evidence.

There are a number of surveys on the economics of invention and innovation and of research and development, and within these surveys some attention is paid to the effects of firm size and industrial structure. These surveys include Freeman (1982) (especially Chapter 6) and Kamien and Schwartz (1982) (especially Chapter 3). We draw heavily on these surveys although it should be noted that the original material on which these surveys are based overlaps substantially.

Research Intensity and Firm Size

In general the research input made by a firm can only be measured if the firm itself identifies part of its activities as research. Then expenditure on research or the number of people employed on research can be used as a measure of research input. Sometimes a proxy measure, such as the number of qualified scientists and engineers employed, is used to indicate the research commitment of a firm or industry. But even such a proxy requires the identification of qualified manpower by the firms involved. Large firms are generally thought more likely than small firms (apart from specialist research firms) to have formal arrangements through which research activity can be identified and measured. Further some technical advance arises from 'learning-by-doing' (see pp. 67–8 above), leading to small modifications to the production process. The sources of such improvements would be very difficult to identify and measure.

Freeman (1982) concludes that research and development programmes are highly concentrated in a relatively few firms, and generally are more concentrated than production or employment. For example, in the United Kingdom in the mid-1960s, the 100 firms with the largest R & D programmes accounted for 69.5 per cent of the total (and this can be compared with a share of the largest hundred firms in net output in manufacturing industry around the same date of about 40 per cent). Research programmes are found to be mainly conducted in large firms, with firms with over 5,000 employees accounting for 90 per cent of all industrial R & D expenditure in the USA (1978), and for around 75 per cent in West Germany and the UK. In contrast, the vast majority (around 95 per cent) of small firms (with less than 200 employees) do not have any specialised research programme.

However, amongst firms which do undertake research, there is no strong evidence for the research intensity (e.g. the ratio of expenditure on research and development to sales) to increase with firm size. Freeman (1982) concludes that

> there is a generally far weaker correlation between the *relative* measure of research activity (research intensity) and size of firm [than between absolute measure of research activity and size of firm] and it is not significant in some industries and countries . . . [Further] in several countries those few small firms who *do* perform R & D have above average R & D intensities.

There has been disagreement in the literature as to whether R & D intensity declines with size amongst the largest firms. For example, Scherer (1965) finds some tendency for research intensity to first rise and then fall with firm size. But Soete (1979), examining data for the USA in the 1970s, found some tendency for R & D intensity to continue to increase with firm size even amongst the largest firms.

We now look at the output of research activity, and begin with the two main ways in which research output has been measured. The first one has been the use of the number of patents taken out. This sees a patentable invention as the end-product of the research process and it relates to invention rather than innovation. But the issue of a patent does not mean that an invention is useful nor that the invention leads to profitable innovation, though the firms taking out the patent are likely to believe that the invention has some commercial potential since there is a cost to taking out a patent. One difficulty with the use of patent statistics is that the propensity to patent an invention may vary with the size of the firm. It has been argued that small firms (particularly very small ones) would be less likely to take out patents because of the expense involved. However the work of Schmookler (1966) indicated that the reverse position seemed to hold, namely that large firms tended to patent proportionately less than small firms (a finding also reported by Pavitt, 1982). The reason for this appears to be that large firms hope to profit by their own use of their inventions and to use commercial secrecy to prevent other firms obtaining information about inventions. Indeed the issue of a patent may serve to warn rivals of the existence of the invention. With a long period elapsing between invention and innovation the rivals may have some chance of catching up if a patent is issued but not if the invention is kept secret. In contrast a small firm may hope to reap most of the profits from an invention by the sale of the knowledge to other firms rather through its own use. The heavy costs of innovation relative to those of invention referred to above may be major cause of this.

Scherer (1965) found that patent output generally increased less than proportionately with sales amongst large firms, and that inventive output as measured by patents did not appear to be related to market power nor to previous profitability. Scherer concluded that his results severely undermine the Schumpeter thesis. He made some allowance for technological opportunities (by classifying the firms in one of four broad industrial categories) and found that differences in technological opportunity were important in explaining differences in patents taken out. Smyth *et al.* (1972) found that the pattern varied between industries, with one industry where patents increased more than proportionately with firm size, one industry where patents increased less than proportionately, and a third where examined patents increased more than proportionately except amongst the largest firms.

Patent statistics make no distinction between significant and insignificant inventions (nor between profitable and unprofitable ones). A measure which seeks to overcome that objection is to use 'important' inventions as assessed by experts or by people involved in the relevant industries, followed by the identification of the source of those important inventions.

Jewkes *et al.* (1958, 1969) look at the source of a number of important inventions, although they do not attempt to make their sample in any sense representative. They considered the source of 61 inventions in their original study, and a further 20 in their follow-up study, drawn from inventions made during the nineteenth and twentieth centuries. They conclude that 'more than one half of the cases can be ranked as individual invention in the sense that much of the pioneering work was carried through by men who were working on their own behalf . . . or where the inventors were employed in institutions, those institutions were . . . of such a kind that the individuals were autonomous, free to follow their own ideas without hindrance'.

Kamien and Schwartz (1982, p. 84) conclude that the relationship between invention and firm size varies between industries, with the chemical industry in particular being cited as exceptional to the general pattern. However, it is possible to conclude that the larger size of firm is not particularly conducive to invention.

Efficiency and Firm Size

The question of the efficiency of research activity has two aspects of interest here, namely whether it is an activity which is subject to increasing or decreasing returns and whether the level of input-output efficiency is related to the size of firm undertaking the research. Efficiency in terms of the relationship of output to input is particularly different to assess, since as we have seen above, the measurement of both inputs and outputs of research activity is fraught with difficulty.

Kamien and Schwartz (1982) survey the available evidence and find that the few studies undertaken on the question of economies of scale in research and development activity have indicated the absence of economies of scale. They also find that 'empirical studies over the last fifteen years have consistently shown that, although there may sometimes be certain advantages of size in exploiting the fruits of R & D, it is more efficiently done in small or medium size firms than in large ones'.

There is also some evidence (Blair, 1972) based on American law suits that some large firms have tried to withhold inventions, presumably on the basis that new inventions threaten the viability of existing products. There may also be differences in the importance of the inventions generated by small and large firms. Hamberg (1966) reviewed evidence on this and concludes that large laboratories tend to produce mainly minor inventions.

Innovation and Firm Size

The relationship between innovation and firm size may be rather different from the one between invention and firm size for the skills involved in invention and in innovation are likely to be different. We can start with the observation of Freeman (1982) that whilst the inventions studies by Jewkes *et al.* (1958) were largely made in small firms, the development of the inventions was largely undertaken by large firms. Freeman indicates that, in Britain in the period 1945 to 1970, the proportion of innovations made by small firms (less than 200 employees) was around 12 per cent, which was well below their share in employment or net output (the latter shares having fallen to 22 per cent and 19 per cent respectively by 1963). However, industries can be classified into two distinct groups: the first includes industries where small firms make virtually no contribution to innovation, and the second (including scientific instruments, electronics, carpets and construction) in which small firms make a significant contribution to innovation, with their share of innovations approaching their share of net output.

Kamien and Schwartz (1982) find, however, that '[b]eyond some magnitude size does not appear especially conducive to either innovational effort or output in either this country [i.e. USA] or in European countries. However, patterns differ by industry'.

Research and Industrial Structure

This aspect of enquiry is particularly difficult to investigate, for in addition to the measurement problems already raised, there is the problem of trying to compare the research intensities of different industries. Substantial differences in research intensity between industries are likely to arise from basic technological differences, which are particularly difficult to measure accurately. However, attempts have been made to allow for 'technological opportunity', although this has often been made by subjective assessment. It may be the case that differences in technological opportunity swamp any differences arising from industrial structures. There may also be difficulties in sorting out the direction, if any, of causation between research and industrial structure. Large-scale capital-intensive industries may be highly concentrated and may have more technological opportunities than other industries. This could lead to a non-causal association between concentration and research and development. Indeed, Johnson (1975) concludes that in all these studies a positive relationship between concentration and R & D intensity was found, but it was much weaker than when no account was taken of technological opportunity. This result arises because research intensities and concentration are both affected by technological opportunity. The correlation between research intensities and concentration may, therefore, contain a spurious element.

Kamien and Schwartz (1982) 'find little consensus . . . [from] reviewing the diverse findings on research efforts and concentration . . . In most instances it has been difficult to discern a statistical relationship among these variables. There is agreement that the relation may vary with the "technological class" of the industry'.

Looking at labour productivity growth as a composite indicator of invention, innovation, 'learning-by-doing' and capital investment has generally led to mixed results. Some authors (e.g. Phillips, 1956) have found a positive relationship between concentration (establishment concentration in the case of Phillips) and productivity change. But Stigler (1956), for example, reached the opposite conclusion.

Turning to more direct measures of research output, Scherer (1965) found no support for a positive relationship between research output (as measured by the number of patents) and industrial concentration amongst large firms after allowing for differences in technological opportunity. Williamson (1965), based on the data of Mansfield (1962) for three industries over two time periods, found that the relative share of innovations contributed by the largest four firms appeared to decline as concentration increased, and that for a concentration ratio (*CR4*) above 30 to 50 per cent (the precise figure depending upon the specification of the estimated equation) the largest firms appear to make less than their proportionate share of innovations.

There have been a few studies on the speed of diffusion of innovations.[2] Before discussing some of these studies, we can mention common findings. These are that the relationship between the number of firms having adopted an innovation and time is approximately a logistic curve. Such a curve (roughly S-shaped) indicates that at first adoption is relatively slow, and then speeds up followed by a flattening out as saturation level (near universal adoption) is approached. Further, there are very considerable time-lags in the adoption of new ideas. Davies (1979b) reports that whilst for four innovations (out of a sample of 22) half or more of the potential adopters had adopted in less than six years, for seven innovations less than half of the potential adopters had actually adopted after 14 years.

Mansfield (1969) deals with innovations regarded by industry sources as important in four major industries (petroleum refining, butuminous coal, railways and steel). In the first three of those industries, he found that the four largest firms accounted for a larger share of the innovations than they did of output, but in steel they accounted for less. Mansfield looked at the nature and size of the innovation, and found that

> the largest four firms seemed to account for a relatively large share of the innovating in cases in which (1) the investment required to in- novate was large relative to the size of the potential users, (2) the minimum size of the firm required to use the innovations profitably was relatively large, and (3) the average size of the largest four firms was much greater than the average size of all potential users of the innovation.

Thus larger firms are innovative-intensive in situations where large in- vestment is required, the type of situation which Galbraith and others have seen as increasing in importance over time.

Davies (1979b) investigates the speed of diffusion of 22 successful pro- cess innovations in UK industries over the period 1945 to the mid-1970s. He concludes that his findings seem to establish 'that the probability of a firm having adopted [an innovation] will be higher, at any point in time, the larger is that firm's size'. But a large firm operates more factories and makes more investment decisions than a small firm does. When a comparison is made between the speed of innovation of a large firm and a number of small firms whose combined size is comparable with the size of the large firm, then the large firms appear, if anything, less pro- gressive than the small firms. Davies also finds that the speed of diffu- sion tends to be faster as the innovation is more profitable, the greater the labour intensity (and growth to a limiting extent) of the adopting in- dustry, the fewer firms in the adopting industry, and the smaller the in- equalities between firms. These last two variables reflect the absolute and relative concepts of concentrations (cf. pp. 29–30 above).

Impact on Industrial Structure

There are likely to be some effects of the results of research and develop- ment on industrial structure — particularly on barriers to entry and con- centration. The first possible effect is that when existing firms compete in terms of product innovation, then potential entrants have to compete in that dimension. It may be difficult for entrants to acquire relevant knowledge for the production of 'new' products because of patents or commercial secrecy. Further new entrants may have to invest themselves in research and development, creating difficulties in raising finance for this particularly risky undertaking.

The second aspect is whether technical change has tended to lead to production techniques which favour large scale rather than small scale. If it has, then the minimum efficient scale of production will rise over time, and again raise barriers to new entry.

Blair (1972) concluded that from the late eighteenth century through to the first third of the twentieth century, technical change had generally encouraged economies of scale and tended to push concentration upwards. But since then newer technologies had tended to reduce plant size.

The third aspect is that the nature of new knowledge may be influenced by the nature of the seekers for that information. In other words, much research effort is likely to be devoted to trying to solve some of the problems currently facing the sponsors of that research. It has been seen that large firms devoted more resources to research and development, and we might anticipate that more resources would be devoted to solving the problems of large firms rather than the problems of small firms.

There are clearly substantial problems in investigating the links between industrial structure and technological advance. However, the thrust of the results discussed above is that there is little support for strong versions of theses like those of Galbraith and Schumpeter which postulate large firms and concentrated industries are necessary for rapid technological advance.

Notes

1. For a brief description of the British patent system, see Johnson (1975), pp. 39–48, and for a detailed discussion see The British Patent System (1970). For a discussion of the American system, see for example Wilcox and Shepherd (1975), Ch. 9. For some proposals for alternatives to the present patent system see *Intellectual Property Rights and Innovations*, Cmnd 9117 (HMSO).

2. See Davies (1979b), Ch. 2, for a survey.

9 PRICES, PRICE CHANGE AND OLIGOPOLY

Introduction

The discussion in earlier chapters has dealt with theories of the determination of prices relative to costs, under the heading or price-cost margin and profitability. This chapter deals briefly with views on how firms decide upon prices, and then at more length with the question of whether industrial structure affects price flexibility and the rate of inflation.

Price Decisions

The level of prices under oligopoly has been implicit in the discussion of profitability in Chapters 2, 6 and 7. Under short-run profit maximisation the price was seen as a mark-up over marginal cost with the mark-up determined by the elasticity of demand, the degree of concentration and the degree of interdependence between firms. Under limit-pricing the mark-up of price over average costs was determined by the height of barriers to entry. In both cases it may be argued that the firms do not attain the price predicted by the theory because they lack the information assumed by the theory. However, the price predicted by the theory could be viewed as the target towards which the firms seek to move, as it is the price they would wish to charge to further their objectives. Actual prices would then sometimes be above and sometimes below the corresponding predicted prices.

It is possible to identify three broad approaches which economists have used in looking at the determination of prices. The first is that indicated in the previous paragraph, namely that prices are determined, relative to costs, by firms in the pursuit of their objectives. In this view, firms are price-makers and set prices in a way which they think will achieve their objectives (subject to constraints arising from demand and cost conditions).

The second approach is that embedded within the theory of perfect competition, namely that firms are effectively price-takers and the interaction between demand and supply in the market set prices. The difficulty with this approach (Arrow, 1959) is that the process of price determination is not discussed. Firms are regarded as price-takers, and hence not in a position to set prices. In theoretical discussion, an auctioneer is often introduced as a price-adjuster, but apart from a few markets there is not such a price-adjuster in practice. Industrial economists have generally not pursued this approach to price determination.

The third approach has been built upon the idea of observing the process of price decision-making and seeking to infer from such observation generalisations on the process of price determination. An early study of this genre was Hall and Hitch (1939). Their view is expressed as 'price [is] based on full average cost (including a conventional allowance for profit)' and full average cost is determined as follows: prime (or direct) cost per unit is taken as the base, a percentage addition is made to cover overheads (or oncost or indirect cost), and a further conventional addition (frequently 10 per cent) is made for profit. Selling costs commonly and interest on capital rarely are included in overheads; 'when not so included they are allowed for in the addition for profits'.

In order to focus discussion and to compare the first and third approaches indicated above, we take a profit-maximising monopolist as an example of the first approach and full-cost pricing as an example of the third.[1] A profit-maximising monopolist would charge a price given by:

$$p = (e/(e - 1)) \cdot mc = (1 + 1/(e - 1)) \cdot mc \tag{1}$$

where e is the elasticity of demand (measured to be positive) and mc is marginal cost. The full-cost pricing firm would charge a price of:

$$p = (1 + m) \cdot adc \tag{2}$$

where m is the mark-up set as indicated in the quote from Hall and Hitch given above, and adc is average direct costs.

The first contrast between the two approaches arises from the determination of the mark-up. In the profit-maximising approach, this is given by $1/(e - 1)$. In the full-cost pricing approach, the mark-up is described (as in the quote given above), but the forces determining that mark-up are not stated. It is often seen as set by convention and to be maintained for substantial periods of time, i.e. to be taken as roughly constant. One difficulty in discriminating between the theories is that under the profit-maximising approach the mark-up would remain constant provided that the firm's perceptions of the elasticities of demand remain unchanged. Once a firm has discovered a mark-up of price over marginal costs which serves its purposes, then it is quite likely that it will maintain that mark-up.

The second contrast between the two approaches would appear to be that marginal costs appear in equation (1) and average direct costs in equation (2). Conceptually, these two types of costs are clearly different from another. In practice, they may be rather similar. Many economists, particularly those working within the third approach indicated above, have argued that average direct costs are roughly constant with respect to output (some of the supporting evidence for this view was discussed in Chapter 4). If that view is taken, then marginal (direct) costs are also constant and equal to average direct costs. The full-cost pricing and similar approaches lead to the view that prices change little with changes in output since the mark-up and average direct costs are taken as constant. In the profit-maximising approach, it is clear that a similar view would emerge if the elasticity of demand and marginal costs were constant with respect to output.

The third contrast to be drawn is that the purpose of the two approaches may be rather different. The first approach seeks to provide a theory of the determination of prices (relative to costs) based on postulated objectives of firms. The third approach can be viewed as seeking to provide a generalised description of the process of price decision-making. The third approach generally leaves open the question of which factors actually determine the mark-up, and further what actions firms and their managers take if the planned mark-up is either not achieved or results in falling sales.

There have been two main methods by which economists have sought to discover the determinants of price. The first has been the case-study approach by which managers are asked how they approach the pricing decision, which are the factors that influence that decision, what their objectives are, etc. Silberston (1970) concluded his survey of empirical studies on pricing by saying that full-cost pricing finds some support though 'there are so many marginalist and behavioural qualifications. It seems clear that the *procedure* of calculating prices very often starts with an average-cost type of calculation, but the qualifications that arise are conerned with the next stages of the process, including the exact method by which full costs are calculated'. Skinner (1970) similarly stated that 'there seems to be little doubt that "cost-plus" pricing is fairly widely used in British industry'. However, there remains the question as to whether the mark-up is modified for changes in demand and in competitors' actions. Skinner states as his main conclusion '. . . that although 70 per cent of the respondents in the survey claim to use cost-plus pricing, great weight is given in fixing prices to competition and demand, although not quite as much weight as to a firm's own costs and profits'.

The second method has been the econometric estimation of price equations. Whilst a variety of approaches have been used within that general method, it is possible to indicate some common aspects. These studies have generally sought to explain price changes by a combination of cost changes and demand pressure variables. The key questions which are addressed by these studies are:

(i) which costs are relevant to pricing decisions? For example do firms cost the inputs used at historic cost (i.e. price paid for the inputs used up in producing current output) or at replacement costs (i.e. pricing of buying equivalent inputs now)?;

(ii) what influence does the level of or change in demand have on pricing decisions?

The econometric studies have generally been undertaken at the industry or economy level rather than at the firm level. The role of competition has generally been ignored in these studies, partly through the difficulties of measuring the degree of competition or rivalry. Below we will review the 'administered price' thesis in which industrial concentration is seen to have a role on price determination.

Coutts, Godley and Nordhaus (1978) argue that firms base prices on 'normalised costs', which are taken to be the level of costs which would occur if output were at its normal level, which can be thought of as the average level of output which a firm thought would be produced when making its investment decisions. Normalised costs can be seen as costs purged of demand effects, and if the mark-up of prices over normalised costs is constant then demand effects have no direct role in the setting of prices.[2] This approach can be seen as a variant of the full-cost pricing theory. It was tested by Coutts, Godley and Nordhaus on price indices for six two-digit level manufacturing industries in the UK over the period 1963 to 1972. They find that a predicted price, based on a constant mark-up over normalised costs, is highly correlated with actual prices, although there is strong evidence that the profit margin did decline over the period studies. They also find that demand factors (measured in a variety of ways) did not have any significant effect on prices.

Sawyer (1983) relates price changes to changes in costs of material inputs and of labour and to demand factors for 40 British three-digit industries over the period 1963 to 1975. That study concluded that there is 'considerable support for the view that price changes, relative to cost changes, are not strongly influenced by short-run fluctuations in demand'.

There would seem little doubt that output price changes are closely associated with changes in the price of inputs. In the sphere of industrial economics, the controversy has largely surrounded the extent to which the mark-up applied to average costs is influenced by demand factors and by the extent of competition. Case studies at the firm level often reveal some influence of demand and competition, but econometric studies at the industry or economy level often do not find demand influences. There is also the question of what forces determine the mark-up and whether the mark-up is derived from maximisation of objectives (e.g. profits) or from satisficing behaviour (as in the full-cost pricing approach).

Structure and Pricing

In this section we examine the relationship between the determination of prices and price changes and industrial structure, particularly concentration. This involves three questions. The first is how often prices are changed, and in particular whether they change more frequently under competitive conditions than under oligopolistic conditions. The frequency of price change is often seen, within the context of macro-economics, to govern the speed with which an ecnomony can overcome a major departure from full employment. The second and related question is: do prices under oligopolistic conditions tend to be rigid downwards? Whilst this may be a relatively unimportant issue during periods of general price rises, it could be of considerable interest in the context of periods, such as the 1930s, when the level of demand was low and prices were generally stable or falling. In particular it is of importance to know whether prices respond to a fall in demand in the manner predicted by conventional theory (i.e. that prices fall in such circumstances), or whether under conditions of oligopoly prices remain constant or increase in circumstances of low demand. The third question is how do prices set under oligopoly conditions move during the course of a trade cycle in relation to prices set under competitive conditions, and how do oligopolistic prices move relative to costs? Again one of the interesting questions is what effect changes in the level of demand have on prices under conditions of oligopoly.

Discussion on these subjects often draws on the notion of 'administered prices'. This term, introduced by Means (1935), has developed two distinct meanings. The first is that producers set prices at which they are prepared to trade and the price is set on a 'take-it-or-leave-it' basis, so that producers do not usually haggle with consumers over the price. Clearly in any price-making situation, prices are made or in other words administered. An 'administered price' will not generally continuously adjust, but only change when the firm makes a decision to change the price. Hence an element of price rigidity is introduced.

The second and more important meaning of 'administered price' is that when firms have discretion over price and price changes, they are likely to use that discretion in pursuit of their objectives. From that general statement we will indicate below how authors have suggested that discretion is used by oligopolists to raise their prices (relative to competitive prices and to costs) during a fall in demand and to lower their relative prices during a rise in demand.

Two main reasons are given for infrequent price changes under oligopolistic conditions. The first is that when prices are administered there are costs of changing price. These costs include those of publishing a revised price list, costs of decision-making, etc. The second reason relies on the kinked demand curve theory (developed by Sweezy, 1939) derived for an industry producing heterogeneous products. The gains from a price change for a firm will depend upon whether or not the other firms make similar price changes. Sweezy postulated that firms believe that their rivals will not follow a price increase, but would match a price decrease. This leads to a kinked demand curve, illustrated in Figure 9.1, with a corresponding gap in the marginal revenue curve. Changes in costs do not lead to changes in price and output, unless it is substantial enough to shift the marginal cost curve out of the gap in the marginal revenue curve.

Under conditions of general inflation, the marginal cost curve will be tending to move upwards as input costs rise. A belief that other firms are ready to raise prices by removing the 'kink' in the demand curve, removes the gap in the marginal revenue curve, and prepares the way for a price rise. Thus under inflationary conditions, rises in the marginal costs curve and/or a belief that other firms are ready to raise prices will lead to price increases. The kinked demand curve does not then stop price increases but points to relatively infrequent adjustments of price.

There are two groups of reasons for postulating that competitive prices and oligopolistic prices behave differently over the trade cycle. The first reason makes a distinction between market-determined and administered prices (Means, 1935). The market-determined group consists of (a) industries in which price is determined by competitive pressures and (b) industries where the price of a major input is determined by competitive pressure. Prices for this group fall in response to a fall in demand — in the first case mentioned the effect of a fall in demand on price is direct, but in the second it works indirectly through the cost of inputs which fall with the decrease in demand. In an inflationary era, price falls should be replaced by the phrase prices rise less slowly than otherwise. Under this head, only oligopolistic industries have administered prices, but the market-determined prices group includes both competitive and some

Figure 9.1: The Kinked Demand Curve and Related Marginal Revenue Curve

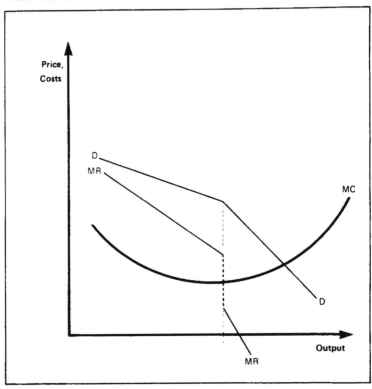

oligopolistic industries.

Price can be portrayed as a mark-up over costs (average or marginal) and variations in price over a trade cycle can be investigated on the basis of variations in the mark-up and/or in costs. The second group of reasons are derived from looking at the mark-up and at the costs. In a general model of oligopoly producing differentiated products and aiming to maximise short-run profits, then the price of firm i is given by $p_i = c_i (e_i - e_i' b)/(e_i - e_i' b - 1)$, where c_i is the marginal cost, e_i the elasticity of demand for firm i's product with respect to its own price, e_i' the cross elasticity of demand between firm i's output and the general level of prices charged by other firms in the industry, and b is the proportionate change in other firms' prices in response to a change in firm i's price.[3]

If firms adhere to this short-run profit-maximising rule, then price will move relative to (marginal) costs with changes in the elasticity of demand (e_i and e_i') and the degree of interdependence (b). The degree of concentration may influence all three of those variables. Over the trade cycle, as demand varies these three factors can vary leading to variations in the mark-up of price over costs. How do these factors vary? With a rise in demand, firms may believe that their rivals are more likely to follow a price rise than during periods of low demand. In the above formulation, with e_i' taken as positive, it can be shown that this effect would lead to a rise in the mark-up following a rise in demand.[4] There is the response of marginal costs. If under conditions of oligopoly there is usually excess capacity, then this would be reflected in declining short-run marginal costs. Then a rise in demand, leading to a rise in output, would generate a fall in marginal costs, and *ceteris paribus* a fall in price.

When firms have a profit mark-up which is either a target (as in the theory of full-cost pricing) or is constrained by external factors (as in the limit-pricing theories), then the mark-up is a constant, and movements in price reflect movements in average costs. For under these circumnstances $p = (1 + m) \cdot ac$, where m is the profit mark-up and ac average costs. However, when firms have a *total* profits target or constraint (e.g. theory of sales revenue maximisation briefly considered in Chapter 11), then increased output means a lower unit profit target or constraint and hence a decline in the profit mark-up.

This discussion indicates that under oligopolistic conditions a rise in demand and output can generate a fall or a rise (relative to what would have happened otherwise) in price. Under atomistic competitive conditions, a rise in demand is anticipated to lead to a rise in price, and a rise in output as well (provided that the supply curve is upward-sloping). When the demand curve shifts then changes in price and changes in output are expected to be positively associated. Thus there is some anticipation that oligopolistic prices will fall relative to competitive prices during periods of rising demand, and rise relatively during periods of falling demand. However, this relies upon being able to identify some competitive industries, and amongst manufacturing industries particularly these may be relatively rare.[5] We can also note that nothing has been said about how variations in the degree of oligopoly would affect changes in price. Yet often empirical investigation seeks to determine the influence of variations in the level of concentration (reflecting variations in the degree of oligopoly).

This discussion has focused on the impact of changes in demand on price. Costs will, in general, be also changing and those changes need to be taken into account. This discussion on the role of changes in demand and prices is of considerable importance for a debate on the control of inflation, for some of these theories indicate that prices may not respond to changes in the level of demand. In other words, the conventional view that reductions in the level of aggregate demand will reduce the pace of inflation may not hold under oligopolistic situations.

Summary of Evidence[6]

There is a considerable amount of conflicting and mainly American evidence on the 'administered price' controversy. The reasons for the conflict in evidence include the following. Results reported by one author often display considerable differences between time periods, indicating that results are sensitive to the time period examined. There are problems of identifying periods of rising demand and periods of falling demand. Investigators often cover a relatively small number of prices and conflicting results may reflect differences in sample selection or data availability. There are difficulties of allocating industries into those with market-dominated prices and those with administered prices, and differences in results may reflect differences in the allocation of industries between the two groups.[7] There are difficulties of construction of price indices, well-illustrated by the study of Stigler and Kindahl (1970). Finally, there has been considerable confusion and disagreement over what the 'administered price' thesis was.

The confusion over the 'administered price' thesis has arisen in two dimensions. First, is the basic dichotomy between high-concentration and low-concentration industries, or between industries which exhibit infrequent price changes and those with frequent price changes? Second, which are the relevant movements in prices claimed to be administered? Some have focused on their absolute movement, some on their movement relative to other prices, and other relative to costs.

The study of DePodwin and Selden (1963) focused on the relationship between price change and concentration over the period 1953 to 1959. With a sample of 322 products, they found little correlation between price changes and concentration (as measured by the Herfindahl index) over the period of generally low demand. However, Weiss (1966) found, over this period for a sub-sample of that used by DePodwin and Selden (dictated largely by availability of other data) and after allowing for cost and output changes, that concentration did have a positive effect on the rate of change of prices. But over the period 1959 to 1963 (which contained periods of expansion and contraction) concentration had a negative but significant effect on the rate of price change.

The debate over administered prices reopened with the publication of Stigler and Kindahl (1970). They looked at the behaviour of prices during periods of contraction and expansion. A brief summary (based on their own price indices) is given in Table 9.1. They argue that broadly these figures support the conventional view that prices fall in periods of falling demand, and rise in periods of rising demand. However, Means (1972) argued that a distinction must be made between market-dominated prices and administered prices, and when only the latter are used then the administered price thesis is supported. This is indicated by the summary of Means (1972) given in the second section of Table 9.1. It should be noted that Means and Stigler and Kindahl differ over the precise dating of the contractions and expansions. Stigler and Kindahl (1973) reply with a rearrangement of the Means figures, and this reply is summarised in the third section of Table 9.1. Stigler and Kindahl argue that these figures (particularly those indicating price reductions by administered price industries during recoveries) do not support the administered price thesis. But it could also be argued that the substantial number of price rises in periods of contraction, and of price falls in periods of recovery, give little support to the atomistic competitive view of prices moving with demand.

Weston *et al.* (1974) look at the differences in price behaviour in terms of increases or decreases for low-, medium- and high-concentration industries. Their results are summarised in the fourth panel of Table 9.1, and conclude that there was no significant differences in the price behaviour between the three groups. They also find that prices in the 50 industries identified by Means as administering prices were 'generally more cyclically flexible that the average of competitive prices'.

Weiss (1977) works over much the same set of statistics, and classifies prices as market-determined, intermediate or administered by the frequency of price change. In our summaries, since the market-dominated group has only three entries, we combine the market-dominated and intermediate prices (which between them contain those prices which change more than once in four months).

The results summarised in the fifth section of Table 9.1, as well as other results reported by Weiss, indicate that there is little relationship between price change and concentration. However, there is a difference in behaviour between the administered prices and other prices, and Weiss concludes that '[t]here does seem to be such a thing as an administered price', and those prices follow 'patterns that support the administered price thesis'. But in some of the periods (e.g. second contraction) the absolute price movements do not fully accord with the anticipations raised by the

Table 9.1: Summary of Some American Studies on the Administered Price Thesis

	Two contractions 5/60-2/62			One expansion 4/58-5/60
	Contraction 7/57-4/58	Recovery 4/58-6/59	Contraction 1/60-1/61	Recovery 1/61-3/62
1. Stigler and Kindahl (1970)				
Number of industries with				
Price increase	18			37
No change	10			14
Price decrease	40			19
2. Means (1972)				
Percentage 'conforming' to 'truncated' administered price thesis[a]	68	66	52	90
3. Stigler and Kindahl (1973)				
Number of industries with				
Price increases	15	17	12	5
No change	19	10	14	16
Price decreases	16	23	24	19
4. Weston et al. (1974)				
Percentage of industries with price increases				
CR < 40%	37.5	43.8	50.0	75.0
40% < CR < 60%	58.6	37.9	44.8	79.3
CR > 60%	66.7	61.1	38.9	88.9

5. Weiss (1977)[b]: Average Percentage change in price

	Contraction 7/57-4/58 %	Time Period Recovery 4/58-5/60 %	Contraction 5/60-2/61 %	Recovery 2/61-3/62 %	Recovery 11/64-66 %
Market dominated and intermediates	-5.7	6.3	-3.0	0.1	10.1
Administered prices	-0.1	1.7	-2.2	-1.9	4.2
CR < 30%	2.3	4.3	-2.0	0.2	5.9
30% ≤ CR ≤ 50%	1.9	-0.3	-2.2	-3.4	5.5
CR > 50%	1.5	2.4	-2.3	-2.6	3.1

a   The truncated administered price thesis is that those prices move counter-cyclically (e.g. fall when demand rises).
b   Some of the figures reported by Weiss appear to be proportions, rather than percentages as stated. In this table we have amended those figures.

administered price thesis, since all prices fall. Weiss also looks at change in price relative to its underlying trend in order to make some allowance for change in costs, which he believes will be reflected in the long-run trend in price. Similar results are obtained in this case.

Eichner (1973) postulates that the rate of increase of prices proceeds more smoothly in oligopolistic industries than in competitive industries. Whilst his reasoning is different from that given above his results can be interpreted in terms of the administered price thesis. Eichner divided industries into high- and low-concentration groups and derived price indices for the two groups. The price index for the high-concentration group shows a more uniform upward trend than that exhibited by the low-concentration group price index, indicating a greater sensitivity of prices in competitive industries to variations in the level of demand than is found for prices in oligopolistic industries.

Aaronovitch and Sawyer (1981) examine a number of the hypotheses outlined above for a sample of 40 UK manufacturing industries for a variety of sub-periods within the period 1963 to 1975. Using the Herfindahl index as a measure of concentration, they find that 'in two of the five [sub] periods there is some support for the administered price thesis in the sense that during the upturn prices appear to have risen less quickly in the more concentrated industries, and during the downturn to have risen more quickly (as compared with less concentrated industries)'. They also find that for a sample of 77 industries there did not appear to be any relationship between the variability of prices and the level of concentration.

Wilder, Williams and Singh (1977) relate price changes for 357 American four-digit industries for each year from 1958 to 1972 to cost changes, a proxy for demand changes and eight-firm concentration ratio. Of the 14 regressions (one for each of the annual price changes covered), the coefficient on the concentration ratio was negative on 12 occasions, of which three coefficients were statistically significant for zero. The authors interpret this result as contradicting the 'administered price thesis'. But it does suggest that concentration sometimes has an effect on price changes, and on some views of the 'administered price thesis' the impact of concentration would be expected to be negative during booms and positive during slumps, and the three negative significant effects of concentration occur during years of high demand.

Sellekaerts and Lesage (1973) investigate the influence of concentration on price change, with allowance for changes in costs and output, for 41 Canadian industries. However, they test two hypotheses which are rather different from those given above. The first is the 'catching up' hypothesis, which is the converse of the administered price thesis, and which suggests a faster rise in oligopolistic prices than in competitive prices during the early phase of a recovery. Sellekaerts and Lesage find the 'catching-up' hypothesis fully supported by the Canadian data during periods beginning in 1957 and extending to 1959, 1961 or 1963.

The second proposition which Sellekaerts and Lesage test, labelled the Galbraith-Ackley hypothesis, postulates that when firms in concentrated industries are working at or near full capacity, they respond to an increase in demand by increasing prices, but with a lag. Apart from the lag, under these conditions, prices in concentrated industries move in line with the general rate of inflation. They find that during the period 1963 to 1966, when demand was generally high in Canada, concentration had no significant effect on price changes, lending support to their second hypothesis.

Phlips (1969) examined the ratio of prices in 1964 to prices in 1958 as a function of concentration and the corresponding ratio of costs for industries in Belgium, France and the Netherlands. The period 1958 to 1964 was chosen as one of generally high demand. For Belgium, concentration generally had a negative effect on the price ratio, and this effect is often statistically significant. But for France and the Netherlands, the effect of concentration is found to be non-significant. Phlips concludes that for Belgium that there is 'no support whatsoever for the administrative inflation hypothesis'. But it must be noted that his interpretation is that this hypothesis indicates that prices in concentrated industries rise relative to those in unconcentrated industries during periods of high demand, which is contrary to our opinion expressed above.[8]

Much of this evidence is further discussed by Lustgarten (1975b), who concludes that the administered price thesis has many interpretations and that the evidence is generally not in accord with his interpretation of the thesis.

Domberger (1983) and Dixon (1983) have adopted a different approach in that they investigate whether the speed with which firms adjust their prices in response to cost changes depends on the industrial structure. Both of these authors find that industrial structure (concentration, number of firms) does have some effect on the speed of price adjustment. However, whilst Dixon's work for Australia finds that 'the rate of adjustment of prices to prime costs is slower the more concentrated the industry', Domberger's work relating to UK industries points in the opposite direction.

Qualls (1979) investigated the degree of fluctuations in the price-cost margin as related to structural characteristics of concentration and entry barriers. This approach, using observed revenue and cost data, overcomes the problem in using list prices that may not correspond to transactions prices. It also incorporates the nature of the cost conditions and the extent to which unit costs change with demand and output. Qualls finds that the price-cost margin tends to fluctuate more in concentrated industries than in less concentrated ones. Clarke (1984), whose work on structure-profitability relationships was discussed in Chapter 6, reports similar conclusions to those of Qualls.

The important question raised by the administered price thesis is whether in an oligopolistic environment prices respond to changes in the level of demand in the same qualitative manner as they would in a competitive env ironment. Clearly, a deflationary macro-economic policy aimed to reduce the rate of inflation requires that the impact of a fall in demand reduces the rate of increase of prices and/or wages. We have looked at the price side here and only at comparisons between oligopolistic industries and others. It could be argued that most, if not all, manufacturing industries operate under oligopolistic conditions, and that comparisons between more oligopolistic and less oligopolistic industries may not resolve the questions posed above, for all of those industries may follow oligopolistic pricing practices. These oligopolistic practices can encompass a wide range covering those based on profit maximisation (as discussed in Chapter 6), on limit-pricing (p. 72), on satisficing behaviour leading to, for example, full cost pricing, and on sales and growth maximisation.

Notes

1. For discussion of the variety of theories of the firm and of industry in terms of price decisions see Sawyer (1983), Ch. 2.
2. There may be demand effects in other parts of the economy which affect the price of inputs and thereby affect prices. Some of that is removed in the calculation of normalised costs, but some may remain. Thus, it is demand effects within the output market which are being examined in this study.
3. For firm i, profits $\pi_i = p_i q_i (p_i, p) - C_i(q_i)$ where q_i is output of firm i, p_i its price, C_i its costs of production and p the general level of prices of other firms. The first order conditions for profit maximisation gives:

$$\frac{\partial \pi_i}{\partial p_i} = q_i + \left(p_i - \frac{\partial C_i}{\partial q_i} \right) \left(\frac{\partial q_i}{\partial p_i} + \frac{\partial q_i}{\partial p} \frac{\partial p}{\partial p_i} \right) = 0$$

Using symbols from the text, this can be written as:

$$\frac{p_t - C_t}{p_t} \cdot \left(\frac{p_t}{q_t} \cdot \frac{\partial q_t}{\partial p_t} + \frac{p_t}{q_t} \frac{\partial p}{\partial p_t} \cdot \frac{p_t}{p} \cdot \frac{\partial q_t}{\partial p} \right) = -1$$

and then as:

$$\frac{p_t - C_t}{p_t} (-e_t + e_t' \cdot b) = -1$$

so that

$$p_i = C_t (e_i - e_t' b)/(e_i - e_t' b - 1).$$

4. With a rise in demand, b increases, and

$$\frac{\partial p_i}{\partial b} = \frac{c_i\, e_i'}{(e_i - e_i' b - 1)^2}$$

which is positive.

5. For example, in Weiss (1977) there are three competitive industries (in his terminology market-dominated industries), 16 intermediate and 43 administered price industries. If non-manufacturing industries are introduced (e.g. agriculture) then comparisons would be much more complicated.

6. For a more extensive survey see Domberger (1983), pp. 36–43, and Sawyer (1983), pp. 81–9.

7. Means (1935) made the distinction between a 'market price . . . which is made in the market as a result of the interaction of buyers and sellers' and an 'administered price . . . [as one] set by administrative action and held constant for a period of time'. Thus frequency of price change would constitute the criteria for allocation between the two groups, although the degree of frequency of change has to be determined. Later, Means (1972) seems to use competitive conditions as the criteria for the market price inudstries and place other industries in the administrative price group. A number of authors have used the level of concentration ('high' and 'low') as a way of identifying administered price industries and market price industries. See Weston *et al.* (1974), p. 232.

8. See also the interchange between Ross (1973) and Phlips (1973).

10 THE STRUCTURE-CONDUCT-PERFORMANCE APPROACH: A CRITIQUE

The central role of the structure-conduct-performance approach to industrial economies and the large volume of empirical work which it has generated have been indicated in the preceding chapters. In this chapter, we look at some of the general criticisms of that approach.

The reader will have to decide for her(him)self the validity of arguments and the status of the empirical results based on the structure-conduct-performance approach.

The structure-conduct-performance approach is, at heart, a short-run static one. The models developed to analyse structure-profitability relationships (Chapter 6) and advertising (Chapter 7) indicate that quite clearly. With a particular structure firms are taken as seeking to maxmise short-run profits, possibly subject to a constraint of limiting entry into the industry. Another crucial feature of this approach is neatly summed up by the words of Caves (1967) when he writes 'market structure is important because the structure determines the behaviour of firms in the industry, and that behaviour in turn determines the quality of the industry's performance'. This indicates that causation runs from structure through conduct to performance and the relationship is essentially deterministic.

The question which arises immediately is: why is the industrial structure as it is? There are a number of answers. The first is that some parts of industrial structure are determined by factors outside the influence of participating firms. This would apply particularly to features like the minimum efficient scale of production. But other parts of industrial structure, like the number of firms and level of advertising, are seen as determined by a series of historic accidents which are not directly relevant to current conduct and performance. In other words, previous conduct and performance do not directly influence current conduct and performance, with any indirect influence coming via current industrial structure. This would mean, for example, that the way in which firms respond to other firms' price and output changes in the past might have an effect on the current structure, particularly the number and size-distribution of firms, but would not influence the way in which firms believe other firms would respond to their price/output changes.

The second possible answer is in some ways an extension of the first answer, whereby technical factors are seen as largely determining the industrial structure, particularly the size of plant, number of firms, the degree of concentration and barriers to entry (see pp. 41–4). This suggests that many of the dimensions of industrial structure on which emphasis has been placed (particularly concentration) are only proximate determinants of performance, and the underlying determinants are technical factors like the minimum efficient scale of production which mould the industrial structure. The studies, like those of Ornstein *et al.* (1973) discussed toward the end of Chapter 3, are concerned with an examination of the determinants of concentration.

The third approach to the question of the determinants of industrial structure emphasises the part played by the past conduct and performance of firms. Since barriers to entry are thought to lead to higher profitability for existing firms, it can be anticipated that firms try to add to barriers to entry in their search for increased profits. Indeed much of the discussion in Chapter 5 can be viewed in this light. Investment in productive capacity (Spence, 1977), advertising and research and development can in various ways lead to changes in the height of barriers to entry. Further mergers and acquisitions (see Chapter 13) can directly affect the degree of concentration. Performance can also have effects on structure which are regarded by existing firms as adverse. The most notable route would be the one whereby high profitability induces entry into the industry and hence changes the industrial size-distribution of firms.

These answers do not necessarily mean that the structure-performance relationships are invalid, but rather may indicate that their usefulness is limited. Phillips (1970) argued that '[w]ithout consideration of the more complete and endogenous relations among these variables, predictions covering any significant periods of time are quite likely to be wrong'. The major limitation is that the structure-performance relationships, based on a short-run static equilibrium approach, can provide at most only a snapshot picture of the forces at work. A more complete picture would require discussion of the evolution of industrial structure through time, and how conduct and performance influences future structure, conduct and performance.

Although labelled the structure-conduct-performance approach, it is evident from much of the preceding discussion that the major emphasis of this approach is on the linkages between structure and performance with the conduct part rather downgraded. In general, the conduct assumption which is made is that of profit maximisation. The downgrading of the conduct part of this approach is intimately linked with the deterministic approach to structure-performance relationships. When firms have elements of discretion, which is the general case under conditions of oligopoly, then that discretion can be used in many different ways, including departure from profit maximisation. The conduct of firms is essentially the way in which firms use the available discretion. Chapter 5 indicated some of the forms in which firms use this discretion. The discussion in that chapter has two important implications for this one. First, conduct influences the ease of entry into the industry and thereby industrial structure. Second, when a range of conduct can emerge from a particular industrial structure then a range of performance can result. Thus when there is some discretion over conduct for the firms there is no longer a one-to-one relationship between structure and performance.

The determinism of the structure-performance relationships can be illustrated by the structure-profitability derived from the general model of oligopoly (pp. 9–20). It can be seen from there that the profit margin depends upon the elasticity of demand, the level of concentration and the degree of collusion. If the degree of collusion is dependent on the level of concentration then a deterministic relationship between the profit margin and concentration would be derived. But if there was no relationship between collusion and concentration, then a stochastic relationship between profitability and concentration would arise.

Departures from profit maximisation would lead to alternative range of outcomes, although, for example, a positive relationship between profit margins and concentration could still be maintained. The departures from profit maximisation could come from the pursuit of other objectives such as sales revenue maximisation. Alternatively, there may be departures from full technical efficiency. But since much of the work underlying the structure-conduct-performance approach rests on the assumption of profit maximisation, the relaxation of that assumption would require a reworking of the various structure-performance relationships. Similar relationships may emerge but that could not be guaranteed ahead of the investigations.

It was seen in Chapter 6 that there is al ernative derivation of the structure-profit relationship based on the notion of limit-pricing. Thus within the structure-conduct-performance approach, there is not a unique approach to the manner in which the structure-performance relationships are determined.

The discussion in the earlier chapters will have indicated that there are many views on how structure can influence performance. In Chapter 6 it was seen that there were two major routes (short-run profit maximisation and limit-pricing) by which structure was postulated to influence profitability. In practice some mixture of these two approaches is used, even though the two approaches involve different objectives for the firms involved. The frequent lack of a clear derivation of the structure-profitability relationship has been forcibly exposed by Cowling (1976), who argues that '[m]ost empirical studies have tested an hypothesis of a direct relationship between concentration and profitability without being very clear about appropriate form of the relationship'. He goes on to discuss a number of problems with the way in which structure-performance relationships have been examined.

Advertising also creates problems for the structure-conduct-performance approach. Chapter 7 indicated that advertising can be seen as an element of structure, of conduct and of performance. At a minimum this creates the problem of not being able to classify advertising under one of the three heads of structure, conduct or performance. It can create simultaneous equation problems discussed below.

The earlier discussion will have indicated that in general the structure-conduct-performance approach proceeds on a variable-by-variable basis. Profitability, advertising, research and development and price change behaviour are dealt with separately rather than within a complete model which determines all elements of performance. Thus it cannot be said that the structure-performance approach provides an overall coherent theory of industrial activity. Instead the structure-conduct-performance approach can be seen as a system of classification for the features of an industry, combined with a set of sub-theories which suggest various linkages between individual terms of structure and performance.

A number of authors (Weiss, 1971, Greer, 1971, Strickland and Weiss, 1976, and others) have argued that the single equation approach to structure-performance relationships is liable to be misleading. In earlier discussion (pp. 113–18 and p. 20) it has been seen that these authors have argued that, for example, concentration affects advertising intensity and advertising influences the level of concentration. The solution to this problem (if indeed it is a problem) is the estimation of a set of simultaneous equations.[1] We should note that the differences between single equation estimates and simultaneous equation estimates have not been substantial.

In the future a widely-accepted general theory of structure-conduct-performance may be developed. However, three broad approaches can be identified, which are unlikely to be reconcilable. The first approach lays stress on existing barriers to entry permitting short-run profit maximisation without fear of new entry in the future. The second lays stress on the limited protection given to existing firms by barriers to entry which leads into limit-pricing behaviour and the like, with current behaviour constrained by the requirement of preventing entry into the industry. The third approach argues that barriers to entry are unimportant so that existing firms can earn at most only normal profits. These firms are then forced into profit maximisation if they are to survive. Industries with insignificant barriers to entry would operate in a manner close to that predicted by atomistic competition (whether perfect or monopolistic competition). This general view is examined in more detail in Chapter 15.

Whilst within each of these approaches it may be possible to work out a coherent overall theory of industrial behaviour and performance, it is difficult to imagine an overall theory which could encompass all three basic approaches. It may happen that cumulated evidence will point strongly to one of these three approaches. But until that happy state of affairs emerges we are left with these three alternatives.

Rivalry and competition between firms tends to be overlooked by the structure-conduct-performance approach. This neglect of rivalry arises from two sources. First, structure-performance relationships are often based, formally or informally, on the notion that situations of perfect competition and monopoly are the extremes and that industries can be placed at points along the spectrum running from perfect competition to monopoly. Since rivalry is not involved in either of the extreme cases, rivalry cannot be involved in the intermediate cases. Second, structure-performance relationships are derived from a consideration of equilibrium positions with little attention being devoted to situations of disequilibrium. Rivalry tends to be of little importance in positions of equilibrium in that equilibrium is a position of 'rest', with each firm achieving the best outcome for that firm in light of the activities of other firms. Attempts to change that equilibrium outcome in order to enhance one's position are ruled out. Rivalry between firms arises in disequilibrium when firms struggle to establish themselves, but the rivalry has been resolved before the situation of equilibrium is reached.

The structure-conduct-performance approach could be interpreted as portraying firms as the essentially passive agents through which industrial structure works its influence on industrial performance. This leads to a down-grading of conduct and the essentially deterministic structure-performance relationship. A further example is given by a firm which operated in three industries, *A*, *B* and *C* would have its conduct in, say, industry *A* influenced if not determined by the structure of industry *A*. The firm's presence in industries *B* and *C*, and the reasons for the firm operating in those industries, would not influence conduct and performance. This firm would in a sense make appearances in each of the industries with each appearance not taking account of the other appearances.

This point leads to another major issue that the structure-performance approach is industry-centred rather than firm-centred. An alternative view is that '[f]irms appear as specific blocs of capital, each engaged in the business of capital accumulation. These blocs of capital are the *loci* of the production process. Capital, in the sense in which we are using the term, is not interested in production as such, but in the possibilities of accumulation. Which market to be in is a tactical question, diversification is not aberrant behaviour' (Aaronovitch, 1977, p. 82). This view places firms at the centre of the stage with industrial structure (widely interpreted) constraining their activities as well as influencing their direction of expansion. For example, a firm in an oligopolistic situation may find that expansion within its own industry effectively blocked by the probable responses of their rivals to a price cut and/or output increase. Then accumulation and further expansion requires diversification, and the direction in which the firm diversifies is likely to be conditioned by its own comparative advantages and the links in demand and supply between its own industry and other industries.

The features of industrial structure are seen as the environment within which the firm pursues its objectives. But the industrial structure, as indicated above, may be malleable by firms for their own advantage, particularly in terms of erection of barriers to entry. Thus the view would emerge that firms seek to mould their environment.

In a private enterprise economy the firm is the basic unit of organisation. Under some forms of central planning the industry may be the basic unit of organisation, with production planned at the industry level. But this is not the case in a private enterprise economy and indeed the industry concept may have a rather tentative existence. The concept of an industry is a theoretical construct of economists felt to be convenient for analysis. But, as indicated in Chapter 2, it may be difficult in practice to draw boundaries around an industry. Firms which are grouped together in one industry by economists or statisticians may not themselves regard themselves as belonging to the same industry. Firms often belong to industrial associations which may not coincide with the industrial boundaries drawn by economists.

In contrast to the discussion in Part I, that in Part II focuses on the firm as the central unit of analysis. Much of Part II deals with approaches which envisage the characteristics of the firm as determining the performance of the firm. The clearest case of this is the managerial theories of the firm where the form of control of the firm (that is whether the firm is owner- or manager-controlled) is of considerable importance in determining the profitability and growth of the firm. Indeed, the theories of Part II can be criticised for the opposite reason to that put forward here in respect of the structure-conduct-performance approach, that is for overemphasising the firm and neglecting the influence of industrial structure and the economic environment in general.

Note

1. Cowling (1976) argues that '[a]lthough recognizing that the structure-performance relation is only one equation embedded within a set of equations in which performance, behaviour and structure are determined, we may, perhaps realistically, view such a system as recursive'. If there were the case, then single equation estimation is acceptable (Kmenta, 1971, p. 586).

PART TWO:

ECONOMICS OF FIRMS

11 MANAGERIAL THEORIES OF THE FIRM

Introduction

Firms are the basic organisations of production within a private enterprise economy. In the structure-conduct-performance approach, little emphasis was paid to individual firms, and instead emphasis was placed on the concept of the industry with industrial structure as the key determinant of firm behaviour and industrial performance. The basic motivation of the firms was taken as a profit maximisation. In this part, firms are emphasised with industrial structure playing a minor role. Further, a wider spectrum of objectives of the firm besides profit maximisation is also considered. In this chapter we consider the evidence for the idea that large firms are controlled by their managers, and not by their owners, and these managerial-controlled firms pursue non-profit objectives. The subsequent two chapters of the part cover the relationship between growth, profitability and size of firms (Chapter 12), and the causes and consequences of acquisitions and mergers (Chapter 13).

Berle and Means (1932) are often acknowledged as the first authors to argue that there was a growing 'divorce of ownership and control' arising from the ownership of corporations being widely spread amongst a large number of shareholders. This led, it was argued, to shareholders with little, if any, involvement in the management of a firm, and a management with little ownership interest. This line of argument and the evidence for it is considered below. Whilst Berle and Means and others (such as Burnham, 1941, and Mason, 1959) speculated on the consequences of this 'managerial revolution', the first explicit economic theory on the objectives of these managerial firms was put forward by Baumol (1959), soon followed by Marris (1964). We begin by briefly outlining these theories with a view to indicating how these theories can be tested. A fuller discussion of managerial theories of the firm can be obtained from textbooks on theories of the firm such as Sawyer (1979a) and Wildsmith (1973).

Theories of Baumol and Marris

Baumol (1959) accepts that large firms are effectively controlled by the

Figure 11.1: Outcome from the Model of Baumol

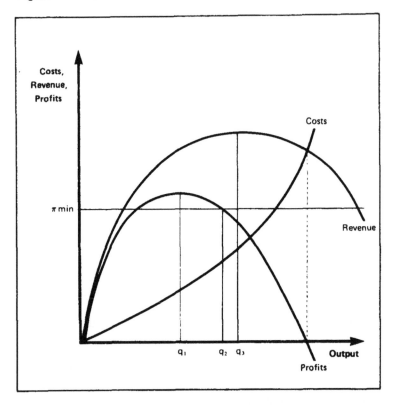

managers and postulates that the basic objective of the managers can be summed up as maximisation of sales revenue subject to the achievement of a minimum level of profits (π_{min}), which is imposed by shareholders on the managers of the firm. The diagrammatic representation of the Baumol model is reproduced in Figure 11.1, where q_1 would be the output of the profit maximisation firm, q_2 would be that of the constrained sales revenue maximiser, and q_3 that of the unconstrained revenue maximiser. There are numerous reasons suggested by Baumol for the pursuit of this objective, but of particular importance here is the notion that managerial salaries are more closely linked to sales than to profits, so that the self interest of the managers promotes the expansion of sales at the expense of profits.

The original theory of Baumol (1959) was a static one-period model, but it was put forward as a static version of an essentially dynamic theory, rather than as a full theory of firm behaviour. A dynamic version in the same vein is Marris (1964). For reasons similar to those given by Baumol, Marris postulates that the managers seek to maximise the growth of sales subject to the avoidance of a take-over by another firm. A firm is assumed to be vulnerable to take-over when the price of its shares falls to a low level relative to its capital worth, so that the firm becomes a bargain to a potential acquirer. Let us look at this in detail. The stock market valuation of the firm is assumed to be determined by the discounted expected future dividends, so that the value $V = \Sigma(1 - r)\pi_t^e/(1 + i)^t$. In this formula r is the retention ratio (the proportion of profits retained by the firm), which is assumed to remain constant over time, π_t^e is the expected profits in time t and i is the rate of discount. The expected level of dividends is then $(1 - r)\pi_t^e$ in period t. When there is steady growth of rate g, with profits and the capital stock (K) growing at the same rate, the rate of profit is constant at ϱ, so that $\pi_t^e = \varrho K_t$ and $\pi^e{}_t = \pi_0(1 + g)^t$. Growth is financed by retained profits so that $r\pi_t = gK_t$ and hence $r \cdot \varrho = g$. Substituting into the formula for V gives $V = (1 - r) \cdot \varrho K \sum\limits_{t=0}^{\infty}$ $(1 + g)^t/ (1 + i)^t$, which equals $(\varrho - g)(1 + i)K/(i - g)$. We define the valuation ratio, v, as the ratio of the market value of the firm to its book value, i.e. $v = V/K = (\varrho - g)(1 + i)/(i - g)$.

The rate of profit is likely to depend upon the rate of growth, with faster growth involving higher costs so that the rate of profit declines. These higher costs derive from the extra costs of developing new products, moving into new markets, costs of internal reorganisation associated with growth and the like. The postulated relationships between the valuation ratio, v, the profit rate and the growth rate are drawn in Figure 11.2. It can be shown by differentiating the above equation for the valuation ratio that the profit rate peaks before the valuation ratio does as the growth rate of the firm is increased (for further discussion see Sawyer, 1979a, pp. 104–5). This means that the valuation ratio-growth rate function and the profit rate-growth rate function have the relationship indicated in Figure 11.2.

The theory of take-overs embedded in this model is examined further in Chapter 13. Here we note that there is a take-over constraint on firms so that in order to avoid take-over firms must keep their valuation ratios above some minimum level $\bar{v}$.

There are two alternative ways of empirically examining this theory. The first way is to divide firms into owner-controlled ones and manager-controlled ones, and to investigate whether the former groups of firms operate with a higher valuation ratio/profit rate and a lower growth rate

Figure 11.2: The Relationship between Valuation Ratio and Profitability and Growth

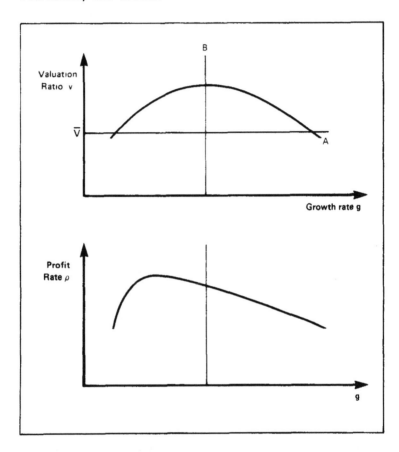

than the latter group. The owner-controlled firms are postulated as mainly interested in the pursuit of profits so operate around point B in terms of Figure 11.2. The manager-controlled firms are assumed to pursue growth up to the limit imposed by the take-over constraint, and in terms of Figure 11.2 operate around point A. From that figure, it is evident that over the range in which firms operate (that is the section AB), a higher valuation ratio is associated with a higher profit rate, and a higher value of both measures is anticipated for owner-controlled firms in comparison with manager-controlled firms. The second alternative, which can only form an indirect test of the theory of Marris, is to investigate whether the valuation ratio (or the profit rate) and growth rate are negatively related. This avoids the need to identify firms as owner- or manager-controlled, which is always a difficult operation and liable to error. Further, it allows for a gradual variation in the emphasis placed on profits and growth by firms. The evidence on this variant is examined in the next chapter (p. 198).

The Evidence on Managerial Control

There are three sets of evidence which we bring to bear on the validity of these managerial theories. First, we examine the evidence on the separation of ownership and control. Second, investigations into differences between owner-controlled and manager-controlled firms are discussed. Third, work on the determinants of managerial income is summarised.

The Separation of Ownership and Control

The position adopted by Berle and Means (1932) was that a firm was owner-controlled only if there were a small group of shareholders who owned a substantial portion of the firm's shares. Thus an archetypal owner-controlled firm is one in which a family or small group of people own at least half of the shares of the firm and effectively determine the policy of the firm. There can be some departure from this archetype before a firm becomes manager-controlled. Berle and Means defined an owner-controlled firm as one in which an individual, family or group of business associates owned at least 20 per cent of the shares. Small shareholders were seen as basically rentiers, lending money to the firm but not participating in any decision-making process within the firm. Small shareholders dissatisfied with the performance of their firm would find the costs of action to change the firm's decisions or operations would far outweigh any benefits which accrue to them individually, even though the shareholders as a whole would receive a net benefit. If there are only people with small holdings of shares, then the managers (assumed to have little, if any, ownership interest in the firm) are not subject to direct control by the shareholders. When a group has a substantial shareholding, the chances of benefits of intervention outweighing the costs increase, and easier communication between its members raises the chances of concerted action.

Berle and Means found on the basis of definitions indicated above that of the largest 200 American firms in 1929, 88 were manager-controlled, 68 were owner-controlled (either minority, majority control or private ownership), 41 were owner-controlled via a legal device, one was in management/minority ownership control and two were in receivership. The 44 per cent of firms in management-control tended to be larger than average, and accounted for 58 per cent of the assets of the largest 200 firms.

Larner (1966) adopted a similar methodology, although he took a 10 per cent share interest (rather than the 20 per cent used by Berle and Means) by a small group as evidence of owner-control. He found that for 1963, 169 of the largest 200 non-financial American corporations were manager-controlled and the remainder owner-controlled, which appeared to confirm Berle and Means' suggestion that the movement toward managerial control would continue.

Florence (1961) used a similar approach in examining the position in the United Kingdom for 1936 and 1951. His criteria for owner-control are

(a) that the largest shareholder had 20 per cent or more of the votes;
(b) that the largest 20 shareholders had 30 per cent or more of the votes;
(c) that either (a) or (b) was satisfied, but these shareholders were companies or 'connected persons';
(d) that the directors had 5 per cent or more of the ordinary shares.

On these criteria, Florence identified 30 out of the largest 98 firms as probably owner-controlled, and for a sample of 268 smaller firms, 89 were owner-controlled. Overall, just under a third of relatively large companies in 1951 were owner-controlled. Florence also found a trend toward increased management-control over the 15 years up to 1951.

It became widely accepted that some type of managerial revolution had occurred in that most large corporations were controlled by their managers rather than their owners, even if the implications were a matter of controversy. One author wrote that 'almost everyone now agrees that in the large corporation, the owner is, in general, a passive recipient, that, typically, control is in the hands of management; and that management normally selects its own replacements' (Mason, 1959). Whilst the passive rentier nature of most shareholders in large corporations has not been disputed, the notion of the dominance of management-control has been recently challenged. The challenge has focused on two areas — the accuracy of the work of Berle and Means and Larner, and on the concepts of owner-control used, and we now look briefly at these two areas.

Burch (1972) and Zeitlin (1974) have pointed out that Berle and Means had reasonably definite and reliable information on at most two-thirds of the companies in their sample. Of the 88 corporations listed as being under management-control, Berle and Means provide no information on 44 which they consider to be 'presumably under management control'. Zeitlin (1974) has shown that some later studies (for example, Lundberg, 1937, Perlo, 1957) classified as owner-controlled some of the corporations listed by Berle and Means as manager-controlled. Zeitlin also argues that further information from other studies and the inclusion of privately-owned firms would raise the number of owner-controlled firms in the largest 500 American corporations from the 95 reported by Larner (1970) to 198.

Two factors had tended to bias upwards the proportion of manager-controlled firms reported. First, information on share ownership and control by connected or related groups of individuals is difficult or impossible to obtain, and previous studies have often used absence of firm evidence on concentration of share ownership as evidence of management control. Second, the statistics refer to public companies and ignore private large companies which, by definition, are owner-controlled.

The general concept of owner-control used by Berle and Means and others has been based on control requiring a given percentage of the voting shares. Some recent work has used 5 per cent as the required percentage for owner-control, rather than the 10 per cent used by Larner (1966) and 20 per cent used by Berle and Means (1932). Further it is argued that control by financial institutions, the particular history of a firm (especially involvement of a specific family over a number of years), as well as reports of control by a small group, need to be investigated. Nyman and Silberston (1978) in their study of 276 largest British companies looked at:

1. The percentage of votes held by a known individual, institution, or cohesive group;
2. the percentage of votes owned by the board of directors and their families;
3. the identity of the Chairman and Managing Director, and their relationship to the firm's founder and his family.

Potential control is assumed to be present with a shareholding of more than 5 per cent.

Burch (1972), in his study of the largest American corporations in the mid-60s used a three-way classification. The first category is firms 'probably under family control', which arises when (a) 'approximately 4–5 per cent or more of the voting stock was held by a family, group of families, or some affluent individual . . .' and (b) 'that there has been either inside or outside representation . . . on part of a family over an extended period of time'. The second is 'possibly family control' when there are 'definite signs of family influence (usually in the form of representation on the board of directors, though occasionally stock owner- ship statistics . . .) but for which there was insufficient available data from which to make a reliable assessment of control status'. The final category is 'probably management control' where there was no evidence of family involvement.

Chevalier (1969) took the ownership of 5 per cent or more of voting shares as *prima facie* evidence of control by ownership interest. But he also considered that when there was 'a group, represented by a board of directors, which seems to wield a decisive influence on the corpora- tion', this corporation should be classified as essentially ownership- controlled.

Cubbin and Leech (1983), Table 1, provide a summary of the varying criteria which have been used to assess whether firms are manager- controlled or owner-controlled. They also argue that two dimensions of control are involved, namely the location of control and the degree of control. Their approach to the classification of firms as manager- or owner-controlled is to pose the question of how large the biggest shareholding needs to be in light of the dispersion of other shareholdings for the largest shareholder to have a reasonable expectation of control, particularly when transfer of control of the company is at stake. This con- trol is seen as the ability to win votes amongst shareholders. On this basis, they classify 38 companies as owner-controlled and 47 as managerial- controlled out of a sample of 85 large UK companies.

A summary of findings of Burch, Chevalier, Nyman and Silberston is given in Table 11.1. It is clear that on their broader definition of owner- control and the more intensive research programme involved that these studies indicate owner-control to be much more extensive than earlier studies. Burch points to up to 60 per cent as under family control ('possibly' plus 'probably' family controlled). Chevalier places 80 of the largest 200 US manufacturing corporations in 1965 as under management- control, and the remaining 120 under some form of owner-control. Nyman and Silberston indicate over 56 per cent as owner-controlled. Of the 111 companies they regard as controlled by ownership interests, 62 were classified as companies in which directors and families held more than 5 per cent of voting shares, and a further 15 with a family chairman or managing director (but with less than 5 per cent of voting shares owned by the family).

Table 11.1: Recent Estimates of Control-status of Large UK and USA Firms

(i) Estimates of control-status of 300 largest American publicly and privately owned industrial concerns: 1963

	Probably management control	Possibly family control	Probably family control
Top 50	58%	22%	20%
Top 300	40%	15.3%	44.7%

(ii) Estimate of control-status of 200 largest American industrial corporations: 1965

- 60 controlled by individuals/families
- 31 controlled by banks and other financial institutions
- 20 controlled by other groups
- 80 controlled by managers

(iii) Estimate of control-status of largest British publicly and privately owned firms: 1975

	Number	%
Owner-controlled	126	56.25
of which family controlled	77	
No known control	98	43.75

Sources: (i) Burch (1972); (ii) Chevalier (1969); (iii) Nyman and Silberston (1978).

There is one particular aspect of share ownership pertinent to the debate over managerial control, and that is the involvement of financial institutions which may have objectives different from those of individuals.[1] Further, institutions may not have the problems of organisation and communication which face individual shareholders if they wish to take action against the current management.

In the United Kingdom, the evidence summarised in Table 11.2 points to a sharp upswing in the proportion of shares owned by financial institutions. Insurance companies, pension funds and unit and investment trusts accounted for almost 38 per cent of shares in 1975. The figures for the United States in Table 11.2 indicate a much lower share and a much lower rate of increase for the shareholdings of financial institutions. However, other calculations have put the share under the control of financial institutions much higher. For example, Kotz (1979) records that bank trust departments held 26.9 per cent of corporate stock in 1974. The figures in Table 11.2 would allocate much of those holdings to the

Table 11.2: Pattern of Share-ownership in UK and USA.
Proportion (%) of shares held by various groups

	1957	1963	1969	1975
(a) United Kingdom				
Persons (including executors and trustees)	65.8	54.0	47.4	43.7
Insurance companies	8.8	10.0	12.2	14.9
Pension funds	3.4	6.4	9.0	15.2
Unit and investment trusts	5.7	8.7	10.5	7.8
Charities	1.9	2.1	2.1	4.2
Overseas	4.4	7.0	6.6	7.3
Others (including banks, public sector)	10.0	11.8	12.2	6.9
(b) United States	1952	1957	1963	1968
Persons	85.7	82.0	81.6	81.0
Insurance companies	3.8	3.8	3.4	3.1
Pension funds	1.0	2.9	4.8	6.0
Investment companies	4.1	5.2	5.4	5.7
Non-profit bodies	3.4	3.8	2.7	2.4
Others	2.0	2.3	2.1	1.8

Source: King (1977).

personal sector ('persons'). Further, the Security and Exchange Commission have estimated that of the 54 corporations with equity values over 1 billion dollars in 1969, 18 had more than 5 per cent of stock held by a single bank trust department, and 17 had 10 per cent or more held by three or less bank trust departments.

What are the implications of the institutional shareholdings for the control of corporations? Inevitably, the evidence on this aspect is difficult to obtain. In Britain, Nyman and Silberston (1978) estimated that nine corporations in their sample of 224 corporations were controlled by a financial institution (and four of these corporations were regarded as controlled by one financial institution — the Prudential Assurance Company). Stanworth and Giddens (1975) investigated the linkages between financial institutions and industrial corporations. A part of the managerial revolution thesis (especially Galbraith, 1969) is the increasing independence of management from both shareholders and other external suppliers of capital, such as banks. However, the evidence of Stanworth and Giddens points in the opposite direction.

One dimension of linkages between corporations and financial institutions through which control over the corporation can be exercised by the financial institution is the holding of directorships on the corporation by a representative of the institution. Stanworth and Giddens (1975) estimate that the number of directorships in the top 50 industry corporations by bank representatives increased from ten in 1906 to 49 in 1946 and reached 67 by 1970. The number of directorships in the same group of firms held by 'City' firms increased from 69 in 1946 to 94 in 1970.

Chevalier (1969) reports that 31 of the largest 200 US manufacturing corporations were controlled by banks and other financial institutions in 1965. Kotz (1979), drawing mainly on the work of a Congressional Inquiry (usually known as the Patman Report), reports that of the 500 largest industrial corporations in 1967, 147 had 5 per cent or more of their common stock held by one of the 49 top bank trust departments. These 49 banks held 768 interlocking directorships with 286 of the largest 500 corporations.

Johnson and Apps (1979) investigated the interlocks between 200 largest industrial and commercial companies and 35 largest financial companies in the United Kingdom. They found a considerable extent of interlocking through directorships, with 55 per cent of the manufacturing companies having links with firms in that sector, and 48 per cent of those companies having links with firms in the financial sector.

Dooley (1969) looked at the directorships in the 250 largest US corporations (including financial companies) and reported that in these companies a total of 4,007 directorships were held by 3,165 men (sic). The holding of multiple directorships meant that only 17 corporations of the 250 investigated did not have at least one director who was a director of another company. Nearly one in eight of these interlocks involved companies which were competitors, even though such interlocking directorships are illegal in the United States.

Interlocking directorships may be a channel through which apparently independent firms competing can co-ordinate their decisions. Thus evidence on concentration needs to be evaluated in conjunction with the evidence on interlocking directorships. The interlocks between financial institutions and other firms are likely to have a bearing on the assessment of the managerial revolution and whether control has passed from individual owners to financial institutions.

Whilst there is general agreement that share ownership in any particular large firm is usually relatively widely dispersed, and that most shareholders play no role in the management of the firm, there is disagreement on the extent of ownership control, ranging from one-tenth to one-fifth (of Larner, 1970) through to near three-fifths (of Burch, Chevalier and Nyman and Silberston). There is substantial evidence of growing involvement of financial institutions in the ownership and control of large industrial corporations, particularly in Britain. A more extensive treatment of the type of evidence discussed in this section is Scott (1979),

Chapters 3 and 4.

Performance Differences between Owner-controlled and Manager-controlled Firms

The theory of Marris, as indicated above, predicted differences in the performance of owner-controlled firms and manager-controlled firms in terms of growth and profitability. A first test of the theory is the examination of the profits and growth record of owner-controlled and manager-controlled firms. A second one used in the next chapter is the examination of the relationship across firms between profitability and growth.

Figure 11.3: Firms With Different Utility Functions Facing Same Opportunities

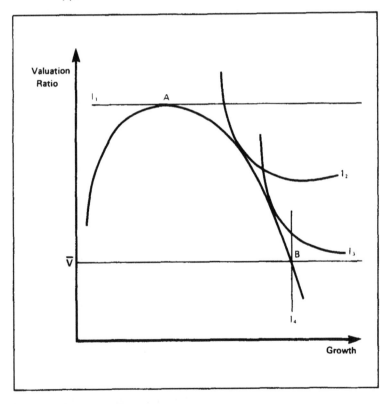

In testing these predictions, researchers are looking at the pooled experience of a number of firms. The predictions, however, relate to a single

firm, and not to a group of firms. Firms are likely to face different opportunities and to have different objectives. Firms and their controllers may gain some utility from a high market value and from growth and we write this as $U(v, g)$. If firms vary in the utility gained from market value and growth, reflected in different utility functions, but face the same set of opportunities, then the trade-off AB in Figure 11.3 will be mapped out by observations on the valuation ratio and profitability of firms. In Figure 11.3 the indifference curves derived from four utility functions have been drawn. The indifference curve I_1 is derived from a utility function which only values the market value of the firm, which is the conventional view of the owner-controlled firms. The indifference curve I_4 is for a firm which values only growth, which is the conventional view of the manager-controlled firm. But such a firm is constrained by the

Figure 11.4: Illustration of Possible Association between Valuation Ratio and Growth Rate

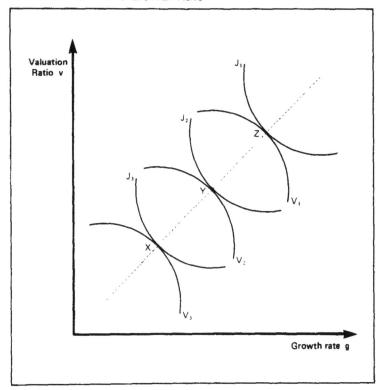

Table 11.3: Summary of Studies on Impact of Control Type on Firm Performance

Author	Nature of sample	Results
Bothwell (1980)	150 large US corporations 1960-67	Comparison of risk-adjusted profit margins on sales allowing for barriers to entry. O.C. firms had higher profit margin than M.C. firms in each barrier to entry grouping
Boudreaux (1973)	3 firms of each control type from each of 12 industries, U.S.A. Annual observations 1952-63	The effect of control type on rate of return and risk is significant, but not on firm size
Holl (1975)	Up to 183 British companies over period 1948-60, with control type as at 1951	In unadjusted sample, the profit rate is higher and growth rate lower for O.C. firms than for M.C. firms, and the differences between the control types is significant. But in a matched sample to control for size and industry differences, the 'results are . . . consistent with the hypothesis that control type has no effect on the performance of the firm'
Kamerschen (1968)	47 American firms over the period 1959-64	Control type does not have a significant effect on profit rate
McKean and Kania (1978)	1,800 largest US corporations assigned to 4-digit industries	No strong inter-industry pattern relating profit performance to control type, though O.C. firms had somewhat higher mean levels of performance

Within Boudreaux (1973) Results:

	ρ	Variability of ρ	Size
O.C.	13.16	4.58	853.4
M.C.	10.45	3.07	923.0

Monsen *et al.* (1968)	Same as Boudreaux above		
		O.C.	ϱ 12.8
		M.C.	7.3
Radice (1971)	89 British firms in foods, electrical engineering and textile industries 1957-67	The effect of control type is significant	

The effect of control type is significant

	ϱ	(average % p.a.) growth of assets
O.C.	16.81	12.42
M.C.	12.40	6.84

$$\varrho = 2.733\, D + 0.348\, g - 0.015\ \text{Size}$$
$$(1.489) \quad (0.116) \quad (0.023)$$

+ Constant + industrial dummies;

$R^2 = 0.199$, where $D = 1$ if firm is O.C., 0 if M.C.

Abbreviations:
O.C. Owner-controlled
M.C. Manager-controlled
g growth
ϱ Rate of return profit (%)

The precise definition of these variables varies from study to study.

requirement of avoiding takeover. Indifference curves I_2, I_3 take intermediate positions.

Let us now look at the case where firms have the same objectives, but face different opportunities. This is illustrated in Figure 11.4, where V_1, V_2, V_3 represent three opportunities which face firms, and J_1, J_2 and J_3 are three indifference curves drawn from one utility function. We can see that under these circumstances maximisation occurs at X, Y, Z for the three groups of firms, and that a positive relationship between the valuation ratio and growth would be traced out.

Thus the interpretation of a set of observations on the valuation ratio and growth rate of firms is difficult. For there is no certainty that the observations are drawn from a single valuation ratio-growth rate curve.

The theory of Marris runs in terms of a firm choosing a steady growth path and its associated rate of profit. But steady growth is not generally observed and instead growth fluctuates from year to year. One year's growth rate may be a poor guide to any underlying growth rate of the firm, and for this reason usually growth over a number of years (often five) is used. Similarly, one year's profit may be a poor guide to the underlying position.

The results of seven studies on the effects of the type of control on firm performance are summarised in Table 11.3. Besides differences which arise from use of different time periods and different countries, some differences may arise from the different statistical techniques used. In all studies the companies included are large and often within the largest 500 in their country. A consensus which emerges is that when the control type is significant, owner-controlled firms earn a higher rate of profit than manager-controlled firms. This result can be less concerned with shareholders' interests as reflected in the rate of return or that they are less efficient.

Some support for the latter view comes from the study of Radice (1971) where the owner-controlled firms have both higher profit and growth rates than measurement-controlled firms. The result of that study does not support the view that firms, whether manager-controlled or owner-controlled, face the same trade-off between profitability and growth, although the initial findings of Holl (1975) would support that position.

Fatemi *et al.* (1983) focused on American management-controlled firms over the period 1968 to 1975,[2] and sought to identify the main goals which these firms and their controllers pursue by the application of canonical correlation analysis applied to a range of performance variables (e.g. profitability, growth). They conclude that large managerial-controlled firms have two important goals, which are those of shareholder wealth maximisation and sales maximisation, with the former being the dominant objective. Possible goals of firms which were tested for but found unimportant were earnings 'smoothing' and liquidity.

A central feature of the managerial theories is that there is a conflict between owner interests (often seen as linked to profits and share-price) and management interest (often linked to sales and growth). Francis (1980), based on questionnaires returned by managers in some large UK companies, can be seen as challenging the validity of that central feature. He concludes that

> although our managers did report satisfaction from the growth of their company . . . their primary sources of satisfaction do not include the other factors commonly expressed by managerialist writers, such as security, status, prestige and service to employees, customers and the community. Moreover whatever interests they have in the fast growth of their company these are not seen to be in conflict with profit-maximising corporate objectives. Profits and growth are both pursued, although growth in profits is given higher priority than growth in sales or assets.

Determinants of Executive Income

An important strand in the reasoning of Baumol, Marris and others on managerial objectives is that managerial income is more closely linked with sales and size than with profitability, thereby creating incentives for managers to pursue sales and size at the expense of profits.

Before looking at the evidence on the determinants of executive income, a few preliminary remarks are needed. First, managers in this context means 'top' management who make the effective decisions on pricing, investment, etc., for this is the group which is faced by any trade-off between size and profits or between growth and profits. In the empirical work summarised below, it is the income of the highest paid director (often labelled the chief executive), or the incomes of the highest paid directors, for which the determinants are sought. Second, we have to consider an alternative explanation of executive income, which could be labelled a neo-classical one. This explanation would postulate that managers vary in ability, with that of a particular manager fixed and easily ascertained, and the more able the manager the higher the income he can command. Managers with more ability are required for larger firms because of the greater problems involved in running a larger firm. Then

Table 11.4: Summary of Findings on the Determinants of Executive Compensation

Author	Brief description of sample, etc.	Summary of conclusions
Cosh (1975)	Over a thousand UK companies quoted and unquoted, annual observations 1969-71	Both size and profitability have significant impact on compensation; significant differences between quoted and unquoted companies and between different industries. Overall regression result: $$\log EC = 7.426 + 0.619D + (0.0045 - 0.0032D)\varrho$$ $$\quad (0.178) \quad (0.0009) \quad (0.0012)$$ $$+ (0.228 - 0.074D) \log K$$ $$\quad (0.010) \quad (0.021)$$ $R^2 = 0.2920$. D is a dummy variable with value 1 if firm is unquoted, 0 if quoted. Units: EC in £, K in thousands of £s.
Ciscel (1974)	210 of the largest 250 US industrial corporations. Annual observations 1969-71	Correlation of executive compensation (both of chief executive and sum of all directors' and officers' salaries) lower with profits than with sales, assets or number of employees.
Llewellen and Huntsman (1970)	50 US corporations for every third year from 1942 to 1963	Find little difference between use of narrow and broad definitions of executive compensation (see text). Find profitability has a significant but sales an insignificant effect on compensation. For example for 1963: $$\frac{EC}{K} = 155.3\frac{1}{K} - 15.6\frac{S}{K} + 677.5\frac{\pi}{K}$$ $$\quad (8.1) \quad (14.4) \quad (173.3)$$ $R^2 = 0.932$ EC in dollars, S, K in millions of dollars

McGuire et al. (1962)	45 US corporations of the largest 100. Annual observations 1953-9	The correlation between executive income and sales revenue is higher than that between income and profits. When the effect of profits is controlled for, correlation between income and sales revenue is 0.248; when sales revenue is controlled for correlation between income and profits is 0.0564
Masson (1971)	Total financial return to top 3-5 executives in 39 companies, 1947-66. For each company, year-to-year changes over the period in compensation related to changes in sales, earnings per share and rate of return on shares	Changes in rate of return have a positive and significant effect on compensation (see text)
Meeks and Whittington (1975)	Over a thousand largest UK companies, annual observations, 1969-71	Both size and profitability have a significant effect in executive income; a typical result for 1971 is $EC =$ constant $+ 4002 \log S + 46 \varrho$ $\quad\quad\quad\quad\quad\quad (156.3) \quad\quad (16.4)$ $R^2 = 0.395$
Roberts (1959)	410 US corporations for the years 1945, 1948 and 1949, 989 corporations for 1950	The most important determinant of executive compensation is sales revenue, and profitability has no significant effect. There are no significant inter-industry differences
Smyth et al. (1975)	500 largest US firms in 1972	Executive compensation related to profits and sales. Both statistically significant. After allowance for heteroskedasticity, they report: $EC =$ constant $+ 1.0371\pi + 0.0251S$ $\quad\quad\quad\quad\quad\quad (0.1139) \quad\quad (0.0056)$ EC in dollars, others in thousands of dollars

Table 11.4 (cont.)

Author	Brief description of sample, etc.	Summary of conclusions
Yarrow (1972)	85 US corporations (mainly amongst the largest 150) for 1963, 1965 and 1968	Overall results show size and selling and administrative expenses are significant influences on income, but profitability is not. For example, for 1968, the regression is: $\log EC = 2.861 + 0.175 \log K + 0.140 \log Ex$ $\qquad\quad (0.391) \quad (0.045) \qquad\quad (0.043)$ $\qquad\quad + 0.036 \log \varrho \; R^2 = 0.461$ $\qquad\qquad (0.078)$ But there are significant industry differences, and when these are allowed for, profitability is sometimes significant. Concludes that profitability may have an effect (see text)

Notes: For all results reported in this table, executive compensation consists of salary and bonuses only.
Symbols used:
EC : executive compensation
K : assets
ϱ : profitability (rate of return on capital)
S : sales revenue
π : profits (total)
Ex : selling and administrative expenses

we would expect to observe a positive association between managerial income and firm size. But this would not create incentives to the manager to increase the size of the firm. For if the size of the firm increases, the degree of managerial ability required increases and the present manager is replaced by a more able and more highly paid manager.

Many investigators have measured executive income by the salary and bonus of the chief executive. However, the salary and bonus may be only a part of the total remuneration of the chief executive. In addition, there can be pension contributions made by the employer, payment in the form of shares or of share options, and dividend income and capital gains from the ownership of shares in the firm. With the exception of the first of those items, these forms of income are influenced by the performance of the firm's share price. Llewellen (1969) argues that the proportion of total post-tax real income of executives which was paid in the form of salary and bonuses declined over the period 1940 to 1963. Based on data for 50 of the largest American corporations, he found that whereas in the early forties the salary and bonus component was over two-thirds, it had declined by the early sixties to around one-half. This change can be seen as a response of executives to the different tax treatments of salary and the other forms of income, or as a deliberate attempt by shareholders to provide profit-linked incentives for their executives.[3]

There have been two basic approaches to investigating the determinants of executive income. The first one has been to see which variables, such as sales, profits and other measures of size, correlate most closely with executive income. Apart from the point that correlation does not imply causation, this method does not indicate the relative quantitative importance of the variables involved. For example, sales could be closely correlated with executive income without creating significant incentive effects if a very large increase in sales were required for a small increase in salary. At most this method can only indicate how much uncertainty is attached to any forecast of higher income resulting from, say, higher profits or sales.

This method has been used by, *inter alia*, Ciscel (1974) and McGuire *et al.* (1962), and a brief summary of their conclusions is given in Table 11.4. These authors find that executive income is less correlated with profits than it is with other measures of firm size. Indeed, McGuire *et al.* find that when the effect of sales revenue is controlled for, the correlation between executive profits and income virtually disappears. One difficulty of interpretation of these results is that they use annual observations, and profits are likely to vary from year to year to a greater extent than the other measures of size.

The second approach has used regression analysis with executive income as the dependent variable and the independent variables including sales, assets, profits or profitability, etc. Five such studies are also summarised in Table 11.4. The two British studies, which cover the same period of time and many of the same firms, agree that both a size variable (such as assets or sales) and profitability (rate of return) have an influence on executive income. Two studies for the United States (Roberts, 1959; Yarrow, 1972) find firm size of significance whereas profitability is not. But Yarrow argues that there are substantial industry differences and, after allowing for these, finds profitability of some significance. The studies generally find that it does not matter materially which measure of size is used. They point to the importance of size in general rather than sales in particular as an influence on executive income.

The third American study (Llewellen and Huntsman, 1970) differs from the others in two respects. They investigate both total remuneration, and salary and bonus as measures of executive income, and have slightly less success in explaining total remuneration than salary and bonus. This may arise from the greater year-to-year fluctuation in total remuneration than in salary, with the former being influenced by fluctuations in profits and share prices. But their results provide some justification for the use of salary and bonus as a measure of executive income. The second different aspect is the form of the equation, with executive income as a function of level of profits and sales. The direct estimation of such an equation encounters problems of heteroskedasticity and multicollinearity, and to overcome these the authors divide the equation through by assets to obtain the form of the equation reported in Table 11.4. Thus their starting point is the influence of profits and size, rather than profitability and size. The results of Smyth *et al.* (1975), from an equation similar to that of Llewellen and Huntsman, point to the effect of both profits and sales on executive income.

The study of Masson (1971) is rather different in that he examines the determinants of the percentage change in executive compensation from year to year in 39 companies. The results reported summarise the experience of all the companies involved. Masson estimates, for example, that in 30 out of the 39 companies, the effect of a change in the rate of return on executive compensation is positive, and the finding of such a proportion is statistically significant from a 'no effect' outcome of one half at the 99.9 per cent confidence level. He also finds that changes in sales have a negligible effect on executive compensation, and 'rejects view that executives are paid to expand sales at the expense of net worth'.

The majority of studies (with those of Llewellen and Huntsman and of Masson forming the minority) find a positive relationship between size and executive income. If executives believe that this positive relationship wil hold for their own firms' expansion, so that increased size leads to increased executive income, incentives for expansion exist. The magnitude of this possible incentive effect can be seen from the calculations of Meeks and Whittington (1975). A doubling of the rate of profit (on capital employed) from 10 per cent to 20 per cent would, according to the results quoted in Table 11.4, raise executive compensation by £460 per annum (at 1971 prices). A doubling of firm size would lead to a rise of £2,774. It is difficult to compare the relative difficulty of raising profitability as compared with increasing size, but at first glance these figures suggest incentives to expand size rather than profitability.

One way in which a rapid increase in size can be obtained in a short time is through acquisition of another firm, and enhanced executive income as a motive for acquisition is discussed in Chapter 13.

Organisational Structure

The idea of a shift from owner control to management control is generally associated with large firms. In part, there is an association between the size of firm and the number of shareholders, and also the need for specialist managers to run large companies. The question arises in the context of large firms of whether there are ways of organising the firm which reduces the difficulties of managing a large organisation.

One of the major difficulties which could arise in large firms is the progressive loss of control (as firm size increases) by the central controllers and decision-makers. Those controllers require an upward flow of information on, for example, sales, advertising, costs, and the downward flow of orders and instructions which are carried out. The general line of argument is that these requirements become more difficult to attain as the size of the firm increases. There are likely to be, for example, more 'layers' of the firm through which information has to pass and orders are handed down. At each 'layer' there is the possibility of inaccuracies coming in, whether by accident or design. Those passing on information or orders would in general have an incentive to present the information or orders in a way which suited them rather than in the manner which was intended.

Some of the advantages of large size stem from a greater extent to which transactions can be conducted internal to the firm. For example, inputs which a small firm has to purchase from another may in the case of a large firm be supplied by one department of the firm to another, and if the input has to be of a particular specification and quality, it may be easier to instruct one department of a firm to produce the input to the required specification and quality rather than to seek to contract with another firm for its supply. This idea is explored more extensively in the next chapter (pp. 198–204).

Williamson (1970) has drawn attention to the various organisational structures which firms can adopt. Although he suggests a number of different structures attention has focused on two particular ones. These have been labelled the unitary form (abbreviated to U-form) and multidivisional form (M-form). In the U-form firm, the firm is organised centrally as a single unit and in terms of functions, e.g. sales department, production department, even though the firm may sell a wide variety of products in many different markets. In contrast, the M-form firm is organised in terms of product groups (divisions). Within each division there will usually be productions, sales etc. departments. There are some functions which are retained at the centre and not decentralised to the divisions, and the most usual central function is the allocation of finance and thereby control over investment allocation. It might also be expected that those functions which are subject to economies of scale over the range of interest to the firm would be centrally organised to reap the benefits of such economies. It is strongly suggested by Williamson's work that for large firms the M-form will be superior to the U-form. As such it would be predicted that firms with M-form structure would be more profitable than those with U-form. Further, large firms would gradually adopt the M-form structure. The limited empirical work on these aspects has confirmed these predictions, and we now review those studies.

Steer and Cable (1978) examine the organisational structure and performance of 82 large UK companies over the period 1964–6 to 1970–2. Following Williamson, they classify these companies into six categories. These are the U-form, M-form and transitional M-form (i.e. in the process of transition from U- to M-form), 'corrupted' M-form (i.e. some but not all features of being M-form), mixed structure and holding company (in which the firm is organised in terms of divisions but lacks central control over divisions). They identify 35 companies as M-form in 1970–2 (a rise from 21 in 1964–6), a further 47 as transitional or corrupted M-form (29 in 1964–6), 14 as holding companies (down from 37), nine as U-form (down from 14) and finally 15 as mixed or uncertain (19 in 1964–6). They further investigate whether the profitability is related to organisational form, after making allowance for size, growth and industry of firm. They distinguish between 'optimal' organisational form as multidivisional structure for large firms and U-form for small or single-product range firms and 'non-optimal' organisational form as the other organisational types. On this basis, the 'optimally organised' firms gain six to nine percentage points on the rate of return on equity as compared with the 'non-optimally' organised firms, and the former gain two to three percentage points on the rate of profit on sales as compared with the latter group.

Thompson (1981) produces some further results using the same sample as Steer and Cable (1978), but using share price return as the measure of performance. His results 'substantiate the [Steet and Cable] findings of a large performance differential in favour of the optimally organised (essentially M-form) firms. [But] . . . much of this difference was attributable to an abnormal short-term decline in the performance of the H-form [holding company] firms'.

Armour and Teece (1981) conducted a similar exercise for American petroleum companies over the period 1950 to 1975, finding that the proportion of M-form firms increased from 13 per cent to 78 per cent in this period. They postulate that, in a period when the M-form was not widely used, firms with that organisational form would be more profitable than those that were not. Over the period 1956 to 1968 they report that M-form firms gained an extra two percentage points on the rate of return on equity (compared with an average return of $7\frac{1}{2}$ per cent). Over the period 1969 to 1973, by which time most firms had adopted the M-form, there was not a significant effect of organisation form on the rate of return. Teece (1981) provides mini-histories of the organisation structure of some large American firms and compares 'the differential performance between the M-form "innovator" in an industry and its principal rival. Application of two non-parametric statistical tests . . . is supportive of the hypothesis that the M-form structure is associated with superior firm performance'. The differential performance induced by the adoption of the M-form is 1.22 percentage points on the rate of return on assets in this sample.

Notes

1. Collett and Yarrow (1976) provide evidence on 85 large British companies on the concentration of shareholdings. They report that, on average, the largest 50 shareholdings account for $45\frac{1}{2}$ per cent of the total. This understates concentration since, for example, the beneficial owners of nominee shareholdings are not identified. They also find that the concentration of shareholdings is negatively related to the size of firm and tends to be positively related to the extent of shareholdings in a company by financial institutions.

2. Management-controlled firms were those where no single party held more than 10 per cent of shares. Of the 749 companies examined, there was insufficient information on 225 of them, a further 198 were identified as not management-controlled, leaving 326 as management-controlled and included in the statistical analysis.

3. The taxation system encourages payment of income which accrues as capital gains on shares, etc., rather than payment in the form of money income, with the former generally taxed at a much lower rate than the latter. Further, some of the income benefits from payment in the form of shares are likely to be received during retirement when income, and hence marginal tax rate, is likely to be lower.

12 THE GROWTH OF FIRMS: SPEED AND SCOPE

Introduction

This chapter has two main purposes. The first is the consideration of the relationships between the rate of growth, rate of profit and size of firms. Under this general heading, we first outline the reasons which have been suggested for particular types of relation between growth, profitability and size, and see how these relationships link with the previous discussions in this book. Then the evidence on these relationships is reviewed. The second purpose is a discussion of the direction in which firms expand and contract. Under this heading, our discussion mainly relates to questions of vertical integration and diversification.

Profitability and Size

Profits are the difference between revenue and costs, and hence the relationship between profits and size is a combination of the relationship between revenue and size and between costs and size. If there are firm-level economies of scale, unit costs fall with increased size, leading to the profits/size ratio rising with size *ceteris paribus*. Market power, widely interpreted to include all factors which lead to higher output prices and lower input prices for larger firms, may rise with size. Thus relating profits to size of firm can only be a partial test for firm-level economies of scale. It may be possible to make some allowance for the market power of larger firms by, for example, allowing for the degree of concentration of the industries in which the firm operates.[1] Alternatively, it could be argued that market power does not decrease with firm size, so on that count profit rates would be expected not to fall with size. Thus any failure of profits to rise at the same pace as firm size would indicate the existence of diseconomies in costs with firm size.

Baumol (1959) argued that profitability will tend to rise with size since there are some things which only large firms can undertake, but large firms can if they wish undertake everything that small firms can do. Then large firms should be at least as profitable as small firms. This effect would reinforce any management desire to increase the size of their firm, and means that there may not be a conflict between managers and owners in that larger size may satisfy managers directly and owners through enhanced profitability. Thus Baumol's line of argument points to profitability rising (or at least not falling) with size.

The usual way in which the profits-size relationship has been explored is by the regression of the profits/capital ratio on some measure of size. The use of the profits/capital ratio avoids problems arising from changes in the degree of capital intensity as size changes.

It is essential that profits and capital employed are measured in a manner which is comparable between companies to ensure that the rate of profit is comparable across firms. In particular the way in which the firm is financed should not in itself affect the measure of profitability. This indicates that interest payments on borrowed capital should not be deducted as a cost from revenue before arriving at profits, for otherwise a firm financed by a high proportion of fixed interest borrowing would, *ceteris paribus*, record a lower level of profits than one financed largely by its shareholders.[2]

The measure of capital usually adopted is capital employed by the firm. This corresponds to the capital stock (or net assets) under the control of the firm, no matter how that capital has been financed. In principle, a piece of capital equipment which has been leased rather than bought should be included in the measure of capital employed (and the leasing charge not included in costs).

The size of a firm can be measured in numerous ways, such as net assets, output or numbers employed. These measures are likely to be highly correlated across firms, and the choice of size measure is unlikely to have any considerable impact on the regression results.[3] It has usually been found preferable to use the logarithm of size rather than size itself in the regression equations. This indicates that any impact of size is such that a given proportionate increase in size has the same influence on profitability no matter what size range is considered, rather than a given absolute increase in size having the same influence.

There may be other influences at work on profitability, and some allowance is generally required for these other factors before the influence of size can be adjudged. However, this may understate the role of firm size, particularly if profitability did indeed rise with size. For example, if one benefit arising from large size is the ability to operate in a particular industry because entry into that industry requires large capital commitment, allowing for the effect of operating in that industry may remove some of the effect of size.

Large firms usually operate in a number of industries, and their diversified operations may reduce the degree of variability of profitability and other dimensions of performance over time. Essentially, large firms may benefit from 'not having all their eggs in one basket'. This can be put more formally. Suppose that firms can be regarded as composed of a number of subdivisions, each of a fixed size, and each of which earns on average a profit rate ϱ. Firms vary in size by variations in the number of subdivisions. The average profit rate, under this regime, will be the same for all firms. But the variability of the profit rate of a firm will depend upon the value of the number of subdivisions, n, and on the correlation of profit rates between the subdivisions. When the variability of profitability over time is measured by the standard deviation of the profit rate this can be demonstrated as follows. Then the standard deviation of the firm of n subdivisions is given by $\sigma_n = ((1 + (n - 1)\tau)/n)^{\frac{1}{2}} \cdot \sigma$, where σ is the common standard deviation of the profit rate of the subdivisions, and τ is the common correlation between profitability of any two different subdivisions.[4] When there is no correlation between the profitability of the subdivisions, so that $\tau = 0$, then the variability declines with $(1/n)^{\frac{1}{2}}$. Then a four-fold increase in firm size would lead to a halving of the variability of profit rates. When $\tau = 1$, $\sigma_n = \sigma$ and there are no gains to be made from diversification in terms of reduced variation in profitability. The value of τ is likely to be influenced by the similarity of the firm's various activities and the extent to which these activities are affected by the same factors (such as the level of aggregate demand). Whilst this discussion has been in terms of profit rates, an analogous argument applies to growth rates.

Two important consequences flow from any tendency for the variability of profits (and other performance indicators) to fall with size. The first one is that if investors are averse to fluctuation of profits then the cost of finance is likely to be lower for a firm with a lower variability of profits. If variability does decline with firm size, then larger firms would have access to cheaper finance than smaller firms.

The second consequence is one for econometric estimation. If the lower variability over time for an individual firm of a particular size-class is translated into a lower variability of profitability across firms within that size-class for a particular time period, then the problem of heteroskedasticity arises. An equation of the form $\log Z_{t+1} = a + b \log Z_t + u$ is often estimated across firms (with u as the random error term), where Z_t is a measure of size at time t and Z_{t+1} size at time $t + 1$. If the variance of $\log Z_{t+1} - \log Z_t$ (i.e. growth) depends on $\log Z_t$, then the variance of u will also depend on $\log Z_t$. In other words $var(u)$ and the independent variable $\log Z_t$ are correlated, which is the problem of heteroskedasticity. In the presence of heteroskedasticity, for which a

correlation is not made, the calculated standard error of the coefficients
is biased. If the variance declines with size (as suggested by the above
argument), then the calculated standard errors are biased upwards (e.g.
Kmenta, 1971, pp. 255–6).

Growth and Firm Size

Interest in the relationship between growth and size may to some extent
arise from an interest in firm-level economies of scale. When there are
severe problems of measurement with profits and capital stock (pp. 88)
there may be advantages to looking at the growth-size relationship rather
than at the profitability-size relationship. The survivor technique for the
estimation of minimum efficient scale (pp. 57–61) argues that cost conditions can be ascertained from an examination of the nature of the firms
who prosper. Interpreting prosperity as growth, then the relationship of
growth and firm size may give some clues to the nature of the underlying cost conditions.

There are also implications of growth and firm size for trends in concentration. It is clear that if on average large firms grow faster than small
firms, concentration will increase over time. It is perhaps less obvious
that the variability of growth may be an important element in changing
concentration.

Our discussion of growth and firm size begins with Gibrat's Law (often
labelled the Law of Proportionate Effect (Hart, 1962; Prais, 1976). The
starting point is the view that there are numerous factors which influence
the growth of any particular firm. These factors influence the *proportionate* change in the size of firms, rather than the *absolute* change. These
influences, which would include the ability of the entrepreneur, changes
in product demand, luck and random factors, are likely to be difficult
to measure. The crucial assumption is that these factors which influence
the rate of growth do not operate systematically with respect to the size
of the firm, so that growth can be viewed as a random process with respect
to firm size. Further, it is assumed that the growth of a firm in one period
is not related to growth in another period. This may be a much stronger
assumption than the first one in that factors such as entrepreneurial ability
are likely to operate in successive periods. Some factors serve to increase
growth, whilst some retard growth. Firms which are particularly lucky
in a given period grow considerably whilst those which are unlucky grow
slowly or decline. These factors act randomly in the sense that there is
no tendency to favour firms of any particular size. This can be formally

expressed as $Z_{t+1} = Z_t (1 + h_t)$ where Z is a measure of size of firm, h_t is a randomly determined variable and t refers to period t. Then we have that $\log Z_{t+1} = \log Z_t + \log (1 + h_t)$. By substitution for $\log Z_t$ in terms of $\log Z_{t-1}$ and so on, we arrive at $\log Z_{t+1} = \log Z_0 + \sum_{j=0}^{t} \log (1 + h_j)$. Thus the size of a firm at time $t + 1$ depends on its initial size and the summation of a number of random factors. As time proceeds, the influence of initial size declines in relative importance, and the influence of the random factors increases. It can be shown that from this random process of growth, the size distribution of firms will tend towards log-normality.[5]

The Law of Proportionate Effect can be tested by an examination of relationship $\log Z_{t+1} = a + c \log Z_t + u$, where u is a random term with the prediction that $c = 1$.[6] An alternative, but not precisely equivalent formulation is derived from $\log Z_{t+1} - \log Z_t = a + (c - 1) \log Z_t + u$ and the left-hand side yields the approximation $\log Z_t (1 + g_t) - \log Z_t = \log (1 + g_t) \doteq g_t$ if g_t is small. Then this gives $g_t = a + b \log Z_t + u$ with prediction that $b = 0$.

From the first formulation, some indication of the role of variability of growth rates on concentration can easily be derived. From the above equation we can obtain $var(\log Z_{t+1}) = c^2 var(\log Z_t) + var(u)$, where $var(\cdot)$ indicates the variance of the variable.[7] Since $var(u)$ is positive (unless there is no variability of growth rates when it is zero), with $c = 1$ the variance of the log of firm size will increase over time. Even if growth rates tend to decline with size, so that $c < 1$, the variance of logs may still increase over time for $var(\log Z_{t+1}) > var(\log Z_t)$ when $var(u) > (1 - c^2)var(\log Z_t)$.

It was indicated above that the operation of random factors on the firm size would generate a log-normal distribution of firm size. In Chapter 3 we indicated that if the size-distribution of firm size is log-normal then the variance of logs is the 'natural' measure of inequality to use, for then measures of concentration can be calculated from a knowledge of the variance of logs and the number of firms in the industry. This random approach often assumes (implicitly) that the number of firms is constant, and under that assumption a rise in the variance of logs implies a rise in other measures of concentration.

This approach finds difficulty in dealing with the birth and death of firms. In the analysis above the identity of the firms involved did not change. The birth of firms can be dealt with by assigning some small but non-zero size to these new firms for the initial period when the firms did not exist. A similar option can be adopted for the death of firms.

But the assignment of arbitrary size to these firms is not a satisfactory solution.

This process can be illustrated with a numerical example. Suppose that there are 81 firms originally of an equal size of 16 units. In any period, some firms grow and some decline, but how many grow and how many decline and by how much are independent of the size of firm. We take the case where, for any size of firm, one third decline by 50 per cent in a period, one third remain the same size, and the remaining third grow by 100 per cent. The distribution of firm size at the end of each five periods is shown in Table 12.1. At the end of the second period, 27 (i.e. one third) of firms have declined by 50 per cent to 8 units, 27 have grown by 100 per cent to 32 units, and the remaining 27 stay at 16 units. In the next period, one third of the 27 firms at 8 units decline by a further 50 per cent to 4 units. Another third of the 8 unit firms remain at that size and are joined by the one third of the 16 unit firms who decline by 50 per cent. The final third of the 27 firms of size 8 units grow by 100 per cent back to 16 units, and are joined by some firms of 16 units who remain unchanged in size and some who decline by 50 per cent from 32 units.

It is clear from Table 12.1 that there is a growing dispersion of firm size over time in this model. In period 0, the five-firm concentration would be 6.2 per cent (i.e. 5/81), whilst at the end of period 4 it had risen to 32 per cent, and would continue to rise thereafter. It is also clear that in this numerical example that growth of a particular firm in one period is assumed to be unrelated to its previous growth.

Table 12.1: Illustration of Effect of Dispersion of Growth Rates on Size-Distribution of Firms

Number of firms size at end of period	1	2	4	8	16	32	64	128	256
0					81				
1				27	27	27			
2			9	18	27	18	9		
3		3	9	18	21	18	9	3	
4	1	4	10	16	19	16	10	4	1

In this process large firms grow at the same average rate as small firms, and that would leave the share of the originally large firms constant. But some small firms overtake previously large firms, boosting the share of the large firms, when the group of large firms is reconstituted to include the fast-growing former small firms and exclude the slow-growing formerly large firms.

This points towards a tendency for concentration to rise because of variation in growth rates between firms. This effect has sometimes been labelled the 'Gibrat effect' (Hannah and Kay, 1977) and sometimes 'spontaneous drift' (Prais, 1976). However, if growth rates tend to decline with size of firms, then concentration may stabilise. The de-concentration effect of slower average growth of larger firms may be balanced by the concentrating effect of the random growth component. In terms of the formulation above, the variance of logs will be constant when $var(\log Z) = var(u)/(1 - c^2)$ requiring that $c < 1$.

The quantitative importance of this Gibrat effect will depend on, besides the values of c and $var(u)$, the role of the factors ignored by this analysis. In particular, the birth of new firms may offset the concentrating effect and death of firms, particularly through acquisition, may enhance the concentrating effect. But some of the variation in growth (and the consequent concentrating effects of that) may arise from variation in acquisition activity between firms of different sizes. The relative importance of the Gibrat effect and of acquisitions has been a matter of fierce debate, and for this debate see Hart and Prais (1956), Prais (1976) and Hart (1979) for the view that the Gibrat effect is important, and Hannah and Kay (1977) for the view that acquisitions have a more important role than the Gibrat effect.

Growth and Profitability

In the previous chapter we saw that one prediction based on the Marris theory of the firm behaviour was that, in steady state, a firm would be operating in the region where profitability and growth were negatively related.[1] But this negative relationship would only be reflected in observations on growth and profitability across firms if firms had access to the same opportunity set.

A 'common sense' view might suggest that efficient dynamic firms would be both more profitable and faster growing than inefficient sluggish firms, and that across firms profitability and growth would tend to be positively related. High profitability means that more internal finance is available for expansion purposes, and is likely to increase the available external finance by, for example, making the issue of new shares easier.

There is one further difference between these lines of argument. There is no causal relationship between profitability and growth in the theory of Marris, but rather it reflects firms making different choices. In the second case, if high growth and profits arise out of more efficiency, again there is no causal mechanism at work. But when profits become the means of finance for growth, then there is a causal relationship for it is high profits which lead to growth and not *vice versa*.

The Evidence

Profitability and Size

It is gratifying to be able to report that this is an area of investigation where consensus has emerged. Eatwell (1971), surveying a considerable amount of American and British work, ends his discussion of the profitability and size relationship by concluding that

> the empirical literature demonstrates that there is no constant relationship between the mean rate of profitability by size classes when individual firms are considered, but the grouping of a large sample of firms may produce certain non-linear relationships. We also note that intra-class variability of profit rates decreases with increasing size, but that this is not a consistently monotonic phenomenon. Finally, if the sample consists solely of (positive) income corporations, there is a weak but significant relationship between profitability and size . . . and the small firms are those that make the largest losses most frequently. Thus, given the *a priori* premises with which we began, the profitable, growing corporation may expect to encounter slightly lower profit rates as it moves into higher size classes; but the certainty of profitability will usually be increased and could reinforce the expansionary process (text in parenthesis added).

Whittington (1980), in a study of around a thousand British quoted companies over the period 1960–74, reaches a similar conclusion that 'average profitability is largely independent of firm size, but such relationship as there is tends to be negative', with the variability of profitability across firms and across time tending to decline with firm size.

However, whilst there is a decline in the dispersion of profit rates with size, it is not usually as rapid a decline as would be indicated by the $1/n^{\frac{1}{2}}$ rule (see p. 191). Some correlation between profitability of different sectors of a firm is indicated, perhaps arising from operation in related markets.

Growth and Size

The evidence on the growth-size of firm relationship indicates that, in general, there is no significant relationship, although most studies relating to Britain during the 1950s show a positive relationship. Prais (1976) (for 1951 to 1958), Samuels (1965) (for 1951 to 1960), Utton (1971) (for 1954 to 1965) and partially Singh and Whittington (1968) (for the sub-period 1954–1960), find a positive and significant relationship between growth and size. However, studies for the 1960s have generally shown a negative but non-significant relationship of growth and firm size (Samuels and Chesher, 1972; Aaronovitch and Sawyer, 1975b).

The general consensus for the fifties needs to be somewhat modified by the findings of Singh and Whittington (1968) when they group the firms in their sample into four industries. They report that:

[The hypothesis that growth rates are independent of firm size] has not been rejected by our data. We have found very few statistically significant differences between average growth rates for different size-classes of companies, although there is a very slight tendency for average growth rates to increase with the size of firms, particularly in the second sub-period [1954–60]. (Text in brackets added.)

Rowthorn (1971) investigates the growth of international firms and reports that '[o]ne conclusion stands out clearly from all this. Growth was not an increasing function of size. Big firms did not grow faster than small firms. On the contrary, during 1962–67 firms which were small by international standards, grew faster than the giants. Apart from this, size and growth seem to have been largely independent of each other'.

When studies have investigated the relationship between dispersion of growth rates and firm size, the usual finding has been that dispersion declines with size, although not always in a uniform manner. Singh and Whittington (1968) find that '[the postulate] that the dispersion of growth rates is the same for all size-classes of firms, has not been found to hold for the companies analysed in this study . . . The variances [of growth rates] tend to be heterogeneous in the smaller size classes, but for companies above a certain minimum size, the variance of growth rates tends to be lower than for smaller companies.'

Another aspect of Gibrat's law is that growth in one period is not related to previous growth. But Singh and Whittington find 'a significant tendency for growth rates to persist in the Engineering, Tobacco and Clothing and Footwear industries, but not in the Food industry'.

Growth and Profitability

Eatwell (1971), in surveying work on the growth-profitability relationship, finds 'that there exists a fairly strong, though somewhat erratic, relationship between growth and profitability of the firm. Significant difference in regression coefficients were identified between industries, small and large firms and intertemporally . . .' But in all the work surveyed the relationship was a positive one.

This has two important implications for our previous discussion. First, it does not provide support for a trade-off between growth and profitability although if inter-firm opportunity differences are important, it may be not inconsistent with individual firms facing declining profitability as the price of increased growth. Second, whilst growth may be independent of size, it may not be 'random' in that profitability may be a significant explanatory variable. However, as indicated above, this is only one interpretation amongst a number of the profitability-growth relationship.

In conclusion, the evidence points against the existence of firm-level economies of scale, with profitability (and to a lesser extent growth) tending not to rise with firm size. However, the evidence points to lower variability of performance as an advantage of increased size.

Horizontal and Vertical Integration

In this and the following section we are examining the reasons suggested as to why firms expand or contract in particular directions, e.g. why do some firms expand through moving into the production of goods or services substantially different to those which they initially produce (i.e. diversify)? Most of the discussion focuses on expansion rather than contraction. Underlying much of the discussion is a presumption that firms will seek to grow. Profitable firms receive a flow of profits each year, which can form the basis of finance for expansion if they wish to grow.

The act of horizontal integration means the integration into a firm's range of some products which while new to that firm are essentially similar to its previous products. These 'new' products may be variations on the existing product range or the sale of its previous range of products in different geographical markets (e.g. regional or national ones). Horizontal integration may come about through the acquisition of a market rival, the development of new products related to the previous ones and the movement into 'new' geographical markets.

The act of vertical integration involves a firm extending its activities to cover some activities which were previously undertaken by its suppliers or customers. Thus the production by a firm of inputs which it previously bought from other firms or the acquisition of a customer firm would count as acts of vertical integration. The extent of vertical integration is often measured by the ratio of net output (value added) by a firm to its gross output (sales). Net output is measured as the sum of the wages, salaries and profits of a firm, whilst gross output is equal to net output plus material inputs purchased from other firms.[9] Clearly if a firm begins to produce some inputs itself which it had previously bought for other firms, then its degree of vertical integration would rise as its net output rises and its purchase of material inputs from elsewhere declines.

The reasons why firms would seek to expand by the production and sale of products similar to those which they currently produce and/or by geographical expansion can be conveniently placed into two groups. The first one, which is of particular importance when the expansion of the firm takes place through acquisition or merger, is the exploitation of enhanced monopoly power. Thus horizontal integration is seen to add to the firm's market share and to any monopoly power which it might possess, and is profitable through exploitation of increased market power.

The second reason, which has been applied particularly in the context of multinational enterprises, is that the firm seeks to gain further benefits from its knowledge and expertise. This expertise may relate to the nature of the particular range of products, e.g. how the product is produced, how it is marketed. The knowledge may be gained through research and development and through the effects of 'learning-by-doing'. The knowledge and expertise which the firm has gained in one geographical market, where it is assumed to have been successful, can then be applied in other geographical markets, e.g. in other regions of the same country or in other countries. Once knowledge of a particular type of market has been gained by a firm from one area, the knowledge can then be utilised in other geographical areas. This general idea has been applied to the study of multinational enterprises, on which see e.g. Hood and Young (1979), Chapter 2 and Casson (1983), especially Chapters 1 to 3.

The general starting point for the discussion on vertical integration is Coase (1937), of which brief mention was made in Chapter 2. One way of introducing this discussion is to pose the question which factors determine whether a firm (say, a car producer) would seek to purchase a particular input which it makes use of (e.g. gear boxes) from another firm or would decide to produce that input itself. A related question is what factors determine whether a firm will hire workers on an employment contract basis or on a task-specific self-employment basis. Under an employment contract, a worker is generally hired for a specified time to perform a range of tasks under the instructions of his/her supervisor. Under a self-employment contract, the workers are contracted to provide a specified range of goods or services. When a firm decides for whatever reason to employ workers to produce an input rather than purchase the input from another firm, or to contract with workers on a self-employment basis, the firm will be measured as larger than otherwise and more vertically integrated than otherwise.

It is convenient to group the reasons suggested for the extent of vertical integration into three groups, although they are not unrelated. These three groups could be labelled technological-, transactions- and hierarchy-based.

Under the heading technological-based reasons, we include the technical nature of a particular production process with which the firm is involved, such that it would be impossible or very inconvenient to break up successive parts of that production process. The example usually cited in this respect is that of the integration of parts of steelmaking whereby blast furnaces and rolling mills are placed side-by-side so that the steel can be transferred in a hot liquid state from one to the other. Similar examples are likely to arise in the chemical industries. A converse case would arise when the production of an input is subject to economies of scale, but the users of the input make small use of the input (relative to the minimum efficient scale). Using our example of a car firm from above, if the production of gear-boxes requires a minimum annual output of, say, 5 million but a car firm requires only, say, half a million annually, then that car firm could not gain the available economies of scale if it produced its own gearboxes (unless it could sell the extra gearboxes).

The technological view points to technical reasons why in the example of steelmaking the blast furnaces and rolling mills should be linked together. The evaluation of this reasoning rests on two questions. First, how extensive are these technological imperatives for integration and do they explain the observed extent of vertical integration? Second, the concept of vertical integration relates to ownership and not geographical proximity. Thus a firm may locate stages of its production process at different geographical locations but would be regarded as highly vertically integrated if its ratio of net output to gross output was high. In the steelmaking example, the blast furnace and rolling mill may need to be built close together, but that does not necessarily mean that they will be owned by the same firm. The alternative is that they are under separate ownership but with contracts between the firms. This leads us into discussion of the second group, that of transactional reasons. The underlying reason can be seen from this steelmaking example, namely that the drawing up of a contract between a blast furnace owner and a rolling mill owner may be too costly and complicated.

The distinction made by Coase (1937) (and extended by Wiliamson, 1975) was between the nature of the allocation of resources between firms and the allocation of resources within firms. The general notion is reflected in the title of Williamson (1975), namely *Markets and Hierarchies*. Coase (1937) described the difference as follows:

> In economic theory we find that the allocation of factors of production between different uses is determined by the price mechanism. The price of factor *A* becomes higher in *X* than in *Y*. As a result, *A* moves from *Y* to *X*, until the difference between the prices in *X* and in *Y*, except in so far as it compensates for other differential advantages, disappears. Yet in the real world we find that there are many areas where this does not apply. If a workman moves from department *Y* to department *X*, he does not go because of a change in relative prices, but because he is ordered to do so.

The transactions view begins with the postulate that the use of the market is not costless, or in other words that there are transactions costs. These costs would include the time and financial costs of discovering a supplier, finding out the price and nature of the goods or services which the seller has on offer and the difficulties of ensuring that the goods or services supplied are of the type and quality required.

The discussion of Williamson (1975) is organised around three key features of the world, which in his view, interact to favour internal production by a firm over market transactions. Market transactions involve a contract (explicit or implicit) between seller and buyer. The three features discussed by Williamson point to the difficulties of agreeing on mutually acceptable contracts between seller and buyer. These three features are:

(1) Bounded rationality, uncertainty and complexity. Bounded rationality refers to human behaviour that is '*intendedly* rational but only *limitedly* so' (Simon, 1961), and can be contrasted with the conventional approach in economies which could be summarised as unbounded rationality. The view of bounded rationality stresses that there are limits on the human capacity to receive, store and process information. Uncertainty about the economic environment (e.g. uncertainty about the quality of a product

which we are considering buying) and the complexity of the world make decision-making very difficult and bring people up against the constraint posed by the limits of human capacity to process information.

(2) Opportunism allied with small numbers. Opportunism relates to one economic agent take advantage of whatever opportunities arise even at the expense of others. The small numbers arise when, as would seem likely, a firm deals only with a few potential suppliers of inputs. Opportunism and small numbers can arise both from market transactions (e.g. one firm gaining at the expense of another) and also within firms. Indeed, within a firm the small number problem may reach its height, for a firm will usually have only one, say, advertising department but would be able to choose from a number of advertising agencies. However, Williamson (1975, pp. 29–30) argues that 'internal organisation enjoys advantages . . . over market modes of contracting in circumstances where opportunism and small-numbers conditions are joined'. These advantages include the easier resolution of disputes within a firm and the ability of a firm to conduct audits into the performance of its own departments, whereas the effective auditing of other firms is not generally possible. Auditing can be used to reduce the use of opportunism by a department of a firm to the detriment of the general interests of the firm.

(3) Information impactedness. This rather ugly phrase refers to cases where relevant information is available to one group but not to others. It will often be the case that the producer of a product will know much more about the product and the way it is made than the purchaser will. Often this differential knowledge may not matter, but, as illustrated below, there will be important cases where this differential does matter.

These three features combine to foster internal production rather than purchase through the market, and hence are seen to encourage vertical integration. We can illustrate these points with reference to research and development. The choice facing a firm seeking to develop a new product could be pictured as lying between undertaking research in-house or sub-contracting the research to a specialist research organisation. The difficulties with contracting-out can arise from each of the three features listed above. The drawing-up of a contract between the two firms would run into the difficulties for the producer firm in specifying exactly the type of research to be undertaken, the new product which is hoped for, and the way in which the research firm should respond as the research proceeds, new ideas are discovered and problems encountered (bounded rationality, uncertainty and complexity). The research firm may not reveal to the producer firm all that is discovered from the research programme (opportunism). If the research fails, the producer firm may find it difficult to find out whether this was because of the nature of the research programme or the incompetence or dishonesty of the research firm (information impactedness). It could be argued that similar problems would arise if the research were undertaken by the producer firm. For example, would the managers of that firm be able to judge whether a failure of the research programme was due to the incompetence or dishonesty of its research staff or the nature of the research programme? This point is recognised by Williamson and others, but the view is held that the problems are reduced by in-house production rather than by contracting-out.

The third view, which we labelled a hierarchy approach, stresses that within a firm control is exercised by the owners and managers over workers. This view has recently been developed as a critique of Williamson (1975) in, for example, Francis (1983). Simply, the difference between workers being hired on an employment basis and on a self-employment basis is not only a difference in the transactions costs involved but also a difference in the control exercised by the firm over the workers. This view has a long history, reflected in the analysis of Marx (e.g. Marx, 1976) of the labour process. Put briefly, once workers have been hired on an employment contract basis, then the interests of the firm are that the workers work as hard as possible to produce as much as possible, whilst the interests of the workers are to work as little as possible since hard work is unpleasant. Thus at the workplace, the interests of the owners of the firm and the workers are in conflict. Further, this view indicates that the level of output will depend upon the extent of control and power which the owners and managers are able to exercise over the workers. Francis (1983) describes the transactions view as

> if A has to transact with B then either they do this in the market place or else move into the hierarchal transaction mode in which case a third party, C, enters the scene. This third party is the bureaucratic mechanism set up, presumably under joint agreement. It is C who stands in hierarchal relationship to both A and B. A and B remain on the same level and both stand to gain the same transaction cost reduction and also lose the same atmospheric benefits of autonomy. However, certainly in the case of the employment relationship and I would argue often in the case of vertical integration, a different hierarchy is instituted. This is one in which A now stands over B or vice versa.

This view would point out that whatever the reason for an increase in vertical integration there is a change in the power relationships involved. Those gaining from the change in power relationships would have an incentive to arrange that the vertical integration happens.

Many of the arguments above point to the advantages of internal production by a firm, and hence imply that a firm would continue to expand by taking over more and more functions. What are the limits to expansion through vertical integration? It could first be noted that the relationship between independent firms may replicate the relationships within a firm by, for example, continuing relationship and trust established between firms. But we can list three main factors which would limit the expansion of a firm.

(1) Economies of scale in the production of an input (for reasons give above, p. 200).

(2) A loss of control by the managers of the firm as the firm expands, particularly as that expansion involves not only increased size but also a larger range of activities.

(3) The comparative advantage held by specialist firms and a reluctance of those firms to be taken over.

Diversification

When a firm extends the range of goods or services which it produces, then the firm has diversified its activities. Diversification usually relates to a firm operating in an industry or market in which it has not previously operated. The diversification may arise through acquisition of another firm (discussed in the next chapter) or through the firm developing new products. In Chapter 2, it was seen that there are difficulties in defining industries and markets. If an industry or market is narrowly defined then firms would be more likely on average to be counted as diversified, i.e. operate in more than one industry or market, than when an industry or market is broadly defined. Usually statistics on the extent of diversification relate to firms operating in more than one three-digit (sometimes two-digit) level industry.

The traditional economic reasoning would suggest that firms would diversify if it were more profitable to do so than remain with the existing range of products, and move in the direction in which they had a comparative advantage. It could be expected that firms would move into activities which bore some relationship with their existing activities. This could involve the production of goods which are sold through the same range of shops as their existing range, thereby exploiting their relationship and knowledge of the existing distribution network. Or it could involve the development of products which use similar inputs (as the current range of output) or which use the waste products of current activities.

The expansion of firms into new geographical markets (regional, national) could be viewed as either horizontal integration or diversification. If we consider multinational enterprises as an example of diversified firms, then we can see diversification as involving the use of the knowledge about the production and marketing of a product gained in one market in other markets. Thus although geographical diversification is involved, nevertheless there are common elements in the goods produced/sold in the different geographical markets, and we have treated this under the heading of horizontal integration above. A conglomerate is a diversified firm, where it appears that the links between the products which the firm produces are very limited. Indeed, the advocates of conglomerates would argue that the benefits of conglomerates are the use of scarce high-quality management talent.

Diversification also involves risk-spreading. A diversified firm is clearly not reliant on the fortunes of a single industry. We have encountered part of this argument above (p. 191) where we reviewed the idea that large firms have lower variability of economic performance than small firms do (see also n. 4).

The measurement of the degree of diversification faces two difficulties. The first one is that mentioned above, namely how are industries and markets defined. The second one is the development of a suitable indicator of a firm's diversification, and it is that problem which we now address. If a diversified firm operated in only two industries, it would be relatively easy to summarise the extent of diversification by noting that the firm is involved in two industries and reporting the relative importance of the major and minor industry (as far as this firm is concerned). But when diversified firms operate in several industries we cannot use that simple measure. A measure of diversification needs to reflect the number of industries in which the firm operates and the extent to which the firm operates outside its main industry. It would also be useful if the measure would reflect the difference between a very small and a significant involvement by a firm in an industry. One measure of diversification which has been widely used and which incorporates these features to some degree is $W = 2(\sum_i p_i) - 1$, where p_i is the proportion of the firm's activities in the industry i when the industries have been ranked in order of importance in the firm's activities (i.e. industry 1 is the one which accounts for the greatest share of the firm's activities, and hence $p_1 >$ $p_2 > p_3$ etc.). A completely specialised firm will have $p_1 = 1$ and hence $W = 1$. A firm which operates to an equal extent in N industries will record a value of $W = N$. The index W can be interpreted on a 'numbers-equivalent' basis (cf. p. 30 above). A diversified firm operating to an unequal extent in a number of industries which records a value of W^* could be interpreted as equivalent to a firm which operated to an equal extent in W^* industries.[10]

Utton (1979) investigates the extent of diversification amongst the largest 200 UK manufacturing firms. Before reporting those results, it should be noted that the degree of diversification may be overstated in this study since vertical integration is included under diversification. On the other hand, diversification by a manufacturing firm outside manufacturing is not captured in these statistics. Diversification is measured at the three-digit industry level. Amongst the largest 200 firms in 1972, Utton (Table 2.2) reports that, on average, nearly 57 per cent of a firm's employment was in its main industry, nearly 15 per cent in its second industry. The weighted (by employment of firms) average of the W index described above was 4.39 and the unweighted average, 3.23. The excess of the weighted average over the unweighted average reflects the fact that larger firms tend to be more diversified than smaller firms. Amongst the largest 200 firms, the largest 50 firms operated in more industries than the smallest 50 firms by a margin of over one industry. Whilst some firms are highly diversified (the largest value of W recorded amongst the firms examined by Utton is 16.67), Utton concludes that 'most of the largest enterprises in the United Kingdom are still fairly cautious in their diversification policies and do not regard anywhere within the manufacturing sector as their natural domain'. The basis of this conclusion is the finding that a larger part of firms' diversification is into industries which are in the same two-digit level industrial group. Utton also finds that there has been a general upward trend in diversification over the period 1935 to 1968.

Goudie and Meeks (1982) examine the role of acquisitions and mergers in leading to diversification amongst UK companies over the period 1949 to 1973. An acquisition is measured to be diversified when a firm allocated to one two-digit level industry acquires a firm allocated to a different two-digit industry, and hence a diversification includes vertical integration. Using the measure of diversification indicated above and some related measures, Goudi and Meeks find that 33 per cent by value and 39 per cent by number of acquisitions and mergers over this period involved diversification.

Notes

1. This would have to assume that all firms within an industry benefit from a high level of concentration, rather than the largest few firms. However, few studies have allowed for the market share of each firm.

2. This does not avoid the problem that the reliance on external finance may vary with firm size. With a perfect capital market in the absence of taxation, the Modigliani-Miller theorem (Modigliani and Miller, 1958) indicates that the cost of finance will be the same whatever the source. But under other circumstances see Prais (1976), Ch. 5.

3. When net assets/capital employed is used as the measure of size the following problem arises. In a regression of the form $\pi/K = f(K)$, K (net assets) appears in the denominator of the left-hand side as well as on the right-hand side. This can generate a spurious negative relationship between profitability and size, for any measurement error in K will have the opposite impacts on π/K and K.

4. Use $V(\cdot)$ to denote variance of a variable. Then the variance of mean of n correlated variables $V(\Sigma x/n) = (nV(x) + n(n-1) C(x_i,x_j))/n^2$ where $C(x_i,x_j)$ is the multiple of deviations of x_i and x_j from their mean, and hence $C(x_i,x_j) = \tau\sigma^2$ where τ is the (common) correlation coefficient between any pair of x_i, x_j. Then $\sigma_n^2 = \sigma^2 (1 + (n-1)\tau)/n$.

5. Appeal is made to the central limit theorem which states that the probability distribution of the sum of n random variables tends to the normal distribution. Thus in this case, the distribution of the logarithm of size of firms tends to a normal distribution, and the size-distribution to log-normality. (For central limit theorem see Feller, 1957, Ch. 10, and Christ, 1966, p. 143.)

6. It also required the examination of other functional relationships (e.g. quadratic) between $\log Z_{t+1}$ and $\log Z_t$ in addition to the linear form indicated in the text.

7. $\log Z_{t+1,i} = a + c \log Z_{t,i} + u_i$ for firm i

then

$$\overline{\log Z_{t+1}} = a + c \overline{\log Z_t}$$

where bar over a variable indicates the mean value of the variable. So

$$(\log Z_{t+1,i} - \overline{\log Z_{t+1}}) = c (\log Z_{t,i} - \overline{\log Z_t}) + u_i$$

and

$$(\log Z_{t+1,i} - \overline{\log Z_{t+1}})^2 = c^2 (\log Z_{t,i} - \overline{\log Z_t})^2$$
$$+ c (\log Z_{t,i} - \overline{\log Z_t})\cdot u_i + u_i^2$$

Taking respective values leads to $var(Z_{t+1}) = c^2 var(Z_t) + var(u)$ since $E [(\log Z_t - \overline{\log Z})\cdot u] = 0$.

8. Marris (1964), Ch. 7, discussed the causes of inter-firm differences in the observed values for growth, profitability (valuation ratio), grouped into Type A (observed even if all firms had same utility function) and Type B (attributable to differences in utility function). The evidence presented by Marris points to a small and positive correlation between growth and profitability.

9. For simplicity we are here ignoring any difference between gross output which a firm produces in, say, a year and sales of that firm. In practice, gross output and sales differ through additions to or subtractions from stocks of finished products and changes in work in progress.

10. For further discussion on this, see Utton (1979), Ch. 2.

13 ACQUISITIONS AND MERGERS

Introduction

In this chapter we indicate the importance of acquisitions and mergers, outline the theories advanced to explain their occurrence and evaluate the evidence on these theories. Then we review the research done on the impact of acquisitions on the profitability of the firms involved, on the efficiency of the economy and on the level of concentration.

Acquisitions refers to cases where one firm purchases another firm from its shareholders, and control of the enlarged firm lies with the acquiring firm. Mergers, on the other hand, relates to cases where two or more companies come together to form a joint new company. The precise dividing line between acquisitions and mergers is not always clear-cut, and the form and substance of an acquisition and a merger may differ little. Thus, for example, it may appear that a merger has taken place with the formation of a new joint company on the basis of two previously independent firms, but the substance may be that one firm has acquired control over another. The number of mergers is small relative to the number of acquisitions, and we shall in this chapter for convenience use the term acquisitions to cover generally both mergers and acquisitions. However, it should be noted that in Chapter 16 on policy, we shall use the convention of talking about merger policy, which covers acquisitions and mergers. It should also be noted that some of the empirical work discussed below uses the term mergers to cover mergers and acquisitions.

The figures in Table 13.1 illustrate a number of features of the quantitative significance of acquisitions in the post-war British economy.[1] The American experience is broadly similar (see Wilcox and Shepherd (1975), p. 233), with a gradual rise in acquisition activity during the 1950s and 1960s and an intensive acquisition boom at the end of the 1960s of the same order of magnitude relative to the size of the economy as the British boom of 1968. There has also been a general slackening of acquisition activity during the 1970s. The boom in acquisition and merger activity in the late 1960s and early 1970s was also experienced in many other Western countries (see Hughes and Singh, 1980 for details).

The first part of Table 13.1 reports the acquisitions in the United Kingdom recorded by the Department of Trade and Industry. For the period 1963 to 1969, this incorporates the number of acquisitions made by companies (mainly the larger quoted ones) whose accounts were analysed by that department. From 1969 onwards, the acquisitions recorded are those on which information was available to the department, mainly derived from information in the financial press. The second, and particularly the third, columns of the first part of this table show the cyclical nature of acquisition activity with peaks of activity in 1967–8 and 1972–3.[2] It is difficult to relate the number of acquisitions made to the number of firms which are potential victims. However, Kuehn (1972) reports that over the period 1957 to 1969 about 47 per cent of quoted companies were taken over. Singh (1975) indicates that nearly one quarter of the sample of quoted companies were acquired during the four years 1967 to 1970. The other side of this coin is indicated by the extent to which companies participated in acquisition activity. Aaronovitch and Sawyer (1975b) report that over the period 1957 to 1967, 80 per cent of large quoted companies who survived the period made some acquisitions.

The final column of the first part of Table 13.1 deflates the amount paid for acquired companies in current prices by the Financial Times 500 Share Index. This seeks to make some allowance for the general variation in the level of share prices, which could be expected to affect the prices paid for acquired companies. Although it is a rather rough calculation, it does introduce an element of expressing the amount paid for acquired companies in constant prices terms.

The second part of Table 13.1 summarises the relationship between expenditure on acquiring subsidiaries (E.A.S.) and first expenditure on fixed assets and second the total uses of funds. Both these latter expenditure figures include E.A.S. and the total use of funds includes expenditure on fixed, current assets, depreciation provision and dividend payments. The first feature of these is the increasing tempo of acquisitions during the 1950s and 1960s and the rather lower levels of activity after 1973. The second feature is the considerable role played by acquisitions in the expansion of fixed assets, particularly during the years 1964 to 1972. It can be seen that over a third of the increase in fixed assets (of surviving companies) during that period can be attributed to acquisitions. We will discuss further below the relative roles of internal growth (expansion through the purchase of new assets) and external growth (expansion through the acquisition of existing assets).

Of the acquisitions and mergers shown in Table 13.1, around one quarter by number and one fifth by value were the sales of a subsidiary by one company to another, and thus did not involve the disappearance of an independent firm. Whilst during the 1960s and early 1970s a high proportion of the expenditure on acquiring other firms was met by the

Table 13.1: Acquisition Activity in the United Kingdom

(i) Acquisition activity amongst industrial and commercial companies

Year	Number of acquisitions	Consideration paid for acquired company	
		£ million	Index[a]
1963–4	914	429	117
1965–6	949	508	143
1967	763	822	216
1968	946	1946	362
1969[b]	907	935	176
1969[b]	846	1069	201
1970	793	1112	238
1971	884	911	164
1972	1210	2532	357
1973	1205	1304	213
1974	504	508	141
1975–6	334	370	74
1977–8	524	982	133
1979	534	1656	187
1980	469	1475	156
1981	452	1144	107
1982	463	2206	178
1983	447	2343	150
1984	507	5243	282

(ii) Expenditure on acquiring subsidiaries by quoted companies in manufacturing and distribution as a percentage of

	Expenditure on fixed assets	Total uses of funds
1949–53	5.3	11.1
1954–58	8.3	14.7
1959–63	15.1	30.9
1964–68	21.3	46.9
1969–72	32.7	14.3
1973–77	13.5	4.3
1978–80	13.1	5.8

a. Consideration in current prices deflated by the Financial Times Actuaries 500 Ordinary Share Index: Index in 1963 = 100.
b. Based on company accounts prior to 1970 and on the financial press and other sources since 1968.
Source: (i) Review of Monopolies and Mergers Policy (1978), updated by author with data from Business Monitor M7 and Financial Statistics.
(ii) Calculated from Business Monitor M3 (various issues).

issue of shares and fixed interest securities, since 1973 cash has been used
to finance over half of the expenditure on acquisitions. The significance
of this point is that when acquisitions were predominantly financed
through the issue of shares and fixed interest securities, then firms could
expand rapidly, provided only that they continued to receive stock market
support in the form of a reasonable share price. Amongst large acquisitions (which are looked at by the Office of Fair Trading, see Chapter
16), the proportion classified as horizontal has fluctuated around two thirds
of the total, with diversified acquisitions counting for around one quarter,
with vertical acquisitions being a minor element. However, it should be
remembered that these figures relate to large firms, which are, in general,
diversified firms (cf. pp. 204–6 above). In these figures, an acquisition
is regarded as horizontal if the two firms involved have their main activities within the same two-digit industry. The figures in the first part
of the table do not include the acquisition of British-based companies
by foreign companies, nor do they include acquisitions made overseas
by UK companies, and these acquisitions were (by value) around 20 per
cent of the domestic acquisitions.[3]

   Why do acquisitions occur? There is an embarrassingly large number
of explanations which have been advanced, many of them relating to particular historical periods and/or focusing on particular features of the stock
market (or, as it is sometimes labelled in this context, the market for
corporate control).[4] Whilst not wishing to dismiss these explanations out
of hand, we deal here only with those theories which arise out of theories
of firm behaviour. We place particular emphasis in our discussion on
deriving the predictions of the theories so that the available evidence on
acquisitions can be brought to bear on the validity of these theories. Four
approaches to acquisition activity are dealt with here, though these approaches are not entirely mutually exclusive.[5]

The Neo-classical Theory

The neo-classical theory begins with the general proposition that one firm
will bid for another firm if the value which the potential acquirer places
on the potential victim is greater than the value placed on it by its current owners. The capital value of a firm can be seen as set by the dis-
counted future expected earnings, so that value $V = \Sigma ((1 - r)/(1 + i)^t) \cdot \pi^e_t$, where π^e_t is expected profits in time period t, i is the rate of
discount and r is the retention ratio. Let us label the value of the firm
to its current owners as V_c, and the value to a potential acquirer as V_a.

The two values placed on the firm can diverge because of differences in r, π^e_t, i or T. The potential acquirer may have a longer time horizon than the present owners, and this would be reflected in the use of a higher value of T leading to a higher value of V. An acquirer which believed that it could increase profits by, say, raising efficiency would also place a higher value on the firm than the current owners.

A further possibility of some importance is that of synergy, sometimes expressed as '2 + 2 = 5'. In other words, the sum of the whole is greater than the sum of the parts so that the post-acquisition firm is able to operate more profitably than the two previously independent pre-acquisition firms. Numerous possibilities for the sources of synergy have been suggested, but two are of some importance. These are the possibility of increased market power and of the reduction in costs arising from rationalisation of surplus capacity leading to lower unit costs.

The price actually paid for a firm by its acquirer can, then, be expected to lie between V_c and V_a. The major emphasis of the neo-classical approach is, however, on differences in the value placed on a firm arising from differences in expected future profitability. Acquisitions are seen as a route through which efficiency and profitability are raised as firms are acquired by new owners who believe they are able to raise profitability. This process would be mutually advantageous to the firms involved. The owners of the acquired firm benefit through realising a higher value for their ownership of the firm than previously, and the acquirers gain through the purchase of the firm at a price less than the value they place on it.

This process is, however, often seen as the major mechanism through which firms and their controllers are pressed towards profit-maximising behaviour. Departure from profit maximisation opens the way for V_a to exceed V_c through differences in current profits and those which the acquirer believes he could achieve. This line of argument is probably more applicable to the case of a quoted company with numerous shareholders than it is to a privately owned firm. In the former case, where the identity of owners and controllers coincide, lower profits and capital value can continue in that any potential acquirer cannot enforce the sale of shares by existing shareholders.

The extent of any gain to the acquiring firm, and the extent to which a firm can allow its value to fall below the maximum achievable, depends upon two factors. First, there are the costs of acquisition. If these costs are, in some relevant sense, large then the chances of an acquisition being profitable for the potential acquirer are reduced.

The second factor is the size of the pool of potential acquirers. If that pool is large, it could be expected that there will be competition amongst the potential acquirers, which tends to bid up the price which is offered for the victim firm. The upper limit to the price would be expected to be that price which leaves it only just worth while for the acquisition to proceed. Hence it could be expected that when there are a large number of potential acquirers, the price is bid up close to that upper limit. In such a case, the shareholders of the acquired firms would gain, and those of the acquiring firm would gain little.

The Theory of Marris

We have outlined the theory of Marris on the behavoiur of corporations in Chapter 11, and it is only necessary here to draw out the implications for acquisitions. The constraint on the managers in their pursuit of growth in this theory arose from the takeover threat. A faster growth rate required a higher retention ratio and lower dividend pay-out ratio, leading to a lower valuation ratio. There were two variants on the takeover threat. First, the probability of being acquired rose with a declining valuation ratio, and second there was a minimum valuation ratio below which the corporation was certain of being acquired.

The clear prediction is that the frequency of acquisition will be greater as the valuation ratio is lower. There may be difficulties in measuring the valuation ratio (the ratio of share market value to the value of the assets of the firm), for both numerator and denominator present measurement problems. Whilst the market value for quoted companies is easily obtainable, the share price fluctuates from day to day, and more importantly the general level of share prices exhibits large fluctuations over time. The denominator can be approximated by the book value of the firm. But firms differ in the extent to which book values and the real value of the assets diverge. This divergence can arise from factors like inadequate accounting for depreciation, and failure to revalue assets to take account of inflation.

There are some common features in the neo-classical theory and that of Marris. Both of them see acquisitions as playing a key role in limiting the extent to which firms can depart from profit maximisation and still survive. Departures from profit maximisation can arise from inefficiencies (reflected in a sub-maximum π) in the formula for V above and/or from sacrificing dividends for growth (which is particularly important in the theory of Marris). Especially in the theory of Marris, a take-over bid is seen as an essentially hostile act at least as far as the present managers are concerned. The threat of acquisition is seen as the major constraint on the current controllers and actual take-over is the punishment for overstepping the mark.

Both of these theories focus on the characteristics of firms which are predicted to be acquired, and say little about the characteristics of the firms predicted to make the acquisitions. For example, the neo-classical theory indicates that firms with profitability below the potential maximum would be a prime candidate for acquisition. This is often translated into a firm with low profitability will tend to be acquired. But whilst the acquirer is expected to raise profitability nothing is said directly about the current profitability of the acquirer (assuming that it is operating another firm). If there is a correlation between the acquirer's pre-acquisition record of profitability and its ability to raise the acquired firm's profitability then it would be expected that the profitability of the acquirer would be relatively high and would tend to be above that of the acquired firm.

The theory of Marris predicts that acquired firms have below average valuation ratios, and the frequency of acquisition rises with declining valuation ratios. On a similar argument to that which concluded the previous paragraph, it could be argued that the valuation ratio of an acquiring firm will be above that of the victim firm.

Market Power Theory

There are a number of approaches to the explanation of acquisitions and mergers which can be loosely grouped under the heading of market power. This approach is taken by, *inter alia*, Aaronovitch and Sawyer (1975a) and George and Silberston (1975). These approaches place the seeking of market power and strengthening of position as key elements. In contrast to the other approaches, these approaches make little of the distinction between acquisition and merger, and view most acquisitions as being agreed by both parties and intended to strengthen the joint position of the firms involved. These market power approaches may not be inconsistent with acquisitions and mergers made to exploit profit oportunities, but rather stress the increased market power as an important source of increased profits. The market power approaches also stress adverse circumstances as a stimulus to the consideration of acquisition and merger as a way of seeking to overcome adversity.

Since there are a number of approaches which are placed under this general umbrella, there are a number of not necessarily consistent strands of thought. We highlight three strands as of particular importance.

The first strand is that acquisitions and mergers are undertaken to increase the market power of the firms involved. This market power may arise in the product market or in the factor markets, and would lead to an ability to charge higher prices for output and/or buy inputs at a lower cost. The search for market power in the product market can only be an explanation for acquisitions and mergers between firms producing similar output. But diversified mergers and acquisitions may still enhance market power in factor markets.

The second and related strand sees adverse changes in the economic climate acting as a trigger in the search for market power. Three particular types of changes have been stressed. The first is a fall in demand, relative to capacity, which leaves the industry with excess capacity and faced with the prospect of price cutting competition and declining profits. The elimination of the excess capacity is achieved with less difficulty after the merger of some of the firms involved, rather than the removal of excess capacity through price competition, profit declines and bankruptcy. The second type is an increase in international competition with the invasion of domestic markets by foreign producers. It has been argued, for example, that the formation of Imperial Tobacco in 1901 from 13 constituent firms was a response to the formation of American Tobacco and the threat of import penetration from that company (Evely and Little, 1960; Monopolies Commission, 1961). Aaronovitch and Sawyer (1975a, Chapter 12) emphasise the destabilising role of increased international competition on British firms and their response of making acquisitions to try to meet the competition and also to reduce rivalry. A third type of change can arise from legislative change, particularly the virtual outlawing of restrictive practices. For then co-operation between independent companies is made illegal, but if acquisitions are not controlled then co-operation between these companies can continue if they are under common ownership.[6]

The third strand stresses the importance of size, particularly size relative to rivals, customers and suppliers. Size may be useful in any protracted battle with rivals and allows a firm to outlast its rivals. It may be useful in bargaining with suppliers and customers. It may help to protect a firm from being acquired by other firms with whom it does not wish to be associated. To the extent to which it is size relative to others, rather than absolute size, which is of importance, there will be a ratchet effect at work. As one firm increases its size and power, it diminishes the relative size and power of other firms providing those other firms with an incentive to merge to restore the balance.

These strands are consistent with the view that the seeking of profits lies behind mergers and acquisitions. But the emphasis is on market power rather than productive efficiency as the source of increased profits. Further, acquisitions are seen as playing a much smaller role in disciplining inefficient firms.

Managerial Interests

The theory of Marris can be extended in a manner which suggests that the pursuit of managerial interests lies behind many acquisitions. That theory suggested that managerial interests can be proxied by growth size and security. One way in which size can be quickly increased is through acquisitions, particularly when financed by share-exchange rather than by cash. The security motive led Marris to argue that a firm must maintain a particular valuation ratio. But if size confers security on a firm by reducing the probability of being acquired then the firm has an incentive to make acquisitions itself in order to avoid being acquired itself. Thus fast growth leading to increased size rather than a higher valuation ratio becomes the route through which security from take-over is achieved. Further, a positive linkage between size of firm and the income of the executives would generate incentives for the executives to promote acquisitions to increase size and thereby their income. In sum, there may be considerable incentives for managers, arising from the advantages to them of increased size of their firm, to promote acquisitions for faster growth and increases in size.

Review of Evidence on Acquisitions[7]

We review the evidence on the characteristics of firms involved in acquisitions in terms of profitability, valuation ratio, growth and size. The studies surveyed here have used a number of different statistical techniques, often of a sophisticated nature, and some of the differences in the results reported may arise from the different techniques used. There may be important differences between different periods of time and different countries. The fluctuations in acquisition activity indicated in Table 13.1 are suggestive that there are times when acquisitions are in fashion and other times when they are not. The reduced pace of acquisition activity in recent years is associated with a much reduced pace of research activity in that area. Much of the research on acquisitions relates to the 1960s and early 1970s.

Profitability

We begin with the profitability of firms involved in acquisitions. Kuehn (1975) investigated the characteristics of all UK quoted companies over the period 1957 to 1969 involving over 3,000 firms each allocated to one of 67 industries. The technique used is a linear probability model in which a dummy variable with a value of zero if the firm was not acquired during the period or of unity if the firm was acquired is regressed on variables describing characteristics of the firm such as profitability, growth, valuation ratio and size (and other variables which do not directly concern us here). Of the 66 industries for which estimation was possible, the number in which profitability had a significant negative impact on the likelihood of being acquired varied between 12 and 22 depending on how profitability and other variables were measured. Kuehn estimated six regressions for each industry involving profitability but only reports the results of the best two regressions for each industry, with one of the regressions involving absolute values of profitability, growth, etc., and one involving relative (to industry average) values of those variables. For the regression result which uses the absolute values for profitability, in 49 of them profitability has a negative impact on the likelihood of being acquired (of which 24 are statistically significant), and a positive impact in the other 17, but only in one case is that impact significant.

Singh (1971) analysed acquisitions amongst quoted companies in four 2-digit-level industries during the years 1955 to 1960. He makes two types of comparisons between firms acquired and those which are not. First, he compares the characteristics of each acquired firm with the corresponding median value of those characteristics for the firm's industry. Second, he forms a sample of non-acquired firms matched with the group of acquired firms in terms of size. Our immediate concern is with the differences in profitability between acquired and non-acquired firms, and with both methods Singh finds a significant difference in profitability in the anticipated direction. Singh (1975) repeats the first type of comparison for the period 1967 to 1970, when the rate of acquisition was much faster (as illustrated in Table 13.1). During that period, the profitability of acquired firms was below the industry median for 58 per cent of acquired firms, and this differs from a 50 per cent for all firms to the extent which is statistically significant at the 10 per cent level only.

Singh (1971) also compares the performance of acquired firms with that of their acquirers. The profit rates of acquiring firms are on average higher than the rates of acquired firms. But there is considerable overlap between profit experience of acquirers and acquired and the profit rate of many acquired firms exceeds that of many acquirers. One measure of overlap is how many firms would be mis-classified if a prediction were made as to which firms would be acquired and which would be acquirers based on profit record. On this basis, 42 per cent of firms would be mis-classified on the basis of their two-year average profit record, and this can be compared with 50 per cent mis-classification if a random prediction were made.[8] However, for the period 1967 to 1970, Singh (1975) finds that whilst on average the profitability of acquiring firms is higher than that of the acquired firms, the difference is not significant.

Newbould (1970) suggests that, for the year 1967–8, there was no significant difference between acquiring and acquired.

Finally, we can look at the profit record of acquisition-intensive firms. Kuehn (1972) focuses on firms who made more than three acquisitions ('raiders') and finds that the profit rates of raiders do not differ significantly from those of all firms. But the profit rate of raiders was significantly lower than that for firms which survived.

Singh (1971) drew up a sample of non-acquiring firms which are matched by year and industry with the population of acquiring firms. The acquiring firm tended to be slightly more profitable than the non-acquiring firm, but the difference in profitability was not significant.

Mueller (1980a) summarises the conclusions of studies undertaken within a common format on the causes and consequences of acquisitions and mergers in seven countries (Belgium, France, Germany, the Netherlands, Sweden, the UK and the USA).[9] Mueller (1980a) concludes that

> in Belgium and the Netherlands the acquiring firms were somewhat less profitable than the control group companies; in France, slightly more so. In the other four countries the two groups appeared to be roughly equal in profitability. In contrast, the acquired firms tended to be either as or less profitable than the control group companies. Thus, the acquiring companies turned out to be as profitable or more profitable than the firms they acquired.

Levine and Aaronovitch (1981) investigated all acquisitions and mergers involving British manufacturing and distribution firms in 1972 in which more than £3 million was paid for the acquired firm. They were largely concerned in making comparisons between the acquiring firms and the acquired firms (on average and a pairwise comparison between each acquiring firm and its victim), and with some comparisons between firms involved in acquisitions and other firms. Their univariate results found 'no evidence of any significant differences between [acquiring], [acquired] and all companies for the profit-related variables [rate of return, earnings per share] and their growth' (text in brackets added). However, in a multivariate analysis, the rate of return did sometimes (depending on which other variables were included) contribute significantly to discriminating between acquiring and acquired firms.

Valuation Ratio

The valuation ratio plays a key role in the theory of Marris, and in particular the lower the valuation ratio the higher the probability of being acquired, with the possibility of a minimum value of the ratio at which acquisition becomes a virtual certainty. The inverse relationship between the valuation ratio and the probability of being acquired is largely supported by the evidence of Kuehn (1975), summarised in Table 13.2, in which the frequency of being acquired for different valuation ratio groups is given. Further, in 59 industries (out of 66 examined) the valuation ratio was found to be a significant determinant of the likelihood of being acquired. Levine and Aaronovitch (1981) report (their Table III) in their sample relating to 1972 that whilst nearly 30 per cent of the acquired firms had a valuation ratio below 1 so did nearly 15 per cent of the acquiring firms. At the other end of the spectrum, 25 per cent of the acquired firms had a valuation ratio of above 2 as did nearly 50 per cent of the acquiring firms. The valuation ratios of the acquiring firms were generally higher than the ratios for the acquired firms (univariate analysis). In a multivariate analysis, after allowances have been made for the size of firm (which appears to influence the valuation ratio of a firm), they find that the valuation ratio is a significant discriminator between acquiring and acquired firms.

Singh (1971) found much less support for the Marris proposition, and states that:

> although the valuation ratio of the taken-over firms is significantly less than that of the non-taken-over firms, there is a very considerable overlap between the two groups. In the period studied, there was a relatively large number of acquired firms with above average valuation ratio, and a similarly large proportion of non-taken-over firms whose valuation ratios were below the average for their respective industries.

When Singh compares acquiring and acquired firms, he finds that 'the acquiring firms have higher valuation ratios than the acquired ones'.

Table 13.2: Frequency of Firms being Acquired by Valuation Ratio

Valuation ratio	Frequency of firms being acquired
0.0–0.5	0.840
0.5–1.1	0.499
1.1–2.0	0.284
2.0–3.0	0.216
3.0–4.0	0.089
over 4.0	0.169

Source: Calculated from Kuehn (1975).

Newbould (1970) similarly finds no basic difference between acquired and acquirer for terms of valuation.

Finally, Kuehn (1972) finds that 'raiders have on average higher valuation ratios than the average for all firms, including those which disappeared, but there is no difference between raiders and other surviving firms'.

Growth

Kuehn (1975) reports that growth of assets has a negative impact on the likelihood of firms being acquired in 60 industries (out of 66 considered), with a significant effect on that likelihood in up to 27 industries. Singh (1971, 1975) finds that whilst growth is a significant determinant of which firms are acquired in the earlier period of 1955 to 1960, it is not in the later period of 1967 to 1970.

Aaronovitch and Sawyer (1975b) report that prior to acquisition the acquiring firm grew (on average) substantially faster than the acquired firm, and in the two years prior to acquisition, in 59 cases out of 77 the acquirer grew faster than the acquired firm.

Singh (1971, 1975) reports significantly higher growth for the acquirer as compared with the acquired firm for the earlier period. But whilst the acquiring firm grew on average by 43 per cent over three years against an average of 28 per cent for the acquired firm in the later period, this difference was not a significant one.

Kuehn (1972) finds that nearly all raiders grew faster than the median rate for their industry. Singh (1971) reports significant higher growth for acquiring firms over non-acquiring firms for his matched sample.

Mueller (1980a) in his summary of seven country studies referred to above finds that

Table 13.3: Proportion of Firms Taken Over by Initial
Size-class of Firms

Asset size in 1954	Percent taken over between 1955 and 1960
Up to £¼ million	20.1
£¼–£½ million	24.5
£½–£1 million	26.0
£1–£2 million	16.6
£2–£4 million	18.3
over £4 million	9.6

Source: Derived from Singh (1971).

a fairly consistent pattern of growth rate differences holds up across all countries. Acquiring firms grow as fast or faster than the size-matched control group non-acquiring firms. Acquired firms grow as fast as their control group companies, except in the United Kingdom where they grow a bit more slowly and in West Germany where they grow considerably more slowly. Acquiring firms thus are generally faster growing than the companies they acquire. The latter proposition holds for every country but France, where acquiring and acquired firms grow at roughly equal rates.

Size

The likelihood of a firm being acquired has often been found to decrease with size, at least amongst relatively large firms. Singh (1971) finds a non-linear relationship between size and frequency of acquisition, and this is illustrated in Table 13.3. Aaronovitch and Sawyer (1975b) find a general decline in the disappearance rate with increasing size, but all the firms in their sample would have been in the top size-class used by Singh. Kuehn (1975) finds that the likelihood only declines with increasing size for the largest firms (although Singh (1976) argues that those results may be misleading in that the size of acquired firms is taken for the year prior to acquisition whereas that of non-acquired firms is the average over the 13-year period). Further, Kuehn finds that only in a few industries does size play a significant role in determining the likelihood of being acquired. However, in the regression results reported by Kuehn, the impact of size is indicated to decrease the likelihood of being acquired in 56 industries out of 66, although the effect is only statistically significant in seven industries. Singh (1971, 1975) finds that for all the periods he considered the size of the acquiring firm is on average greater than that of the acquired firm, with the difference in mean size statistically significant.

Indeed, Singh (1971) concludes that 'the most important feature distinguishing the acquiring firm from the acquired appears to be their much higher rate of growth and very much larger size'. This view is also reflected in the conclusion of Levine and Aaronovitch (1981), who point to 'the overwhelming importance of size for picking out potential raiders as opposed to potential victims in takeovers . . . '. Mueller (1980a) also reports that in the seven country studies surveyed there is a consistent pattern with 'acquiring firms . . . larger than randomly selected firms from their industries, larger than the average firm in their industries, and larger than the firms they acquire'.

Of the four characteristics examined, the first two (profitability and valuation ratio) can be thought of as particularly relevant in the first two approaches described above (the neo-classical and Marris theories). The second two characteristics (growth and size) are seen as particularly relevant by the second two approaches. The evidence presented above has been conflicting, but it would on the whole appear to give rather more support to the importance of growth and size than it does to the importance of profitability.

Evidence on Impact of Acquisitions

We now review some of the impacts of acquisition on the firms involved and on the rest of the economy. The four types of impacts singled out for attention are on the profitability of firms involved, on the wealth of shareholders, on efficiency and on the level of concentration. The first three, of course, are related. A change in profitability, which could arise from a change in the efficiency of the firm, is likely to affect the share price of the firm. But increases in profits following an acquisition may arise from increases in market power. Further, the shareholders of the acquired firm gain more than the shareholders of the acquiring firm when a premium price is paid for the acquired firm.

The effects of acquisitions at the firm level have been discussed almost exclusively in terms of profits, growth and efficiency, with little regard for the possibly important effects on employment, regional development, etc. When mergers and acquisitions increase efficiency they involve changing the balance between inputs and outputs, and this will often mean a reduction in inputs rather than an increase in output. Any reduction in inputs will generally mean a reduction in employment of labour in the firms concerned. The impact which that reduction has on unemployment will clearly depend upon the state of the labour market, but will often involve some transitional unemployment. The costs of this unemployment has then to be set against benefits from the efficiency gains. One study (Cowling *et al.*, 1980, Chapter 8) of the merger of AEI, English Electric and GEC estimated that the unemployment generated by the rationalisation which followed the merger was equivalent to over 1,500 person-years.[10]

There is a temptation in the investigation of the impacts of acquisitions to assume that acquisitions always have the same impacts when they occur for a variety of reasons and may have different consequences. Thus an unambiguous answer to questions like what is the impact of acquisitions on concentration may not be possible.

The major problem is assessing the consequences is that a counterfactual alternative is required with which the actual outcome can be compared. When investigating the impact of acquisitions on profitability, the general approach has been to compare the experiences of firms involved in acquisitions with those not involved. In making such comparisons often some of the acquiring firms have to be omitted. The comparisons require the experience of profitability of the acquiring firms during a period when the effect of the acquisition on the firm has been absorbed and during which its operations are not disturbed by further acquisitions. Thus, for example, Utton (1974b) compared the experience of firms *uninvolved* in acquisitions with firms which were very active acquirers in the period 1961–5 and relied mainly on internal growth in the next five years.

Acquisitions may be a response to a deteriorating situation.[11] This would imply that in the absence of acquisition profits were expected to fall, and so the experience of firms uninvolved in acquisitions may not be relevant for the experience of firms involved in acquisitions.

On Profitability

Utton (1974b) surveys 13 studies of the impact of acquisitions on profitability and classifies five of them as suggesting that acquisition worsened the profit situation of the acquiring firms, six studies indicating no difference between acquiring firms and non-acquirers and two showing an improvement in profitability. However, whilst some of these studies looked at the rate of return on assets employed, others were concerned with the behaviour of the share price (e.g. change in share price, growth in share price plus dividends). These share-price measures are more concerned with the benefits to the shareholders than with profitability directly. Movements in the share price can reflect many influences including the stock market's assessment of the profitability of the acquisition and the division of benefits from acquisition between the shareholders of the acquired firm and those of the acquiring firm.

The studies surveyed by Utton (and most of them are also surveyed by Meeks (1977), Appendix C) were mainly American and covering various periods of this century. The two studies which indicated improved profitability were both for the post-war period in the USA.[12]

Utton's own study focuses on the effect of acquisitions during the period 1954 to 1965 on the rate of return on assets during the period 1966–70. He compares a sample of 39 acquisition-intensive firms with a matched sample of 39 companies which grew mainly from internal sources. The acquisition-intensive firms were required to have obtained at least one-fifth of their assets in 1965 by acquisition and to have made considerable acquisitions during the period 1961 to 1965. Given the manner of constructing the samples, it is perhaps not surprising that the acquisition-intensive group grew much faster than the non-acquisition group during the period 1961 to 1965. But in the subsequent period of 1966 to 1970 there was no significant difference between the growth experience of the two groups. The average profit rate of the non-acquiring group was however significantly higher than the rate for the acquisition-intensive group, in both periods examined. For example, in the second period the acquisition-intensive group had an average rate of profit of 11.5 per cent whereas the non-acquiring group had a rate of 14.2 per cent, and this difference was statistically significant at the 1 per cent level.

The price paid by the acquiring firm for the acquired firm often exceeds the book value of the acquired firm. Thus the assets of the acquired firm enter the balance sheet of the acquiring firm with a higher value than they entered the balance sheet of the acquired firm before acquisition. If profits remain unchanged, the measured rate of profit is lower because the assets are now more highly valued. The study of Meeks (1977) made some allowance for such effects and standardised for the profitability of the industries in which the firms operate. The method adopted by Meeks was to compare the profitability, adjusted and standardised as indicated above, of the merging firms before and after acquisition. Thus, implicitly, the profit experience of firms involved in acquisitions is compared with the profit experience of other surviving firms. One problem of this approach is that firms which are very acquisition-intensive are omitted from the analysis since the post-acquisition profit experience is only calculated up to the year prior to a second acquisition. Partly as a result of that, the analysis covers roughly one-third of all acquisitions of one quoted company made by another during the period 1964 to 1972. The results of this study are summarised by Table 13.4 and show a decline in profitability after acquisition, apart from the year in which the

Table 13.4: Post-acquisition Profitability and Proportions of
Firms showing a Decline in Profits

Year after acquisition	Number of firms	Change in profitability[a]	Per cent of firms with lower profits
0	213	0.148[b]	34
1	192	−0.015	54
2	174	−0.010	52
3	146	−0.058[b]	53
4	103	−0.098[b]	66
5	67	−0.110[b]	64
6	44	−0.067	52
7	21	−0.073	62

a. Profitability of the amalgamation adjusted and standardised as described
in text less 3-year pre-merger profitability of the amalgamation (similarly
standardised).
b. Significantly different from zero at 1 per cent level.
Source: Meeks (1977).

acquisition is made which Meeks argues could be attributed to remaining measurement problems. The declining number of firms as the number of years after acquisition increases reflects both the participation of acquirers in further acquisitions and that the number of years for which post-acquisition data are available is limited by data only being available up to the end of 1972.

Cosh, Hughes and Singh (1980) examine acquisitions and mergers involving large UK companies in the years 1967 to 1969. They find that, for a variety of measures of profitability, there is little difference between acquiring firms and a control group of firms. In the case of post-tax profitability on equity there is 'weak evidence that merging firms are more profitable in the post-merger period than the matched control group companies'.

The survey of Mueller (1980b) referred to above indicates that the impact of mergers and acquisitions on profitability does not show a consistent pattern between countries.

Firth (1979) investigated whether the shareholders of the acquirer and acquired gain or lose from the take-over acquisition. From a study of acquisition during the period of 1972 to 1974 in the United Kingdom, he concluded that the stock market performance of the acquired firm prior to the take-over bid had been poor. But on the day of the take-over bid, the share price of the potential acquisition leapt by an average of 22 per cent. In contrast, acquiring firms had slightly better pre-bid stock market performance but their share prices generally fell on the day of the bid. Firth calculated that in four-fifths of the acquisitions the shareholders of the acquiring firm suffered a loss through the take-over bid. The average loss to shareholders (per firm) was around £3 million, which was almost exactly balanced by the gain to shareholders of the acquired firm.[13] In contrast Halpern (1973) in his investigation of acquisitions of firms quoted on the New York Stock Exchange, found the gains arising from the acquisitions were divided equally between the shareholders of the two firms involved.

On Efficiency

Discussion of the impact of acquisitions on efficiency can draw on the studies of the impact on profitability to some extent. If profits decline after an acquisition there is a presumption that efficiency has declined also. An increase in profits does not necessarily carry the connotation of increased efficiency since the increase may have arisen through the exploitation of increased market power. The work of Cowling *et al.* (1980) focused more directly than other studies on changes in efficiency and market power. They investigated nine important horizontal acquisitions which occurred in the period 1966–9. They find a 'wide diversity in the performance of firms after merger, and that to attempt generalisations is rather ambitious'. However, 'efficiency gains from mergers are in general not found. Market power has been enhanced and we have some specific indications of its use. The judgement must therefore be against mergers'.

The results reported by Newbould (1970) are not dissimilar. Based on a survey of managers in 38 public companies which had made acquisitions during 1967 and 1968, the study records that after 2 years 17 companies reported no beneficial effects of any kind.

On Growth

When the impacts of acquisitions on growth and on concentration are being assessed, counter-factual alternatives have again to be presented. For the acquiring firm the question is what would have been done with the resources used in making the acquisition. Where the payment for the acquisition is made in cash, the acquiring firm could have used the cash for the purchase of other assets. In that case, the immediate size of the firm (in terms of assets) is unaffected by the acquisition, although later growth may be affected by the acquisition. However, many acquisitions are paid by share exchange in which the acquiring firm issues new shares which are taken by the shareholders of the acquired firm in exchange for their previous shareholding. In this case it is unlikely that the acquiring firm would have issued the same volume of new shares or have been able to sell them in the absence of an acquisition. Most studies have implicitly assumed that the resources obtained by the acquiring firm through acquisition are net additions to the firm's assets.

Aaronovitch and Sawyer (1975b) calculate that between one-quarter and one-third of growth of surviving firms during the period 1958 to 1968 can be attributed to acquisitions. Meeks (1977) finds that over the period 1948 to 1964, internal growth of quoted companies averaged 6.1 per cent per annum and external growth averaged 2.9 per cent per annum, but during the period 1964 to 1970 acquisitions became more important and raised external growth rate average to 6.0 per cent, whilst the internal growth rate slipped slightly to 5.8 per cent per annum.

Aaronovitch and Sawyer (1975b) investigated whether internal and external growth were substitutes or complements for each other, and found some weak support for the complementary view. They also find that the overall growth rate of firms increased with the proportion of growth attributed to acquisitions. Meeks (1977) finds rather stronger evidence for the complementarity of internal and external growth, and reports that '[t]he active acquirer appears then to have invested more heavily than average in new fixed assets too'.

Kumar (1981) investigated a related question of the impact of acquisitions on the level of investment. His investigation covered the period 1967 to 1974 and involved 354 acquisitions. He compared the pre-acquisition and post-acquisition investment (relative to investment in the industry of the firm concerned) and found that 'the marked feature of the results . . . is that the *average* investment share of merging [acquiring and acquired] firms shows an improvement over the pre-merger level for all post-merger years'. The rise in post-merger investment was more pronounced for non-horizontal mergers and for firms making multiple acquisitions and relatively small acquisitions.

On Concentration

The calculated impact of acquisitions on concentration is sensitive to the measure of concentration used. With the n-firm concentration ratio, an acquisition by one of the largest n firms will increase the ratio by the extent of the acquisition. For an acquisition by a firm outside the largest n there will be no measured impact unless the acquisition brings the acquiring firm into the largest n when the ratio would increase by the excess of the post-acquisition share of the acquirer and the share of the nth firm. For the Herfindahl index, an increase will always be registered following an acquisition. If firm i acquired firm j, then the contribution of these firms to the index changes from $s_i^2 + s_j^2$ to $(s_i + s_j)^2$, an increase of $2s_i s_j$, with the contribution of the other firms remaining unchanged.

Table 13.5: Estimates of the Contribution of Acquisitions to the Growth of Concentration

Study	Aaronovitch and Sawyer (1975b)	Hart, Utton and Walshe (1973)	Hannah and Kay (1977)		Utton (1971)
Time period	1958–67	1958–63	1957–69	1969–73	1954–65
Level of aggregation, coverage, etc.	Manufacturing and distribution. Large quoted companies	Sample of 30 manufacturing industries	Manufacturing companies		Large companies
Measure of concentration[a]	CR 100	CR5	Numbers-equivalent based on Herfindahl index		Variance of logs
Percentage of the increase in concentration attributed to acquisitions	62%	One-third of industries were categorised as 'increasing concentration with mergers'. Concentration increases in those industries accounted for 82% of total increases	133%[b]	Concentration did not change. The impact of acquisitions would have reduced numbers-equivalent from 78 to 74	41–49%

a   The studies often use a number of measures, of which one is selected for reporting here.
b   I.e. concentration would have declined in the absence of acquisitions.

However, for the Gini coefficient and the variance of logs the joining together of two small firms reduces inequality, for the resulting firm is closer to the average than the two component firms were. The acquisition by a firm above average size has two impacts — the increased size of the acquiring firm increases inequality but the disappearance of the acquired firm may decrease inequality if that firm is well below average size.[14]

A summary of the calculated impact of acquisitions on concentration is given in Table 13.5. In addition to those studies, Hart and Clarke (1980), using a case study approach, concluded for the period that 'mergers were primarily responsible for increases in concentration in fourteen products out of a sample of 27 . . . It is not possible to estimate with much precision but our results, based on the case studies, suggest that mergers were responsible for about half of the average increase in product concentration from 1958 to 1968'.

From our discussion above, it will be appreciated that some of the differences indicated in Table 13.5 may arise from the use of different measures of concentration. But it is clear that for Britain acquisitions have been an important part of increasing concentration.

Another way of looking at the impact of acquisitions on concentration is to see to what extent acquisitions can be said to have crated or strengthened a situation of monopoly. Using the definition of a monopoly as a firm having more than a 25 per cent share of a market (which is the definition used in British monopoly legislation), it has been estimated that of the nearly 1800 proposed acquisitions considered by the Mergers Panel over the period 1965 to 1978 for possible reference to the Monopolies and Mergers Commission, some 22 per cent were creating or strengthening a monopoly position.

Notes

1. There are numerous ways of measuring the importance of acquisition activity. A full list of proposed measures is given in Aaronovitch and Sawyer (1975a), Ch. 7.

2. For attempts to relate the cyclical movements in acquisition and merger activity, see Aaronovitch and Sawyer (1975a), Ch. 12 (for the UK) and Nelson (1959) (for the United States).

3. The discussion in this paragraph is based on calculations made from *Business Monitor M7* (various issues) and the Annual Report of the Office of Fair Trading; these publications can be referred to for up to date information on these subjects.

4. For discussion of some other approaches see Gort (1969).

5. For an alternative review of theories on acquisitions and mergers see Hughes and Singh (1980).

6. Elliot and Gribbin (1977) calculate that in industries where restrictive practices had been struck down in the previous few years, the level of concentration (*CR5*) increased by 10 percentage points over the period 1958–68, as compared with an increase of 6.73 percentage points in other industries.

The views of a manager intimately involved in a merger are of interest:

> A subsidiary reason for considering a merger lay in the break up of the Standard Metal Window agreement. . . . A financial merger between Hope's and Crittall, even if they traded as separate companies, would allow the two companies to agree common selling prices between themselves without breaking the law. Hopefully this might do something towards maintaining the fragile price level of the standard metal window trade (Hope, 1976).

7. For a tabulation and discussion of much relevant evidence which overlaps with this review, see Levine and Aaronovitch (1981), especially Appendix 2.

8. The differences between the means of two samples can be statistically significant but there can still be considerable overlap between the two samples. For example, suppose we know that the standard deviations for two populations, A and B, are equal at 10, and that with a sample of 100 from each population the sample means are 12 and 14.5 respectively. Then the standard deviation for the difference of the mean size is $10/(100)^{\frac{1}{2}}$, i.e. 1. Hence the *t*-ratio for the difference of the means of 2.5 which indicates statistically significant difference at the 5 per cent level. But the overlap between the two samples would be such that 45 per cent would be mis-classified if a given observation were assigned to population A or B on the basis of whether it was above or below the median of the 200 observations.

9. The seven country studies are published in Mueller (1980b), of which Mueller (1980a) is one of the concluding chapters.

10. Calculated from their Table 8.3.

11. For example, Newbould (1970) reports that in a sample survey of 38 larger public companies, which acquired other firms during 1967 and 1968, in seven cases the acquired company had approached the acquiring company, mainly because of deteriorating business conditions.

12. However, Honeycutt (1975) queries the conclusions of one of those studies (Lev and Mandelker, 1972) and argues that merging firms were less profitable than non-merging firms.

13. Franks *et al.* (1977) investigated acquisitions in the breweries and distillery sector. The gains to the shareholders of the acquired company were similar to those found by Firth (1979). The shareholders in the acquiring company did not receive any sustained gains.

14. For further discussion on measures of concentration and the impact of acquisitions on concentration, especially in connection with the variance of logs, see Sawyer (1979b).

PART THREE:

ECONOMICS OF POLICY

14 THE WELFARE LOSS OF MONOPOLY

The Measurement of Welfare Loss Under Monopoly

The traditional case against monopoly has been that a monopoly charged a higher price and produced a lower output than an atomistically competitive industry would have done. The measurement of monopoly welfare loss is an attempt to quantify the losses arising from these higher prices and lower output levels.

We begin by looking at the basis of the conventional way of calculating the welfare loss of monopoly. In this case, it is assumed that production takes place at constant unit costs, which are the same under monopoly as they would be under atomistic competition. The monopolist, in terms of Figure 14.1, charges a price p_m and produces output q_m. Under perfect competition, price p_c would be equal to marginal cost, and with constant costs assumption this is equal to average cost (ac). Thus price is higher under monopoly to the extent of $p_m - p_c$, and output lower to the extent of $q_c - q_m$.

The loss of consumer surplus arising from a monopoly situation rather than an atomistic competitive one is given by the area $A + B$ in Figure 14.1.[1] However, the equivalent of the area B is transferred from consumers to the monopolist in the form of monopoly profits, since the area $B = (p_m - ac) \cdot q_m$. Thus the net social welfare loss is equivalent to the area A.

The visual impression given by Figure 14.1 is that the area A is much smaller than the area B, and this is generally confirmed by other calculations. For the area A is $\frac{1}{2}(p_m - p_c) \cdot (q_c - q_m)$, so that the relative size of the area A to the area B is $\frac{1}{2}(q_m - q_c)/q_m$.

Monopoly welfare loss calculations are intended to relate to the *net* loss to the economy arising from monopoly. But that net loss is the balance between gains to monopolists and losses to consumers, and hence the net figures hide the redistribution of income between consumers and firms (as compared with a perfectly competitive outcome).

The monopoly welfare loss is equivalent to $\frac{1}{2}(p_m - p_c) \cdot (q_m - q_c)$. The calculation of the welfare loss requires information on the four magnitudes involved. The values of p_m and q_m are observable, and p_c is taken as equivalent to average costs ac. The remaining variable, q_c, is more difficult to locate. But given the price change (between perfect

233

Figure 14.1: The Conventional Measurement of the Welfare Loss
of Monopoly

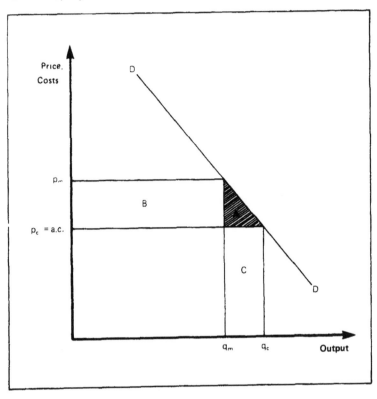

competition and monopoly) the change in output can be calculated if the
elasticity of demand is estimated or assumed. Information on the elasticity
of demand is sparse, and most estimates of monopoly welfare loss are
based on *assumed* elasticities of demand.

The ratio of monopoly welfare loss (*MWL*) to sales (*S*) is $\frac{1}{2}\Delta p\Delta q/p\cdot q$,
where Δ refers to the change in the relevent variable. Now define pseudo-
elasticity $E_H = p\cdot\Delta q/q\cdot\Delta p$, and by substitution obtain $MWL/S =$
$\frac{1}{2}\cdot E_H\cdot(\Delta p/p)^2 = \frac{1}{2}\cdot E_H\cdot(\pi/S)^2$. Thus for a given profit-sales ratio (π/S),
the welfare loss rises directly with the pseudo-elasticity E_H. Essentially
this reflects the point that, for a given profit-sales ratio, and hence a given
difference between monopoly price and the competitive price, the higher
the elasticity the greater will be the difference between the monopoly
output and the competitive output. It will also be noted that for a given

pseudo-elasticity of demand the loss rises with the square of the profit-sales ratio.

The profit-sales ratio and the pseudo-elasticity of demand may not be independent. For if the monopolist is maximising profits, then those variables are related by the equation $\pi/S = 1/E_H$. Then $MWL = \frac{1}{2}\pi$, and monopoly welfare loss is one-half of monopoly profits in this case.

In a number of studies a relatively low value is placed on the elasticity of demand and $E_H = 1$ is often used. It can be seen from the preceding equation that estimates of welfare loss for another value of E_H can be obtained by multiplying the welfare loss for $E_H = 1$ by that other value of E_H. The assumption of elasticity of unity implies a marginal revenue of zero, and a profit maximising firm would not normally be operating where its marginal revenue was zero.

In this derivation, a number of simplifying assumptions have been made. First, the level of costs under the two regimes being compared is assumed to be the same. Thus any tendency for costs to be higher under monopoly through, for example, technical inefficiency (or X-inefficiency) is excluded from consideration. Second, unit costs are taken as being constant. But if unit costs are actually rising then the conventional calculations of welfare loss outlined above with constant costs assumed would overstate the monopoly welfare loss (and conversely for falling unit costs). This arises because, *ceteris paribus*, the rise in output between a monopoly position and a competitive one will be larger for the constant cost case than for the rising cost case. Thus monopoly imposes a larger output fall when there are constant costs than when there are increasing unit costs.

This simple model has been developed for a single industry, without paying regard to the rest of the economy. Under monopoly output is lower than under atomistic competition, and correspondingly the use of inputs is reduced by the equivalent of the area C in Figure 14.1. It is implicitly assumed that the resources released by the new monopolised industry are re-employed elsewhere in the economy, and yield consumers real income equivalent to the area C. But the actual calculations do not build in this requirement, so that the actual resource use under monopoly may be less than under perfect competition. However, the simple model is applied to the whole economy and not just to a single industry. The general equilibrium nature of the problem is partially recognized in the way in which the competitive price (= average cost) is calculated. Average costs must include an allowance for the cost of capital, since they are long-run costs. There are two basic alternatives for the cost of capital. One alternative is the supply price of finance representing the cost of finance capital to a competitive industry. The other alternative is the use of the average rate of return on capital. In this way, with some industries with above-average rates of return and others with below-average rates of return, some observed prices will be above the competitive level and others below the competitive level. Consequently some industries will have output below the competitive level, whilst others have output above the competitive level. In this way, general equilibrium features are taken into account in that some industries increase output and input use, whilst others reduce output and input use. But it leaves monopoly welfare loss as a loss arising from price dispersion rather than from monopoly *per se*. Indeed, the welfare comparison is between the existing monopoly situation and one in which there is an equal degree of monopoly in all industries (i.e. where the mark-up of price over costs is the same: Cowling and Mueller, 1978).[2]

Estimates of Monopoly Welfare Loss

Some results of applying the conventional method are given in Table 14.1. The first four results indicate monopoly welfare loss of the order of upwards of $3\frac{1}{2}$ per cent of net output or national income. The remaining results suggest that the welfare loss from monopoly is rather small, of the order of less than one-tenth of a percent of net output or national income. Some of the differences can be explained by the use of the profit maximising assumption in the first group of studies reported. But this does not explain all of the differences. For example, Kamerschen's estimates based on $E_H = 1$, corresponding to the estimates reported in Table 14.1 for the profit maxmisation case, are 1.03 per cent and 2.66 per cent, respectively. Another source of difference is that in some studies (e.g. Harberger, 1954) the welfare loss in one sector (usually manufacturing industries) is related to the whole of national output, whereas in other studies (e.g. Cowling and Mueller, 1978) the welfare loss within a sector is related to the net output of that sector.

   The estimates of Masson and Shaanan (1984) can be related to their estimates of the monopoly welfare loss which would arise if there were monopoly situations or oligopoly with joint profit maxmisation uninhibited by potential entrants. That monopoly welfare loss they estimate would be 11.6 per cent of sales, and they attribute just over half of the difference between actual and maximum welfare loss to effects of potential competition and the remainder to actual competition amongst existing firms.

Table 14.1: Estimates of Monopoly Welfare Loss

Author	Elasticity assumption		Welfare loss %	Comments
UK				
Cowling and Mueller (1978)	(a) $E_H = 1$		0.21	Relates to 1968/9, and uses firm level
	(b) Profit maximisation		3.86	data (103 firms)
			of gross corporate product	
Sawyer (1980)	(a) $E_H = 1$		0.95	Relates to 1963, and uses industry data
	(b) Profit maximisation		6.93	
USA				
Cowling and Mueller (1978)	(a) $E_H = 1$		0.40	Relates to 1963/6 and uses firm level
	(b) Profit maximisation		3.96	data (734 firms)
Kamerschen (1966)	Profit maximisation	(a)	3.87	Uses post-tax unadjusted profit data
		(b)	6.52	Uses pre-tax adjusted profit data
Harberger (1954)	$E_H = 1$		0.08	Relates to 1929
Masson and Shaanan (1984)	Profit maximisation		2.9 of shipments	
Schwartzman (1960)	$E_H = 2$		0.1	
Siegfried and Tiemann (1974)	$E_H = 1$		0.073	
Worcester (1973)	$E_H = 2$	(a)	0.203 to 0.440	Range of losses for years 1957–68
		(b)	0.443 to 0.728	Includes allowance for higher wages and advertising under monopoly

Notes: Authors generally provide many estimates, and only a selection is reported in this table. Welfare loss is given as a percentage of national income, unless otherwise stated.

An Alternative Approach

A general equilibrium approach has been proposed by Bergson (1973). The essential idea is that the welfare loss of monopoly can be measured by finding the variation in income which would just compensate consumers for the higher prices of monopoly (i.e. the compensating variation). The analysis starts from the existing level of income under monopoly (I_m) and the utility which would be derived from that income if there were competitive prices (p_c) and label that utility $U(p_c, I_m)$.[3] The idea is to find the level of income I^* which would enable consumers faced with monopoly prices (p_m) to obtain the level of utility described above, so that $U(p_m, I^*) = U(p_c, I_m)$. Then $I^* - I_m$ would compensate consumers for having to pay monopoly rather than competitive prices. Bergson focuses on the coefficient of net compensating variation (*CNCV*) defined as $(I^* - I_m)/I_m$.

This approach has so far been at a rather general level, and cannot be used as it stands to derive estimates of welfare loss. Bergson uses a specific form of the community utility function, which leads to a relatively simple formula for *CNCV*. In terms of the goods, the utility function is taken to be $U(x_1, x_2, \ldots, x_{n+1}) = \sum_{i=1}^{n} A_i x_i^{(1 - 1/\sigma)}$. With this utility function, the own-price elasticity of demand for good $i = \sigma - \gamma_i (\sigma - 1)$ where γ_i is the share of the good i in total expenditure. Thus the utility function used here imposes price elasticities for different goods which are broadly similar, differing only by the term $\gamma_i(\sigma - 1)$.

From this utility function, Bergson derives the *CNCV* as

$$\left(\sum_{i=1}^{n+1} \gamma_i \lambda_i^{\sigma - 1} \right)^{1/\sigma - 1} \cdot \left(\sum_{i=1}^{n+1} \gamma_i \lambda_i^{-1} \right) - 1$$

where λ_i are the prices under monopoly (scaled so that they would be each unity under perfect competition), and there is one sector (the $n + 1$th) which produces under perfectly competitive conditions.[4]

This formula as it stands is not particularly illuminating, and some illustrative figures may help. Take the case where there are four sectors in the economy, with prices under monopoly of 1.3, 1.2, 1.1 and 1. (i.e. the last sector is competitive), respectively. A value of σ of unity yields a value for *CNCV* of 0.49 per cent, and values of 2, 5 and 10 for σ give values of *CNCV* for 0.97 per cent, 2.37 per cent and 4.47 per cent, respectively. An important feature of the Bergson approach is that it incorporates the constraint that the level of resource utilisation is maintained at the same level under monopoly as under competition, in that the calculation of $U(p_c, I_m)$ is based on finding a vector of competitive outputs x_c which involves the same resource use as the vector of monopoly output (x_m). However, the nature of the utility function used reduces the role of substitution between different goods. Whilst there is indirect substitution in that an increase in the purchase of one good leads to a reduction in the purchase of other goods within a budget constraint, there are no direct substitution effects.

Despite appearances, this approach does not differ much from the previous output. Further, this approach essentially measures the welfare loss arising from the existing unequal degrees of monopoly compared with a situation involving an equal degree of monopoly. This can be seen from the following features. First, although Bergson made the assumption that $\lambda_{n+1} = 1$ (that the $n + 1$th sector is perfectly competitive), this is not a vital assumption in that the relaxation of the assumption does not affect the outcome. Second, an equal degree of monopoly (that is one where the mark-up over the competitive price is the same everywhere), by substituting the condition that $\lambda_1 = \lambda_2 = \ldots = \lambda_n$ into the formula for *CNCV* above (and remembering that $\Sigma\gamma_i = 1$ by definition) would give a *CNCV* of zero. Third, by examining the partial derivative of *CNCV* with respect to a price λ_i, it can be shown that an increase in a price will decrease *CNCV* (and hence monopoly welfare loss) if the price has a 'below-average' monopoly mark-up, and increase *CNCV* if the price has an 'above-average' mark-up.[5]

In principle, the welfare loss of monopoly relates to the mis-allocative effects of monopoly as compared with atomistic competition. But, in practice, the comparison is between a situation of unequal degrees of monopoly across industries and one with equal degrees of monopoly everywhere.[6]

General Remarks on Monopoly Welfare Loss

We conclude this section with raising some general criticisms of the approaches to the measurement and concept of monopoly welfare loss. The first point is to note that calculations of monopoly welfare loss rely on a comparison between the existing outcome, which is taken as a monopoly outcome, with a hypothetical perfect competitive outcome. The comparison is undertaken using the tools of conventional welfare economies. We have seen above (p. 235) some of the difficulties involved in the construction of a hypothetical competitive alternative, which is comparable in terms of resource usage with the actual outcome. Further, these calculations of welfare loss implicitly accept the desirability of a perfectly competitive outcome, and also incorporate the strengths and weaknesses of standard welfare economics.

Second, we can note that the economy is assumed to be in long-run equilibrium such that all super-normal profits can be attributed to monopoly power. Littlechild (1981) attacks this view essentially on two grounds.[7] The first ground is to raise the question of whether long-run equilibrium and monopoly are compatible. For example, would not the existence of monopoly profits attract firms into the industries with such profits, thereby undermining the monopoly position as well as the notion that the economy was in long-run equilibrium? The second ground is to argue that the economy is never in a long-run equilibrium (in line with the Austrian approach discussed in Chapter 15), and that positive profits arise from superior efficiency, foresight, good luck etc. (with negative profits arising for the converse reasons). Further, these profits are regarded as generally temporary, acting as a spur for other firms to follow suit in terms of efficiency or to seek to produce better products. It can be seen that this line of criticism rests on making a different interpretation of the underlying causes of above-average profits.

Third, the distributional aspects of monopoly profits are ignored in these types of calculations (as generally in welfare economies). Little is known about the distribution of monopoly profits, though it is known that in developed capitalist economies, the richest 10 per cent of households receive around 25 per cent of total income but 50 per cent of investment income.[8] Comanor and Smiley (1975) have argued that 'past and current degrees of monopoly have a major impact on the current degree of inequality in [the household wealth] distribution'. Their estimate for the United States is that the wealthiest 0.27 per cent would have a share of between 3 and 10 per cent of wealth in the absence of monopoly profits, in contrast to an actual share of over 18 per cent (in 1962).

There can be other losses arising from monopoly other than the misallocative losses discussed, and we now turn to a brief look at these other possible losses.

Costs of Monopolisation

The analysis above of the losses arising from monopoly concentrates on the effect of the degree of monopoly, without asking how that monopoly came into existence, or how it is maintained. When expenditure is undertaken to create and/or preserve monopoly and the subsequent profits, then that expenditure needs to be brought into the picture. The expenditure may be to help create barriers to entry (like advertising, research and development) or on making acquisitions to create a monopoly position. Before examining such expenditure for its welfare implications, we look at the approach of Posner (1975).

The basis of this approach is that the pursuit of a monopoly position is a competitive activity, to which firms will devote resources up to the point at which the expected marginal gains and the expected marginal costs are equal. Let us take an extreme example, where the government awards a monopoly position (and its attendant profits) through a lottery. What price would a firm pay to be included in the lottery? If the capitalist monopoly profits were W, then a firm would be prepared to pay up to $f \cdot W$, which are the expected profits, with f the probability of being awarded the monopoly position. Now if entry into the lottery is a competitive activity, then firms competing for a place in the lottery will bid up the entry price to $f \cdot W$. The probability of winning is the inverse of the number of firms entering, so that the total entry payments will be $(1/f) \cdot f \cdot W = W$. The analysis could be amended to deal with the probability of success depending on the amount of expenditure by allowing firms to buy as many lottery tickets as they wish, but this would not alter the basic conclusion. This is that the expenditure which firms are prepared to undertake to secure a monopoly position is the capital value of the monopoly position, which is the discounted future monopoly profits. The annualised value of this capital is the flow of profits, and thus the monopoly profits correspond to the annualised cost of securing the monopoly position.

The costs to the firms involved of gaining and securing a monopoly more generally include the costs of driving rivals out of the market (and the costs to those firms who get driven out), and the costs of erecting barriers to entry. There are two important questions concerning the nature of these costs. The first is whether these costs enter the profit and loss accounts of the firms involved. When the expenditure was incurred in the past, and does not affect the firm's valuation of its capital stock, then those costs will not enter current costs. In particular, those costs which fell on unsuccessful firms are unlikely to appear as current costs anywhere in the system.[9]

The effect which costs of monopolisation have on the calculations of welfare loss is indicated in Figure 14.2. The same analysis would apply if costs are higher under monopoly than under competition through inefficiencies under monopoly. The observed costs under monopoly are ac_m, and with prices p_m, the welfare loss is calculated as the area $B1$. But if competitive costs are ac_c, then the 'true' welfare loss is area $B1$ +

Figure 14.2: Illustration of Some Costs Associated with Monopoly

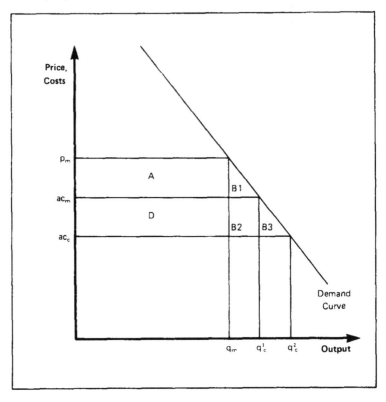

B2 + B3, so that the welfare loss is understated by the extent of *B2* + *B3*. Further there are extra costs under monopoly equivalent of the area *D*1. The monopoly profits are *A* + *D*1, of which *A* is recorded as monopoly profits, and *D*1 is dissipated in maintaining, securing monopoly position and/or in technical inefficiency.

The second question is whether the extra private costs under monopoly yield any benefits. To return to the lottery example, the extra costs on the firms yield revenue to the government, from which the government would be able to finance public goods and services. Discussion in earlier chapters on the nature of barriers to entry indicates that some of the expenditure on erecting barriers to entry generates a gain to the consumers (e.g. product improvement arising from research and development, informative advertising). But other expenditure on erecting barriers, such as the costs of excess capacity and persuasive advertising, do not generate gains to the consumers. In terms of Figure 14.2, the area $D1$ represents a cost to the monopolist and part of it is likely to correspond to a social loss.

In the analysis of Posner given above, when monopolisation is a competitive activity, firms pay monopolisation costs which are equal to discounted future monopoly profits. Monopoly profits in a year are the annual return on the investment in monopolisation, and can be seen as equivalent to the annualised cost of monopolisation. When the costs of monopolisation do not enter current costs, and when these monopolisation costs do not confer any benefit on society, then the above argument indicates that current monopoly profits are equal to the annualised costs of monopolisation. For some further discussion see Cowling *et al.* (1980), Chapter 2.

The impact of this line of thought can be seen from some of the calculations undertaken by Cowling and Mueller (1978). First, they deduct advertising expenditure from costs, since advertising may be a monopolisation activity. In other words, they accept advertising expenditure as raising costs from ac_c to ac_m in terms of Figure 14.2. Under the assumption of profit maximisation, the omission of advertising expenditure from costs raises the estimated welfare loss for the UK from 3.86 to 4.36 per cent. Second, they add on the (post-tax) monopoly profits as a measure of the costs of monopolisation, and they arrive at an estimated 7.20 per cent for the total loss of monopoly.

Conclusion

Until recently, the general consensus was that the welfare losses associated with monopoly were rather small, of the order of one-tenth of a per cent of *GNP*. But some of the recent estimates summarised in Table 14.1, and the discussion in the last section, have upset the general consensus.

Notes

1. For discussion of consumer surplus, see any text on welfare economics, for example Barnett (1985), Ng (1983), Winch (1971).
2. This point and some other problems with the conventional approach are dealt with in Sawyer (1980).
3. This assumes that there is a utility function which can represent social welfare. In particular, distributional aspects are suppressed.

4. When $\sigma = 1$, the utility function becomes $U(x_1, x_2, \ldots, x_{n+1}) = A \prod_{i=1}^{n+1} x_i^{\gamma_i}$ where $\prod_{i=1}^{n+1}$ is the multiplicative equivalent of the additive $\sum_{i=1}^{n+1}$ (i.e. $U = A x_1^{\gamma_1} x_2^{\gamma_2} \ldots x_{n+1}^{\gamma_{n+1}}$).

Then the $CNCV = \left(\prod_{i=1}^{n+1} \lambda_i^{\gamma_i}\right) \left(\sum_{i=1}^{n+1} \gamma_i \lambda_i^{-1}\right) - 1.$

5. With an equal mark-up everywhere $\lambda_1 = \lambda_2 = \ldots = \lambda_{n+1} = a$ (say) then

$$CNCV = \left(\sum_{i=1}^{n+1} \gamma_i\, a^{\sigma-1}\right)^{1/\sigma-1} \cdot \left(\sum_{i=1}^{n+1} \gamma_i a^{-1}\right) - 1$$

$$= (a^{\sigma-1})^{1/\sigma-1} \cdot \left(\sum_{i=1}^{n+1} \gamma_i\right)^{1/\sigma-1} \cdot a^{-1} \left(\sum_{i=1}^{n+1} \gamma_i\right) - 1$$

$$= a \cdot a^{-1} - 1 = 0 \text{ since } \sum_{i=1}^{n+1} \gamma_i = 1$$

$$\partial CNCV/\partial \lambda_j = 1/(\sigma - 1) \cdot \left(\sum_{i=1}^{n+1} \gamma_i \lambda_i^{\sigma-1}\right)^{(1/\sigma-1)-1} \cdot \left(\sum_{i=1}^{n+1} \gamma_i \lambda_i^{-1}\right).$$

$$(\sigma - 1) \lambda_j^{\sigma-2} - \left(\sum_{i=1}^{n+1} \gamma_i \lambda_i^{\sigma-1}\right)^{1/\sigma-1} \cdot (\gamma_j \lambda_j^{-2})$$

$$= \left(\sum_{i=1}^{n+1} \gamma_i \lambda_i^{\sigma-1}\right)^{1/\sigma-1} \gamma_j \lambda_j^{-2} \cdot \left\{\left(\sum_{i=1}^{n+1} \gamma_i \lambda_i^{\sigma-1}\right)^{-1} \sum_{i=1}^{n+1} \gamma_i \lambda_i^{-1} \cdot \lambda_j^\sigma - 1\right\}.$$

This is positive or negative as $\left(\sum_{i=1}^{n+1} \gamma_i \lambda_i^{\sigma-1}\right)^{-1} \left(\sum \gamma_i \lambda_i^{-1} \lambda_j\right)$

is greater or less than 1, i.e. as $\sum_{i=1}^{n+1} \gamma_i \lambda_i^{-1} (\lambda_j^\sigma - \lambda_i^\sigma)$

is greater than or less than zero. 'Above average' prices are defined in this context, when this last expression is positive; and similarly 'below average' prices when the expressive is negative.

6. In the production sector, an equal degree of monopoly yields zero welfare loss. But there is a loss compared with perfect competition, arising from consideration of the factor market. Under an equal degree of monopoly case, the labour-output price ratio facing supplies of labour is the real wage = marginal revenue product of labour. But the labour input-output conversion factor by firms is equal to the marginal physical product of labour.

7. Littlechild (1981) makes some specific criticisms of the approach of Cowling and Mueller (1978), whose calculations are used in Table 14.1; for a response see Cowling and Mueller (1981).

8. See, for example, Sawyer (1976), Tables 7 and 14.

9. In the lottery example, it could be argued that the unsuccessful firms write off their lottery entry price since it has not realised them any profit. Thus their expenditure does

not appear in their costs in any way in subsequent periods. For the successful firm the picture is different, for it has acquired an asset, namely the monopoly position. Suppose the expenditure was E, then this firm could increase its capital assets by E, and this raises its costs in any period by $i \cdot E$, where i is the competitive rate of return on capital. Alternatively, it may value the monopoly position at its full value, W, and then the capital value of the firm rises by an amount W, and its costs (including the cost of capital) by $i \cdot W$.

15 COMPETITION AND INTERVENTION

Introduction

Debates over the appropriate role of competition and government intervention in industry and over the role of private, public and cooperative ownership are ultimately parts of a much wider debate on the nature of the
desirable politico-economic system. In this chapter we cannot hope to
deal with the broader debate. Instead the focus is on four basic approaches
to the roles of competition and intervention, with a stress on the economic
arguments underlying each of these approaches. The discussion relates
to economies which are essentially private enterprise ones, although it
will become clear that implementation of the policies derived from the
fourth approach would move such economies towards forms of public
ownership and intervention. A complete consideration of the alternatives
would require discussion of central planning and of firms of decentralised planning in an economy with large elements of public ownership, and
such a discussion is not attempted here. Indeed, in general this chapter
does not consider the detailed problems of implementation of policies
derived from these four approaches, although the general problem of
whether any interventionist policies are feasible is considered. In the next
chapter some of the problems of implementation which have arisen with
the industrial policies pursued in the post-war period are considered within
a general discussion of those policies.

Atomistic Competition

We begin with a consideration of policy approaches based on the view
that the equilibrium outcome in the model of perfect competition has some
desirable properties. The use of this conclusion lies behind many recommendations by economists in favour of increased competition. This concept of competition is essentially in terms of structural characteristics,
such as a large number of relatively small firms, absence of substantial
economies of scale and unimpeded entry into the industry. This structural concept of competition must be distinguished from those concepts
of competition which are used in the other approaches discussed below.

   The arguments for the desirability of perfect competition stem from one of the fundamental theorems of welfare economics.[1] The starting point is the acceptance of the Pareto criteria for an improvement in social welfare which states that social welfare is improved if the welfare of some individuals (in their estimation) is improved whilst the welfare of others is not diminished (again in their own estimation). A situation is then said to be Pareto optimal if no change can be made which would be judged as an improvement under the Pareto criteria. Then it can be shown, under certain assumptions, that a perfect competition equilibrium is Pareto optimal and conversely that for any Pareto optimal configuration there is a distribution of factors and initial endowments which would lead via perfectly competitive outcome to the given configuration. This assumptions required for this result include:

(a) diseconomies of scale beyond a 'small' level of output (such that firms of the cost minimising size are so small that they cannot affect price);
(b) no externalities in production or consumption.

There are numerous perfectly competitive equilibria, and each one is based on a particular distribution of factors of production and initial endowments (between individuals). When input and output prices have been determined for the general equilibrium, then the distribution of income (both in terms of the size-distribution and the factor shares distribution) becomes determined.

The desirability of atomistic competition rests on the properties of equilibrium under perfect competition and the assumptions set out above, with a particular distribution of initial endowments (and so a particular resulting distribution of income). Much of the opposition to the use of this optimality result arises from a judgement that the resulting distribution of income may be undesirable and from views that the crucial assumptions indicated above do not hold. A further reason is that the actual operation of a private enterprise economy may not approximate a perfect competitive equilibrium.

The conclusions of the desirability of perfect competition based on the Pareto criteria relates to the general equilibrium of the whole economic system. For policy towards a single industry, we would still need to know whether moving an industry towards a perfectly competitive structure (by, for example, increasing the number of firms) would lead to improvements. Lipsey and Lancaster (1956) have shown as a general proposition that if perfect competition does not operate in one sector of the economy (say because of the presence of economies of scale in that sector) then moving another sector toward perfect competition will not necessarily improve matters. However, the practical importance of this result, usually referred to as the theory of second best, has been doubted by Mishan (1962) who argued that usually moves towards perfect competitive structure will lead to improvements.

There is the major question of whether the economy can be regarded as perfectly competitive or not. One group, particularly associated with the Chicago school, argue that most of the economy is competitive, and that most if not all of monopoly persists only with the active support of government. For example, Stigler (1949) says that for the American economy 'it is my present judgement that competition declined moderately from the Civil War to the end of the nineteenth century, and thereafter increased'. He estimates that 81 per cent of the American economy is competitive and 19 per cent monopolistic, a view which clearly places industries at either the competitive or monopolistic ends of the structure spectrum, with no reference to intermediate cases of oligopoly. Friedman (1962) argues that 'probably the most important source of monopoly power has been government assistance, direct or indirect'.

This view would indicate that industrial concentration would be expected to be fairly low and to exhibit no upward trend over time. Barriers to entry into an industry would generally be expected to be low with government activity seen as a major cause of most substantial entry barriers. The virtual absence of barriers to entry into an industry leads to prices pushed toward the level of average costs, and removes any monopoly profits.

An alternative view is that whilst perfect competition has desirable properties atomistic competition is absent from a substantial number of industries, and that government policy should be geared towards moving those industries in the competitive direction. This type of policy is often labelled a non-discretionary or anti-trust. Such a policy would involve the break-up of existing situations of monopoly and oligopoly, and the prevention of mergers which would lead to oligopolies, and the prevention of mergers leading to the formation of further oligopolies.

Crew and Rowley (1970) argue that '[a]nti-trust policy may be viewed in such circumstances, as an unambiguously appropriate device for improving social welfare by replacing monopoly by competition'. They propose that

all cases of conspiracy might well be prohibited with severe penalties for transgression, on the principle that scale benefits can rarely be significant whereas consumer losses and X-inefficiency may be extensive. Similarly, all mergers might be prohibited which would raise the market share (properly defined) of the resulting combine above an acceptable limit (say 50 per cent). Where individual companies already employed a market share in excess of 50 per cent (again properly defined) a solution would be less tractable. In a growing market, absolute limits on size might be imposed . . .

or if they did not work then reduction of tariffs or as a last resort government regulation. However, they expect that 'in the longer term, technological progress might help to erode the market power of those companies which initially escaped the full impact of the anti-trust policy'.

This type of approach requires the definition of markets and the setting of limits to firms' market shares. But if markets were narrowly defined and the limits to market shares placed relatively low, then an anti-trust policy could involve considerable intervention by governments in the economy.

There are two basic difficulties with this approach. First, a system of competition relies on using incentives of individual gain to bring about efficient production. Under an anti-trust approach, an efficient firm earns relatively high profits and can grow relatively fast, but if that growth leads to a size which is judged large enough to constitute a monopoly or oligopoly position, then the firm is to be broken up. Evidently a firm is to be encouraged to be successful but not *too* successful (Marris, 1972).

A second difficulty is more the theoretical problem of how the emergence of oliopolies and monopolies is to be explained. The theory of perfect competition has nothing indicating any tendency towards the formation of oligopoly.[2] Thus the emergence of oligopoly stands in contrast to the predictions of the theory of perfect competition, and could indicate the inappropriateness of that theory.[3]

Another response to the 'optimality' of perfect competition result has been the use of perfect competition as a blue-print for the organisation of a socialist economy. An early proponent of this view was Lange (1937), who argued that 'the actual capitalist system is not one of perfect competition; it is one where oligopoly and monopolistic competition prevail. This adds a much more powerful argument to the economists' case for socialism'. Lange also saw the 'distribution of the ownership of the ultimate productive resources [as] . . . a very unequal one', and the resulting inequality in the distribution of profits could be avoided under socialism since profits (social dividend in Lange's terminology) could be distributed according to need rather than according to ownership of capital.

Contestable Markets

An idea which has attracted considerable attention in recent years is that of 'perfectly contestable markets'. The ideas on this are developed at length in Baumol, Panzar and Willig (1982), and a summary is given in Baumol (1982).[4] In this section we seek to draw out the important aspects of this idea for industrial policy.

A 'perfectly contestable' market is one in which there is completely free entry and exit. The entry into an industry may only be potential but, as will be seen, it is potent in constraining the behaviour of existing firms. In this context, the type of barriers to entry which would inhibit entry are the costs of entry and exit, rather than, for example, economies of scale. If a firm could enter an industry at will and then leave without incurring losses, there would be free entry and exit. Thus, for a perfectly contestable market, there has to be an absence of significant lags between a decision to enter and the entry occurring, and an absence of losses on exit. A major way in which there could be losses on exit would arise if there were capital value losses on resale of the capital equipment specific to the industry concerned. Expenditure on some items (e.g. advertising) may be irrecoverable. The assumption of free entry and exit leads to the possibility of 'hit-and-run' entry, that is firms entering the market for brief spells when profits can be gained, and then leaving. This hit-and-run entry is seen to constrain existing firms to normal profits. In general, the ability of firms to entry the industry in response to above-average profits and then to leave if necessary without incurring losses means that incumbent firms are unable to gain above-average profits.

The theory of contestable markets also leads to the view that the industrial structure resulting from the operation of perfectly contestable markets will tend to the optimal (in the sense of involving least cost production), with firms exploiting any economies of scale but at the same time constrained in their pricing activities. There will be an 'absence of any sort of inefficiency in production in industry equilibrium' (Baumol, 1982). The simple argument here is that if there were unexploited economies of scale, then firms (incumbent or entrant) would expand to gain the lower costs and higher profits resulting from a large scale of production.

This theory, like that of perfect competition, can be treated in three ways. It could be treated as a welfare ideal, against which the real world would be judged and policies recommended to try to move industries closer to that ideal. Alternatively, it could be treated as a theory relevant to some or all industries in the real world. The third possible treatment is to build a theory with perfectly contestable markets as one end of the range of possibilities, with the performance of the industry (e.g. in terms of profits) linked to some measure of the divergence of the structure of that industry from being that of free entry and exit. The analogy in the case of perfect competition is the general structure conduct performance where the performance is linked to the extent of departure on the structural side from perfect competition. These different treatments are evidence in the work on contestable markets. Baumol (1982) states that 'perfect contestability . . . serves not primarily as a description of reality, but as a benchmark for desirable industrial organisation . . .'. Spence (1983) discusses contestable markets largely in terms of a welfare ideal. Bailey and Panzar (1981) have, for example, applied the idea to the study of the deregulation of the American air-travel market (though Graham, Kaplan and Sibley (1983) argue that, contrary to the predictions of contestable markets approach profitability on airline routes was related to industrial concentration). Davies and Davies (1984) apply the idea of contestable markets to banking. Schwartz and Reynolds (1982) discuss the question of whether the predictions of perfectly contestable markets will be gradually approached as the conditions of entry and exit approach costless and instantaneous entry and exit. Shepherd (1984) indicates some empirical tests which could be undertaken in this area.

The main policy implication of the contestable markets literature is that internal structural characteristics of an industry are not particularly relevant to performance but that the conditions of entry and exit into an industry are. This would lead to concern over entry conditions rather than with concentration. The regulation by governments of entry of firms into particular industries (e.g. restrictions on which airlines can fly particular routes in many countries) would be condemned as enhancing the power of existing firms.

In comparison with earlier discussion on barriers to entry (cf. Chapter 5 above), three features of the contestable market approach are of interest. First, economies of scale do not constitute an entry barrier in this approach. This highlights the nature of the free entry and exit assumption (cf. Spence (1983), Weitzman (1982), for further discussion). Suppose that there were economies of scale such that 1 million units a year of the good concerned was the minimum efficient scale of production. Under the hit-and-run entry view, a firm could produce 100,000 units a year at the minimum efficient scale by producing for one tenth of the year only, and selling the output over the whole year. Entry at any scale, however small, is then possible by this method of producing for a sufficiently short period of time (though the good does have to be storable).

The second contrast with preceding treatments of entry is that the theory of contestable markets does not investigate the response of existing firms to actual entry. Indeed, the theory of contestable markets is built on the view that the existing firms will not respond. By reference to Chapter 5, it can be seen that existing firms can seek to deter entry to convincing potential entrants that the existing firms will lower their prices if entry occurs, thereby making entry less inviting.

The third contrast relates to the nature of entry barriers. In Chapter 5, we saw that traditional industrial economics focused on economies of scale, product differentiation, absolute cost advantage and excess capacity as important entry barriers. The contestable market approach dismisses, as we saw above, economies of scale as an entry barrier, and ignores product differentiation. The absolute cost advantage type of barrier is not developed in the contestable markets approach. Further, stress is placed on the conditions of exit as influencing entry conditions. It could also be noted that it would seem likely that entry into an industry by 'already established' firms from other industries would be easier than entry by new firms (cf. p. 74). Thus, in the case of airlines in the USA to which the contestable markets approach has been applied, the entry onto a particular route by an already established airline may be much easier than entry by a new airline.

Workable Competition

Workable competition is 'competition which works', indicating that an industry is to be judged in terms of performance rather than structure. In the previous approach, a 'good structure' was identified with an atomistic competitive one, and from that structure a 'good performance' would, it was believed, result. With workable competition, it is more a matter of defining 'good' performance, and then finding the structure which will generate that performance. Thus, in some versions, workable competition is the policy arm of the structure-conduct-performance approach. For if the structure-performance relationships were well established, then it would be possible to work back from 'desired' performance to find the appropriate 'desired' structure. Public policy would then be seen as a means of establishing the 'desired' structure.

There are numerous versions of the notion of workable competition. However, at the centre of the general concept of workable competition is the belief that perfect competition is not a *worthwhile attainable ideal*. Advocates of the concept of workable competition place varying emphasis on those three italicised words. For some, perfect competition is an ideal, which is costly to implement fully, and they feel that it is possible to get close enough to the performance benefits of perfect competition without fully attaining the structural characteristics of perfect competition. Clarke (1940), an originator of the concept of workable competition, argued that '"perfect competition" does not and cannot and has presumably never existed' and that perfect competition was 'an unreal or ideal standard which may serve as a starting point of analysis and a norm with which to compare actual competitive conditions'. But the use of perfect competition as a standard 'has seemed at times to lead to undesirable results, in that it does not afford reliable guidance to the factors which are favorable to the closest available working approximation to that ideal, under actual conditions'.

For others, some of the features of the real world which are assumed away by the theory of perfect competition are of crucial importance. These features could include uncertainty, lack of information and dynamic investment considerations. Clarke (1940) puts forward a second-best type of argument when he argues that when one or more of the conditions for perfect competition are absent then it may no longer be desirable to strive for the remaining conditions to operate.

Finally, perfect competition may not even be an ideal. An example would be when economies of scale are significant so that only a few firms are required for production at minimum average cost. A further example would arise when importance is attached to the benefits of product differentiation, which would be lost under a strict perfectly competitive regime.

Numerous aspects of performance have been suggested by writers on workable competition as relevant to the consideration of an industry. Sosnick (1958) provides an extensive summary of the various performance indices and norms which have been suggested. Norms have varied from 'operations should be efficient', to 'quality should conform to consumers' interests' and on to 'excessive political and economic power should not rest in the hands of small groups' and 'employees' welfare should not be neglected'. Thus each author has a number of criteria or norms, and between the authors a large number of criteria and norms have been advocated.

Each author usually provides a number of criteria for desired performance, but does not generally indicate how much weight must be given to each dimension of performance. For each dimension, the criteria was pitched in terms of satisfactory or accepted levels of performance, so leaving another element of ambiguity.

Figure 15.1: Illustration of Gains and Losses arising from a Merger

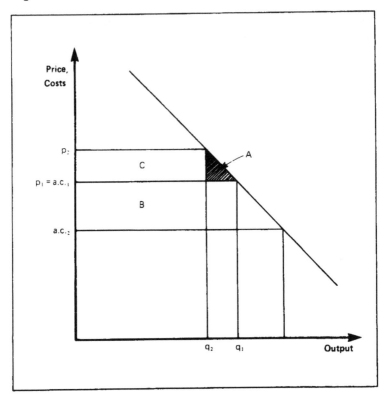

Within the broad approach of workable competition, two distinct strands can be identified. The first strand leads to industrial policies which have often been described as discretionary or case-by-case. Under this type of policy, an industry is examined to see whether in some sense its performance has been acceptable (or in the case of a proposed merger whether it would lead to acceptable performance). If the performance is found to be unacceptable, then policies to change structure, behaviour and performance would follow. British monopoly and merger policy can be seen as in this mould, whereby a firm with more than 25 per cent market share can be referred to the Monopolies and Mergers Commission for an examination as to whether it is operating in the 'public interest'.

A simple example of the use of the discretionary approach, based on Williamson (1968), illustrated how this approach could operate if the relevant performance criteria were precisely defined and measurable. When there are economies of scale an increase in concentration is expected to lead to a fall in unit costs but a rise in the price-cost margin. These two effects can be formally compared in the following way. For simplicity, assume that in the unconcentrated case, price p_1 is equal to average costs $(a.c._1)$ and output q_1 results, as illustrated in Figure 15.1. In the concentrated case price is higher at p_2, though average cost is lower at $a.c._2$ and output contracts to q_2. The loss of consumer surplus in the concentrated case as compared with the unconcentrated case would be $A + C$, of which C would accrue as monopoly profits. The saving in resources is reflected by the area B, which is assumed to be employed in other sectors of the economy. The net change in welfare is then represented by the area B-A.

Obvious simplifying assumptions were made in this analysis, so that costs and benefits of a rise in concentration were relatively easy to evaluate. In a more realistic example, there would be many other changes (e.g. in the level of advertising, expenditure on research and development) of which the costs and benefits are much more difficult to evaluate. Further the comparison being made is inevitably between an existing situation and a potential one, and the difficulties of predicting future developments in an industry with changes in the extent of competition are particularly acute.

Wilcox and Shepherd (1975) support this approach in writing that 'a correct or optimal policy will increase competition up to the margin at which benefits of extra competition are just offset by the lost technical economies of scale. Perfect competition is not sought or expected. Rather agencies operate in the great middle range, where a greater degree of healthy competition and rivalry is usually worth seeking'.

The assessment of costs and benefits of changes in industrial performance arising from changes in industrial structure would generally lead to proposals for changes in the structure. These changes may involve the break-up of existing firms or the encouragement of mergers. Thus the existing level of industrial concentration may be judged too high or too low. The basis of any judgement is the *social* costs and benefits of a change in structure, whereas the firms are presumed to be interested in the difference between *private* benefits and costs (i.e. profits). If social benefits and costs coincide with private benefits and costs, there is little problem in persuading the firms involved of the benefits of the change. But such a coincidence could often lead the firms to make the change anyway. When there are differences between social net benefits and private net benefits, difficulties of implementation arise. For example, it is difficult to imagine firms merging in the 'public interest' if the merger were believed by the participants to be unprofitable.[5] Wilcox and Shepherd (1975) note that '[g]enerally, any public policy which would reduce profits will be resisted *up to the point at which the marginal rate of return on resistance expenditures just equals the opportunity cost of capital*' (italics in original).

Underlying this approach is the view that the existing structure in an industry is not likely to correspond with the 'optimal' structure. Shepherd (1970), for example, argues that '[m]arket power will tend to grow unnecessarily large, rather than to settle spontaneously at minimal or optimal levels . . . Therefore, the actual status of the monopoly problem is a series of open questions subject to empirical answers'.

The second strand within the broad approach of workable competition emphasises that 'good' performance arises from industrial structure other than that of atomistic competition. Further, it postulates that there is a tendency for the actual industrial structure to evolve towards the 'optimal' structure. Thus here the pursuit of private profit is seen to lead to a structure which is not only privately but also socially desirable. The argument is that any monopoly power is limited and temporary. The profits from a monopoly position are soon eroded by entry of firms in pursuit of those profits. This entry will not only push profits downwards but also move industrial structure towards the 'optimal' one.

Evidence which suggested that there was little relationship between concentration and profitability, and that concentration was subject to considerable changes (particularly decreases in industries with high concentration), would be consistent with this approach. The policy recommendations arising from this approach are of a non-interventionist form. This essentially *laissez-faire* policy also arises from the next approach considered, and indeed the two approaches tend to merge into one another.

Laissez-faire

The view that governments should not intervene in the operation of markets and industries arises from at least three distinct theoretical positions. The first two of these are variants of the two approaches discussed above. The first is the view that perfect competition is both desirable and widespread in the economy. To this could be added the view which sees perfectly contestable markets as desirable and free entry and exit as typical of many industries. The second is the view within the workable competition approach that the actual structure is close to the optimal one. The third, which can be labelled the Austrian or neo-Austrian approach, derived from the work of Hayek, von Mises and others, is discussed now. Shand (1984) provides an introduction to the Austrian approach, and Chapters 5 to 9 and 15 are particularly relevant to this section.

The first theme is concerned with the role of profits. The existence of profits, particularly high profits, is seen as an indicator that the firms involved are particularly efficient in terms of productive efficiency and satisfying consumer demands. High profits are not to be associated with market power, but rather any coincidence of monopoly involved. Hence a particularly efficient firm will have both large market shares and high profits. But such a firm may not possess monopoly power in that rivals exist who try to enter the industry or to develop close substitution. In general, high profits are seen as temporary, eroded as new firms enter and as new substitutes are introduced. High profits are seen as the necessary inducement in the short run for the introduction of new ideas, products and techniques. A typical sequence could be seen as follows. An entrepreneur manufactures a new product in which the entrepreneur has a temporary monopoly, and earns high profits if the new product is successful. The prospects of high profits were the spur for the entrepreneur to make the innovation. However, gradually other entrepreneurs will respond to these high profits by copying the idea or by introducing a close substitute, and as this proceeds profits will decline. Whilst this particular product may settle down to a kind of equilibrium, new products will be developed elsewhere in the economy. In some respects, this corresponds to the 'perennial gale of creative destruction' postulated by Schumpeter (1954) in his discussion of technical innovation (p. 129 above).

An important assumption in this line of argument is the general absence of any long-term barriers to entry, so that profits are bid down to their 'normal' level by entry or the threat of entry. Any barriers to entry are usually attributed to government actions like licensing.

The second theme is that competition is a process rather than a state. In the first approach considered above emphasis was placed on the structure of the industry, and the properties of competitive equilibrium. The Austrian approach views competition as 'mobility, not equilibrium. We ought to mean the unbarred movement of factors of production' (Reekie, 1979, pp. 10–11). This line of argument leads on to the view that 'in a world of uncertainty, changing tastes and evolving technologies *no* structural equilibrium *qua* equilibrium can be optimal. In fact, in such a world the world "equilibrium" really has no meaning' (Reekie, 1979).

The third theme is that there are few externalities (such as pollution) which cannot be internalised. In other words, when the activities of one firm impose costs on other firms, then it is argued that the firms on whom the costs fall can, if the legal framework is adequate, pass those imposed costs back to the cost-imposing firm (or alternatively pay that firm not to impose the cost). Another type of externality which is imposed on consumers arises from monopoly, since the private benefit to the firm (marginal revenue) deviates from the social benefit to consumers (= price). This form of externality is, as indicated above, thought by this school to arise rarely.

The fourth theme is the importance of property rights and of the entrepreneur. The first theme indicated the role of profit. If the entrepreneur is to seek after profits, then (s)he must have the claim to those profits. Thus the property rights to those profits must be assigned to the entrepreneur. Alchian and Demsetz (1972) argue that five aspects of property rights are important. These are the rights to be a residual claimant, to observe input behavoiur, to be the central party common to all contracts with inputs, to alter the membership of the team and to sell these rights. The first of these rights clearly is the right to the profits. The next three rights essentially mean that the owner of these property rights has full control over the production process and over the workforce.

This fourth theme has important implications for the existence of a 'managerial revolution'. The first and fifth property rights would legally reside with the shareholders, whereas if there has been a 'managerial revolution' some or all of the middle three rights would reside with the managers. Mises (1949) argued that in the final analysis the entrepreneur is the owner (of the firm), for the manager can never be the entrepreneur since the manager 'cannot be made answerable for the losses incurred'. In the context of the large corporation, this poses two problems. First, who is the entrepreneur from amongst the thousands of shareholders? Second, are the shareholders able to impose their demands on the managers? The approach under discussion asserts that the owners are able to do so. For example, Reekie (1979), states that '[t]o ensure that [the owner] retains these property rights the market in corporate control must be subject to effective competition. The divorce of ownership from control must, if society is to be optimally served by the entrepreneurial function, be a fiction. The reality should be a marriage of convenience between the internal labour market and the entrepreneur'.

The fifth theme is that the world is one of very limited information, but that the exploitation by entrepreneurs of the information which they have is one of the engines of the system. Indeed this exploitation of information by entrepreneurs is seen as the basis of profits in the system. Thus, it is argued that 'the ultimate source from which entrepreneurs' profit and loss are derived is the uncertainty of the future constellation of demand and supply. If all entrepreneurs were to anticipate correctly the future state of the market, there would be neither profits nor losses' (Mises, 1949).

There are three clear implications from this approach for the empirical evidence. First, no systematic relationship between concentration and profitability is anticipated, and even if such a relationship were found its interpretation would not be straightforward. Second, there is no 'divorce of ownership from control'. Mises (1949) argued that '[a] successful corporation is ultimately never controlled by hired managers. The emregence of an omnipotent managerial class is not a phenomenon of the unhampered market economy. The entrepreneur determines alone, without any managerial interference, in what lines of business to employ capital and how much capital to employ'. Third, advertising is seen as a method of spreading information and not persuasion. Mises (1949) says that '[i]t is a widespread fallacy that skilful advertising can talk the consumer into buying anything that the advertiser wants them to buy' and that '[t]o convey to [the consumer] information about the actual state of the market is the task of business propaganda . . . Business propaganda must be obtrusive and blatant'.

The policy implications are fairly clear. Any government policy should be solely directed towards the encouragement of entrepreneurship, and the removal of restrictions on entry into industries (e.g. by licensing) and on trade (e.g. tariffs). The emphasis placed on the role of entrepreneurship in pursuit of profits leads to a strong preference for private enterprise and a strong distaste for public provision of goods and services. Although we have no space here to develop the argument, the public sector is usually seen as being particularly inefficient and unresponsive to changes in tastes and technology.

Public Intervention and Ownership

The three broad approaches examined so far have taken the existing system of private ownership as a basic datum, and have argued about the relative merits of different forms of structure and how that system actually operates. The first two approaches may lead to substantial intervention by the government in order to change industrial structure, but it is assumed, implicitly or explicitly, that private ownership is inviolate.[6] The general approach discussed in this section makes no such assumption and often leads to recommendations for the extension of public ownership and control. Limitations of space means that our discussion cannot extend into the area of the operation of public enterprise in a mixed economy nor of the organisation and co-ordination of a socialist economy.[7] The discussion of the latter topic would require an investigation into the relative merits of centralised and decentralised planning, the uses of the price mechanism, and the role of the worker-managements and control of co-operative enterprises.[8] Thus this discussion is limited to the essentially negative arguments in favour of increased public intervention and ownership arising from the problems of private enterprise economy, without any discussion of positive arguments arising from a consideration of the operation of public enterprise.

The arguments put forward in favour of public ownership and intervention tend to be rather diverse, and are often related to specific industries. Different authors stress different aspects and arguments, and we can only summarise here some of the main strands of thought.

The first and basic strand is the view that a developed capitalist economy is fundamentally oligopolistic. There may be areas where something like atomistic competition prevails, but in the bulk of the economy and particularly in key sectors oligopoly prevails. Thus Aaronovitch (1977) argues that '[w]ithout any exception, giant firms dominate the key industrial and financial sectors of all advanced capitalist economies'.

The motivation of the oligopolies is profits and accumulation. Whilst this approach agrees with the Austrian approach considered above that the pursuit of private profit is the major objective of firms, the two approaches part company on the interpretation of the effect of private profit-seeking. However, the divergence between social benefits and costs and private benefits and costs means that the maximisation of private profits which are equal to the difference between private benefits and private costs cannot be translated over into the maximisation of social net benefits (the difference between social benefits and costs). This does not imply acceptance of the conventional methods of assessing social benefits and costs. Such an assessment would be seen as impossible in the presence of monopoly power, inequalities of income and wealth, advertising and sales promotion, etc.

There are also considerable losses arising from the market power possessed by oligopolists. These losses would include monopoly welfare losses (discussed in Chapter 14), higher costs and inefficiencies arising under monopoly and the costs of advertising, sales effort and other expenditure associated with firms protecting their position against rivals.

This approach would see industrial structure moulded by firms in their pursuit of profits. Barriers to entry would be erected to preserve oligopoly positions. Thus there is no sense in which an 'optimal' structure will emerge. Indeed this approach incorporates many of the arguments put forward against the structure-conduct-performance approach which were considered in Chapter 10.

The emphasis on the firm rather than the industry leads to the prediction that a large firm will usually operate in several industries. Diversification may arise from attempts to increase vertical integration as a form of entry barrier or because growth of one firm at the expense of another is likely to be difficult in an oligopolised industry leading to oligopolies expanding to other industries (on this point see Aaronovitch, 1977; Aaronovitch and Sawyer, 1975a, pp. 40–3).

The high levels of concentration and the associated market power of the firms involved are expected to persist for significant periods of time.[9] Thus in contrast to the Austrian approach, high concentration is not expected to decline generally, but rather oligopolists are expected to defend their position by the erection of barriers to entry and by mergers and acquisitions. There may be cases where concentration declines through miscalculation and inefficiency of the established firms, but these cases will be relatively rare. Some decreases in concentration offset by some increases in concentration do not overturn the general notion of an oligopolistic structure for the economy as a totality.

The emphasis on the firm rather than the industry means that aggregate concentration as well as industrial concentration is considered to be of relevance. The level of aggregate concentration helps to indicate the degree of centralisation of decision-making in the economy and the economic power of large firms.

This leads into the second strand of centralisation of economic power. This centralisation has several dimensions. Power within a market over the determination of prices, quality, etc., is seen as concentrated on a few important oligopolists, and not dispersed as envisaged by atomistic competition. The power of the large firms and their importance and controllers extends into the labour market where power arises from restricted employment opportunities and from control over the production process (Braverman, 1974). Arising from high levels of aggregate concentration there is the economic power over investment decision, location decisions and the like. There is also the political power of the large firms arising from their economic importance. This power may be the ability to influence governments and international organisations to institute favourable trade policy (e.g. tariffs on 'cheap' imports, removing restrictions on capital movements to aid multi-nationals, etc.). It may be the ability to extract concessions from governments eager to obtain investment in their country or in particular regions.

Within an economy with a high level of concentration, decisions on prices, investment exports, etc., are effectively in the hands of a few individuals. Further, within each firm these key decisions are likely to be in the hands of a few individuals. However, there would not be any sharp distinctions of interests between managers and shareholders, for managers are often shareholders themselves, and also managers are often drawn from the same social class and have the same basic interests as major shareholders.

The third strand indicates that there may still be considerable rivalry between firms despite the high levels of concentration. This rivalry may be latent for much of the time, but the possibility of the outbreak of rivalry leads firms to prepare for it by seeking to make their position secure (Rothchilds, 1947). Again firms and their pursuit of profits is central, and rivalry *and* collusion arise as a consequence of that pursuit of profits. In other words, the pursuit of profits is fundamental, and whether rivalry or collusion result depends upon the firms' assessments of the relative advantages of the alternatives. This does not rule out the miscalculation by firms of the advantages involved.

In Chapter 4 there was a discussion of economies of scale, and some indication of possible benefits of increased size to the firms involved. In Chapter 12 some results indicated that larger firms faced a lower variability of profit and growth rates, and this was one possible reason why larger firms faced lower costs of capital. Chapter 13 indicated that size was often found to be an important determinant of which firms were acquired, with increased size tending to reduce the likelihood of being acquired. These give indications of some advantages derived from size. Another one may be important in the context of rivalry. This is the idea that the larger a firm is the better able it is to withstand an outbreak of competition. The clearest case is the large diversified firm which can withstand an outbreak of competition in one market by the use of profits gained from other markets. Bargaining power may be a function more of relative size than of absolute size. If that is so then a ratchet effect is created. One firm's relative expansion is another firm's relative decline. Rapid increases in size are usually only obtainable from acquisition, so that this ratchet effect may have particular consequences there (see pp. 214–16 above and Aaronovitch and Sawyer, 1975a, Chapter 10).

The fourth strand stressed the destabilising element in the operation of capitalist markets, rather than the equilibrating mechanism normally stressed. A noted advocate of this view is Myrdal (1957), who wrote 'the idea I want to expound . . . is that, on the contrary in the normal case there is no such tendency towards automatic self-stabilisation in the social system'. The destabilising effect or cumulative process have been particularly applied to regional and national development. 'If things were left to market forces unhampered by any policy interferences, industrial production, commerce, banking, insurance, shipping and, indeed, almost all those economic activities which in a developing economy tend to give a bigger than average return . . . would cluster in certain localities and regions, leaving the rest of the country more or less in a backwater'. Once a region has started growing '[t]hereafter the ever increasing internal and external economies — interpreted in the widest sense of the word to include, for instance, a working population trained in various crafts, easy communications, the feeling of growth and elbow room and the spirit of new enterprise — fortified and sustained their continuous growth at the expense of other localities and regions where relative stagnation or regression become the pattern'. Resources of labour and capital will be drawn towards the successful areas as those areas offer employment and investment opportunities. The growth areas are helped by trade for those areas have advantage derived from the economies of scale (broadly defined) arising from their larger scale of experience and production. Kaldor (1972) puts forward a similar line of argument.

Policies arising from this approach vary considerably. At one level, these arguments indicate reasons why the private sector does not operate in a socially desirable manner, and thus provides a rationale for government intervention designed to push firms towards a socially desirable outcome. This may evolve controls over profit margins, level of advertising, rate of price increases, etc., and changes in industrial structure, particularly the level of concentration. These types of policy recommendations may not differ substantially from those arising from the second approach considered above. However, the policy recommendations arising from the current approach differ from those of the second approach in a number of important respects. First, the spectrum of policies considered are broader, and extend past the emphasis placed on policies aimed at structure arising from the second approach. Second, the policies are not just concerned with dealing with the divergence between private and social costs and benefits, but are concerned with reducing the centralisation of economic power. Third, the government is not pictured as the neutral observer of the public good who can manipulate industrial structure in the public interest. Instead '[t]he massive centralisation of capital which exists in all advanced capital countries helps to explain the critical role of big business in the formulation and execution of state policies' (Aaronovitch, 1977). Thus any policies which are designed to reduce or contain the economic power of large firms and to push those firms to operate in ways which reduce their profits will encounter fierce resistance. Consequently such policies can only be implemented if a counter-weight to the political-economic power of the large firms is developed, including the mobilisation of public pressure and of the trade unions.

However, at another level control over profit margins and the like and changes in industrial structure may not be sufficient, and extensions of public ownership are required. Industries where there are considerable economies of scale always pose problems of market power if the economies of scale are to be exploited, and public ownership is one solution to that dilemma. The provision of public funds to private firms in order to stimulate investment or regional development and to finance high technology projects leads to problems of accountability which may be partially soluble through government ownership stake. Effective government intervention requires considerable unbiased information which present very considerable difficulties to the government, which can be partially resolved by a government ownership stake. These reasons amongst others lie behind the policy suggestions of authors like Holland (1975).

Assumptions about Cost Conditions

Whether increasing, constant or decreasing returns to scale are the typical case in most industries is of considerable importance in the debate over competition and intervention. Clearly if there are increasing returns to scale (up to a size which is substantial in relation to the industry) then production at lowest average cost requires a small number of producers. But a few large firms would pose problems of market power and monopoly profits. If there are decreasing returns after a level of output which is relatively small then that dilemma between benefits of scale and costs of monopoly does not arise. The advocates of the first approach, and to a lesser extent the advocates of the second and third approaches, argue that decreasing and constant returns are widespread. Then anti-trust policy which reduced the size of firms would not involve heavy costs arising from sub-optimal size of firms. In the second approach the cost conditions influence the 'optimal' structure, and there may be a requirement for regulation and control in industries with substantial economies of scale. In the third approach, economies of scale may lead to a single firm situation but the pressure of other firms, prepared to enter the industry if profits are high, serves to restrict profits whilst achieving cost minimisation.

In the fourth approach, economies of scale are seen as a force leading to oligopoly and to its maintenance.

Can Industrial Policies be Implemented?

There are two particular aspects of this question which we explore. The first one, which applies to any policy of an interventionist nature, is whether the power of the firms involved is such that any effective action is precluded. At the point of implementation, an interventionist policy would often adversely affect specific firms whose lobbying ability and politico-economic power may be strong enough to rule out any action by the government. The losses from action can include loss of profits to shareholders, as well as loss of employment prospects and wages for the workers. These groups have strong reason to lobby against the proposed action. The gainers from the proposed action would be consumers, other firms (and their shareholders and workers), but the gains may be very dispersed and the gain to any single individual or group rather small. In total benefits may be judged to outweigh costs, but the benefits are widely spread whereas the costs are concentrated. Thus a number of authors have argued that the balance is liable to swing in favour of the firm and little action taken.[10] But the general power possessed by firms *vis-à-vis* government may preclude the introduction of any such interventionist policy.

A second and related aspect arises when multi-nationals are involved. The extra dimension of power of such firms arises from their ability to relocate in different countries and in the process deprive other countries of the investment and employment involved. When threatened by government policy in respect of its behaviour and performance the multi-national can threaten to withdraw its operations (or more likely threaten not to expand and not to replace depreciated assets). Further in the case of foreign-owned multi-nationals, the government of the country of origin of the multi-national may seek to protect that firm. Whilst this protection may amount to little over attempts to, say, modify advertising expenditures or control prices, it may be substantial if nationalisation or splitting off of some of the assets of the firm were proposed.[11]

This chapter has reviewed four broad approaches to industrial policy, and indicated the underlying rationale and the nature of the policy prescriptions. We now turn to a discussion in the next chapter of the type of industrial policies pursued in the United Kingdom and the United States in the past 30 years.

Notes

1. This is spelt out in a text on welfare economics, e.g. Barnett (1985), Ng (1983), Winch (1971).

2. In equilibrium there would be no potential gains left to be gained from increased size or from merger. This does not apply to a situation of monopolistic competition, where under conditions of equilibrium for the existing range of firms there may be profit incentives for mergers, which may help to explain the emergence of oligopoly. For further discussion, see Aaronovitch and Sawyer (1975a), pp. 22–3.

3. It could be argued that perfect competition never existed, and that the current state of oligopoly developed from one of monopoly. For example, a firm may have introduced a new product, and later other firms entered the industry leading to a situation of oligopoly. In this case, there would be no strong reason to think that the model of perfect competition would be applicable to that industry, merely a hope.

4. For detailed review of Baumol, Panzar and Willig see Spence (1983), Brock (1982); for critical comments see Weitzman (1982), Schwartz and Reynolds (1982) and Shepherd (1984), and George (1985) (on the policy relevance of the contestable markets approach).

5. A policy of encouraging mergers was pursued in Britain in the second half of the 1960s with the creation of the Industrial Reorganisation Corporation (see pp. 288–9 below). This policy could be interpreted in part as ensuring that firms knew of profitable opportunities from mergers, and in part as seeking to ensure that, for various reasons, in a contested takeover bid the bidding firm with the largest resources did not necessarily win.

6. 'The theory of workable competition is best understood as an attempt to indicate which practically attainable states of affairs are socially desirable in individual *capitalistic* markets' (Sosnick, 1958) (emphasis added).

7. See, for example, Webb (1973), on nationalised industries, and the readings in Nove and Nuti (1972) on socialist economies.

8. See, for example, Vanek (1975), Jones and Svejnar (1982) for work on co-operative enterprises, and Ellman (1979) on central planning.

9. Terms like high concentration, persistence for significant periods of time, etc., are rather imprecise. Consequently, different approaches can each accept the same piece of evidence as consistent with their apparently conflicting approaches. Suppose, for example, that a firm held a monopoly position which was gradually eroded over a period of 20 years. The *laissez-faire* approach might see this as evidence of the ultimate triumph of competitive forces. The interventionist approach might point to the years of market power during which considerable monopoly profits may have been gained.

10. 'Since anti-trust is rarely if ever a central facet of government policy, politicians tend to be ill-informed on voter preferences. In such circumstances a vote-conscious, risk-averse government would introduce inconsistent legislation, obstructing in one statute the action laid down in the other, or more cynically, would legislate for anti-trust and then refuse to vote the funds necessary for its effective implementation. Furthermore, any pro-competitive platform would quickly encounter producer pressure groups designed to maintain existing market power. Advocates of *laissez-faire* take a pessimistic view of any anti-trust programme weathering successfully the combined pressures of uncertainty in the political market place and sustained producer lobbying' (Rowley, 1973, p. 74).

11. A number of examples are given in Hood and Young (1979), pp. 348–52. The most well-known case is probably that of the activities of ITT in Latin America. In 1965 ITT lobbied the American Secretary of State to intervene on their behalf with the government of Peru who were seeking to reorganise the telephone industry in that country. In Chile in 1970–1, ITT was actively involved with the Central Intelligence Agency in trying to bring down the government through economic sanctions, social disorder, etc., partly in order to preserve its interests in the Chilean telephone system.

16 ASPECTS OF RECENT INDUSTRIAL POLICY

Introduction

This chapter reviews some aspects of industrial policy pursued in the past 40 years, particularly in Britain but with some looks at the United States and the EEC competition policy. The aim is not to discuss these policies in terms of the details of implementation but to examine the main thrusts of the policies and to indicate the nature of the evidence on the results of these policies. Our discussion of industrial policy is restricted to policies which have attempted to change industrial structure (like the Industrial Reorganisation Corporation or the current privatisation programme), or to change industrial behaviour (like the Restrictive Practices Policy) in an attempt to improve industrial performance. Policies such as those on regional development and investment, usually regarded as macro-economic policies, are not discussed here. The distinction, although inevitably somewhat arbitrary, is basically between micro-economic policies which are discussed and macro-economic policies which are not discussed here.

Each of the broad approaches to policy discussed in the previous chapter has had some influence on British policy. Elements of non-discretionary policy are found in the post-1956 restrictive practices policy. The monopoly and mergers policy has been discretionary in nature. A *laissez-faire* policy with little government intervention operated during the fifties (though with some exceptions) and in areas where monopoly policy did not apply because the sectors were excluded from the legislation or because firms did not have a large enough market share to be covered by the legislation. Finally, there have been elements of the fourth approach, with extensions of public ownership (particularly during periods of Labour government), experiments with price control, although this was more related to anti-inflation policy than to industrial policy, and some proposals for planning agreements and for an industrial strategy (under the Labour government of 1974–9).

The legal framework for policy in the United States indicates a non-discretionary/anti-trust type of approach. However, there have been variations in interpretation of the law and the vigour with which the law has been implemented, and there are many indications of an essentially non-discretionary approach. For example, whilst the law outlaws monopolisation, the implementation of the law has paid some regard to the effect of monopolisation. There are also many sectors of the economy which are effectively exempt from the operations of anti-trust laws. In some of those, the government has intervened in other ways through, for example, price support programmes in agriculture and regulation of profits in public utilities.

It is not surprising that the declared industrial policies have varied with changes of the political party in power and in the political climate. Further, there are likely to be differences between the declared policy and the actual policy and variations in those differences. The British legislation on monopolies and mergers, for example, is essentially permissive in that considerable discretion is availble to ministers and the official bodies involved on the extent to which the monopolies and mergers are investigated. Even with the apparently non-discretionary American policy there are variations in the degree to which the law is enforced and in the interpretation placed on the law by the courts.

There are a number of themes which continually arise in discussion of industrial policy reflecting the underlying conflicts involved. The first theme is the benefits of larger firms (and hence fewer firms) in terms of economies of scale, rationalisation, etc., relative to the costs of less firms in terms of market power, lack of competitive pressures and the like. Fluctuations in policy have arisen from fluctuations in beliefs about the relative size of these benefits and costs. The second half of the sixties was probably the period in which belief in the benefits of increased scale was strongest. A second theme is whether industrial structure should be changed in order to lead to improvements in performance, or whether more direct action should be taken to improve industrial performance. A third theme is: what is meant by competition? In discussion of industrial policy, the term competition has at least two meanings. Competition policy can mean a policy which seeks to change industrial structure towards an atomistic competitive structure by reducing the level of concentration. But competition policy can mean removal of restrictions on firms in respect of prices, output, etc. These limitations may have arisen from government action (e.g. licensing) or from restrictive practice agreements between the firms themselves. This type of competition policy by removing some limits of the expansion of firms may encourage an increase in concentration. This can particularly arise if agreements between independent firms are outlawed without parallel action to restrict mergers and acquisitions.

Our discussion of industrial policy is divided into five sections. The first section reviews policies in respect of restrictive practices and cartels, whilst the second section discusses monopoly policy. The third section investigates policies on mergers and acquisitions, whilst the fourth section outlines policies designed to restructure industries. Finally, we look at other government policies towards industry, such as price control. Space precludes discussion here of policy in these areas in other countries and for a brief review, the reader is referred to Review of Monopolies and Mergers Policy (1978).

Restrictive Practices and Cartels

UK Policy[1]

Until 1948 there was no legislation directed against restrictive practices or monopolies, although there were some generally ineffective common law doctrines of monopoly, conspiracy and contracts in restraint of trade. But it is generally felt that government involvement with industry during the first half of this century had favoured cartelisation and the development of restrictive agreements.[2] Elliot and Gribbin (1977) have estimated that in 1958, just before the restrictive practices legislation of 1956 began to bite, 50 to 60 per cent of UK manufacturing output was subject to cartel regulations. Swann *et al.* (1974) concluded that the restrictive agreements were generally effective, and often covered more than 80 per cent of sales in those industries which had restrictive agreements.

The first stage of restrictive practice policy lasted from 1948 to 1956, during which cartels covering more than one-third of a market could be referred to the Monopolies and Restrictive Practices Commission (hereafter MRPC) for investigation.[3] The approach was essentially discretionary with each case to be judged in terms of the effect on the 'public interest', with no general presumption against cartels. Some of the references to the MRPC were chosen 'to provide a body of evidence about monopolies and restrictive practices which would guide the Government in framing its policy in the years ahead' (Allen, 1968, p. 64). A general report on collective discrimination (Monopolies and Restrictive Practices Commission, 1955) strongly influenced the legislation introduced in 1956, which formed the basis for the second and current stage of policy on restrictive practices.[4] This legislation established a general presumption against restrictive practices and created the Restrictive Practices Court (hereafter RPC) to adjudicate cases brought before it by the Registrar of Restrictive Trade Practices. The legislation did not cover services and applied to agreements on price, terms and conditions of sale, quantity to be supplied and manufacturing process.

Although the general presumption was against restrictive practices, the Act laid down seven conditions under which an agreement could be allowed to continue.[5] These 'gateways' are:

  (i) the agreement was necessary to protect the public against injury,
 (ii) its removal would deny consumers specific and substantial benefits;
(iii) it was necessary to counteract measures which would restrict competition;
 (iv) it was necessary to yield countervailing power against monopolies or other cartels;
  (v) its removal would lead to serious and persistent unemployment in an area;
 (vi) its removal would lead to a substantial fall in exports,
(vii) it was necessary to maintain the viability of other acceptable agreements.

Another 'gateway' was added in 1968 to the effect that if the agreement did not restrict competition to any material degree it could continue. Even if a restrictive agreement passed through one of the 'gateways', then it still had to pass the 'tailpiece' which required that the Court was satisfied that the balance of advantages and disadvantages resulting from the agreement was favourable.

In 1968, information agreements were placed under the same restrictions as restrictive agreements. Information agreements, under which, for example, firms would swap information on prices, were believed to be a widely used method of circumventing the restrictive practices legislation. Other changes since 1956 have included the extension of the legislation to cover the supply of services as well as goods, and the role of the Registrar of Restrictive Trading Agreements being taken over by the Director-General of Fair Trading (DGFT).

The general argument in favour of a non-discretionary policy with a presumption against restrictive practices is that such practices would generally lead to dis-benefits. On the one hand, the expected benefits to be derived from competition in terms of improved resources allocation, improved efficiency and lower prices were being held back by the cartel, whilst on the other hand there were not (and could not be) benefits from economies of scale (whether in production, research and developments or wherever).

There is some evidence that there was an 'announcement effect' from the introduction of legislation in 1956, for Swann *et al.* (1974) indicate that 13 per cent of a sample of restrictive agreements were abandoned before the legislation came into full effect. Once the RPC began to operate, it became apparent that a 'tough' interpretation was being placed on the seven 'gateways'. This led to a high proportion of the registered agreements being abandoned (or at least substantially modified) without a hearing before the Court.

The impact of restrictive trade practices legislation is now examined in three related areas. The first impact which is on the scale of restrictive agreements in operation, is indicated to some degree by the figures given in Table 16.1. These figures show that a substantial proportion of agreements were abandoned. The Court has upheld 11 restrictive agreements relating to the supply of goods, and the remaining difference between registered agreements and terminations of agreements indicates those agreements allowed to continue as being of trivial importance and agreements which the Office of Fair Trading or the Court are still considering. Restrictive agreements on the supply of services have only been covered since 1976. By the end of 1983, six agreements involving services had been referred to the Court. In one case (travel agents)[6] part of the restrictive agreement was allowed to continue. Another case, relating to the Stock Exchange, was taken out of the hands of the RPC and the OFT by the government. An act of parliament was passed exempting the Stock Exchange from the restrictive trade practices legislation in exchange for a number of concessions by the London Stock Exchange, the most important of which was the scrapping of minimum commission rates. The other cases were still outstanding at the end of 1983.

It is, not surprisingly, difficult to gain information on illegal restrictive practices, collusion and unregistered agreements. The Review of Restrictive Trade Practices Policy (1979) states that 'the evidence from the investigatory work of the MMC [Monopolies and Mergers Commission] and Price Commission shows that unregistered agreements continue to operate'. The Director General of Fair Trading is required by law to investigate the substance of evidence of unregistered agreements which should be registered, which often comes to light as a result of investigations relating to other matters. For example, in 1979, 24 local agreements on the supply of concrete and 47 on construction materials were discovered, and in 1983, 165 agreements on the price and distribution of milk.[7] In 1984, the OFT announced that two cases (involving bookmakers and ferry operators) were being taken to the RPC partly on the basis that registered agreements were said to be involved. In addition, conscious parallelism, price leadership and the like may replace formal agreements (Monopolies Commission, 1973).

The second impact is the indirect one on the level of concentration.

Table 16.1: Cumulative Numbers of Agreements Registered under the Restrictive Trade Practices Act

Date	Goods Registered terminations		Services Registered terminations	
November 1957	1200	—		
December 1959	2240	723		
June 1969	2660	2370		
December 1978	3678	3089	321	40
December 1983	4132	3269	846	272

Source: Review of Restrictive Trade Practices Policy (1979), Annual Report of the Office of Fair Trading, 1983.

Whilst agreements amongst independent firms were effectively outlawed in 1956, the merging of firms was in no way limited up to 1965, and after 1965 subject to only rather limited restriction (as indicated below). Thus incentives towards mergers are thereby increased concentration were created. The evidence on this aspect is mixed. Elliot and Gribbin (1977) were able to investigate the changes during the years 1958 to 1968 in industries in which there were products on which agreements had been terminated with industries in which there had not been any agreements. Their results, summarised in Table 16.2, suggest a faster rise in concentration following the termination of an agreement than in those industries where restrictive practices had not operated.

Table 16.2: Changes in Concentration in Products with and without Terminated Restrictive Agreements

	Level of CR5	Changes in CR5		
		1958–63	1958–68	1963–8
Products with terminated agreements	56.3	3.18 (90)	10.0 (90)	7.04 (142)
Products not subject to agreements	56.8	2.53 (64)	6.73 (64)	3.22 (127)
Difference	0.5	0.65	3.27*	3.82*

CR5   Five-firm concentration ratio (sales).
Number in parenthesis gives number of industries involved.
* Difference statistically significant at 5 per cent level.
Source: Elliot and Gribbin (1977).

Swann *et al.* (1974) in their study of industries where there had been agreements suggested that 'one of the most noticeable features of many of the industries studied in detail has been the decline in the number of firms producing particular products', and that mergers were a major factor in this decline. But the number of firms was declining in most industries and concentration increasing, and in a later study (O'Brien *et al.*, 1979) involving many of the same authors it was concluded that 'industries [where price agreements had been removed] were no more merger-intensive than other industries and that the higher level of merger activity which we [i.e. Swann *et al.*, 1974] observed was due, almost entirely, to the fact that the period of our previous study coincided with the 1960s merger boom' (text in brackets added).

The third impact is on efficiency in terms of the levels of costs and the overall allocation of resources and on the related areas of prices and profits. The study of Heath (1961) on the short-term consequences of the termination of 159 price agreements found the reported effects to be small, and about one-third of respondents thought that prices had fallen as a result of the termination. The study found there were some improvements in efficiency, though the effects were reduced by the substitution of information agreements for the restrictive agreements.

Swann *et al.* (1974) found that of the 34 cases examined where a restrictive agreement had been abandoned, there were between 18 and 21 industries where it would be said that a competitive or partially competitive situation (in respect of price, quality or service, etc.) had been established. In the short run price falls of up to 26 to 30 per cent occurred following the end of an agreement, though this size of fall applied in only a few industries. The price reductions often took up to six years to be completed. The reduction in prices places pressure on profits, and in some cases leads to reductions in costs. In sum the Restrictive Trade Practices Act can, they conclude, 'be judged to have improved resource allocation, however incompletely, and to have done very little harm'.

Whilst the Restrictive Trade Practices Act of 1956 prohibited collective resale price maintenance, this was not extended to individual resale price maintenance (hereafter RPM) until the Resale prices Act, 1964. With RPM suppliers make a condition of supply of goods to retailers that the retailers charge at least some minimum price. Under the Act such refusal to supply became illegal, except where the supplier has reason to believe that the retailer would use the goods as a 'loss leader' (that is sold at a loss for the purpose of attracting customers likely to purchase other goods). This legislation created a presumption against RPM, with the possibility of exemptions being granted by the RPC on grounds similar to those outlined above for the restrictive practices legislation.[8]

It is generally thought that RPM has declined substantially, with only two cases (books and medicaments) being upheld by the Court, although again here it is difficult to be sure that practices which have been declared illegal do actually disappear. The Office of Fair Trading (hereafter OFT) receives about 30 complaints a year to the effect that the provisions of the Resale Prices Act, 1976 have been broken in that producer firms are imposing conditions on the minimum price to be charged by retailers or wholesalers before supplying goods to them.[9]

The effect of the ending of legal RPM (with a few exceptions) would appear to be

> smaller than opponents or proponents of the practice had anticipated and that the net outcome has been beneficial. Although retail prices probably declined less than critics of resale price maintenance had predicted it does seem that on balance prices were lower — but only markedly so in the long run for a limited number of products. The decline in the number of retail outlets which followed the Act may also in part reflect the Act's operation as consumers were not prepared to pay for the additional services and convenience which the previous range of shops had provided. Thus it seems likely that whereas the legislation contributed to efficiency in the short run by accelerating structural change it also promoted efficiency in the long run (Review of Restrictive Trade Practices Policy, 1979, p. 24).[10]

US Policy

Competition policy in the United States has a much longer history than in the United Kingdom. Legislation started in 1890 with the passing of the Sherman Act, with major extensions made in 1914 (Clayton Act, Federal Trade Commission Act) and 1936 (Robinson-Patman Act). The enforcement of this legislation is the responsibility of the Anti-Trust Division of the Department of Justice and the Federal Trade Commission. A brief outline of American policy is given in the Review of Monopolies and Mergers Policy (1978), Annex C, and a more extensive discussion is given in Neale (1960) and in Wilcox and Shepherd (1975), Part II. The latter provides an interesting outline of the many problems of implementing a non-discretionary policy operated through the courts and subject to the process of law.

The Sherman Act declared every contract, combination or conspiracy in restraint of trade or commerce against state borders illegal. Following extensions of the law and the interpretations of the law by the courts, collusion over price fixing, market sharing and the exclusion of competitors are now regarded as illegal activities, and others like exclusive dealing and reciprocal dealing have been attacked by the courts. In the case of collusion, it is only necessary for the plaintiffs to show that collusion has occurred, and no consideration is given to effects of the collusion for good or ill. The Anti-Trust Division usually brings the case to court, although private plaintiffs can do so. Besides penalties imposed by the court, individuals and firms which have been harmed by the conspiracy can sue for damages claims up to three times the damages incurred.

The other aspect of firm behaviour which is unlawful is price discrimination between different purchasers of goods of 'like grade and quality', where the effect may be 'substantially to lessen competition or tend to create a monopoly or to injure, destroy or prevent competition', although price differentials which reflect differences in costs of supply (because of, for example, different locations of buyers) are permitted.[11] However, this legislation (the Robinson-Patman Act) was introduced as a response to fears of small retail shops that they were losing out to large supermarket chains. The latter, through greater bargaining power *vis-à-vis* the suppliers, were able to achieve lower prices than the small retail shops. This illustrates one of the fundamental problems of competitive policy, that rivalry between firms can lead to the emergence of monopoly, and that in order to protect competition in a structural sense it may be necessary to limit competition in the sense of rivalry between firms.

The apparent severity of the American law in respect of restrictive practices is modified in two respects. First, it has been estimated (Wilcox and Shepherd, 1975, p. 120) that the numerous exceptions to universal coverage that have been made, either by the courts or by Congress, have led to the anti-trust laws covering less than one-half of the economy. Second, the implementation of the law requires sufficient resources available to the agencies charged with the discovery and prosecution of collusive activity, price discrimination, etc. Wilcox and Shepherd (1975) argue that 'the agenices have always been small, even microscopic, in comparison with their tasks . . . The total budget and expert staffs are slender, and much of them are taken up by secondary chores. They contend with private resources which routinely dwarf them'.

There has been little assessment of the effects of restrictive practices legislation in the United States. Some restrictive practices continue as evidenced by the cases brought to the courts each year and continue in areas untouched by the legislation. But evidence on the economic effect is lacking, and even if we accept the frequent argument of economists that the ending of restrictive practices has benefits and no costs we still do not know the order of magnitude of the benefits.

Monopoly Policy

UK Policy[12]

In contrast to the post-1956 policy on restrictive practices, policy in respect of monopolies has been operated on an essentially discretionary basis. A statutory monopoly is defined as a situation where either a single firm accounts for more than one-quarter (one-third until 1973) of the market for the supply or purchase of particular goods or services or when a number of firms which together have one-quarter market share operate so as to restrict competition, although restrictive practices which fall under the jurisdiction of the RPC are excluded from consideration in this context. The relevant sales or purchases can be in a local or national market, and in the case of sales can include exports. A firm or group of firms suspected of being a statutory monopoly can be referred by the Director-General of Fair Trading, subject to a veto by the responsible minister,[13] to the Monopolies and Mergers Commission (hereafter MMC) for investigation.

This policy is one of identifying a monopoly situation by structural characteristics (i.e. market share of one-quarter) with the presumption that some aspects of behaviour and performance of a firm in a monopoly position may not be in the public interest. Thus structure identifies an industry for investigation, but the investigation itself is concerned with behaviour and performance.

The scope of monopoly policy has gradually been extended. Initially only monopolies in respect of goods were covered by the legislation, with services, the professions, nationalised industries and trade unions explicitly excluded. The legislation was extended to services and professions in 1965 and to nationalised industries in 1980.

Investigations by the MMC have often taken a number of years to complete. Whilst since 1973 the reference to the MMC has usually contained a time limit for the investigations of 18 months or 2 years, before 1973 an investigation typically took 2 to 3 years. The costs and uncertainty created by these investigations as well as their length, have been a frequent criticism of the MMC and its operations.[14]

In the first phase of operation up to the time when the 1956 Act became effective, the MRPC completed 20 reports, of which 18 related to cartels, although in half of those cases evidence of the existence of a statutory monopoly was found. In the second phase, from 1957 to 1964, the number of cases referred fell to an average of less than two a year. The third phase, from 1965 to date, has seen the scope of the MMC extended to cover more industries (as indicated above), to investigate some proposed mergers and anti-competitive practices and to conduct efficiency audits into nationalised industries as discussed below. In the period since 1959 there have been six general references, covering parallel pricing, refusal to supply professional services, recommended resale prices, 'full-line' forcing and tie-sales and aspect of discount to retailers. There have been (by the end of 1984), 68 reports on monopoly or complex monopoly situations and on restrictive practices in service industries.

The first part of the investigation by the MMC is to see whether a statutory monopoly exists. This may not be a simple undertaking since the boundaries of the market in which the firm (or firms) is thought to hold a monopoly position have to be drawn (see pp. 20–4). The definition of the market has in one sense been dealt with prior to the investigations of the MMC by the specification in the reference to the MMC of the goods and services to be considered. No formal criteria have been laid down for the definition of the appropriate market, and a 'common sense' approach has been adopted.

When a firm is shown to have a monopoly position, the MMC moves to the second stage of scrutinising the firm to determine whether the 'things done' (in the words of the 1948 Act) by the firm have operated against the 'public interest'. Whilst the 'public interest' is intended to be the basic guide, successive Acts have indicated that regard should be paid to efficient production and distribution, a balanced distribution of industry and employment within the United Kingdom, increase of efficiency and encouragement of new enterprise, etc. The only change of significance in the list of factors which the MMC should take into account has been the specific mention of the desirability of competition *per se* in the Fair Trading Act of 1973. However, the guidance given to the MMC on what constitutes the public interest is rather sparse. A former member of the Monopolies Commission, Allen (1968), argues that 'the guidance given by the Act consisted of a string of platitudes which the Commission found valueless, and it was left for members themselves to reach their own conclusions by reference to the assumptions, principles or prejudices which their training and experience caused them to apply to economic affairs' (p. 66).

In its reports the MMC gives its judgement and usually makes recommendations for changes in the firm's behaviour, though the implementation of any such recommendations is in the hands of the responsible minister. In the overwhelming majority of cases, the MMC has made some criticisms of the practices of the firms under investigation. Predominant in terms of number of times reported amongst the practices which have been condemned are restriction of sale of competitors' goods, price notification agreements, monopoly pricing and profits and discriminatory pricing (for a summary of practices found against public interest see Review of Monopolies and Mergers Policy 1978, p. 73).

In none of their reports did the MMC condemn a monopoly position as such and recommend structural change. The nearest the MMC came to recommending structural change was in the case of roadside advertising services.[15] Ten companies had set up and owned a company called British Posters Ltd., and the MMC made the recommendation, which was carried out, that this company be disbanded. Most of the practices found to be against the public interest were aspects of behaviour which either operated to make life more difficult for (actual or potential) competitors without benefiting consumers through the supply of 'better' products or the charging of lower prices. These types of behaviour include supplying a retail outlet only if that outlet agreed not to sell competitors' goods and the favouring of some firms at the expense of others by discriminatory pricing. Excessive profits and prices have generally been condemned, particularly when reinforced by entry barriers and restrictions on competition.[16] In the past few years, increasing attention has been given by the MMC to the effects which an existing monopoly or oligopoly position has on competition and on the possibility of new entry into the industry concerned. The majority of those recent MMC reports on monopoly situations which have found activities against the public interest have included the restriction of competition amongst the activities against the public interest.

The case-by-case approach of British monopoly policy, operating without a well-defined legal background and not building up case law, is liable to have severe problems of maintaining consistency. In the British policy context, changes in the membership of the MMC and the use of a subgroup of members for each investigation are likely to aggravate the consistency problems. Some of these difficulties of maintaining consistency arise when a legal firm is used, as the USA and EEC policies indicate. The views held by the MMC and the government (as reflected to some degree in the legislation and to some degree in the people appointed to the MMC) on what constitutes the public interest have changed over time. In the 1960s, there was much emphasis on the technical progressivity and export performance of firms, whereas in the 1980s there has been an emphasis of the impact of monopoly positions on competition.

Sutherland (1969) studies six reports of the MMC on monopolies and eight on proposed mergers. On the monopoly reports, he concludes that there was one major inconsistency in decision-making, with some inconsistencies in methods and approaches. On the merger reports, he finds that

> [i]t is therefore not possible to say much in detail about inconsistency, for the appropriate criteria have still to evolve . . . At the present stage it does not seem to me to be possible, therefore, to distinguish between inconsistency of approach and differing assessments by the MC [Monopolies Commission] of evidence submitted in the various cases.

When the actions of firms in monopoly situations have been judged as against the public interest, what steps have been taken to correct the position? In the British context, it is necessary to distinguish between the recommendations of the MMC for corrective action and the action actually taken by the government. Up to 1973, the responsible government department conducted the discussions with firms in order to secure voluntary undertaking to amend their actions which had been found to be against the public interest. Since 1973, discussions have been largely conducted by the OFT, although the final decisions rest with the responsible minister.[17] When the government department involved is also concerned with fostering relations with larger firms in attempts to increase exports, improve regional development and the like, the possible conflict of interest is clear. The firms involved are also afforded opportunities to negotiate and to bring pressures to bear so that the final undertakings fall short of the original MMC recommendations. Allen (1968) argues that 'the governments of the 1950s did not retain a consistent interest in the monopoly problem, and they treated most of the recommendations of the Commission with scant respect' (p. 124). One of the reasons for the establishment of the OFT was that this body would have a continuing interest in competition and consumer affairs. The OFT is now responsible for monitoring undertakings given by firms following monopoly investigations.

There have been few studies on the effectiveness of British monopoly policy.[18] A recent study (Shaw and Simpson, 1985) indicates that in 30 markets, where firms had been subject to monopoly investigation during the period 1959–73, the share of the dominant firm declined over the ten-year period following the MMC report from an average of 60 per cent to one of 52 per cent. However that decline may have occurred anyway. From eight case studies (taken from the 30 markets referred to above), those authors conclude that the MMC criticisms and recommendations, and the resulting under-takings given to the government, had only a minor impact on the process of competition. In all four markets where the leading firms clearly lost market share in the years following the MMC report the evidence suggests that competitive forces largely independent of the MMC were primarily responsible. Similarly, in the four markets where the leading firm or group largely retained its dominant position increases in competitive pressure often arose from changes independent of the MMC.

US Policy

At first glance, American law prohibits monopoly as a form of industrial structure. Section 2 of the Sherman Act states that '[e]very person who shall monopolize, or attempt to monopolize . . . shall be deemed guilty of a misdemeanour'. But the strictness of this, as other anti-monopoly legislation, depends on the definition of monopoly adopted and the breadth of markets used, in addition to the vigour with which the law is enforced. Whilst monopoly has not been defined, the consensus of opinion indicates that a market share of at least 60 per cent is considered necessary by the courts. The definition of the relevant market has, as might be expected, been the subject of intense debate with conflicting evidence presented to the courts. The main test applied by the courts appears to have been in terms of cross-elasticity of demand expressed as reasonable interchangeability of products. The geographic market has varied from a single city to the whole country, in part reflecting general differences between products and in part reflecting ambiguities of interpretation. A further consideration is that the law refers to the act of monopolisation rather than the position of monopoly *per se*, and thus aspects of conduct are involved. Thus the courts have looked for evidence of the intention to monopolise as well as at evidence on the existence of economies of scale which would not only explain the emergence of a monopoly position but would imply a loss from the break-up of that monopoly.

The use of a legal framework has still presented problems of fluctuations over time in the approach to monopoly policy. This has arisen from variation in the resources and attitude of the agencies appointed to enforce the law and from variations in the interpretations of the law by the courts.

In respect of established monopolies, American anti-trust policy has settled down to a very minor role. Wilcox and Shepherd (1975) conclude that 'restructuring by public policy has virtually ceased'. The legal framework has meant that the burden of proof lies with the prosecuting agencies who often lack the means of formal proof of, for example attempts at monopolisation. The legal process is subject to considerable delay, with the average time taken by an anti-trust case being 5½ years. Wilcox and Shepherd (1975) conclude that '[t]he agencies must, in practice, establish that a change will be enough superior to the existing structure to justify conviction and the costs of transition'. The earlier parts of this book will have demonstrated that it is difficult to predict accurately and with confidence what the consequences of a change in industrial structure would be in general and even more difficult for a particular industry. Thus the establishment of the case against monopoly in a court of law becomes extremely difficult.

Phillips (1971) argues that anti-trust policy leaves a 'good trust' largely unaffected and tends to protect business interests at the expense of the consumer. Thus a monopoly which 'does not threaten or coerce customers, suppliers or actual or potential rivals . . . is immune from anti-trust prosecution' (Phillips, 1971) and the policy operates like a discretionary policy focusing on behaviour and performance rather than structure. The protection of business interests at the expense of consumers can arise when there are economies of scale so that large firms can undercut small firms.

The limited action taken on the monopoly front and the absence of restructuring proposals (e.g. divestment) leads to the conclusion that any impact of American monopoly policy has been slight in recent years.

EEC Policy

In this section we deal briefly with the main thrust of EEC policies on restrictive practices and monopolies. Two important exclusions from our discussion are the ECSC (Steel and Coal) policy and industrial policy involving restructuring and protection against imports. The relevant parts of the Treaty of Rome are Articles 85 (dealing with cartels and restrictive trade practices) and 86 (monopoly). These articles refer to interstate trade, which would appear to exclude any cartels or monopolies affecting only within country trade, but agreements and actions which serve to limit imports from one EEC country to another would be covered by these articles.

The implementation of competition policy is in the hands of the European Commission, with cases which appear to break Articles 85 or 86 being taken to the European Court of Justice. There is a similarity with British policy in the area of cartels and restrictive practices in that there is a presumption that they are against the public interest with the possibility of exemptions being granted.[19] Article 85 covers agreements, decisions and concerted practices which may affect trade between member states and which have been the effect of restricting or distorting competition. The article specifically mentions agreements and practices which fix prices, limit production, share out markets between firms or which charge discriminatory prices. In practice, the Court and Commission have placed a 'tough' interpretation on Article 85. However, the implementation of the article is subject to a *de minimis* rule under which agreements involving firms with a combined market share below 5 per cent or with a combined annual turnover below 50 million UA (around £30 million) are excluded from consideration. Firms do not have to register any restrictive trade agreements, but may notify the Commission of agreements. The incentive to notify an agreement is that 'if, when the Commission comes to investigate the agreement, it decides to prohibit it then fines can be imposed for the period between entry into operation and the date of notification' (Swann, 1983).

Article 86 deals with the abuse of market dominance rather than with monopoly *per se*, and with those abuses which affect trade between member states. In the Article, particular abuses mentioned are:

(a) directly or indirectly imposing unfair purchase or selling prices or other unfair trading conditions;

(b) limiting production, markets or technical development to the prejudice of consumers;

(c) applying dissimilar conditions to equivalent transactions with other trading parties, thereby placing them at a competitive disadvantage.

(d) making the conclusion of contracts subject to acceptance by the other parties of supplementary obligations which, by their nature or according to commercial usage, have no connection with the subject of such contracts.[20]

The Treaty of Rome does not define dominanance but the Court has looked at both market share and actions before arriving at a view as to whether there is dominance in a particular case. A market share as low as 40 per cent has been used as partial evidence of dominance. There is here, as elsewhere, the problem of finding an appropriate definition of the market, and this problem is exacerbated in the EEC context since the question arises as to whether the appropriate market area is the whole of the EEC or is one particular country or region. Mergers are not explicitly covered by the Treaty of Rome, and indeed there has been debate over whether mergers were covered. However, the European Court has ruled that Article 86 does cover mergers, partly on the grounds that Article

85 (on restrictive practices) could be sidestepped by firms merging (rather than operating illegal agreements amongst themselves). However, there has not actually been a formal decision of the Court prohibiting a merger.

Merger Policy

In the UK, USA and the EEC, the policies on mergers operate within the same institutional framework as the corresponding monopoly policy. In policy discussion, the term merger is used to cover acquisitions as well as fusions, and we follow that usage here (though it goes against the usage followed in Chapter 13).

UK Policy

Since 1965, a proposed merger which would create or enhance a monopoly position, or which involves the acquisition of assets above a specified size, is evaluated by the government. The definition of a monopoly position is the same as that used in the monopoly policy, i.e. a market share of more than 25 per cent since 1973. The size requirement for a merger to be evaluated was initially set at £5 million, raised to £15 million in 1980 and further raised to £30 million in mid-1984. The initial evaluation of a proposed merger is made by a panel of civil servants (the Mergers Panel), who consider whether there should be a referral of the merger to the MMC for further investigation. The decision on referral is taken by the responsible minister (see note 13 on p. 299), although advice is given by the DGFT.[21] It is known that firms contemplating a merger may take informal advice from the OFT. Any investigation by the MMC is normally expected to be completed within six months, during which time the takeover bid usually lapses (under the conditions of the Stock Exchange Takeover Code).[22]

The details on the number and value of mergers in the UK have been given in Table 13.1 above, though those figures cover all acquisition and mergers which occur, and not just those which are examinable under the mergers legislation. From that table it can be seen that the pace of mergers did not slacken after 1965, and indeed tended to increase substantially in the late 1960s and early 1970s (encouraged to some extent by other aspects of goverment policy like the Industrial Reorganisation Corporation discussed below). Merger activity has been, however, rather lower since 1973.

The limited impact of merger policy is evident from the proportion of proposed mergers investigated by the MMC. During the period 1965 to 1978, only 45 mergers (about 2½ per cent) out of 1791 scrutinised by the Mergers Panel were referred to the MMC for more detailed consideration, with the remainder allowed to proceed. In the period 1979 to 1983, 774 mergers fell within the scope of the legislation (which would have been only 626 if the £15 million asset criteria had been in operation throughout the period), of which 29 potential mergers were referred to the MMC.[23] In the period 1965–78, of the 45 mergers considered by the MMC, 14 were declared against the public interest, 15 were declared as not against the public interest and 16 were abandoned by the firms involved before the MMC reported and the referral was withdrawn. For the mergers referred in the period 1979–84, nine were declared against the public interest, 17 were allowed to proceed and seven were abandoned (and one outstanding at the time of writing).[24]

The extent to which mergers were abandoned during the investigation of the MMC can be compared with the proportion of one seventh of proposed mergers considered by the Mergers Panel which were abandoned (Pickering, 1978). Thus the effect of referral on the abandonment of mergers is less than it may appear at first sight. Further, the recipients of an unwelcome takeover bid may seek referral to the MMC as a means of at least delaying the merger, with the possibility that their hostility to the merger will be one factor used by the MMC in arriving at a decision on whether the merger should proceed (for further discussion see Fairburn, 1985). There is, however, a possible deterrent effect on mergers arising from confidential advice given by the OFT to firms contemplating mergers.

The level of merger activity and the rate of referral of mergers to the MMC both fluctuate over time. The ability of the MMC to pursue investigations does not fluctuate correspondingly, leaving open the possibility that some mergers are allowed to proceed in periods of high merger activity through a lack of resources of the MMC to investigate. In the period 1965 to 1973 there was an average of three referrals a year, rising to an average of five to six a year in the period 1974 to 1975 (when the overall number of mergers was lower than in the earlier period), and the average of five to six a year has been largely maintained in the period 1979 to 1983.

Merger policy has been subject to two governmental reviews in recent years. The first was part of a general review of monopolies and mergers policy (Review of Monopolies and Mergers Policy, 1978), and argued that

a more critical policy towards mergers be adopted. The evidence does not justify a complete reversal of the presumption on mergers . . . Instead, the policy should be shifted to a neutral approach, within the existing legislation and institutional framework, recognising the dangers of reduced competition and increased concentration, but also the benefits that may result from improved industrial structure.

It was estimated that such a shift in emphasis would lead to around a fourfold increase in the number of referrals of mergers to the MMC. However, the policy proposal was never implemented, in part because there was a change of government about a year after this review was published.

The second review, which has not been published, did not lead to any suggestions for major changes in merger legislation but led to indications that policy 'has been and will continue to be to make references [on mergers] primarily on competition grounds'.[25]

The operation of mergers policy faces many of the problems which arise with the operation of monopoly policy as discussed in the last section. In two respects the problems are intensified in the case of mergers policy. First, mergers policy has to assess future consequences of a merger, whereas monopoly policy assesses past behaviour and performance. Second, the inconsistency problem is heightened by the speed with which a decision has to be taken, and the involvement of the Mergers Panel, MMC, OFT and the responsible minister.

The figures given above indicate that mergers policy could be said to have stopped about 2 per cent of mergers (those abandoned during period of reference plus those declared against the public interest). There may, however, have been some indirect discouragement effects on mergers. Pickering (1983) reports 'it seems that between 1965 and 1975 some 50 major proposed mergers were abandoned following receipt of confidential guidance [from the OFT] and no doubt a number of those were abandoned because of the possibility of reference to the MMC'. But unless those indirect effects were very large, the impact of mergers policy must be judged to have been rather small. This leaves any assessment of the worthwhileness or otherwise of mergers, the evidence for which was reviewed in Chapter 13.

US Policy

The agencies and procedures for the enforcement of American mergers policy parallels those for monopoly and restrictive practices policy. The law (Section 7 of the Clayton Act as amended by the Celler-Kefauver Act) indicates that it is illegal to acquire the shares or assets of competing firms or tend to create a monopoly. As before it is necessary to examine how the law has been interpreted by the agencies and the courts.

In 1968, the Department of Justice published guidelines indicating the cases where a merger would probably be challenged, and indicating their interpretation of the terms substantially lessening competition or tending to create a monopoly. These guidelines (reproduced in Howe (1972); Rowley (1973), pp. 86–7; Wilcox and Shepherd (1975), p. 241) indicate that benefits claimed for a merger arising from economies of scale, etc. will not usually prevent a challenge to that merger. The main features of the guidelines were that for horizontal mergers, even relatively small mergers will be challenged. For example, in a highly concentrated industry (four firms with a combined market share above 75 per cent), the proposed acquisition of a firm with a 1 per cent market share by a firm with a 5 per cent market share would be challenged, or the proposed acquisition of a firm with a 1 per cent market share with one with a 15 per cent share. Vertical mergers which are seen as foreclosing competition are likely to be challenged. Cases which would be challenged included, for example, mergers involving one firm that is a customer for a product and makes 6 per cent of the purchases of that product and another firm supplying the product and making 10 per cent of the sales (unless the merger raised no significant barriers to entry). The guidelines on conglomerate mergers indicate that any acquisition by one of the largest 200 industrial firms of any significant-sized firm (in the early 1970s this meant a firm with assets of over $10 million) would be challenged. Whilst that would slow down acquisition activity by the largest firms, it also serves to make them virtually immune themselves from being acquired. These guidelines focused on the structural characteristics of the firms and industries involved.

The guidelines of 1968 have now been superseded by 1982 and 1984 guidelines (see George (1985) for some discussion). Whereas the 1968 guidelines focused on structural considerations, with some allowance for the effect of merger on efficiency, the 1982 and 1984 guidelines further widen the factors which are taken into account in interpreting concentration and market share data so much so that in introducing them the Attorney General was able to say that

> the revisions clarify that the aim of our merger policy is to take into account all relevant factors . . . [in these] guidelines the emphasis has swung towards recognising that most mergers do not threaten competition; that many are in fact pro-competitive and enhance efficiency, thus leading to lower prices to consumers. The current emphasis

is thus on the need for economic evidence of harm or potential harm to competition before a merger will be challenged (US Department of Justice).

'To this extent at least merger policy in the UK and US is now at one' (George, 1985).

Restructuring Industry

The policies discussed above are essentially passive responses to the existing situation or proposals. However, in Britain there have been many active policies designed to change the structure of industry. These activist policies have mainly, but not entirely, been associated with periods of Labour government. This type of approach has been largely absent from the United States.

These activist policies can be divided into three categories. The first category consists of policies designed to restructure specific industries, often linked with the aim of reducing capacity in declining industries. The second category contains policies designed to promote general structural change, and are typically firm-centred rather than industry-centred. The third category is that of nationalisation. We look briefly at the extent of policies in each of these three categories.

The restructuring of the cotton industry under the Cotton Industry Act of 1959 was designed to reduce physical capacity by about half and to encourage re-equipping.[26] One effect of this policy was to reduce substantially the number of firms in the industry and was accompanied by substantial increases in concentration so that by 1969 the four largest firms controlled 30 to 40 per cent of output in most main sectors of industry (Miles, 1976, p. 201) and six major companies had acquired between 100 and 150 smaller companies between 1960 and 1966 (Mottershead, 1978, p. 473). Substantial restructuring through the encouragement of mergers took place in the aircraft and shipbuilding industries, to be subsequently followed by nationalisation in the mid-seventies.[27] Following the Shipbuilding Act of 1967, 24 firms were merged into seven groups (each based on a particular geographic region), and in the aircraft industry eight firms were formed from 21 firms.

Whilst the reorganisation of these industries aimed to remove excess capacity and raise efficiency, in structural terms the effect was to increase the level of concentration.

The major agency designed to promote general structural change was the Industrial Reorganisation Corporation (hereafter IRC) which formally came into existence in December 1966, and its operations effectively ended by the close of 1970.[28] The IRC operated mainly through the promotion of mergers. The aims of the IRC have been summed up by Graham (1972) as 'threefold. First, they aimed to increase productivity by improving the logical structure of industry . . . Secondly, they aimed to promote (or at least not harm) regional development. Thirdly, they aimed at retaining company control in the UK'.

The arguments advanced in favour of bodies such as the IRC draw at some stage on the view that market forces are inadequate. McClelland (1972) states that one of the propositions 'on which the case for the IRC rests is that market forces would not have cured these structural inadequacies quickly enough. In theory, where there are economies of scale to be exploited, or where one company's management is inadequate, the stock market provides a mechanism whereby a takeover bid will occur. In practice, the mechanism is often ineffective. Shareholders are inadequately informed, directors have vested interests; having regard to the risks for any particular party, finance may not be forthcoming.'

The IRC's 'principal purpose was to bring about mergers which would not otherwise have taken place' (McClelland, 1972). The two weapons in its armoury were persuasion and money. It could talk to firms about potential mergers in order to encourage certain mergers in a way which could not have been undertaken by commercial merchant banks, who would be acting in the interest of their client firms. This persuasion could, of course, be backed with financial support. But the financial support of the IRC became more important in cases of contested take-over bids, where the IRC supported one of the bids. This happened in cases where the IRC favoured a smaller, rather than a larger, firm to make the acquisition, but where it was felt that the assets of the larger firm would be decisive in a take-over battle.[29] It also happened in order to prevent foreign ownership of domestic firms.[30]

These has been little work on a direct evaluation of the work of the IRC. As with merger policy an evaluation of the work of the IRC is in part an evaluation of the benefits or otherwise of mergers, though it could be argued that the IRC's sponsorship of mergers was on a highly selective basis.[31] Other complications of any evaluation include the ending of the IRC which meant that its monitoring role, regarded as an essential ingredient of its operations by the IRC, did not continue. This complication is reinforced by the long time period which was believed to be needed before positive benefits would appear.

In terms of its immediate objectives, the IRC could be said to have succeeded. In a number of industries, such as nuclear construction and heavy electrical engineering, the IRC substantially changed the industrial structure. It also 'borrowed public funds but earned a surplus even after paying for its running expenses, its tax, its interest on its borrowings from National Loans Fund and the dividend on its borrowings from Public Dividend Capital . . . the indications were that a body like the IRC could not only be self-supporting, but could earn something approaching a commercial rate of return on its operations' (Young with Lowe, 1974).

McClelland (1972) made a loose assessment of the record of the IRC and reckoned that in early 1971 it looked as though of the 70 projects undertaken by the IRC 16 were struggling a bit and 54 were 'undoubtedly successful'. He writes that 'a score of 8 out of 10 must be regarded as good' and 'notwithstanding its short life, the IRC must be accounted a success'.

Another assessment of the IRC is made by Hindley and Richardson (1983), in which they focus on the share performance of the firms with which the IRC was involved over the period December 1966 (before the IRC began its operations) to December 1979. Their assessment relates to 54 projects with which the IRC management were involved of their own volition.[32] They divide those projects into three groups, namely 31 sponsored mergers or acquisitions without financial involvement by the IRC (on which there was usable data in 19 cases), 18 sponsored mergers with financial involvement (usable data in 11 cases) and five involving loans but not involving mergers or acquisitions (usable data in two cases). Their main finding is that there is no statistically significant difference between the share performance of the first two groups mentioned in the previous sentence and the average market performance of other firms, apart from the fact that the first group (sponsored mergers without provision of finance) showed significantly greater capital gains than other groups.

The National Enterprise Board (hereafter NEB) was conceived originally (Holland, 1975; Labour Party, 1973) as part of a considerable extension of public ownership and government intervention in the economy (see Hindley and Richardson (1983b) for outline of background to NEB). The role of the NEB was to be to act as a state holding company of 25 large companies which would be nationalised as part of the extension of public ownership. It actually performed two rather different roles during its period of activity from 1975 to 1979 (and it formally disappeared as a separate entity in 1981) (Parr, 1979). The first one, which involved the bulk of its funds, was to act as a holding company for the government stake in companies such as British Leyland and Rolls Royce, which had come into public ownership through government rescue of large companies in danger of going bankrupt. The second role was that of filling a gap in the capital market through the provision of finance to firms involved in areas of advanced technology and to medium-sized firms to foster regional development. Hindley and Richardson (1983b) provide an outline of the activities of the NEB.

Whilst the policy on mergers operating through the MMC has been designed to slow down the pace of mergers, many other policies have speeded up the pace of mergers and restructuring. These two aspects of government policy could be rationalised by the argument that if industrial structure is not optimal, then to reach an optimal structure may sometimes require a move towards increased concentration and sometimes towards decreased concentration. Nevertheless, the net effect of British government activity has probably been to encourage, rather than discourage, concentration.

A similar conflict of policies can be seen over collusion between firms. Whilst restrictive practices legislation has been discouraging agreements between firms, there have been other aspects of government activity which have encouraged agreements and information exchange. Swann *et al.* (1974), for example, argue that '[a]part from the government, the National Economic Development Council was centrally involved in exerting pressure for more scope for collective action . . . It soon became apparent that the NEDC was in the vanguard of the movement to modify the 1956 Act'. NEDC (1967) argued that 'the experience of a number of EDC's has revealed that the strong bias in the Restrictive Trade Practices Act against all forms of restrictive agreements and its rigid interpretation in the Restrictive Practices Court can frustrate co-operative action which would be in the national interest'. Partly as a result of pressure from NEDC, a provision was introduced into law in 1968 which enabled the Secretary of State to exempt from registration certain agreements designed to hold down prices. The EDC's (Economic Development Committees) set up under the auspices of the NEDC for particular industrial sectors provide a forum for firms to discuss their common concerns.

Privatisation

The major programme of nationalisation in the post-war period was undertaken by the Labour Government of 1945–51. During that period, industries such as coal-mining, railways, part of road haulage (later denationalised), gas, electricity and the Bank of England were nationalised.

Nationalisation in the 1960s and 1970s was concentrated on industries in long-term decline (such as steel, shipbuilding and aerospace). Individual firms such as part of Rolls-Royce and British Leyland came into public ownership more by accident than by design as a response by the government to the threat of the extinction through bankrupcy of those firms.

The general trend in the direction of nationalisation has been sharply broken over the past few years. Whilst there was some limited sale of nationalised firms during the Conservative Government of 1970–74, these were restricted to the sale of a travel agency (Thomas Cook) and state-owned public houses in the Carlisle area. At the time of writing, privatisation occupies a key place in the government's policy proposals, although the substantial sale of publicly owned assets has occurred too recently for any appraisal to be given.

The term 'privatisation' has been used to cover a number of different policies. It is convenient to distinguish three policies which have sometimes been included under the heading of privatisation.[33] The first type of policy is the sale of assets which the government had previously owned, and this would constitute the narrow definition of privatisation.[34] In some cases, as in the first stages of the privatisation programme, the assets sold were largely those which had been relatively recently acquired by the government and often as part of a rescue programme. This part of privatisation was largely a selling off of those assets which had been acquired by the National Enterprise Board under the preceding Labour government. In other cases (notably the sale of part of British Telecom), the privatisation involved sale of firms which had been nationalised for long periods of time.

The second type of policy, often labelled 'contracting-out', is the provision to public bodies (government departments, nationalised industries, publicly owned hospitals and schools) of certain goods and services by private firms, which had previously been provided by the public bodies themselves. Public bodies have always purchased goods and services from the private sector, and this policy of 'contracting-out' aims to increase the extent to which that is done. An example of 'contracting-out' is the use of private-contract cleaning firms by hospitals instead of the hospitals hiring their own cleaning staff.

The third type of policy included under this heading does not necessarily involve any change of ownership that would be implied by the term privatisation and could be more accurately labelled deregulation or liberalisation. This policy involves the removal of some of the restrictions on which firms can provide certain types of goods or services (for example, limits on companies which are able to provide local bus services). The link between privatisation and deregulation is that the firms eligible to provide the goods and services have often been publicly owned.[35]

The sale of assets by the government has been treated as 'negative' public expenditure, and serves to reduce the measured level of public expenditure and the public sector borrowing requirement (the difference between public expenditure and government revenue). There are clearly macro-economic aspects of the privatisation programme which fall outside of the scope of this chapter. The change of ownership can also affect the position of workers in the industries concerned. Some advocates of privatisation have argued that the power of trade unions will be reduced. The argument here is that the power of trade unions in the public sector arises from a combination of a protected market position of the nationalised industries and from the view that nationalised industries would not be allowed to go bankrupt. Thus, it is argued, trade unions can push up wages more easily in nationalised industries than in the private sector. Heald and Steel (1982) provide a critical assessment of this and other arguments for privatisation. Further, the wages of people employed in the public sector would generally be determined by national collective bargaining. When a private firm is bidding for a contract to provide services previously supplied by the public sector, that firm would not be constrained to pay that level of wages.

As it is not possible to provide an empirical assessment of the effects of this change of policy, instead we relate the policy to our previous discussions.[36] In the case of the second aspect, we can relate that to our discussion in Chapter 12 on the scope of firms. The arguments in favour of 'contracting-out' activities previously undertaken within the public sector are twofold. First, the profit motive is introduced to that sphere of activity under the belief that the profit motive leads to a more efficient operation than previously. Second, there are the gains from specialisation with specialised firms providing the services in question, rather than those services being provided within a large organisation which is undertaking a wide range of activities.

The disadvantages are almost exactly the reverse of the advantages. First, it is argued that the pursuit of profits will lead to the provision of inferior services. Whereas the advocates of privatisation argue that the pursuit of profits in a competitive environment will be to the benefit of comsumers, the opponents of privatisation would argue that there is a conflict between service to consumers and profits. Second, the nationalised undertaking may be able more easily to specify its requirements to its own employees than it can to an independent firm (cf. discussion above, pp. 199–204). The contract between a nationalised industry or local authority and the subcontractors may include specified levels of 'performance' which are to be achieved under the contract, and this has to be monitored.

Much of the debate over the sale of productive assets by the public sector to the private sector revolves around the question of the relevance or otherwise of type of ownership to the performance of a firm. This debate can be considered in a number of stages. First, it is argued that it is the degree of competition that a firm faces which determines its behaviour and performance. In that case, the actual ownership of the firm would not be relevant to that firm's behaviour and performance. However, one threat to a firm which arises from competition is the threat of bankruptcy. Advocates of privatisation would argue that the threat of bankruptcy and the resulting spur to efficiency is not present in nationalised industries, in the sense that a government could bail out a nationalised industry threatened with bankruptcy. However, the government may have other ways of penalising unsuccessful management, most notably sacking them. It may also be asked whether a government would actually be prepared to allow important firms to go bankrupt.

The promotion of competition imposes limits on the sale of nationalised firms, in that if a competing firm purchased the privatised firm then competition would be reduced rather than increased. Thus, in the case of the sale of British Rail's cross-channel ferry operations, limits were placed on who was allowed to bid for the purchase of those operations.

Second, it is argued that the effect of privatisation will be the introduction of the profit motive into the previously nationalised firms, and thereby efficiency in those firms will be raised. This line of argument was discussed in Chapter 15 (pp. 256–9). The validity of this argument rests on the view that those who own a firm will be interested in the profits of the firm, and will ensure that their firm pursues profit maximisation. The debate (cf. Chapter 11) on the managerial revolution indicated that managerialists put forward the proposition that in large corporations managers rather than owners were in control. The discussion in Chapter 13 indicates that it is often argued that a major constraint on the behaviour of private firms is the threat of takeover. The question arises as to whether large privatised firms would be subject to an effective takeover threat. This consideration arises in part from the sheer size of the firms involved (cf. discussion in Chapter 13 on the role of size in takeovers). Another aspect is the restrictions placed on who can be the owners of privatised firms by the government (e.g. that the ownership should not leave the

UK), and in some cases the retention of part ownership by the government.

Third there is the empirical question of whether ownership and control makes any difference to the efficiency of a firm. This is a far from settled question, on which we touched briefly in Chapter 11. We can report that Millward and Parker (1983) conduct a wide-ranging survey on the available evidence, and indicate the extensive difficulties in making comparisons between privately owned and publicly owned firms. They conclude that 'while the results are rather mixed, there is some evidence that competition does reduce the costs of public firms and regulation raises the costs of private firms. Neither finding is inconsistent with the finding about the effects of "ownership" on costs — namely that, . . . there is no general indication that private firms are more cost efficient than public firms'. Beesley and Littlechild (1983) provide a more limited survey and arrive at contrary conclusions, namely that private firms operate more efficiently than publicly owned firms.

Efficiency Investigations

Government-sponsored investigations into the efficiency of firms, outside the ambit of monopoly policy, have arisen from the operation of prices and incomes policies. Whilst the introduction of these policies has been as an anti-inflation weapon, they have often involved efficiency audits. The operation of a prices policy will generally involve the monitoring of proposed price increases by an examination of unit costs and of profit margins.[37] Thus it is almost inevitable that the body monitoring price increases is drawn into an assessment of efficiency (reflected in the unit costs) and of monopoly power (reflected in the profit margin).

The two bodies which were created as part of a prices and incomes policy and which became involved in efficiency investigations were the National Board for Prices and Incomes (hereafter NBPI) (in effective operation from 1965 to 1970) and the Prices Commission (in effective operation from 1973 to 1979).

The precise role of the NBPI and the specific conditions of the prices and incomes policy within which it operated varied (see Fels, 1972, for further details). It was not only concerned with the investigation of proposed price increases. The relevant government department would refer cases to the NBPI for investigation, within three months, and the investigation would be undertaken against the background of the criteria laid down by the government for wage and price increases.

Pickering (1971), in his study of the impact of the NBPI on private sector prices, concludes that the guiding principles for the NBPI include the view '[w]here possible, market forces should control prices. Prices should not be based on collusive arrangements between firms. Less competitive markets will require closer attention to questions of costs and efficiency; countervailing power or the imposition of direct price controls may be necessary. A price leader should be the firm best able to absorb price increases, not the least efficient. "Umbrella" pricing should be avoided'.

In one sense the NBPI cast its net widely. Fels (1972), in his study of the NBPI, argues that '[i]ndustry-wide matters — the scope for mergers and other structural change, the effects of uncompetitive practices and the need for reform of collective bargaining institutions — were also regarded as highly relevant (to their assessment of a price increase)'. But, nevertheless, Fels concludes tha 'there were no references in which the NBPI judged a firm or industry's profit level to be "too high" or "unfair" '.[38]

The Price Commission was established to help control prices as part of an anti-inflationary policy. Its role was changed substantially in 1977, away from price control toward efficiency audit. Its effective life ended with the fall of the Labour Government in May 1979. We focus on its role during the period 1977 to 1979 when there were two major elements in the operation of the Price Commission.[39] First, large firms were required to give 28 days' notification of any intention to raise prices. The Commission selected some of the proposed increases for a three-month investigation, during which prices were frozen or increases limited if profits fell below a specified level. The Price Commission made its recommendations to the Secretary of State for Prices and Consumer Affairs, who decided whether to impose restrictions on prices or profit margins for up to 12 months. Second, the Secretary of State could direct the Commission to carry out investigations of anything concerning prices and changes in a sector or industry. Here there were no price restrictions during the investigation. But restrictions, which with parliamentary approval could last for any length of time, could be required afterwards, by the Secretary of State within the limit that the limits placed on the firms were not more restrictive than those proposed by the Price Commission.

The Price Commission Act, 1977, set out the criteria by which the Commission was to judge a proposed price increase or the level of prices and profit margins. The Commission was 'to have regard to all matters . . . relevant with a view to restraining prices of goods and charges for services so far that appears to the Commission to be consistent with the making of adequate profits by efficient suppliers of goods and services'.

The Commission was given a list of eight matters which it could take into account. These included the desirability of cost reductions through increased efficiency, of maintaining quality of goods and services, and of maintaining a balance between demand and supply. A further matter to be considered was the promotion of competition between suppliers or when competition 'must be restricted or cannot be promoted (either because certain suppliers control a substantial share of the relevant market or for any other reason), by restricting prices and charges' (Price Commission Act, 1977).

During the two years of effective operation under the 1977 Act, the Price Commission made 44 reports on investigations of proposed price increases, and a further 19 reports on prices and charges in a sector of industry. Thus the scale of operation of the Price Commission in terms of number of firms and industries investigated was much greater than that of the MMC.

Competition Act 1980

The Competition Act of 1980 signalled a number of important changes in the approach of government to industrial policy and, as the title of the Act would suggest, reflected the new Conservative government's declared belief in the benefits of competition and of the use of the market over government intervention. The first part of the Act abolished the Price Commission, whose function was discussed above. The second part of the Act, which we now outline, is the control of anti-competitive practices. This aspect of the Act had to some extent been foreshadowed in the previous government's Review of Monopolies and Mergers Policy (1978) which recommended that 'consideration should . . . be given to dealing with such [anti-competitive practices] as a more general basis than can be provided by MMC monopoly investigations'. In the words of the preamble to the Competition Act, an anti-competitive practice is defined as 'a course of conduct which has or is intended to have or is likely to have the effect of restricting, distorting or preventing competition in the United Kingdom', although restrictive practices, covered by the legislation on those practices discussed above, are excluded from consideration under the Competition Act.

The framework within which the Competition Act is implemented is that initially the DGFT can initiate an investigation into any activities which (s)he believes may amount to anti-competitive practices (subject to a possible veto by the relevant government minister). The findings of such investigations are published with recommendations on the next steps to be taken. When no anti-competitive practices, or practices with only insignificant effect, are found, then the investigation is at an end. In other cases, the DGFT can seek an undertaking from those identified as engaging in anti-competitive practices to desist from those practices. In the event of an undertaking being given, the DGFT monitors the observance of the undertakings given (which have generally been for periods of five to ten years). In the event of no undertaking being given, the case is referred to the MMC, for that body to form a view on whether the anti-competitive practices are against the public interest. Finally, if the MMC finds that the practices are against the public interest, those involved can, if necessary, be legally compelled to desist from those practices by order of the Secretary of State for Trade and Industry.

In the years since 1980, there has been an average of four investigations a year by the DGFT into possible anti-competitive practices. Of the first 16 investigations undertaken (those completed by the DGFT by the end of 1983), five were found not to involve significant anti-competitive practices, in six cases undertakings were given by the firms involved to desist from anti-competitive practices, whilst in five cases reference was made to the MMC. Of the five cases referred to the MMC, one was outstanding at the time of writing, and the other four were all found to involve anti-competitive practices of which two were found to be against the public interest. The volume of investigations under this part of the Competition Act can be seen to be small both in absolute terms and relative to the annual 20 to 30 cases which were envisaged when the Act was introduced (cf. speech by DGFT reported in *British Business*, 11 April 1980).

The practices which have been regarded as anti-competitive and against the public interest have largely been practices such as refusal to supply certain shops, trying to prevent dealers selling the products of competitors and limiting access of car-hire firms to railway stations and airports.[40]

The third part of the Competition Act falls outside the scope of this chapter, but is mentioned here for completeness. This part broadened the scope of monopoly legislation to include nationalised industries. Further, in addition to monopoly-style investigations, the MMC now conduct efficiency audits into the operation of parts of the nationalised industries. The selection of nationalised industries for investigation is made by government ministers. Since the inception of this legislation, the MMC have dealt with an average of four to five efficiency investigations into nationalised industries each year.

Conclusion

Industrial policy has taken many forms, not all of which we have been able to discuss in this chapter. Shifts in policy have partly reflected changes in the political party in power. There has been an underlying trend towards more concern over industrial policy, which may be seen as a response to the continuing relative decline of the British economy. But the nature of industrial policy has changed a number of times during the post-war period. Recently much more emphasis has been placed by the government on the virtues of the market and of competition, whereas in earlier periods the emphasis was more on restructuring industries and efficiency audits. In contrast American policy in the post-war period has generally been restricted to the continued operation of the established monopoly and restrictive practices legislation, with some shift in recent years towards deregulation (e.g. of airlines). However, as will be evident from the preceding discussion, there has been rather little evidence produced as to whether the variety of industrial policies pursued have had the desired effects.

Notes

1. Stevens and Yamey (1965) provide a description of the policy and of the debate surrounding the introduction of restrictive practices legislation. This legislation is also described by Allen (1968), Chs. 7 and 8, and in A Review of the Restrictive Trade Practices Policy (1979).

2. For details see Allen (1968), Ch. 4 and A Review of Restrictive Trade Practices Policy (1979), para 2.4–2.10.

3. The legislation applicable to this period was the Monopolies and Restrictive Practices (Inquiry and Control), Act, 1948.

4. The legislation was the Restrictive Trade Practices Act, 1956.

5. The full details of these 'gateways' is given in A Review of Restrictive Trade Practices Policy (1979), para. 3.10.

6. The members of the Association of British Travel Agents (ABTA) are involved in exclusive dealing arrangements whereby ABTA tour operators only sell through ABTA agents, and the agents only sell the services of the ABTA tour operators.

7. Source of this and similar information is the annual reports of the Office of Fair Trading.

8. Exemptions can be granted

if it appears to the Court:
(a) that in the absence of minimum resale prices one of the following detriments to the public would occur: a substantial reduction in the quality or variety of the goods available; a substantial reduction in the number of retail establishments; an increase in retail prices in general and in the long run; sale under conditions likely to cause dangers to health through misuse of goods by the public; and a substantial reduction in necessary services provided with the goods; and
(b) that these detriments would outweigh the detriments of RPM. (Source: A Review of Restrictive Trade Practices Policy, 1979).

9. The Resale Prices Act is the current legislation covering resale price maintainance. Information on the number of complaints is taken from annual reports of the Office of Fair Trading. Usually the evidence is considered by the OFT to be inconclusive, but on occasion written undertakings are obtained from the producers to the effect that they will not continue to impose minimum price or resale conditions.

10. The review makes reference to the study of Pickering (1976).

11. Quotes from Robinson-Patman Act, (1936).

12. The institutional arrangements were changed in 1973, and the details given in the text refer to the post-1973 position. But there has been relatively little change in the main thrust of monopoly policy.

13. Since 1973, the responsible minister has been at times the Secretary of State for Trade and Industry, for Prices and Consumer Affairs and for Trade.

14. 'Monopoly investigations impose a considerable burden on the firm under investigation in terms of both cost and time and effort of senior management. This too has been the subject of criticism from industry . . . the fact that companies are frequently legally represented when giving evidence to the MMC can increase the cost and time involved' (Review of Monopolies and Mergers Policy, para. 4.24).

15. For details, see Monopolies and Mergers Commission (1981c).

16. There are numerous problems in identifying excessive or monopoly profits, which have usually been examined in terms of a high rate of profit on capital. Profits can be measured pre-tax or post-tax, net or gross of depreciation, etc. Problems of measuring capital have been discussed in Chapter 4, 6 and 11. High profitability also has to be defined. Generally, the MMC has compared the profitability of the firm under investigation with the profitability of the median firm or of the upper quartile of firms (ranked by profitability). Rowley (1969) concluded that the rate of return has been regarded as the most significant indicator of economic performance by the MMC. But that 'the empirical work is strong . . . that the choice of guidepost does make a difference in the examination of the rate of return on capital performance of dominant firms'. See also the vitriolic exchange between Sutherland (1971) and Rowley (1971). In recent years, the rate of return has played much less of a role in the deliberations of the MMC.

17. 'The Secretary of State [following an MMC report] has wide powers [including the powers to order divestment and splitting up of companies] exercisable by Order to such an extent as he considered requisite to remedy the adverse effects found by the MMC . . . These Order-making powers are not normally exercised . . . But the outcome usually takes the form [of the Secretary of State] asking the DGFT to obtain undertaking from the firms concerned, instead of making an Order' (Review of Monopolies and Mergers Policy (1978), p. 25; text in brackets added).

18. Sutherland (1969) lists the actions recommended by the Monopolies Commission and the undertakings secured by the government from the firms involved arising from the reports he surveyed. Graham (1972) concludes that 'it was rare for the recommendations of the Monopolies Commission to be carried out by the Government in anything like their original form'.

19. See, for example, Swann (1983) for discussion of the exemptions (pp. 88–9). The exemptions arise when four conditions are all met. These conditions relate to the argument making a contribution to efficiency or technical progress, consumers must share in the benefits arising from the agreement, only restrictions indispensable to achievement of the two previously given objectives to be included, and agreement must not permit elimination of competition. For further discussion of EEC policy see Review of Monopolies and Mergers Policy (1978).

20. Quote is from Article 86 of the Treaty of Rome, quoted from Swann (1983).

21. Over the period 1973 to 1983, it has been reported that nine referrals proposed by the DGFT were turned down by the responsible minister, whilst two mergers were referred to the MMC against the advice of the DGFT (*Investors Chronicle*, 9 December 1983).

22. For recent outlines of merger policy see Fairburn (1985) (who discusses some

recent cases) and Kay and Silberston (1984).

23. In the figures for both periods, it is the number of potential takeovers which are countered, so that when one firm is subject to two or more bids that is counted as one referral. In the period 1965 to 1978, amongst the cases referred to the MMC there was one case where a firm was subject to two or more takeover bids, and six cases in the period 1979 to 1983.

24. One of the mergers abandoned was declared not against the public interest by the MMC. The mergers declared not against the public interest include one case where a majority of four to two of the members of the MMC investigating the merger declared it against the public interest. The responsible minister can overrule the MMC if their decision does not carry a majority of more than two thirds, and he did so in this one case. In a further case which was eventually allowed to proceed, the MMC concluded that the proposed merger was against the public interest through the part-ownership of the bidding company (Pleasurama) by another (Grand Metropolitan). When Grand Metropolitan disposed of its shareholding in Pleasurama, the bid was allowed to proceed.

25. The quote in the text is taken from a speech by Trade and Industry Secretary Norman Tebbit on 5 July 1984; for report see *British Business*, 13 July 1984, p. 381.

26. For a detailed discussion and evaluation of policy see Miles (1968).

27. For further discussion of policy see Mottershead (1978).

28. Young with Lowe (1974) deal at length with the IRC, its method of operation and its effects. McClelland (1972) provides the view of one of the directors of the IRC on its operations and effect. Papers by Graham (1972) and Mottershead (1978) cover industrial policy in general and include a discussion of the IRC. Hindley and Richardson (1983) also discuss the political background to the introduction of the IRC and a list of firms with which the IRC were involved.

29. The best-known example of this being the takeover of Cambridge Instruments. The IRC supported the bid by George Kent against the bid of the much larger Rank Organisation.

30. For example, the IRC managed to block a bid from the Swedish-owned Skefco for the British-owned ball-bearings company of Ransome and Marles (see Young with Lowe, 1974, p. 234).

31. An evaluation of the two largest mergers sponsored by the IRC is given in Cowling *et al.* (1980), Ch. 6, with one (GEC) judged broadly successful and one (British Leyland) judged unsuccessful.

32. Hindley and Richardson (1983a) indicate 74 projects with which the IRC was involved. Of these, five were surveys of particular industries undertaken at the request of the government, one was a recommended merger which did not go ahead, four related to applications for finance for re-equipment, three related to agreements made by British firms with foreign companies and seven were requests from the government that assistance be given.

33. For some discussions on privatisation see Symposium on Privatisation and After, *Fiscal Studies*, vol. 5, no. 1, Kay and Silberston (1984), Shackelton (1984) and Beesley and Littlechild (1984).

34. In some cases (e.g. proposed sale of Trustee Savings Bank), the government was not previously regarded as the owner of the asset. In the example given, there were not previously any formal owners.

35. Beesley and Littlechild (1983), for example, argue that 'for political reasons, privatization may be a necessary accompaniment to competition'.

36. We are excluding from consideration here the sale of council houses since in our view different considerations are involved which fall outside the scope of this book. However in the period 1979 to February 1984 the sale of council houses raised over £6 billion out of a total of over £9 billion raised through sale of government assets (for details see Buckland and Davis, 1984).

37. This is only a general feature, for policies such as a general price freeze (e.g. in the periods July to December 1966, November 1972 to May 1973) do not usually involve investigation of proposed price increases.

38. Fels notes one possible exception to that (Mallory Batteries) and also notes that during the period when the NBPI was operating profit rates were generally declining.

39. A further discussion of the role of the Price Commission is Gribbin (1979).

40. For a critique of the first MMC investigation into anti-competitive practices and the argument that the investigations have been into trivial practices, see Kay and Sharpe (1982).

BIBLIOGRAPHY

Aaronovitch, S. (1977) 'The Firm and Concentration' in F. Green and P. Nore (eds.), *Economics: An Anti-Text*, Macmillan

Aaronovitch, S. and Sawyer, M. (1974) 'The Concentration of British Manufacturing', *Lloyds Bank Review*, no. 114

Aaronovitch, S. and Sawyer, M. (1975a) *Big Business: Theoretical and Empirical Aspects of Concentration and Mergers in the United Kingdom*, Macmillan

Aaronovitch, S. and Sawyer, M. (1975b) 'Mergers, Concentration and Growth', *Oxford Economic Papers*, vol. 27

Aaronovitch, S. and Sawyer, M. (1981) 'Price Change and Oligopoly', *Journal of Industrial Economics*, vol. 30

Adams, W.J. (1980) 'Producer-Concentration as a Proxy for Seller-Concentration: Some Evidence from the World Automotive Industry', *Journal of Industrial Economics*, vol. 29

Alchian, A.A. and Demsetz, H. (1972) 'Production, Information Costs and Economic Organisation', *American Economic Review*, vol. 62

Allard, R.J. (1974) *An Approach to Econometrics*, Philip Allan, Deddington

Allen, G.C. (1968) *Monopoly and Restrictive Trade Practices*, Allen and Unwin

Armour, H.O. and Teece, D. (1978) 'Organizational Structure and Economic Performance: A Test of the Multidivisional Hypothesis', *Bell Journal of Economics*, vol. 9

Armstrong, A. and Silberston, A. (1965) 'Size of Plant, Size of Enterprise and Concentration in British Manufacturing Industry', *Journal of Royal Statistical Society (Series A)*, vol. 128

Arndt, J. and Simon, J.L. (1983) 'Advertising and Economies of Scale: Critical Comments on the Evidence', *Journal of Industrial Economics*, vol. 32

Arrow, K. (1959) 'Towards a Theory of Price Adjustment' in M. Abramovitz (ed.), *The Allocation of Economic Resources*, Stanford U.P.

Arrow, K. (1962) 'Economic Welfare and the Allocation of Resources for Invention' in N.B.E.R., *The Rate and Direction of Inventive Activity*, Princeton U.P.

Ayanian, R. (1983) 'The Advertising Capital Controversy', *Journal of Business*, vol. 56

Baden-Fuller, C. (1983) 'The Implications of the "Learning Curve" for Firm Strategy and Public Policy', *Applied Economics*, vol. 15

Bailey, E.E. and Panzar, J. (1981) 'The Contestability of Airline Markets During the Transition to Deregulation', *Law and Contemporary Problems*, vol. 44

Bain, J.S. (1951) 'Relation of Profit Rate to Industry Concentration in American Manufacturing', *Quarterly Journal of Economics*, vol. 65

Bain, J.S. (1956) *Barriers to New Competition: Their Character and Consequences in Manufacturing Industries*, Harvard University Press, Cambridge, Mass.

Bain, J.S. (1969) 'Survival Ability as a Test of Efficiency', *American Economic Review*, vol. 59

Baran, P. and Sweezy, P. (1967) *Monopoly Capital*, Penguin, Harmondsworth

Barnett, R. (1985) *Welfare Economics: A Paretian Approach*, Wheatsheaf Books, Brighton

Baumol, W.J. (1959) *Business Behaviour, Value and Growth*, Macmillan

Baumol, W.J. (1982) 'Contestable Markets: An Uprising in the Theory of Industry Structure', *American Economic Review*, vol. 72

Baumol, W.J., Panzar, J. and Willig, R.D. (1982) *Contestable Markets and the Theory of Industry Structure*

Beesley, M. and Littlechild, S. (1983) 'Privatization: Principles, Policies and Priorities', *Lloyds Bank Review*, no. 149

Bergson, A. (1973) 'On Monopoly Welfare Losses', *American Economic Review*, vol. 63

Berle. A.A. and Means, G.C. (1932) *The Modern Corporation and Private Property*, Macmillan

Blackaby, F. (ed.) (1978) *British Economic Policy, 1960-1974*, Cambridge University Press

Blair, J.M. (1972) *Economic Concentration, Structure, Behaviour and Public Policy*, Harcourt, Brace, Jovanovich, New York

Bloch, H. (1974) 'Advertising and Profitability: A Reappraisal', *Journal of Political Economy*, vol. 82

Bothwell, J.L. (1980) 'Profitability, Risk and the Separation of Ownership from Control', *Journal of Industrial Economics*, vol. 28

Boudreaux, K.J. (1973) ' "Managerialism" and Risk-Return Performances', *Southern Economic Journal*, vol. 34

Boulding, K. and Stigler, G.J. (eds.) (1953) *Readings in Price Theory*, Allen and Unwin

Bradburd, R. and Caves, R.E. (1982) 'A Closer Look at the Effect of Market Growth on Industries' Profits', *Review of Economics and Statistics*, vol. 64

Bradford, W.D. (1978) 'The Performance of Merging Savings and Loans Associations', *Journal of Business*, vol. 51

Braverman, H. (1974) *Labour and Monopoly Capital*, Monthly Review Press, New York

British Patent System, The (1970) *Report of the Committee to Examine the Patent System and Patent Law* (Chairman M.A.L. Banks), Cmnd 4407, HMSO

Brock, W. (1983) 'Contestable Markets and the Theory of Industrial Structure: A Review Article', *Journal of Political Economy*, vol. 91

Brozen, Y. (1970) 'The Anti-trust Force Deconcentration Recommendation', *Journal of Law and Economics*, vol. 13

Brozen, Y. (1971) 'Bain's Concentration and Rates of Return Revisited', *Journal of Law and Economics*, vol. 14

Brozen, Y. (1974) 'Concentration and Profits: Does Concentration Matter?', *Anti-Trust Bulletin*, vol. 19

Brush, B.C. (1976) 'The Influence of Market Structure on Industry Advertising Intensity', *Journal of Industrial Economics*, vol. 25

Buckland, R. and Davis, E.W. (1984) 'Privatisation Techniques and the PSBR', *Fiscal Studies*, vol. 5

Burch, P.H. (1972) *The Managerial Revolution Reassessed*, Lexington Books, Lexington, Mass.

Burnham, J. (1941) *The Managerial Revolution: What is Happening in the World*, John Day

Buxton, A., Davies, S. and Lyons, B.R. (1984) 'Concentration and Advertising in Consumer and Producer Markets', *Journal of Industrial Economics*, vol. 32

Cable, J. (1972) 'Market Structure, Advertising Policy and Intermarket Differences' in Cowling (1972)

Casson, M. (ed.) (1983) *The Growth of International Business*, Allen and Unwin

Caves, R.E. (1967) *American Industry: Structure, Conduct and Performance* (2nd edn.), Prentice-Hall

Caves, R.E. (1983) *Multinational Enterprises and Economic Analysis*, Cambridge University Press

Caves, R. and Porter, M. (1978) 'Market Structure, Oligopoly and Stability of Market Shares', *Journal of Industrial Economics*, vol. 26

Caves, R.E., Khalilizadeh-Shirazi, J. and Porter, M.E. (1975) 'Scale Economies in Statistical Analyses of Market Power', *Review of Economics and Statistics*, vol. 57

Chenery, H.B. (1949) 'Engineering Production Functions', *Quarterly Journal of Economics*, vol. 63

Chevalier, J.M. (1969) 'The Problem of Control in Large American Corporations', *Anti-Trust Bulletin*, vol. 14

Christ, C. (1966) *Econometric Models and Methods*, John Wiley

Ciscel, D.H. (1974) 'Determinants of Executive Income', *Southern Economic Journal*, vol. 40

Clarke, J.B. (1940) 'Towards a Concept of Workable Competition', *American Economic*

Review, vol. 30

Clarke, R. (1984) 'Profit Margins and Market Concentration in UK Manufacturing Industry: 1970-6', *Applied Economics*, vol. 16

Clarke, R. and Davies, S. (1983) 'Aggregate Concentration, Market Concentration and Diversification', *Economic Journal*, vol. 93

Clarke, R., Davies, S. and Waterson, M. (1984) 'The Profitability-Concentration Relation: Market Power or Efficiency?', *Journal of Industrial Economics*, vol. 32

Coase, R.H. (1937) 'The Nature of the Firm', *Economica*, vol. 4

Collett, D. and Yarrow, G. (1976) 'The Size Distribution of Large Shareholdings in Some Leading British Companies', *Oxford Bulletin of Economics and Statistics*, vol. 38

Comanor, W.S. and Smiley, R.H. (1975) 'Monopoly and the Distribution of Wealth', *Quarterly Journal of Economics*, vol. 89

Comanor, W.S. and Wilson, T.A. (1967) 'Advertising, Market Structure and Performance', *Review of Economics and Statistics*, vol. 49

Comanor, W.S. and Wilson, T.A. (1974) *Advertising and Competition*, Harvard University Press, Cambridge, Mass.

Comanor, W.S. and Wilson, T.A. (1979) 'The Effect of Advertising on Competition: A Survey', *Journal of Economic Literature*, vol. 17

Corden, W. and Fels, G. (eds.) (1976) *Public Assistance to Industry*, Macmillan

Cosh, A. (1975) 'The Remuneration of Chief Executives in the United Kingdom', *Economic Journal*, vol. 85

Cosh, A., Hughes, A. and Singh, A. (1980) 'The Causes and Effects of Takeovers in the United Kingdom: An Empirical Investigation for the Late 1960s at the Microeconomic Level' in Mueller (1980b)

Coutts, K., Godley, W. and Nordhaus, W. (1978) *Industrial Pricing in the United Kingdom*, Cambridge University Press

Cowling, K. (ed.) (1972) *Market Structure and Corporate Behaviour*, Gray-Mills

Cowling, K. (1976) 'On the Theoretical Specification of Industrial Structure-Performance Relationships', *European Economic Review*, vol. 6

Cowling, K., Cable, J., Kelly, M. and McGuiness, T. (1975) *Advertising and Economic Behaviour*, Macmillan

Cowling, K. and Mueller, D. (1978) 'The Social Costs of Monopoly Power', *Economic Journal*, vol. 88

Cowling, K. and Mueller, D. (1981) 'The Social Costs of Monopoly Power Revisited', *Economic Journal*, vol. 91

Cowling, K. and Waterson, M. (1976) 'Price-Cost Margins and Market Structure', *Economica*, vol. 43

Cowling, K. *et al.* (1980) *Mergers and Economic Performance*, Cambridge University Press

Crew, M.A., Jones-Lee, M. and Rowley, C. (1971) 'X-Theory versus Management Discretion Theory', *Southern Economic Journal*, vol. 38

Crew, M.A. and Rowley, C.K. (1970) 'Anti-Trust Policy: Economics versus Management Science', *Moorgate and Wall Street*, Autumn 1970

Cubbin, J. (1981) 'Advertising and the Theory of Entry Barriers', *Economica*, vol. 48

Cubbin, J. and Leech, D. (1981) 'The Effect of Shareholding Dispersion on the Degree of Control in British Companies: Theory and Measurement', *Economic Journal*, vol. 91

Curry, B. and George, K. (1983) 'Industrial Concentration: A Survey', *Journal of Industrial Economics*, vol. 31

Dalton, J.A. and Penn, D.W. (1976) 'The Concentration and Profitability Relationships: Is there a Critical Concentration Ratio?', *Journal of Industrial Economics*, vol. 25

Davies, G. and Davies, J. (1984) 'The Revolution in Monopoly Theory', *Lloyds Bank Review*, no. 153

Davies, S. (1979a) 'Choosing Between Concentration Indices: the Iso-Concentration Curve', *Economica*, vol. 46

Davies, S. (1979b) *The Diffusion of Process Innovation*, Cambridge University Press

Davies, S. (1980) 'Minimum Efficient Size and Seller Concentration: An Empirical Problem', *Journal of Industrial Economics*, vol. 28

DePodwin, H.J. and Selden, R.T. (1963) 'Business Pricing Policies and Inflation', *Journal of Political Economy*, vol. 71

Demsetz, H. (1973) 'Industry Structure, Market Rivalry, and Public Policy', *Journal of Law and Economics*, vol. 16

Demsetz, H. (1974) 'Two Systems of Belief About Monopoly' in H.J. Goldsmith, H.M. Mann and J.F. Weston (eds), *Industrial Concentration: The New Learning*, Little, Brown

Dixon, R. (1983) 'Industry Structure and the Speed of Price Adjustment', *Journal of Industrial Economics*, vol. 32

Domberger, S. (1983) *Industrial Structure, Pricing and Inflation*, Blackwell, Oxford

Dooley, P.C. (1969) 'The Interlocking Directorate', *American Economic Review*, vol. 59

Dorfman, R. and Steiner, P.O. (1954) 'Optimal Advertising and Optimal Quality', *American Economic Review*, vol. 44

Eatwell, J.L. (1971) 'Growth, Profitability and Size: The Empirical Evidence', Appendix A in Marris and Wood (1971)

Eichner, A.S. (1973) 'A Theory of the Determination of the Mark-up', *Economic Journal*, vol. 83

Ekelund, R.B. and Maurice, C. (1969) 'The Empirical Investigation of Advertising and Concentration: A Comment', *Journal of Industrial Economics*, vol. 18

Elliot, D. and Gribbin, D. (1977) 'The Abolition of Cartels and Structural Change in the United Kingdom' in Jacquemin and de Jong (1977)

Ellman, M. (1979) *Socialist Economic Planning*, Cambridge University Press

Esposito, L. and Esposito, F.F. (1971) 'Foreign Competition and Domestic Industrial Profitability', *Review of Economics and Statistics*, vol. 53

Evely, R. and Little, I. (1960) *Concentration in British Industry*, Cambridge University Press

Fairburn, J.A. (1985) 'British Merger Policy', *Fiscal Studies*, vol. 6

Fatemi, A.M., Ang, J.S. and Chua, J.H. (1983) 'Evidence Supporting Shareholders' Wealth Maximisation in Management Controlled Firms', *Applied Economics*, vol. 15

Feller, W. (1957) *An Introduction to Probability Theory and its Applications*, vol. 1 (2nd edn), J. Wiley

Fels, A. (1972) *The British Prices and Incomes Board*, Cambridge University Press

Ferguson, J. (1974) *Advertising and Competition: Theory, Measurement, Fact*, Ballinger, Cambridge, Mass.

Firth, M. (1979) 'The Profitability of Takeovers and Mergers', *Economic Journal*, vol. 89

Florence, P.S. (1961) *Ownership, Control and Success of Large Companies: An Analysis of English Industrial Structure and Policy, 1936-1951*, Sweet and Maxwell

Florence, P.S. (1972) *The Logic of British and American Industry: A Realistic Analysis of Economic Structure and Government* (3rd edn), Routledge and Kegan Paul

Fraas, A. and Greer, D. (1977) 'Market Structure and Price Collusion: An Empirical Analysis', *Journal of Industrial Economics*, vol. 26

Francis, A. (1980) 'Company Objectives, Managerial Motivations and the Behaviour of Large Firms: an Empirical Test of the Theory of "Managerial" Capitalism', *Cambridge Journal of Economics*, vol. 4

Francis, A. (1983) 'Markets and Hierarchies: Efficiency or Domination?' in Francis *et al.* (1983)

Francis, A., Turk, J. and Willman, P. (eds) (1983) *Power, Efficiency and Institutions*, Heinemann

Franks, J.R., Broyles, J.E. and Hecht, M.J. (1977) 'An Industry Study of the Profitability of Mergers in the United Kingdom', *Journal of Finance*, vol. 32

Freeman, C. (1982) *The Economics of Industrial Innovation* (2nd edn), Frances Pinter

Friedman, M. (1953) *Essays in Positive Economics*, University of Chicago Press, Chicago

Friedman, M. (1962) *Capitalism and Freedom*, University of Chicago Press, Chicago

Galbraith, J.K. (1952) *American Capitalism*, Houghton Mifflin, Boston, Mass.

Galbraith, J.K. (1969) *The New Industrial State*, Penguin, Harmondsworth
George, K.D. (1985) 'Monopoly and Mergers Policy', *Fiscal Studies*, vol. 6
George, K.D. and Joll, C. (eds) (1975) *Competition Policy in the UK and EEC*, Cambridge University Press
George, K.D., McNabb, R. and Shorey, J. (1977) 'The Size of the Work Unit and Labour Market Behaviour', *British Journal of Industrial Relations*, vol. 15
George, K.D. and Silberston, A. (1975) 'The Causes and Effects of Mergers', *Scottish Journal of Political Economy*, vol. 22
George, K.D. and Ward, T.S. (1975) *The Structure of Industry in the EEC: An International Comparison*, Cambridge University Press
Geroski, P.A. (1981) 'Specification and Testing the Profits-Concentration Relationship: Some Experiments for the UK', *Economica*, vol. 48
Geroski, P.A. (1982) 'Simultaneous Equations Models of the Structure-Performance Paradigm', *European Economic Review*, vol. 19
Gort, M. (1969) 'An Economic Disturbance Theory of Mergers', *Quarterly Journal of Economics*, vol. 82
Goudie, A.W. and Meeks, G. (1982) 'Diversification by Merger', *Economica*, vol. 49
Graham, A. (1972) 'Industrial Policy' in Beckerman (1972)
Graham, D., Kaplan, D.R. and Sibley, D.S. (1983) 'Efficiency and Competition in the Airline Industry', *Bell Journal of Economics*, vol. 14
Gratton, C. and Kemp, J.R. (1977) 'Some New Evidence on Changes in UK Industrial Market Concentration', *Scottish Journal of Political Economy*, vol. 34
Greer, D. (1971) 'Advertising and Market Concentration', *Southern Economic Journal*, vol. 38
Gribbin, J.D. (1978) 'The Post-War Revival of Competition as Industry Policy', *Government Economic Service Working Paper*, no. 19
Gribbin, J.D. (1979) 'The Role of Competition in the 1977 Price Commission Act', *Government Economic Service Working Paper*, no. 21
Griliches, Z. and Hurwich, L. (eds) (1972) *Patents, Invention and Economic Change*, Harvard University Press, Cambridge, Mass.
Haldi, J. and Whitcomb, D. (1967) 'Economies of Scale in Industrial Plants', *Journal of Political Economy*, vol. 75
Hall, R. and Hitch, C. (1939) 'Price Theory and Business Behaviour', *Oxford Economic Papers*, no. 2
Halpern, P.J. (1973) 'Empirical Estimates of the Amount and Distribution of Gains to Companies in Mergers', *Journal of Business*, vol. 46
Hamberg, D. (1966) *R and D: Essays in the Economics of Research and Development*, Random House
Hannah, L. and Kay, J. (1977) *Concentration in Modern Industry*, Macmillan
Hannah, L. and Kay, J.A. (1981a) 'The Contribution of Mergers to Industrial Concentration: A Reply to Professor Prais', *Journal of Industrial Economics*, vol. 29
Hannah, L. and Kay, J.A. (1981b) 'The Contribution of Mergers to Concentration Growth: A Reply to Professor Hart', *Journal of Industrial Economics*, vol. 29
Harberger, A.C. (1954) 'Monopoly and Resource Allocation', *American Economic Review*, vol. 44
Hart, P.E. (1962) 'The Size and Growth of Firms', *Economica*, vol. 29
Hart, P.E. (1971) 'Entropy and Other Measures of Concentration', *Journal of the Royal Statistical Society (Series A)*, vol. 134
Hart, P.E. (1975) 'Moment Distributions in Economics: An Exposition', *Journal of the Royal Statistical Society (Series A)*, vol. 138
Hart, P.E. (1979) 'On Bias and Concentration', *Journal of Industrial Economics*, vol. 27
Hart, P.E. (1980) 'Log Normality and the Principle of Transfers', *Oxford Bulletin of Economics and Statistics*, vol. 42
Hart, P.E. (1981) 'The Effects of Mergers on Industrial Concentration', *Journal of Industrial Economics*, vol. 29

Hart, P.E. and Clarke, R. (1980) *Concentration in British Industry 1935-1975*, Cambridge University Press

Hart, P.E. and Morgan, E. (1977) 'Market Structure and Economic Performance in the UK', *Journal of Industrial Economics*, vol. 25

Hart, P.E. and Prais, S.J. (1956) 'The Analysis of Business Concentration: A Statistical Approach', *Journal of the Royal Statistical Society (Series A)*, vol. 119

Hart, P.E., Utton, M. and Walshe, G. (1973) *Mergers and Concentration in British Industry*, Cambridge University Press

Harvey, R.A. (1976) 'Learning in Production', Paper presented to the Royal Statistical Society Conference, Swansea, September 1976

Heald, D. and Steel, D. (1982) 'Privatising Public Enterprise: An Analysis of the Government's Case', *Political Quarterly*, vol. 53

Heath, J.B. (1961) 'Restrictive Practices and After', *Manchester School*, vol. 31

Heath, J.B. (ed.) (1971) *International Conference on Monopolies and Restrictive Practices*, HMSO

Hindley, B. and Richardson, R. (1983a) 'United Kingdom: An Experiment in Picking Winners — the Industrial Reorganisation Corporation', in Hindley (1983)

Hindley, B. and Richardson, R. (1983b) 'United Kingdom: Pulling Dragon's Teeth — the National Enterprise Board', in Hindley (1983)

Hindley, B. (ed.) (1983) *State Investment Companies in Western Europe*, Macmillan

Hines, H.H. (1957) 'Effectiveness of "Entry" by Already Established Firms', *Quarterly Journal of Economics*, vol. 71

Hirschey, M. (1981) 'The Effects of Advertising on Industry Mobility', *Journal of Business*, vol. 54

Hitiris, T. (1978) 'Effective Protection and Economic Performance in UK Manufacturing Industry 1963 and 1968', *Economic Journal*, vol. 88

Holl, P. (1975) 'Effect of Control Type on the Performance of the Firm in the UK', *Journal of Industrial Economics*, vol. 23

Holland, S. (1975) *The Socialist Challenge*, Quartet Books

Holtermann, S.E. (1973) 'Market Structure and Economic Performance in UK Manufacturing Industry', *Journal of Industrial Economics*, vol. 22

Honeycutt, T.C. (1975) 'Microeconomic Consequences of Corporate Mergers: A Comment', *Journal of Business*, vol. 48

Hood, N. and Young, S. (1979) *The Economics of Multinational Enterprise*, Longman

Hope, M. (1976) 'On Being Taken Over by Slater Walker', *Journal of Industrial Economics*, vol. 24

Horowitz, A. and Horowitz, I. (1968) 'Entropy, Market Process and Competition in the Brewing Industry', *Journal of Industrial Economics*, vol. 16

Howe, M. (1972) 'British Merger Policy Proposals and American Experience', *Scottish Journal of Political Economy*, vol. 19

Hughes, A., Mueller, D.C. and Singh, A. (1980) 'Hypotheses about Mergers', in Mueller (1980b)

Hughes, A. and Kumar, M. (1984a) 'Recent Trends in Aggregate Concentration in the United Kingdom Economy', *Cambridge Journal of Economics*, vol. 8

Hughes, A. and Kumar, M. (1984b) 'Recent Trends in Aggregate Concentration in the United Kingdom Economy: Revised Estimates', *Cambridge Journal of Economics*, vol. 8

Hughes, A. and Singh, A. (1980) 'Mergers, Concentration, and Competition in Advanced Capitalist Economies', in Mueller (1980b)

Imel, B. and Helmberger, P. (1971) 'Estimation of Structure-Profit Relationships with Application to the Food Processing Sector', *American Economic Review*, vol. 61

Jacquemin, A. and de Jong, H.W. (eds) (1977) *Welfare Aspects of Industrial Markets*, Leidin Nijhoff, Amsterdam

Jewkes, J., Sawers, D. and Stillerman, R. (1958) *The Sources of Invention*, Macmillan (2nd edn 1969)

Johansen, L. (1972) *Production Functions*, North-Holland, Amsterdam
Johnson, P.S. (1975) *The Economics of Invention and Innovation*, Martin Robertson
Johnson, P.S. and Apps, R. (1979) 'Interlocking Directorates among the UK's Largest Companies', *Anti-Trust Bulletin*, Summer 1979
Johnston, J. (1960) *Statistical Cost Analysis*, McGraw-Hill
Jones, D.C. and Svejnar, J. (eds) (1982) *Participatory and Self-Managed Firms*, Lexington Books, Lexington, Mass.
Jones, J.C.H., Landadio, L. and Percy, M. (1977) 'Profitability and Market Structure in Canadian Manufacturing Industry: Some Cross-Section Results', *Canadian Journal of Economics*, vol. 6
Jones, J.C.H., Landadio, L. and Percy, M. (1977) 'Profitability and Market Structure: A Cross-Section Comparison of Canadian and American Manufacturing Industry', *Journal of Industrial Economics*, vol. 25
Kaldor, N. (1950) 'The Economic Aspects of Advertising', *Review of Economic Studies*, vol. 18
Kaldor, N. (1972) 'The Irrelevance of Equilibrium Economics', *Economic Journal*, vol. 82
Kamerschen, D.R. (1966) 'An Estimation of the Welfare Losses from Monopoly in the American Economy', *Western Economic Journal*, vol. 14
Kamerschen, D.R. (1968) 'The Influence of Ownership and Control on Profit Rates', *American Economic Review*, vol. 58
Kamien, M.I. and Schwartz, N.L. (1982) *Market Structure and Innovation*, Cambridge University Press
Kay, J. and Sharpe, T.A. (1982) 'The Anti-Competitive Practice', *Fiscal Studies*, vol. 3
Kay, J. and Silberston, Z.A. (1984) 'The New Industrial Policy — Privatisation and Competition', *Midland Bank Review*, Spring 1984
Khalilzadeh-Shirazi, J. (1974) 'Market Structure and Price-Cost Margins in United Kingdom Manufacturing Industries', *Review of Economics and Statistics*, vol. 56
Khalilzadeh-Shirazi, J. (1976) 'Market Structure and Price-Cost Margins: A Comparative Analysis of UK and US Manufacturing Industries', *Economic Inquiry*, vol. 14
King, M. (1977) *Public Policy and the Corporation*, Chapman and Hall
Kmenta, J. (1971) *Elements of Econometrics*, Collier-Macmillan
Kotz, D. (1979) 'The Significance of Bank Control over Large Corporations', *Journal of Economic Issues*, vol. 13
Kuehn, D.A. (1972) 'Takeover Raiders and the Growth-Maximisation Hypothesis', in Cowling (1972)
Kuehn, D.A. (1975) *Takeovers and the Theory of the Firm*, Macmillan
Kumar, M.S. (1981) 'Do Mergers Reduce Corporate Investment? Evidence from United Kingdom Experience', *Cambridge Journal of Economics*, vol. 5
Kwoka, J.E. (1981) 'Does the Choice of Concentration Measure Really Matter?', *Journal of Industrial Economics*, vol. 29
Labour Party (1973) *Labour's Programme*, Labour Party
Lambin, J.J. (1970) 'Advertising and Competitive Behaviour: A Case Study', *Applied Economics*, vol. 2
Lange, O. (1937) 'On the Economic Theory of Socialism', *Review of Economic Studies*, vol. 4
Larner, R.J. (1966) 'Ownership and Control in the 200 Largest Non-Financial Corporations, 1929 and 1963', *American Economic Review*, vol. 56
Larner, R. (1970) *Management Control and the Large Corporation*, University Press, Dunellen, Cambridge, Mass.
Lawriwsky, H.I. (1984) 'Some Tests of the Influence of Control Type on the Market for Corporate Control in Australia', *Journal of Industrial Economics*, vol. 32
Leak, H. and Maizels, A. (1945) 'The Structure of British Industry', *Journal of the Royal Statistical Society (Series A)*, vol. 108
Leibenstein, H. (1966) 'Allocative Efficiency vs. X-efficiency', *American Economic Review*, vol. 56

Leibenstein, H. (1975) 'Aspects of the X-efficiency Theory of the Firm', *Bell Journal of Economics*, vol. 6

Lev, B. and Mandelker, G. (1972) 'The Microeconomic Consequences of Corporate Mergers', *Journal of Business*, vol. 45

Levine, P. and Aaronovitch, S. (1981) 'The Financial Characteristics of Firms and Theories of Merger Activity', *Journal of Industrial Economics*, vol. 30

Lieberman, M.B. (1984) 'The Learning Curve and Pricing: the Chemical Processing Industries', *The Rand Journal of Economics*, vol. 15

Lipsey, R.G. and Lancaster, R.K. (1956) 'The General Theory of the Second Best', *Review of Economic Studies*, vol. 25

Littlechild, S. (1981) 'Misleading Calculations of the Social Cost of Monopoly Power', *Economic Journal*, vol. 91

Llewellen, G. and Huntsman, B. (1970) 'Managerial Pay and Corporate Performance', *American Economic Review*, vol. 60

Llewellen, W.G. (1969) 'Management and Ownership in the Large Firm', *Journal of Finance*, vol. 24

Lloyd, B. (1970) 'Invention, Innovation and Size', *Moorgate and Wall Street*, Autumn 1970

Locksley, G. and Ward, T. (1979) 'Concentration in Manufacturing in the EEC', *Cambridge Journal of Economics*, vol. 3

Lundberg, F. (1937) *America's Sixty Families*, Vanguard, New York

Lustgarten, S.H. (1975a) 'The Impact of Buyer Concentration in Manufacturing Industry', *Review of Economics and Statistics*, vol. 67

Lustgarten, S.H. (1975b) 'Administered Inflation: A Reappraisal', *Economic Inquiry*, vol. 13

Lyons, B. (1980) 'A New Measure of Minimum Efficient Plant Size in UK Manufacturing Industry', *Economica*, vol. 47

Maddala, G.S. (1977) *Econometrics*, McGraw-Hill

Mann, H.M., Henning, J.A. and Meehan, J.W. (1967) 'Advertising and Concentration: An Empirical Investigation', *Journal of Industrial Economics*, vol. 16

Mann, H.M., Henning, J.A. and Meehan, J.W. (1969a) 'Testing Hypothesis in Industrial Economics: A Reply', *Journal of Industrial Economics*, vol. 18

Mann, H.M., Henning, J.A. and Meehan, J.W. (1969b) 'Statistical Testing in Industrial Economics: A Reply on Measurement Error and Sampling Procedure', *Journal of Industrial Economics*, vol. 18

Mansfield, E. (1962) 'Entry, Gibrat's Law, Innovation and the Growth of Firms', *American Economic Review*, vol. 52

Mansfield, E. (1969) *Industrial Research and Technological Innovation: An Econometric Analysis*, Longman, Green

Marcus, H. (1969) 'Advertising and Changes in Concentration', *Southern Economic Journal*, vol. 36

Markham, J.W. and Papanek, G.F. (eds) (1970) *Industrial Organisation and Economic Development — Esays in Honor of E.S. Mason*, Houghton Miffling, Boston, Mass.

Marris, R. (1964) *The Economic Theory of 'Managerial' Capitalism*, Macmillan

Marris, R. (1972) 'Why Economics Needs a Theory of the Firm', *Economic Journal*, vol. 82

Marris, R. and Wood, A. (eds) (1971) *The Corporate Economy*, Macmillan

Martin, S. (1979) 'Advertising, Concentration and Profitability', *Bell Journal of Economics*, vol. 10

Marx, K. (1976) *Capital Vol. 1*, Penguin Books, Harmondsworth

Mason, E.S. (ed.) (1959) *The Corporation in Modern Society*, Harvard University Press, Cambridge, Mass.

Masson, R.T. (1971) 'Executive Motivation, Earnings and Consequent Equity Performance', *Journal of Political Economy*, vol. 79

Masson, R.T. and Shaanan, J. (1984) 'Social Costs of Oligopoly and the Value of Competition', *Economic Journal*, vol. 94

McClelland, W.G. (1972) 'The Industrial Reorganisation Corporation 1966/71: An Experimental Prod', *Three Banks Review*, no. 94

McFetridge, D.G. (1973) 'Market Structure and Price-Cost Margins: An Analysis of the Canadian Manufacturing Sector', *Canadian Journal of Economics*, vol. 6

McGuire, J.W., Chiu, J.S.Y. and Elbing, A.D. (1962) 'Executive Income, Sales and Profits', *American Economic Review*, vol. 52

McKean, J.R. and Kania, J.J. (1978) 'An Industry Approach to Owner-Manager Control and Profit Performance', *Journal of Business*, vol. 51

Means, G.C. (1935) 'Industrial Prices and their Relative Inflexibility', *U.S. Senate Document 13, 74th Congress, 1st Session*, Washington, DC

Means, G.C. (1972) 'The Administered-Price Thesis Reconfirmed', *American Economic Review*, vol. 62

Meehan, J. and Duchesneau, T. (1973) 'The Critical Level of Concentration: An Empirical Analysis', *Journal of Industrial Economics*, vol. 22

Meeks, G. (1977) *Disappointing Marriage: A Study of Gains from Merger*, Cambridge University Press

Meeks, G. and Meeks, J.G. (1981) 'Profitability Measures as Indicators of Post-Merger Efficiency', *Journal of Industrial Economics*, vol. 29

Meeks, G. and Whittington, G. (1975) 'Directors' Pay, Growth and Profitability', *Journal of Industrial Economics*, vol. 24

Miles, C. (1968) *Lancashire Textiles: A Case Study of Industrial Change*, Cambridge University Press

Miles, C. (1976) 'Protection of the British Textile Industry' in Corden and Fels (1976)

Miller, R.A. (1969) 'Market Structure and Industrial Performance: Relation of Profit Rates to Concentration, Advertising Intensity and Diversity', *Journal of Industrial Economics*, vol. 17

Millward, R. and Parker, D.M. (1983) 'Public and Private Enterprise: Comparative Behaviour and Relative Efficiency' in Millward *et al.* (1983)

Millward, R. *et al.* (1983) *Public Sector Economics*, Longmans

Mises, L. von (1949) *Human Action: A Treatise on Economics*, Hodge

Mishan, E.J. (1962) 'Second Thoughts on Second Best', *Oxford Economic Papers*, vol. 14

Modigliani, F. (1958) 'New Developments on the Oligopoly Front', *Journal of Political Economy*, vol. 66

Modigliani, F. and Miller, M.H. (1958) 'The Cost of Capital, Corporation and Finance and the Theory of Investment', *American Economic Review*, vol. 48

Monopolies Commission (1961) *Cigarettes and Tobacco and Cigarette and Tobacco Machinery*, HC218, HMSO

Monopolies Commission (1965) *Petrol (Supply to Retailers)*, HMSO

Monopolies Commission (1973) *Parallel Pricing*, Cmnd 5330, HMSO

Monopolies and Mergers Commission (1979) *Ice Cream and Water Ices*, Cmnd 7632, HMSO

Monopolies and Mergers Commission (1981a) *Full-line Forcing and Tie-in Sales*, HC 212, HMSO

Monopolies and Mergers Commission (1981b) *Roadside Advertising Services: A Report on the Supply in the UK of Roadside Advertising Services*, HC 365, HMSO

Monopolies and Mergers Commission (1981c) *Discounts to Retailers*, HC 311, HMSO

Monopolies and Restrictive Practices Commission (1955) *Collective Discrimination*, Cmnd 9504, HMSO

Monsen, R.J., Chiu, J.S. and Colley, D.E. (1968) 'The Effects of Separation of Ownership and Control on the Performance of the Large Firm', *Quarterly Journal of Economics*, vol. 82

Mottershead, P. (1978) 'Industrial Policy', in Blackaby (1978)

Mueller, D. (1980a) 'A Cross-National Comparison of the Results', in Mueller (1980b)

Mueller, D. (ed.) (1980b) *The Determinants and Effects of Mergers*, Oelgeschlager, Gunn and Hain, Cambridge, Mass.

Mueller, W.F. and Hamm, L.G. (1974) 'Trends in Industrial Concentration 1947 to 1970', *Review of Economics and Statistics*, vol. 56

Myrdal, G. (1957) *Economic Theory and Underdeveloped Regions*, Duckworth
Nadler, G. and Smith, W.D. (1963) 'Manufacturing Progress Functions for Types of Processes', *International Journal of Production Research*, vol. 2
National Economic Development Council (1967) *Rationalisation and the Restrictive Practices Act*, NEDC
Neale, A.D. (1960) *The Anti-Trust Laws of the United States of America*, Cambridge University Press
Nelson, P. (1974) 'Advertising as Information', *Journal of Political Economy*, vol. 82
Nelson, R.S. (1959) *Merger Movements in American Industry, 1895 to 1956*, N.B.E.R., Princeton U.P., Princeton
Nerlove, M. and Arrow, K.J. (1962) 'Optimal Advertising Policy under Dynamic Conditions', *Economica*, vol. 29
Newbould, G. (1970) *Management and Merger Activity*, Guthstead
Ng, Y.K. (1983) *Welfare Economics*, Macmillan
Nickell, S. and Metcalf, D. (1978) 'Monopolistic Industries and Monopoly Profits or Are Kellogg's Cornflakes Overpriced?', *Economic Journal*, vol. 88
Nove, A. and Nuti, D.M. (eds) (1972) *Socialist Economics*, Penguin, Harmondsworth
Nyman, S. and Silberston, A. (1978) 'The Ownership and Control of Industry', *Oxford Economic Papers*, vol. 30
O'Brien, D.P., Howe, W.S. and Wright, D.M., with O'Brien, R.J. (1979) *Competition Policy, Profitability and Growth*, Macmillan
Ornstein, S.I. (1976) 'The Advertising-Conentration Controversy', *Southern Economic Journal*, vol. 43
Ornstein, S.I., Weston, J.F. and Intriligator, M.D. (1973) 'Determinants of Market Structure', *Southern Economic Journal*, vol. 39
Packard, V. (1957) *The Hidden Persuaders*, D. MacKay, New York
Palmer, J. (1973) 'The Profit-Performance Effects of the Separation of Ownership from Control in Large U.S. Industrial Corporations', *Bell Journal of Economics*, vol. 4
Parr, M. (1979) 'The National Enterprise Board', *National Westminster Bank Quarterly Review*, February 1979
Pavitt, K. (1982) 'R and D, Patenting and Innovative Activities: a Statistical Exploration', *Research Policy*, vol. 11
Peltzman, S. (1977) 'The Gains and Losses from Industrial Concentration', *Journal of Law and Economics*, vol. 21
Perlo, V. (1957) *The Empire of High Finance*, International, New York
Phillips, A. (1970) 'Structure, Conduct and Performance — and Performance, Conduct and Structure', in Markham and Papanek (1970)
Phillips, A. (1971) 'The Objectives of Economic Policy: The Contribution of Anti-Trust', in Heath (1971)
Phillips, A. (1972) 'An Econometric Study of Price-Fixing, Market Structure and Performance in British Industry in the Early 1950s', in Cowling (1972)
Phlips, L. (1969) 'Business Pricing Policies and Inflation — Some Evidence from EEC Countries', *Journal of Industrial Economics*, vol. 18
Phlips, L. (1973) 'Illusion in Testing for Administered Prices: A Reply', *Journal of Industrial Economics*, vol. 21
Pickering, J.P. (1971) 'The Prices and Incomes Board and Private Sector Prices: A Survey', *Economic Journal*, vol. 81
Pickering, J.F. (1976) 'The Abolition of Resale Price Maintenance in Great Britain', *Oxford Economic Papers*, vol. 26
Pickering, J.F. (1978) 'The Abandonment of Major Mergers in the UK', *Journal of Industrial Economics*, vol. 27
Pickering, J.F. (1983) 'The Causes and Consequences of Abandoned Mergers', *Journal of Industrial Economics*, vol. 31
Posner, R.A. (1975) 'The Social Costs of Monopoly', *Journal of Political Economy*, vol. 83

Prais, S.J. (1976) *The Evolution of Giant Firms in Britain*, Cambridge University Press

Prais, S.J. (1981) 'The Contribution of Mergers to Industrial Concentration: What Do We Know?', *Journal of Industrial Economics*, vol. 29

Prateen, C.K. (1971) *Economies of Scale in Manufacturing Industry*, Cambridge University Press

Qualls, T.D. (1979) 'Market Structure and the Cyclical Flexibility of Price-Cost Margins', *Journal of Business*, vol. 52

Radice, H. (1971) 'Control Type, Profitability and Growth in Large Firms: An Empirical Study', *Economic Journal*, vol. 81

Ravenscraft, D.J. (1983) 'Structure-Profit Relationships at the Line of Business and Industry Level', *Review of Economics and Statistics*, vol. 65

Reekie, W.D. (1975) 'Advertising and Market Structure: Another Approach', *Economic Journal*, vol. 85

Reekie, W.D. (1979) *Industry, Prices and Markets*, Philip Allan, Deddington

Rees, R.D. (1973) 'Optimum Plant Size in United Kingdom Industries: Some Survivor Estimates', *Economica*, vol. 40

Rees, R.D. (1975) 'Advertising, Concentration and Competition: A Comment and Further Results', *Economic Journal*, vol. 85

Review of Monopolies and Mergers Policy (1978) *A Consultative Document*, Cmnd 7198, HMSO

Review of Restrictive Trade Practices Policy (1979) *A Consultative Document*, Cmnd 7512, HMSO

Rhoades, S.A. and Cleaver, J.M. (1973) 'The Nature of the Concentration-Price/Cost Margin Relationship for 352 Manufacturing Industries, 1967', *Southern Economic Journal*, vol. 40

Roberts, D.R. (1959) *Executive Compensation*, Free Press, Glencoe, Illinois

Robinson, E.A.G. (1958) *The Structure of Competitive Industry*, Cambridge University Press

Ross, H.N. (1973) 'Illusions in Testing for Administered Prices', *Journal of Industrial Economics*, vol. 21

Rothchilds, K.W. (1947) 'Price Theory and Oligopoly', *Economic Journal*, vol. 57

Rowley, C.K. (1969) 'The Monopolies Commission and the Rate of Return on Capital', *Economic Journal*, vol. 79

Rowley, C.K. (1971) 'The Monopolies Commission and the Rate of Return on Capital: A Reply', *Economic Journal*, vol. 81

Rowley, C.K. (1973) *Anti-Trust and Economic Efficiency*, Macmillan

Rowthorn, R. (with S. Hyman) (1971) *International Big Business 1957-1967*, Cambridge University Press

Samuels, J.M. (1965) 'Size and Growth of Firms', *Review of Economic Studies*, vol. 32

Samuels, J.M. and Chesher, A.D. (1972), 'Growth, Survival and Size of Companies, 1960-69', in Cowling (1972)

Saving, T.R. (1961) 'Estimation of Optimum Size of Plant by the Survivor Technique', *Quarterly Journal of Economics*, vol. 75

Sawyer, M. (1971) 'Concentration in British Manufacturing Industry', *Oxford Economic Papers*, vol. 23

Sawyer, M. (1976) 'Income Distribution in OECD Countries', *OECD Economic Outlook Occasional Studies*, July 1976

Sawyer, M. (1979a) *Theories of the Firm*, Weidenfeld and Nicolson

Sawyer, M. (1979b) 'The Variance of Logarithms and Industrial Concentration', *Oxford Bulletin of Economics and Statistics*, vol. 41

Sawyer, M. (1980) 'Monopoly Welfare Loss in the United Kingdom', *Manchester School*, vol. 50

Sawyer, M. (1983) *Business Pricing and Inflation*, Macmillan

Scherer, F.M. (1965) 'Firm Size, Market Structure, Opportunity and the Output of Patented Inventions', *American Economic Review*, vol. 55

Schmookler, J. (1966) *Invention and Economic Growth*, Harvard University Press, Cambridge, Mass.

Schmookler, J. (1972) 'The Size of Firms and the Growth of Knowledge', in Griliches and Hurwicz (1972)

Schumpeter, J.A. (1954) *Capitalism, Socialism and Democracy* (4th edn), Allen and Unwin

Schwartz, M. and Reynolds, R. (1983) 'Contestable Markets: An Uprising in the Theory of Industry Structure: Comment', *American Economic Review*, vol. 73

Schwartzman, D. (1960) 'The Burden of Monopoly', *Journal of Political Economy*, vol. 68

Scott, J. (1979) *Corporations, Classes and Capitalism*, Hutchinson

Sellekaerts, W. and Lesage, R. (1973) 'A Reformulation and Empirical Verification of the Administered Prices Inflation Hypothesis: The Canadian Case', *Southern Economic Journal*, vol. 39

Shackleton, J.R. (1984) 'Privatisation: The Case Examined', *National Westminster Bank Review*, May 1984

Shand, A. (1984) *The Capitalist Alternative: An Introduction to Neo-Austrian Economics*, Wheatsheaf Books, Brighton

Shaw, R. and Simpson, P. (1985) 'The Monopolies Commission and the Process of Competition', *Fiscal Studies*, vol. 6

Shepherd, W. (1967) 'What Does the Survivor Technique Show about Economies of Scale', *Southern Economic Journal*, vol. 34

Shepherd, W. (1970) *Market Power and Economic Welfare*, Random House, New York

Shepherd, W. (1982) 'Causes of Increased Competition in the U.S. Economy', *Review of Economics and Statistics*, vol. 64

Shepherd, W. (1984) 'Contestability vs. Competition', *American Economic Review*, vol. 74

Shipley, D.D. (1981) 'Pricing Objectives in British Manufacturing Industry', *Journal of Industrial Economics*, vol. 29

Shrieves, R.E. (1978) 'Market Structure and Innovation: A New Perspective', *Journal of Industrial Economics*, vol. 26

Siegfried, J.J. and Tiemann, T.K. (1974) 'The Welfare Cost of Monopoly: An Inter-Industry Analysis', *Economic Inquiry*, vol. 12

Silberston, A. (1970) 'Surveys of Applied Economics: Price Behaviour of Firms', *Economic Journal*, vol. 80

Silberston, A. (1972) 'Economies of Scale in Theory and Practice', *Economic Journal*, vol. 82 (Supplement)

Singh, A. (1971) *Takeovers: Their Relevance to the Stock Market and the Theory of the Firm*, Cambridge University Press

Singh, A. (1975) 'Takeovers, Economic Natural Selection and the Theory of the Firm: Evidence from the Post War United Kingdom Experience', *Economic Journal*, vol. 85

Singh, A. (1976) Review of Kuehn (1975) in *Journal of Economic Literature*, vol. 14

Singh, A. and Whittington, G. (1968) *Growth, Profitability and Valuation*, Cambridge University Press

Skinner, R. (1970) 'The Determination of Selling Prices', *Journal of Industrial Economics*, vol. 19

Smyth, D., Boyes, W.J. and Peseau, D.E. (1975) *Size, Growth, Profits and Executive Compensation in the Large Corporations*, Macmillan

Smyth, D.J., Samuels, J.M. and Tzoannas, J. (1972) 'Patents, Profitability, Liquidity and Firm Size', *Applied Economics*, vol. 2

Soete, L.L. (1979) 'Firm Size and Intensive Activity: the Evidence Reconsidered', *European Economic Review*, vol. 12

Sosnick, S.H. (1958) 'A Critique of the Concepts of Workable Competition', *Quarterly Journal of Economics*, vol. 82

Spence, A.M. (1977) 'Entry, Capacity, Investment and Oligopolistic Pricing', *Bell Journal of Economics*, vol. 8

Spence, A.M. (1983) 'Contestable Markets and the Theory of Industrial Structure', *Journal of Economic Literature*, vol. 21

Stanworth, P. and Giddens, A. (1975) 'The Modern Corporate Economy: Interlocking Directorships in Britain, 1956-1970', *Sociological Review*, vol. 23

Steer, P. and Cable, J. (1978) 'Internal Organisation and Profit: An Empirical Analysis of Large U.K. Companies', *Journal of Industrial Economics*, vol. 27

Stevens, R.B. and Yamey, B.S. (1965) *The Restrictive Practices Court*, Weidenfeld and Nicolson

Stigler, G.J. (1949) *Five Lectures on Economic Problems*, Macmillan, New York

Stigler, G.J. (1956) 'Industrial Organisation and Economic Progress', in L.D. White (ed.), *The State of the Social Sciences*, Chicago U.P., Chicago

Stigler, G.J. (1958) 'The Economies of Scale', *Journal of Law and Economics*, vol. 1 (reprinted in Stigler, 1968)

Stigler, G.J. (1963) *Capital and Rates of Return in Manufacturing Industries*, Princeton University Press, Princeton, New Jersey

Stigler, G.J. (1964) 'A Theory of Oligopoly', *Journal of Political Economy*, vol. 72

Stigler, G.J. (1968) *The Organisation of Industry*, Irwin, Holmewood, Illinois

Stigler, G.J. and Kindahl, J.K. (1970) *The Behaviour of Industrial Prices*, National Bureau for Economic Research, New York

Stigler, G.J. and Kindahl, J.K. (1973) 'Industrial Prices as Administered by Dr. Means', *American Economic Review*, vol. 63

Stonebraker, R.J. (1979) 'Turnover and Mobility among the 100 Largest Firms: An Update', *American Economic Review*, vol. 69

Stoneman, P. (1979) 'Patenting Activity: A Re-evaluation of the Influence of Demand Pressures', *Journal of Industrial Economics*, vol. 27

Stopford, J.M. and Dunning, J.H. (1983) *Multinationals: Company Performance and Global Trends*, Macmillan

Strickland, A. and Weiss, L. (1976) 'Advertising, Concentration and Price-Cost Margins', *Journal of Political Economy*, vol. 84

Sutherland, A. (1969) *The Monopolies Commission in Action*, Cambridge University Press

Sutherland, A. (1971) 'The Monopolies Commission: A Critique of Dr. Rowley', *Economic Journal*, vol. 81

Sutton, C. (1974) 'Advertising, Concentration and Competition', *Economic Journal*, vol. 84

Sutton, C. (1975) 'Advertising and Market Structure: A Reply and Some Further Comments', *Economic Journal*, vol. 85

Swann, D. (1983) *Competition and Industrial Policy in the European Community*, Methuen

Swann, D., O'Brien, D.P., Maunder, W.P.J. and Howe, W.S. (1974) *Competition in British Industry*, Allen and Unwin

Sweezy, P.M. (1939) 'Demand Under Conditions of Oligopoly', *Journal of Political Economy*, vol. 47

Taylor, C.T. and Silberston, Z.A. (1973) *The Economic Impact of the Patent System: A Study of the British Experience*, Cambridge University Press

Teece, D.J. (1981) 'Internal Organisation and Economic Performance: An Empirical Analysis of the Profitability of Principal Firms', *Journal of Industrial Economics*, vol. 30

Telser, L.G. (1964) 'Advertising and Competition', *Journal of Political Economy*, vol. 56

Telser, L.G. (1966) 'Supply and Demand for Advertising Messages', *American Economic Review*, vol. 56

Telser, L.G. (1969) 'Another Look at Advertising and Competition', *Journal of Industrial Economics*, vol. 20

Thompson, R.S. (1981) 'Internal Organisation and Profit: A Note', *Journal of Industrial Economics*, vol. 30

Tucker, I.B. and Wilder, R.P. (1977) 'Trends in Vertical Integration in the U.S. Manufacturing Sector', *Journal of Industrial Economics*, vol. 26

Utton, M. (1971) 'The Effects of Mergers on Concentration in UK Manufacturing Industry, 1954-65', *Journal of Industrial Economics*, vol. 20

Utton, M. (1974a), 'Aggregate versus Market Concentration', *Economic Journal*, vol. 84
Utton, M. (1974b) 'On Measuring the Effects of Industrial Mergers', *Scottish Journal of Political Economy*, vol. 21
Utton, M. (1979) *Diversification and Competition*, Cambridge University Press
Vanek, J. (ed.) (1975) *Self-Management*, Penguin, Harmondsworth
Wallis, K. (1973) *Topics in Applied Economics*, Gray-Mills
Walters, A. (1963) 'Production and Cost Functions: An Econometric Survey', *Econometrica*, vol. 31
Waterson, M. (1980) 'Price-Cost Margins and Successive Market Power', *Quarterly Journal of Economics*, vol. 94
Webb, M.G. (1973) *The Economics of Nationalised Industries: A Theoretical Approach*, Nelson
Weiss, L.W. (1966) 'Business Pricing Policies and Inflation Reconsidered', *Journal of Political Economy*, vol. 74
Weiss, L.W. (1971) 'Quantitative Studies of Industrial Organisation', in M. Intriligator (ed.), *Frontiers of Economics*, North-Holland
Weiss, L.W. (1977), 'Stigler, Kindahl and Means on Administered Prices', *American Economic Review*, vol. 67
Weitzman, M. (1983) 'Contestable Markets: An Uprising in the Theory of Industry Structure: Comment', *American Economic Review*, vol. 73
Weston, J.F., Lustgarten, S. and Grottke, N. (1974) 'The Administered-Price Thesis Denied: A Note', *American Economic Review*, vol. 64
White, L.W. (1979) 'What has been Happening to Aggregate Concentration in the United States', *Journal of Industrial Economics*, vol. 29
Whittington, G. (1980) 'The Profitability and Size of United Kingdom Companies', *Journal of Industrial Economics*, vol. 28
Wibe, S. (1984) 'Engineering Production Functions: A Survey', *Economica*, vol. 51
Wilcox, C. and Shepherd, W.G. (1975) *Public Policies towards Business* (5th edn), Irwin, Holmewood, Illinois
Wilder, R., Williams, C. and Singh, D. (1977) 'The Price Equation: a Cross-Section Approach', *American Economic Review*, vol. 67
Wildsmith, J.R. (1973) *Managerial Theories of the Firm*, Martin Robertson
Wiles, P.J.B. (1956) *Price, Cost and Output*, Blackwell
Williamson, O.E. (1964) *Economics of Discretionary Behaviour: Managerial Objectives in a Theory of the Firm*, Kershaw
Williamson, O.E. (1965) 'Innovation and Market Structure', *Journal of Political Economy*, vol. 73
Williamson, O.E. (1967) 'Hierarchal Control and Optimum Firm Size', *Journal of Political Economy*, vol. 75
Williamson, O.E. (1968) 'Economics as an Anti-Trust Defense', *American Economic Review*, vol. 78
Williamson, O.E. (1970) *Corporate Control and Business Behaviour*, Prentice-Hall, Englewood Cliffs, New Jersey
Williamson, O.E. (1975) *Markets and Hierachies: Analysis and Antitrust Implications*, The Free Press, New York
Winch, D.M. (1971) *Analytical Welfare Economics*, Penguin, Harmondsworth
Worcester, D. (1973) 'New Estimates of the Welfare Loss to Monopoly: US 1956-69', *Southern Economic Journal*, vol. 40
Yarrow, G.K. (1972) 'Executive Compensation and the Objectives of the Firm', in Cowling (1972)
Young, S. with Lowe, A. (1974) *Intervention in the Mixed Economy*, Croom Helm
Zetlin, M. (1974) 'Corporate Ownership and Control', *American Journal of Sociology*, vol. 79

SUBJECT INDEX

perfect competition 9, 74, 127–8,
    233–40 *passim*, 246–50, 253, 255
performance 11–12, 156–7
persuasion 106–7
Price Commission 295–6
Price Commission Act 1977 295–6
price-cost margin 10, 72, 77, 81–6
    passim, 111, 139, 145
price decisions 138–42
price leadership 79
prices 9–10, 71–2
privatisation 290–4
product differentiation 11, 21–2, 73,
    107, 110, 252
profit maximisation 9–10, 70, 77, 85,
    104–5, 111, 144, 152, 156
profit rate 174–9 *passim*
profitability 154–60 *passim*; and ac-
    quisitions 217–19, 223–6; and
    advertising 107–11, 120–2; and
    growth 164–7, 195–6, 198; and size
    of firm 189–92, 196; and structure
    81–102; measures of 85
profits 55, 71, 155, 164, 240, 257, 260
property rights 258
proportionate effect, law of 192–5
public ownership 259–64 *passim*

R^2 13
regional dispersion 87
Registrar of Restrictive Trade Practices
    70, 269–70
relative measures of concentration 30
resale price maintenance 273–4
research intensity 130–3
response of rivals 9–10, 77, 81–2, 113
restrictive practices 76–7
Restrictive Practices Court (RPC) 269,
    290
restrictive practices policy 267, 269–76,
    281–2
restructuring industry 287–90
retention ratio 165
rivalry 158, 262
Robinson-Patman Act 1936 274–5

sales maximisation 145, 163–5
Schumpeter thesis on research 129
science push 124
second-best, theory of 247–8
separation of ownership and control
    167–74
Sherman Act 1890 274, 280
Shipbuilding Act 1967 287
short-run cost conditions 65
simultaneous equation approach 88–9,
    157
single equation approach 88–9, 157
size of firms and acquisitions 221–2
size-distribution of firms 11, 25–6
specialisation index 22
standard errors 14
statistical cost curves 51–6, 61
stock market 165
structure 8, 11–12, 154–5; and pricing
    142–6; and profitability 81–102; and
    research 134–7
structure-conduct-performance 8–10,
    154–60, 252–3
superior efficiency 86
survivor technique 57–61, 64–7
synergy 212

t-distribution 14–15
take-overs 165
tie-in sales 75
transactions approach 201–3
Treaty of Rome 281–2

unitary (U-) form 186–7

valuation of firms 88, 165, 211–12
valuation ratio 165, 175, 178, 213–14;
    and acquisitions 219–20
variance of logarithms 31–2, 228–9
vertical integration 198–204

welfare loss of monopoly 233–45
workable competition 252–6

X-inefficiency 71, 88, 235, 241

AUTHOR INDEX

For Product Safety Concerns and Information please contact our EU
representative GPSR@taylorandfrancis.com
Taylor & Francis Verlag GmbH, Kaufingerstraße 24, 80331 München, Germany